The DAMA Guide to The Data Management Body of Knowledge (DAMA-DMBOK Guide)

First Edition

Mark Mosley, Editor – Development

Michael Brackett, Editor – Production

Susan Earley, Assistant Editor

Deborah Henderson, Project Sponsor

Published by:

Technics Publications, LLC

Post Office Box 161

Bradley Beach, NJ 07720 U.S.A.

www.technicspub.com

ISBN, print ed.   978-1-9355040-2-3

ISBN, CD ed.   978-0-9771400-8-4

First Printing CD ed. 2009

Second Printing print ed. 2010

Printed in the United States of America

Library of Congress Control Number: 2009942515

Dedicated to all the professionals contributing to development
of a data management profession.

Contents

Figures

Tables

Foreword

This truly is a monumental piece of work!

The book is an exhaustive compilation of every possible subject and issue that warrants consideration in initiating and operating a Data Management responsibility in a modern Enterprise. It is impressive in its comprehensiveness. It not only identifies the goals and objectives of every Data Management issue and responsibility but it also suggests the natural organizational participants and end results that should be expected.

Having said that, I would not call this a "how to" book, although there is considerable advice about what to do and what not to do relative to many practices surrounding Data Management and particularly, Data Development. Still, it is not a technical treatise. It does have a plethora of references to technical, "how to" books that would literally fill a library for those who are interested in the technical details of Data Management.

I have been associated with DAMA from its very inception and have seen the evolution of this Body of Knowledge, both in its practice as well as in this document over the many years, which now approximates nearly 50!! The publication began as a non-trivial, sorely needed compilation of articles and substantive facts about the little understood subject of data management orchestrated by some folks from the DAMA Chicago Chapter. It was unique at the time, as there was little substantive reference material on the subject. It has grown to become this pragmatic practitioner's handbook that deserves a place on every Data Management professional's bookshelf. There is a wealth of information for the novice data beginner, but it is also invaluable to the old timer as a check-list and validation of their understanding and responsibilities to ensure that nothing "falls through the cracks"! It is impressive in its breadth and completeness.

The stated goals of the book in short are:

1. To build a consensus …
2. To provide standard definitions …
3. To identify guiding principles …
4. To overview commonly accepted good practices …
5. To briefly identify common issues …
6. To clarify the scope and boundaries …
7. To guide readers to additional resources for further understanding.

I would say it succeeds handsomely in accomplishing its goals.

The "DAMA Guide to The Data Management Body of Knowledge (DAMA-DMBOK Guide) deserves a place on every Data Management professional's bookshelf. It will serve as a guide for setting expectations and assigning responsibilities for managing and practicing what has become the very most critical resource owned by an Enterprise as it (the Enterprise) progresses into the Information Age … DATA!

Thank you to all the contributors and especially to the editors of this monumental undertaking.

Thank you to all the present and future Data Managers who are blazing trails into the complexities of the Information Age. This piece of work will be for you, a valuable Guide.

John A. Zachman
Glendale, California
November, 2008

Preface

It is well known that truth and good advice varies with its context. Because of this phenomenon, it may seem bold to attempt to capture a Body of Knowledge, Best Practices or Principles. Ultimately though, it is the variety of opinion and the dependency on context that makes the subjects rich and deep.

We at DAMA International have been working on a Data Management Body of Knowledge Guide (DAMA-DMBOK Guide) in various forms for many years in our *Guidelines for Implementing Data Resource Management* (Versions 1 through 4) and now in our more formalized structured Guide. It has been a complex project envisioned, sponsored and run by DAMA International VP Education and Research Deborah Henderson. The advisory DAMA-DMBOK Editorial Board supported the process and advocated for the finished product.

The DAMA-DMBOK Guide in its form has been in development for over four years and is a complete overhaul of the earlier Guidelines mentioned above. Starting in a winter storm in 2004, Deborah Henderson traveled to the Chicago DAMA Chapter meeting and presented the first structured framework for a 'body of knowledge' for data management. She asked for input and volunteers to bring this big vision into reality. Mark Mosley stepped up as Editor—Development and began with a white paper framework published as a free download on our DAMA website. That white paper went through three major revisions to date. Updates on progress have been given at regular intervals to the DAMA Board and the membership at meetings and conferences. The interest and input in the revisions of the initial framework is truly global with over 3500 downloads in three languages from over 78 countries, and still climbing.

We quickly discovered that understanding our own language was a very important pre-requisite. Development of a Glossary for the Guide started in 2007 and it soon became a substantial work in itself; indeed it could stand by itself. DAMA responds strongly to limited and dated definitions of data-centric terms that have been propagated since the 1960s and 1970s. Data Management is not 'using an application', or a synonym for 'database administration'. The DAMA-DMBOK Dictionary, published separately in 2008, is the glossary for the Guide and is now a companion to the DAMA-DMBOK Guide. The Dictionary has been received with enthusiasm. We heard back from many users of the Dictionary, some of whom have decided to leverage it across their corporations for its completeness and authority.

The DAMA-DMBOK Guide was written based on the Framework paper, and was developed in a collaborative manner involving many primary and secondary contributors and many draft peer review sessions as well as its own development website. Over 40 reviewers participated in the draft review sessions. Assistant Editor Susan Earley doggedly followed up, incorporating the comments into the second level drafts. These drafts proceeded, chapter by chapter, into copy editing and manuscript development.

The current DAMA-DMBOK Guide is a baseline edition. DAMA International intends to mature the Guide with regular future editions. It is developed as a 'guide' and readers should expect that it covers data management functions at a certain depth augmented with chapter focused bibliographies of significant further reading.

Our work at DAMA International parallels the development of the data management profession itself. The maturity of the profession is reflected in the emerged DAMA certification program and the DAMA continuing education program. It is also reflected in the DAMA involvement with other organizations and government bodies to influence and partner their activities such as curriculum development for data management professional education and international data management standards. The DAMA-DMBOK is part of this overall integrated push to represent Data Management profession world-wide.

Publication of the DAMA-DMBOK Guide has been the most pressing issue from our data community. We hope it doesn't disappoint that community. We will correct any errors by omission or commission in future editions. Looking ahead, DAMA intends to update the DAMA-DMBOK Guide by publishing regularly scheduled revisions. As it evolves we will be more tightly coupling our certification, education and research and industry programs.

The DAMA-DMBOK Guide is truly a journey not to be represented in just one edition. As new perspectives develop in data management we will be there, updating and challenging the best practices in our profession. Your comments, concerns and contributions are welcome, as we are already planning our next edition. Please contact the editors at info@dama.org.

The mission of the DAMA Foundation (a nonprofit 501(c)3 organization, #602-388-362 State of Washington, 2004) is to foster awareness and education within the Data Management industry and profession. Donations to support this mission are needed to continue to grow this focused and valued community. All moneys will be used for development programs and fundraising as well as general operations. Monetary tax deductible gifts may be sent to the DAMA Foundation, 19239 N. Dale Mabry Highway #122, Lutz, Florida 33584 U.S.A.

Deborah Henderson
DAMA-DMBOK Guide Sponsor
VP Education and Research DAMA International
President DAMA Foundation
Toronto, Canada

John Schley
President DAMA International
Des Moines, Iowa, USA

Acknowledgements

We want to thank our DAMA-DMBOK Guide Planning Committee for the almost weekly meetings for months on logistics and progress review and coordination. The core committee of Deborah Henderson, Mark Mosley, Michael Brackett, Eva Smith, Susan Earley and Ingrid Hunt, supported by DAMA Administration Kathy Hadzibajric, really brought the Guide to fruition through many, many personal, committed, volunteer hours.

Thanks, also, to the primary contributors who took the Framework vision and, within the tightly defined format and on a volunteer basis, were able to deliver the wonderful chapter material in-time and on-schedule, for which we are truly grateful.

We particularly wish to thank Mark Mosley for his sound theory, personal fortitude, and endless hours spent, and Michael Brackett for his sound advice, production, and manuscript miracle. Special thanks to John Zachman, Len Silverston and Ben Hu, our DAMA Advisors, for their enthusiasm.

Finally, we want to recognize the families of all the volunteers on this project, who sacrificed personal time with loved ones involved in this second non-paying job.

Deborah Henderson
DAMA-DMBOK Guide Sponsor
VP Education and Research, DAMA International
President DAMA Foundation
Toronto, Canada

John Schley
President, DAMA International
Des Moines, Iowa, USA

The DAMA-DMBOK Guide resulted from the contributions of many DAMA members. Without the contribution of these people, the DAMA-DMBOK Guide would not have been possible. The profession owes a great deal of gratitude to these DAMA members for their participation in a monumental piece of work.

DAMA International, the DAMA International Foundation, and the DAMA Chapter Presidents' Council sponsored the DAMA-DMBOK Guide project. Their vision, insight, patience, and continued support lead to the establishment and continuation of this project.

Deborah Henderson, President of the DAMA Foundation and VP of Educational Services for DAMA International, is the Project Sponsor for the DAMA-DMBOK Guide. It was her idea from the beginning and she has been a dedicated project sponsor through the entire project. Publication of this document is a result of her unwavering vision, enthusiasm, confidence, and support.

Four people contributed substantial time and effort pulling all aspects of development, review, and production of the DAMA-DMBOK Guide together.

Deborah Henderson, Project Lead
Michael Brackett, Editor-Production

Mark Mosley, Editor-Development
Susan Earley, Assistant Editor

The DAMA-DMBOK Guide Editorial Board provided comments on the direction of the DAMA-DMBOK Guide, reviewed chapters, and provided valuable insights, edits, and enhancements to the manuscript. They represented the front line of professionals contributing to the development of a data management profession. The Editorial Board members are listed below in alphabetical order with their role and affiliation.

Michael Brackett, Editor—Production (Puget Sound)
Larry Burns (Puget Sound)
Patricia Cupoli (Philadelphia)
Mike Connor (Wisconsin)
Alex Friedgan (Chicago)
Dagna Gaythorpe (UK)
Mahesh Haryu (New York)
Cynthia Hauer (GEIA)
Deborah Henderson, Chair (Toronto)
Steve Hoberman (New Jersey)
Ben Hu (China)
Ingrid Hunt, Marketing (San Francisco)
Gil Laware (Chicago)
Wayne Little (Portland)
Tom McCullough (NCR)
Jim McQuade (Pittsburg)
Mark Mosley, Editor—Development (Chicago)
Catherine Nolan (Chicago)
John Schley (DAMA I)
Anne Marie Smith (Philadelphia)
Eva Smith, Infrastructure (Puget Sound)
Loretta Mahon Smith (NCR)
Glenn Thomas (Kentucky)
James Viveralli (IDMA)

The DAMA-DMBOK Guide Planning Committee handled the vast multitude of details necessary to bring the manuscript to publication. Many of these details were behind the scenes, but were critical for production of the DAMA-DMBOK Guide. Without their constant, daily, participation, the DAMA-DMBOK Guide would not exist today.

Michael Brackett	Kathy Hadzibajric	Deborah Henderson
Ingrid Hunt	Mark Mosley	Eva Smith

The contributing authors wrote the initial drafts for each chapter. These draft chapters were circulated for review and returned to the author and the Assistant Editor for enhancement. The contributing authors are the professionals contributing to the development of a data management profession.

Larry Burns	Mike Connor	Patricia Cupoli
Mahesh Haryu	Deborah Henderson	Steve Hoberman
Michael Jennings	Wayne Little	David Loshin
Michael G. Miller	Mark Mosley	Erik Neilson
Mehmet Orun	Anne Marie Smith	Gwen Thomas
John Zachman		

Many DAMA Members reviewed the draft chapters and provided significant comment that led to improvement of those chapters. These reviewers are another wave of professionals contributing to the development of a data management profession.

Michael Brackett	Larry Burns	Kris Catton
John Cheffy	Deborah Coleman	Mike Connor
Charmane Corcoran	Patricia Cupoli	Neena Dakua
Satyajeet Dhumme	Susan Earley	Cynthia Edge
Gary Flaye	Marty Frappolli	Alex Friedgan
Dagna Gaythorpe	Wafa Handley	Mahesh Haryu
David Hay	Deborah Henderson	Bill Hoke
Steve Hoberman	Rich Howery	Ben Hu
Chris Jones	David Jones	Gary Knoble
Gil Laware	Jeff Lawyer	Wayne Little
Shahidul Mannan	Pete Marotta	Danette McGilvray
Ray McGlew	Jim McQuade	Mark Mosley
Catherine Nolan	Annette Pence	Terence Pfaff
Michelle Poolet	Ghada Richani	John Schley
Anne Marie Smith	Eva Smith	Loretta Mahon Smith
Stan Taylor	Glenn Thomas	Gwen Thomas
Jim Viveralli	Jim White	Gwen Yung

Many DAMA Members logged on to the DAMA-DMBOK Guide web site but did not submit any comments as part of the review process.

Sid Adelman	Davida Berger	Maureen Bock
Robert Cathey	Jamie Deseda	Gordon Everest
Lowell Fryman	Jim Goetsch	Deborah Gouin
Jean Hillel	Jeff Ilseman	Emiel Janssens
Mattie Keaton	Beverly King	Josef Martin
Tom McCullough	Dennis Miller	Prashant Natarajan
Cynthia Nie	Brand Niemann	Mehmet Orun
Andres Perez	David Plotkin	Fabio Prando
Jie Shi	Kimberly Singleton	Fran Suwarman Sjam
William Tucker	Karen Vitone	Robert Weisman
Manfred Wennekes		

The coeditors sincerely thank all of those DAMA members involved in the DAMA-DMBOK Guide project. Their contributions were invaluable in creating the DAMA-DMBOK Guide and for furthering the development of a data management profession. We sincerely apologize for the unintentional omission of any person who provided support for the DAMA-DMBOK Guide.

Mark Mosley, Editor—Development
Chicago, Illinois
January, 2009

Michael Brackett, Editor—Production
Lilliwaup, Washington
January, 2009

1 Introduction

Chapter 1 introduces the importance of data assets in the information age, the data management function, the data management profession, and the goals of the DAMA-DMBOK Guide. It sets the stage for presenting a Data Management Overview in the next chapter.

1.1 Data: An Enterprise Asset

Data and information are the lifeblood of the 21st century economy. In the Information Age, data is recognized as a vital enterprise asset.

"Organizations that do not understand the overwhelming importance of managing data and information as tangible assets in the new economy will not survive."

Tom Peters, 2001

Money and people have long been considered to be enterprise assets. Assets are resources with recognized value under the control of an individual or organization. Enterprise assets help achieve the goals of the enterprise, and therefore need to be thoughtfully managed. The capture and use of such assets are carefully controlled, and investments in these assets are effectively leveraged to achieve enterprise objectives.

Data, and the information created from data, are now widely recognized as enterprise assets.

No enterprise can be effective without high quality data. Today's organizations rely on their data assets to make more informed and more effective decisions. Market leaders are leveraging their data assets by creating competitive advantages through greater knowledge of their customers, innovative uses of information, and operational efficiencies. Businesses are using data to provide better products and services, cut costs, and control risks. Government agencies, educational institutions, and not-for-profit organizations also need high quality data to guide their operational, tactical, and strategic activities. As organizations need and increasingly depend on data, the business value of data assets can be more clearly established.

The amount of data available in the world is growing at an astounding rate. Researchers at the University of California at Berkeley estimate that the world produces between 1 and 2 billion bytes of data annually. It often seems we are drowning in information.

Yet for many important decisions, we experience information gaps – the difference between what we know and what we need to know to make an effective decision. Information gaps represent enterprise liabilities with potentially profound impacts on operational effectiveness and profitability.

Every enterprise needs to effectively manage its increasingly important data and information resources. Through a partnership of business leadership and technical expertise, the data management function can effectively provide and control data and information assets.

1.2 Data, Information, Knowledge

Data is the representation of facts as text, numbers, graphics, images, sound or video. Technically, data is the plural form of the word Latin word *datum*, meaning "a fact." However, people commonly use the term as a singular thing. Facts are captured, stored, and expressed as data.

Information is data in context. Without context, data is meaningless; we create meaningful information by interpreting the context around data. This context includes:

1. The business meaning of data elements and related terms.

2. The format in which the data is presented.

3. The timeframe represented by the data.

4. The relevance of the data to a given usage.

Data is the raw material we interpret as data consumers to continually create information, as shown in Figure 1.1. The resulting information then guides our decisions.

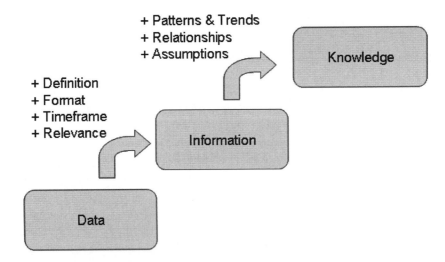

Figure 1.1 Data, Information, and Knowledge

The official or widely accepted meanings of commonly used terms also represent a valuable enterprise resource, contributing to a shared understanding of meaningful information. Data definitions are just some of the many different kinds of "data about data" known as *meta-data*. Meta-data, including business data definitions, helps establish the context of data, and so managing meta-data contributes directly to improved information quality. Managing information assets includes the management of data and its meta-data.

Information contributes to *knowledge*. Knowledge is understanding, awareness, cognizance, and the recognition of a situation and familiarity with its complexity. Knowledge is information in perspective, integrated into a viewpoint based on the recognition and interpretation of patterns, such as trends, formed with other information and experience. It may also include assumptions and theories about causes. Knowledge may be explicit—what an enterprise or community accepts as true–or tacit– inside the heads of individuals. We gain in knowledge when we understand the significance of information.

Like data and information, knowledge is also an enterprise resource. Knowledge workers seek to gain expertise though the understanding of information, and then apply that expertise by making informed and aware decisions and actions. Knowledge workers may be staff experts, managers, or executives. A learning organization is one that proactively seeks to increase the collective knowledge and wisdom of its knowledge workers.

Knowledge management is the discipline that fosters organizational learning and the management of intellectual capital as an enterprise resource. Both knowledge management and data management are dependent on high quality data and information. Knowledge management is a closely related discipline, although in this document, knowledge management is considered beyond the scope of data management.

Data is the foundation of information, knowledge, and ultimately, wisdom and informed action. Is data truth? Not necessarily! Data can be inaccurate, incomplete, out of date, and misunderstood. For centuries, philosophers have asked, "What is truth?", and the answer remains elusive. On a practical level, truth is, to some extent, information of the highest quality – data that is available, relevant, complete, accurate, consistent, timely, usable, meaningful, and understood. Organizations that recognize the value of data can take concrete, proactive steps to increase the quality of data and information.

1.3 The Data Lifecycle

Like any asset, data has a lifecycle, and to manage data assets, organizations manage the data lifecycle. Data is created or acquired, stored and maintained, used, and eventually destroyed. In the course of its life, data may be extracted, exported, imported, migrated, validated, edited, updated, cleansed, transformed, converted, integrated, segregated, aggregated, referenced, reviewed, reported, analyzed, mined, backed up, recovered, archived, and retrieved before eventually being deleted.

Data is fluid. Data flows in and out of data stores, and is packaged for delivery in information products. It is stored in structured formats–in databases, flat files, and tagged electronic documents–and in many less structured formats–e-mail and other electronic documents, paper documents, spreadsheets, reports, graphics, electronic image files, and audio and video recordings. Typically, 80% of an organization's data assets reside in relatively unstructured formats.

Data has value only when it is actually used, or can be useful in the future. All data lifecycle stages have associated costs and risks, but only the "use" stage adds business value.

When effectively managed, the data lifecycle begins even before data acquisition, with enterprise planning for data, specification of data, and enablement of data capture, delivery, storage, and controls.

Projects accomplish the specification and enablement of data, and some of the planning for data. The System Development Lifecycle (SDLC), shown in Figure 1.2, is not the same as the data lifecycle. The SDLC describes the stages of a project, while the data lifecycle describes the processes performed to manage data assets.

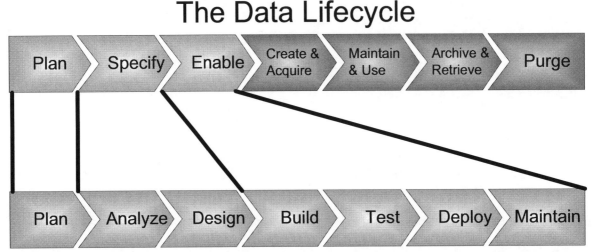

Figure 1.2 The Data Lifecycle and the System Development Lifecycle

However, the two lifecycles are closely related because data planning, specification and enablement activities are integral parts of the SDLC. Other SDLC activities are operational or supervisory in nature.

1.4 The Data Management Function

Data management (DM) is the business function of planning for, controlling and delivering data and information assets. This function includes

- The disciplines of development, execution, and supervision

- of plans, policies, programs, projects, processes, practices and procedures

- that control, protect, deliver, and enhance

- the value of data and information assets.

Data management is known by many other terms, including:

- Information Management (IM).

- Enterprise Information Management (EIM).

- Enterprise Data Management (EDM).

- Data Resource Management (DRM).

- Information Resource Management (IRM).

- Information Asset Management (IAM).

All these terms are generally synonymous, but this document consistently refers to Data Management.

Often the word "enterprise" is included in the function name to emphasize the enterprise-wide focus of data management efforts, i.e., Enterprise Information Management or Enterprise Data Management. Enterprise-wide data management is a recommended best practice. However, data management may also be performed effectively in a local context without an enterprise-wide mandate, although with less business benefit.

The data management function includes what is commonly referred to as database administration–database design, implementation, and production support–as well as "data administration". The term "data administration" was once a popular way to vaguely refer to all the functions of data management except database administration. However, as the data management function matures, its specific component functions are better understood. The data management function is important to enterprises regardless of their size and purpose.

The scope of the data management function and the scale of its implementation vary widely with the size, means, and experience of organizations. The nature of data management remains the same across organizations, even as implementation details widely differ.

1.5 A Shared Responsibility

Data management is a shared responsibility between the *data management professionals* within Information Technology (IT) organizations and the *business data stewards* representing the collective interests of data producers and information consumers. Data stewards serve as the appointed trustees for data assets. Data management professionals serve as the expert curators and technical custodians of these data assets.

Data stewardship is the assigned accountability for business responsibilities in data management. Data stewards are respected subject matter experts and business leaders appointed to represent the data interests of their organizations, and take responsibility for the quality and use of data. Good stewards carefully guard, invest, and leverage the resources entrusted to them. Data stewards ensure data resources meet business needs by ensuring the quality of data and its meta-data. Data stewards collaborate in partnership with data management professionals to execute data stewardship activities and responsibilities.

Data management professionals operate as the expert technical custodians of data assets, much like bank employees and money managers serve as the professional custodians of financial resources for their owners and trustees. While data stewards oversee data assets, data management professionals perform technical functions to safeguard and enable effective use of enterprise data assets. Data management professionals work in Data Management Services organizations within the Information Technology (IT) department.

Data is the content moving through the information technology infrastructure and application systems. Information technology captures, stores, processes, and provides data. The IT infrastructure and application systems are the "pipes" through which data flows. As technological change has exploded over the past fifty years, IT organizations have traditionally focused primarily on maintaining a modern, effective hardware and software infrastructure, and a robust application system portfolio based on that infrastructure. Most IT organizations have been less focused on the structure, meaning, and the quality of the data content flowing through the infrastructure and systems. However, a growing number of IT executives and business leaders today recognize the importance of data management and the need for effective Data Management Services organizations.

1.6 A Broad Scope

The overall data management function, shown in Figure 1.3, encompasses ten major component functions:

- Data Governance: Planning, supervision and control over data management and use.

- Data Architecture Management: Defining the blueprint for managing data assets.

- Data Development: Analysis, design, implementation, testing, deployment, maintenance.

- Data Operations Management: Providing support from data acquisition to purging.

- Data Security Management: Insuring privacy, confidentiality and appropriate access.

- Data Quality Management: Defining, monitoring and improving data quality.

- Reference and Master Data Management: Managing golden versions and replicas.

- Data Warehousing and Business Intelligence Management: Enabling reporting and analysis.

- Document and Content Management: Managing data found outside of databases.

- Meta-data Management: Integrating, controlling and providing meta-data.

Figure 1.3 Data Management Functions

1.7 An Emerging Profession

The management practices for established assets like money and people have matured over many years. Data management is a relatively new function and its concepts and practices are evolving rapidly.

Within the IT community, data management is an emerging profession–an occupational calling requiring specialized knowledge and skills. Specialized data management roles require unique skills and experienced judgments. Today's data management professionals demonstrate a sense of calling and exceptional commitment to managing data assets.

Creating a formal, certified, recognized, and respected data management profession is a challenging process. The current environment is a confusing mixture of terms, methods, tools, opinion, and hype. To mature into an established profession, the data management community needs professional standards: standard terms and definitions, processes and practices, roles and responsibilities, deliverables and metrics.

Standards and recognized best practices can improve the effectiveness of data stewards and data management professionals. Moreover, standards help us communicate with our teammates, managers, and executives. Executives especially need to fully understand and embrace fundamental data management concepts in order to effectively fund, staff and support the data management function.

1.8 A Growing Body of Knowledge

One of the hallmarks of an emerging profession is the publication of a guide to a recognized consensus body of knowledge. A "body of knowledge" is what is generally accepted as true in a professional field. While the entire body of knowledge may be quite large and constantly growing, a guide to the body of knowledge introduces standard terms and best practices.

1.9 DAMA–The Data Management Association

The Data Management Association (DAMA International) is the *Premiere organization for data professionals worldwide*. DAMA International is an international not-for-profit membership organization, with over 7500 members in 40 chapters around the globe. Its purpose is to promote the understanding, development, and practice of managing data and information to support business strategies.

The DAMA Foundation is the research and education affiliate of DAMA International, dedicated to developing the data management profession and promoting advancement of concepts and practices to manage data and information as enterprise assets.

The joint mission of DAMA International and the DAMA Foundation, collectively known as DAMA, is to *Lead the data management profession toward maturity*. DAMA promotes the understanding, development, and practice of managing data, information, and knowledge as key enterprise assets, independent of any specific vendor, technology, and method.

DAMA International seeks to mature the data management profession in several ways. A few of these efforts include:

- DAMA International conducts the annual DAMA International Symposium, now the Enterprise Data World, the largest professional data management conference in the world, in partnership with Wilshire Conferences. Workshops, tutorials, and conference sessions at the Symposium provide continuing education for data management professionals.

- DAMA International conducts the annual DAMA International Conference Europe, the largest professional data management conference in Europe, in partnership with IRMUK. Workshops, tutorials, and conference sessions at the Conference provide continuing education for data management professionals.

- DAMA International offers a professional certification program, recognizing Certified Data Management Professionals (CDMP), in partnership with the Institute for Certification of Computing Professionals (ICCP). CDMP certification exams are also used by The Data Warehouse Institute (TDWI) in the Certified Business Intelligence Professional (CBIP) program.

- The DAMA International Education Committee's Data Management Curriculum Framework offers guidance to US and Canadian colleges and universities regarding how to teach data management as part of any IT and MIS curriculum in the North American higher education model.

1.10 Purpose of the DAMA-DMBOK Guide

DAMA International produced this document, <u>The Guide to the Data Management Body of Knowledge</u> (the DAMA-DMBOK Guide), to further the data management profession. The DAMA-DMBOK Guide is intended to be a definitive introduction to data management.

No single book can describe the entire body of knowledge. The DAMA-DMBOK Guide does not attempt to be an encyclopedia of data management or the full-fledged discourse on all things related to data management. Instead, this guide briefly introduces concepts and identifies data management goals, functions and activities, primary deliverables, roles, principles, technology and organizational / cultural issues. It briefly describes commonly accepted good practices along with significant alternative approaches.

1.11 Goals of the DAMA-DMBOK Guide

As a definitive introduction, the goals of the DAMA-DMBOK Guide are:

1. To build consensus for a generally applicable view of data management functions.

2. To provide standard definitions for commonly used data management functions, deliverables, roles, and other terminology.

3. To identify guiding principles for data management.

4. To overview commonly accepted good practices, widely adopted methods and techniques, and significant alternative approaches, without reference to specific technology vendors or their products.

5. To briefly identify common organizational and cultural issues.

6. To clarify the scope and boundaries of data management.

7. To guide readers to additional resources for further understanding.

1.12 Audiences of the DAMA-DMBOK Guide

Audiences for the DAMA-DMBOK Guide include:

- Certified and aspiring data management professionals.

- Other IT professionals working with data management professionals.

- Data stewards of all types.

- Executives with an interest in managing data as an enterprise asset.

- Knowledge workers developing an appreciation of data as an enterprise asset.

- Consultants assessing and helping improve client data management functions.

- Educators responsible for developing and delivering a data management curriculum.

- Researchers in the field of data management.

1.13 Using the DAMA-DMBOK Guide

DAMA International foresees several potential uses of the DAMA-DMBOK Guide, including:

- Informing a diverse audience about the nature and importance of data management.

- Helping standardize terms and their meanings within the data management community.

- Helping data stewards and data management professionals understand their roles and responsibilities.

- Providing the basis for assessments of data management effectiveness and maturity.

- Guiding efforts to implement and improve their data management function.

- Pointing readers to additional sources of knowledge about data management.

- Guiding the development and delivery of data management curriculum content for higher education.

- Suggesting areas of further research in the field of data management.

- Helping data management professionals prepare for CDMP and CBIP exams.

1.14 Other BOK Guides

Several other professions have published a Body Of Knowledge document. Indeed, the existence of a Body of Knowledge document is one of the hallmarks of a mature profession (see Chapter 13).

The primary model for the DAMA-DMBOK Guide is <u>A Guide to the Project Management Body of Knowledge</u> (PMBOK® Guide), published by the Project Management Institute (PMI®). PMI® is a professional organization for project managers. Among its many services, PMI® conducts the Project Management Professional (PMP) certification program.

Other Body of Knowledge documents include:

- <u>A Guide to the Software Engineering Body of Knowledge</u> (SWEBOK), published by the Institute of Electrical and Electronic Engineers (IEEE). IEEE has begun to offer a certification program for software engineers.

- <u>The Business Analysis Body of Knowledge</u> (BABOK), published by the International Institute of Business Analysis.

- <u>The Common Body of Knowledge</u> (CBK) published by the International Information Systems Security Certification Consortium ((ISC). The CBK is the information tested to achieve the Certified Information Systems Security Professional (CISSP) designation.

- <u>The Canadian Information Technology Body of Knowledge</u> (CITBOK) is a project undertaken by the Canadian Information Processing Society (CIPS) to outline the knowledge required of a Canadian Information Technology Professional.

1.15 The DAMA Dictionary of Data Management

The <u>DAMA Dictionary of Data Management</u> is a companion volume to the DAMA-DMBOK Guide. Originally developed as an extensive Glossary for the DAMA-DMBOK Guide, DAMA International published it separately due to its size and business value. Definitions for terms found in the Dictionary are consistent with their usage in the DAMA-DMBOK Guide. The Dictionary is available for purchase as a CD-ROM.

1.16 The DAMA-DMBOK Functional Framework

In planning for the DAMA-DMBOK Guide, DAMA International recognized the need for:

- A comprehensive and commonly accepted process model for the data management function, defining a standard view of activities. This process model is presented in Chapter 2 and further explained in Chapters 3-12.

- An organizational environment, including goals, principles, activities, roles, primary deliverables, technology, skills, metrics, and organizational structures.

- A standard framework for discussing each aspect of data management in an organizational culture.

The DAMA-DMBOK Functional Framework is an organizing structure that promotes consistency within the DAMA-DMBOK Guide to meet the above needs. Version 3 of the Framework, shown in Figure 1.4, identifies 10 data management functions and the scope of each function.

In addition to identifying the 10 data management functions, the Framework also identifies seven Environmental Elements, shown in Figure 1.5. The scope of each of the environmental elements is shown in Figure 1.6.

The basic Environmental Elements are:

- Goals and Principles: The directional business goals of each function and the fundamental principles that guide performance of each function.

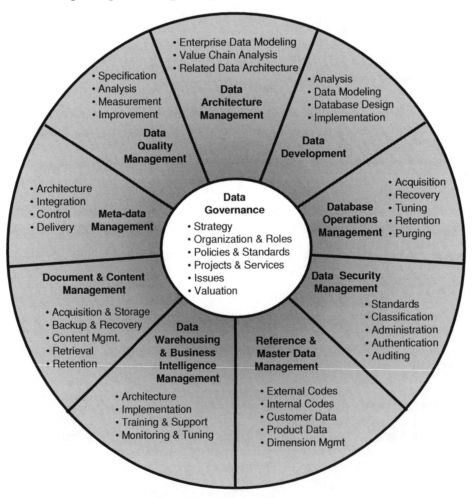

Figure 1.4 Data Management Functions – Scope Summary

- Activities: Each function is composed of lower level activities. Some activities are grouped into sub-activities. Activities are further decomposed into tasks and steps.

- Primary Deliverables: The information and physical databases and documents created as interim and final outputs of each function. Some deliverables are essential, some are generally recommended, and others are optional depending on circumstances.

- Roles and Responsibilities: The business and IT roles involved in performing and supervising the function, and the specific responsibilities of each role in that function. Many roles will participate in multiple functions.

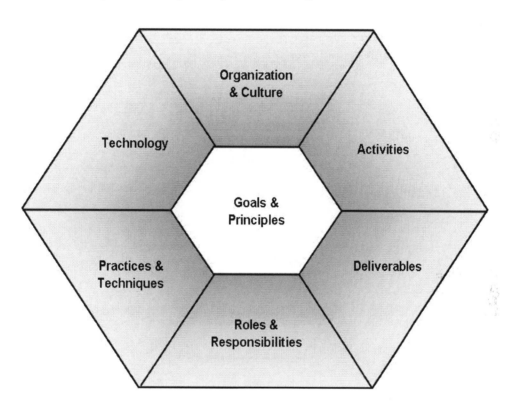

Figure 1.5 The Environmental Elements

The supporting Environmental Elements are:

- Practices and Techniques: Common and popular methods and procedures used to perform the processes and produce the deliverables. Practices and Techniques may also include common conventions, best practice recommendations, and alternative approaches without elaboration.

- Technology: Categories of supporting technology (primarily software tools), standards and protocols, product selection criteria and common learning curves. In accordance with DAMA International policies, specific vendors or products are not mentioned.

- Organization and Culture: These issues might include:
    o Management Metrics–measures of size, effort, time, cost, quality, effectiveness, productivity, success, and business value.
    o Critical Success Factors.
    o Reporting Structures.
    o Contracting Strategies.
    o Budgeting and Related Resource Allocation Issues.
    o Teamwork and Group Dynamics.
    o Authority and Empowerment.
    o Shared Values and Beliefs.
    o Expectations and Attitudes.
    o Personal Style and Preference Differences.
    o Cultural Rites, Rituals and Symbols.
    o Organizational Heritage.
    o Change Management Recommendations.

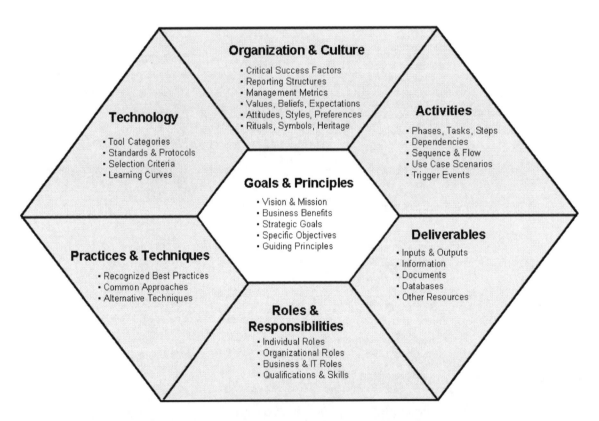

Figure 1.6 Environmental Elements – Scope Summary

The DAMA-DMBOK Functional Framework is conceptually a two-dimensional matrix, shown in Figure 1.7, with the functional decomposition of the data management function on its vertical axis and the set of environmental elements on its horizontal axis.

1.17 Structure of the DAMA-DMBOK Guide

Chapter 1 introduced:

- The importance of data assets in the Information Age.

- The data management function.

- The data management profession.

- The goals of the DAMA-DMBOK Guide.

Data Management Functions	Goals and Principles	Activities	Primary Deliverables	Roles and Responsibilities	Technology	Practices and Techniques	Organization and Culture
Data Governance							
Data Architecture Management							
Data Development							
Data Operations Management							
Data Security Management							
Reference and Master Data Management							
Data Warehousing and Business Intelligence Management							
Document and Content Management							
Meta-data Management							
Data Quality Management							

Figure 1.7 The DAMA-DMBOK Functional Framework, Version 3

Chapter 2 presents an overview of data management, including:

- The overall mission, goals, and benefits of data management.

- The component activities of each of the ten data management functions.

- The primary data management deliverables of each data management function.

- Data management roles.

- Classes of data management technology.

- Applying the DMBOK functional framework in organizations.

Chapters 3 through 12 each address one of the ten data management functions. One or more subject matter experts contributed to each chapter. Each chapter includes:

- A brief *Introduction* to the function, including definitions of key terms, a context diagram for the function, and a list of the business goals of the function.

- A description of *Concepts and Activities,* including associated deliverables, responsible roles and organizations, best practices, common procedures and techniques, and supporting technology.

- A *Summary* including a list restating guiding principles, a table recapping the activities, deliverables and responsibilities of the function, and a brief discussion of organizational and cultural issues.

- A selective list of books and articles suggested as *Recommended Reading*.

Chapter 13 addresses the data management profession and describes personal professional development practices for individual data management professionals.

1.18 Recurring Themes

The DAMA-DMBOK Guide refers to several recurring themes:

- Data Stewardship: Shared partnership for data management requires the ongoing participation of business data stewards in every function.

- Data Quality: Every data management function contributes in part to improving the quality of data assets.

- Data Integration: Every data management function contributes to and benefits from data integration techniques, managing data assets through minimizing redundancy, consolidating data from multiple sources, and ensuring consistency across controlled redundant data with a "golden version".

- Enterprise Perspective: Whenever possible, manage data assets consistently across the enterprise. Enterprise Information Management (EIM) is a best practice for data management.

- Cultural Change Leadership: Adopting the principles and practices of data management within an organization requires leadership from change agents at all levels.

2 Data Management Overview

Chapter 1 presented the concept of data management within the overall concept of the enterprise and information technology. Chapter 2 provides a detailed overview of data management that includes:

- An introduction to the mission, goals, and business benefits of data management.

- A process model for data management, identifying ten functions and the component activities of each function.

- An overview of the format used in the context diagrams that describe each function.

- An overview of the roles involved in activities across all ten data management functions.

- An overview of the general classes of technology that support data management.

Chapters 3 through 12 explore each of the ten data management functions and their component activities in more detail. Each chapter begins with an introduction that includes that function's context diagram. The rest of each chapter explains key concepts, and the activities in the diagram in depth. The last part of each chapter includes some guiding principles, organizational and cultural discussions, followed by a bibliography.

Finally, Chapter 13 covers topics related to professional development for data management professionals. All of these chapters together provide a basic body of knowledge regarding the data management profession, and data management functions and activities.

This chapter will cover process, people, and technology as it relates to overall data management. Chapters 3 through 12 concentrate on the process of each data management function.

2.1 Introduction

Data management is a function that is also known as a high-level business process. It consists of:

- The planning and execution of

- policies, practices, and projects that

- acquire, control, protect, deliver, and enhance the value of

- data and information assets.

Data management may also be the name of a program, which is an on-going initiative that includes several related projects. The term "data management program" can be substituted for "data management function". The major elements of data management are summarized in the context diagram shown in Figure 2.1.

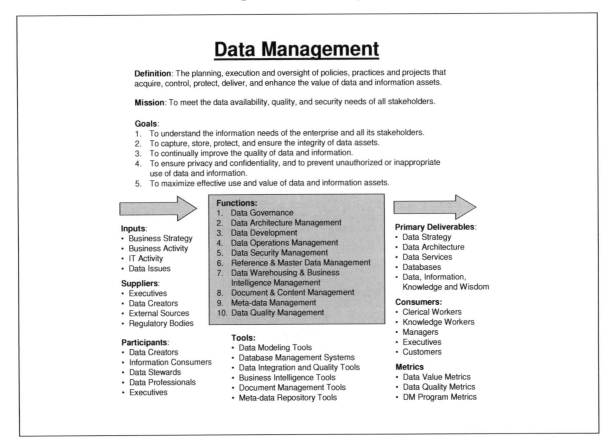

Figure 2.1 Data Management Context Diagram

2.2 Mission and Goals

The mission of the data management function is to meet and exceed the information needs of all the stakeholders in the enterprise in terms of information availability, security, and quality.

The strategic goals of the data management function are:

1. To understand the information needs of the enterprise and all its stakeholders.

2. To capture, store, protect, and ensure the integrity of data assets.

3. To continually improve the quality of data and information, including:
   o Data accuracy.
   o Data integrity.
   o Data integration.
   o The timeliness of data capture and presentation.
   o The relevance and usefulness of data.
   o The clarity and shared acceptance of data definitions.

4. To ensure privacy and confidentiality, and to prevent unauthorized or inappropriate use of data and information.

5. To maximize the effective use and value of data and information assets.

Other non-strategic goals of data management include:

6. To control the cost of data management.

7. To promote a wider and deeper understanding of the value of data assets.

8. To manage information consistently across the enterprise.

9. To align data management efforts and technology with business needs.

While the goals of data management are constant and consistent across enterprises, the objectives for data management at any enterprise vary from year to year. Objectives should be "SMART"–specific, measurable, achievable (or actionable), realistic, and timely, with a specified target timeframe.

2.3 Guiding Principles

Overall and general data management principles include:

1. Data and information are valuable enterprise assets.

2. Manage data and information carefully, like any other asset, by ensuring adequate quality, security, integrity, protection, availability, understanding, and effective use.

3. Share responsibility for data management between business data stewards (trustees of data assets) and data management professionals (expert custodians of data assets).

4. Data management is a business function and a set of related disciplines.

5. Data management is also an emerging and maturing profession within the IT field.

2.4 Functions and Activities

The process of data management is captured in functions and activities. The ten component functions of data management are:

1. Data Governance: The exercise of authority and control (planning, monitoring, and enforcement) over the management of data assets. Data Governance is high-level planning and control over data management.

2. Data Architecture Management: Defining the data needs of the enterprise, and designing the master blueprints to meet those needs. This function includes the development and maintenance of enterprise data architecture, within the

context of all enterprise architecture, and its connection with the application system solutions and projects that implement enterprise architecture.

3. Data Development: Designing, implementing, and maintaining solutions to meet the data needs of the enterprise. The data-focused activities within the system development lifecycle (SDLC), including data modeling, data requirements analysis, and design, implementation, and maintenance of databases' data-related solution components.

4. Data Operations Management: Planning, control, and support for structured data assets across the data lifecycle, from creation and acquisition through archival and purge.

5. Data Security Management: Planning, development, and execution of security policies and procedures to provide proper authentication, authorization, access, and auditing of data and information.

6. Reference and Master Data Management: Planning, implementation, and control activities to ensure consistency with a "golden version" of contextual data values.

7. Data Warehousing and Business Intelligence Management: Planning, implementation, and control processes to provide decision support data and support for knowledge workers engaged in reporting, query and analysis.

8. Document and Content Management: Planning, implementation, and control activities to store, protect, and access data found within electronic files and physical records (including text, graphics, images, audio, and video).

9. Meta-data Management: Planning, implementation, and control activities to enable easy access to high quality, integrated meta-data.

10. Data Quality Management: Planning, implementation, and control activities that apply quality management techniques to measure, assess, improve, and ensure the fitness of data for use.

Many data management activities overlap in scope with other recognized functions, within and outside IT. The DAMA-DMBOK Guide does not attempt to identify which processes are exclusive to a data management function. The only objective is to describe the full scope and context of data management.

Many data management activities described here are not performed in every enterprise. In fact, few organizations have plans, policies, and programs in each of the ten functions. In a given enterprise, certain functions will be more relevant, at least at any one point in time, and will receive higher priority than other functions. The enterprise will rightly invest more attention, time, and effort in some functions and less in others.

How each enterprise implements these activities varies widely. Each organization must determine an implementation approach consistent with its size, goals, resources, and complexity. However, the essential nature and the fundamental principles of data management remain the same across the spectrum of enterprises.

2.4.1 Data Management Activities

Each of these functions decomposes into activities. In a few cases, the activities further decompose into sub-activities. While noun phrases name functions, verb phrases name activities and sub-activities.

1. **Data Governance**
    1.1. Data Management Planning
        1.1.1. Understand Strategic Enterprise Data Needs
        1.1.2. Develop and Maintain the Data Strategy
        1.1.3. Establish Data Professional Roles and Organizations
        1.1.4. Identify and Appoint Data Stewards
        1.1.5. Establish Data Governance and Stewardship Organizations
        1.1.6. Develop and Approve Data Policies, Standards, and Procedures
        1.1.7. Review and Approve Data Architecture
        1.1.8. Plan and Sponsor Data Management Projects and Services
        1.1.9. Estimate Data Asset Value and Associated Costs
    1.2. Data Management Control
        1.2.1. Supervise Data Professional Organizations and Staff
        1.2.2. Coordinate Data Governance Activities
        1.2.3. Manage and Resolve Data Related Issues
        1.2.4. Monitor and Ensure Regulatory Compliance
        1.2.5. Monitor and Enforce Conformance with Data Policies, Standards and Architecture
        1.2.6. Oversee Data Management Projects and Services
        1.2.7. Communicate and Promote the Value of Data Assets

2. **Data Architecture Management**
    2.1. Understand Enterprise Information Needs
    2.2. Develop and Maintain the Enterprise Data Model
    2.3. Analyze and Align With Other Business Models
    2.4. Define and Maintain the Database Architecture (same as 4.2.2)
    2.5. Define and Maintain the Data Integration Architecture (same as 6.3)
    2.6. Define and Maintain the DW / BI Architecture (same as 7.2)
    2.7. Define and Maintain Enterprise Taxonomies and Namespaces (same as 8.2.1)
    2.8. Define and Maintain the Meta-data Architecture (same as 9.2)

3. **Data Development**
    3.1. Data Modeling, Analysis, and Solution Design
        3.1.1. Analyze Information Requirements
        3.1.2. Develop and Maintain Conceptual Data Models
        3.1.3. Develop and Maintain Logical Data Models
        3.1.4. Develop and Maintain Physical Data Models
    3.2. Detailed Data Design
        3.2.1. Design Physical Databases

6.2. Identify Master and Reference Data Sources and Contributors

6.3. Define and Maintain the Data Integration Architecture (same as 2.5)

6.4. Implement Reference and Master Data Management Solutions

6.5. Define and Maintain Match Rules

6.6. Establish "Golden" Records

6.7. Define and Maintain Hierarchies and Affiliations

6.8. Plan and Implement Integration of New Data Sources

6.9. Replicate and Distribute Reference and Master Data

6.10. Manage Changes to Reference and Master Data

7. **Data Warehousing and Business Intelligence Management** *

7.1. Understand Business Intelligence Information Needs

7.2. Define and Maintain the DW / BI Architecture (same as 2.6)

7.3. Implement Data Warehouses and Data Marts

7.4. Implement BI Tools and User Interfaces

7.5. Process Data for Business Intelligence

7.6. Monitor and Tune Data Warehousing Processes

7.7. Monitor and Tune BI Activity and Performance

8. **Document and Content Management**

8.1. Documents / Records Management

8.1.1. Plan for Managing Documents / Records

8.1.2. Implement Documents / Records Management Systems for Acquisition, Storage, Access, and Security Controls

8.1.3. Backup and Recover Documents / Records

8.1.4. Retain and Dispose of Documents / Records

8.1.5. Audit Documents / Records Management

8.2. Content Management

8.2.1. Define and Maintain Enterprise Taxonomies (same as 2.7)

8.2.2. Document / Index Information Content Meta-data

8.2.3. Provide Content Access and Retrieval

8.2.4. Govern for Quality Content

9. **Meta-data Management**

9.1. Understand Meta-data Requirements

9.2. Define the Meta-data Architecture (same as 2.8)

9.3. Develop and Maintain Meta-data Standards

9.4. Implement a Managed Meta-data Environment

9.5. Create and Maintain Meta-data

9.6. Integrate Meta-data

9.7. Manage Meta-data Repositories

---

* These activities do not include actual Business Intelligence activities performed by knowledge workers.
- Perform Ad-Hoc Querying and Reporting
- Perform Multi-dimensional Analysis
- Perform Statistical Analysis
- Perform Data Mining
- Model "What If" Scenarios
- Monitor and Analyze Business Performance

9.8. Distribute and Deliver Meta-data

9.9. Query, Report, and Analyze Meta-data

10. **Data Quality Management**

10.1. Develop and Promote Data Quality Awareness

10.2. Define Data Quality Requirement

10.3. Profile, Analyze, and Assess Data Quality

10.4. Define Data Quality Metrics

10.5. Define Data Quality Business Rules

10.6. Test and Validate Data Quality Requirements

10.7. Set and Evaluate Data Quality Service Levels

10.8. Continuously Measure and Monitor Data Quality

10.9. Manage Data Quality Issues

10.10. Clean and Correct Data Quality Defects

10.11. Design and Implement Operational DQM Procedures

10.12. Monitor Operational DQM Procedures and Performance

2.4.2 Activity Groups

Each activity belongs to one of four Activity Groups:

- Planning Activities (P): Activities that set the strategic and tactical course for other data management activities. Planning activities may be performed on a recurring basis.

- Development Activities (D): Activities undertaken within implementation projects and recognized as part of the systems development lifecycle (SDLC), creating data deliverables through analysis, design, building, testing, preparation, and deployment.

- Control Activities (C): Supervisory activities performed on an on-going basis.

- Operational Activities (O): Service and support activities performed on an on-going basis.

Each data management activity fits into one or more data management activity groups, as shown in Table 2.1.

Functions	Planning Activities (P)	Control Activities (C)	Development Activities (D)	Operational Activities (O)
1. Data Governance	1.1 Data Management Planning	1.2 Data Management Control		
2. Data Architecture Management	2. Data Architecture Management (all)			

Functions	Planning Activities (P)	Control Activities (C)	Development Activities (D)	Operational Activities (O)
3. Data Development	3.3 Data Model and Design Quality Management	3.3 Data Model and Design Quality Management	3.1 Data Modeling, Analysis, and Solution Design 3.2 Detailed Data Design 3.4 Data Implementation	
4. Data Operations Management	4.1 Database Support 4.2 Data Technology Management	4.1 Database Support 4.2 Data Technology Management		4.1 Database Support 4.2 Data Technology Management
5. Data Security Management	5.1 Understand Data Security Needs and Regulatory Requirements 5.2 Define Data Security Policy 5.3 Define Data Security Standards	5.5 Manage Users, Passwords, and Group Membership 5.6 Manage Data Access Views and Permissions 5.7 Monitor User Authentication and Access Behavior 5.8 Classify Information Confidentiality 5.9 Audit Data Security	5.4 Define Data Security Controls and Procedures	

Functions	Planning Activities (P)	Control Activities (C)	Development Activities (D)	Operational Activities (O)
6. Reference and Master Data Management	6.1 Understand Reference and Master Data Integration Needs 6.2 Understand Reference and Master Data Sources and Contributors 6.3 Define the Data Integration Architecture	6.5 Define and Maintain Match Rules 6.6 Establish "Golden" Records 6.7 Define and Maintain Hierarchies and Affiliations	6.4 Implement Reference and Master Data Management Solutions 6.8 Plan and Implement Integration of New Data Sources 6.10 Manage Changes to Reference and Master Data	6.9 Replicate and Distribute Reference and Master Data
7. Data Warehousing and Business Intelligence Management	7.1 Understand Business Intelligence Information Needs 7.2 Define and Maintain the DW / BI Architecture	7.6 Monitor and Tune Data Warehousing Processes 7.7 Monitor Business Intelligence Activity and Performance	7.3 Implement Data Warehouses and Data Marts 7.4 Implement BI Tools and User Interfaces	7.5 Process Data for Business Intelligence
8. Document and Content Management	8.1 Documents / Records Management 8.2 Content Management	8.1 Documents / Records Management 8.2 Content Management		8.1 Documents / Records Management 8.2 Content Management
9. Meta-data Management	9.1 Understand Meta-data Requirements 9.2 Define the Meta-data Architecture 9.3 Develop and Maintain Meta-data Standards	9.6 Integrate Meta-data 9.7 Manage Meta-data Repositories 9.8. Deliver and Distribute Meta-data	9.4 Implement a Managed Meta-data Environment	9.5 Create and Maintain Meta-data 9.9 Query, Report, and Analyze Meta-data

Functions	Planning Activities (P)	Control Activities (C)	Development Activities (D)	Operational Activities (O)
10. Data Quality Management	10.4 Define Data Quality Metrics 10.5 Define Data Quality Business Rules 10.7 Set and Evaluate Data Quality Service Levels	10.8 Continuously Measure and Monitor Data Quality 10.9 Manage Data Quality Issues 10.12 Monitor Operational DQM Procedures and Performance	10.2 Define Data Quality Requirements 10.3 Profile, Analyze, and Assess Data Quality 10.6 Test and Validate Data Quality Requirements 10.11 Design and Implement Operational DQM Procedures	10.1 Develop and Promote Data Quality Awareness 10.10 Clean and Correct Data Quality Defects

Table 2.1 Activities by Activity Groups

2.5 Context Diagram Overview

Each context diagram in this Guide contains a definition and a list of goals at the top of the diagram. In the center of each diagram is a blue box containing the list of that function's activities, and in some cases, sub-activities. Each chapter describes these activities and sub-activities in depth.

Surrounding each center activity box are several lists. The lists on the left side (flowing into the activities) are the Inputs, Suppliers, and Participants. The list below the box is for Tools used by the Activities. The lists on the right side (flowing out of the activities) are Primary Deliverables, Consumers, and sometimes Metrics.

These lists contain items that apply to that list's topic. By no means are they exhaustive, and some of the items will not apply to all organizations. These lists are meant as a context framework, and will grow over time as the data management profession grows and matures.

For convenience of comparison, all of the contents of each function list are included in appendices.

2.5.1 Suppliers

Suppliers are the entities responsible for supplying inputs for the activities. Several suppliers relate to multiple data management functions. Suppliers for data management in general include Executives, Data Creators, External Sources, and

Regulatory Bodies. The suppliers for each data management function are listed in Appendix A1.

2.5.2 Inputs

Inputs are the tangible things that each function needs to initiate its activities. Several inputs are used by multiple functions. Inputs for data management in general include Business Strategy, Business Activity, IT Activity, and Data Issues. The inputs for each data management function are listed in Appendix A2.

2.5.3 Participants

Participants are involved in the data management process, although not necessarily directly or with accountability. Multiple participants may be involved in multiple functions. Participants in data management in general include Data Creators, Information Consumers, Data Stewards, Data Professionals, and Executives. The participants in each data management function are listed in Appendix A3.

2.5.4 Tools

Data management professionals use tools to perform activities in the functions. Several tools are used by multiple functions. Tools for data management in general include Data Modeling Tools, Database Management Systems, Data Integration and Quality Tools, Business Intelligence Tools, Document Management Tools, and Meta-data Repository Tools. The tools used by each data management function are listed in Appendix A4.

2.5.5 Primary Deliverables

Primary deliverables are the tangible things that each function is responsible for creating. Several primary deliverables are created by multiple functions. The primary deliverables for Data Management in general include Data Strategy, Data Architecture, Data Services, Databases, and Data, Information, Knowledge and Wisdom. Obviously, ten functions would have to cooperate to provide only eight deliverables. The primary deliverables of each data management function are listed in Appendix A5.

2.5.6 Consumers

Consumers are those that benefit from the primary deliverables created by the data management activities. Several consumers benefit from multiple functions. Consumers of data management deliverables in general include Clerical Workers, Knowledge Workers, Managers, Executives, and Customers. The consumers of each data management function are listed in Appendix A6.

2.5.7 Metrics

The metrics are the measurable things that each function is responsible for creating. Several metrics measure multiple functions, and some functions do not (in this edition) have defined metrics. Metrics for data management include Data Value Metrics, Data Quality Metrics, and Data Management Program Metrics. The metrics for each data management function are listed in Appendix A7.

2.6 Roles

The people part of data management involves organizations and roles. Many organizations and individuals are involved in data management. Each company has different needs and priorities. Therefore, each company has a different approach to organizations, and individual roles and responsibilities, for data management functions and activities. Provided here is an overview of some of the most common organizational categories and individual roles.

Suppliers, participants, and consumers, as mentioned in the context diagrams, may be involved in one or more data management organizations, and may play one or more individual roles. It would be beyond the scope of this work to identify and define all possible suppliers, participants, and consumers, and all the roles and organizations that would apply. However, it is possible to outline the high-level types of organizations and individual roles.

2.6.1 Types of Organizations

Table 2.2 includes descriptions of the most common types of data management organizations.

Types of Data Management Organizations	Description
Data Management Services organization(s)	One or more units of data management professionals responsible for data management within the IT organization. A centralized organization is sometimes known as an Enterprise Information Management (EIM) Center of Excellence (COE).
	This team includes the DM Executive, other DM Managers, Data Architects, Data Analysts, Data Quality Analysts, Database Administrators, Data Security Administrators, Meta-data Specialists, Data Model Administrators, Data Warehouse Architects, Data Integration Architects, and Business Intelligence Analysts.
	May also include Database Administrators (DBA), although DBAs are found within both Software Development organizations and Infrastructure Management organizations. May also include Data Integration Developers and Analytics / Report Developers, although often they remain in Software Development organizations with other developers.

Types of Data Management Organizations	Description
Data Governance Council	The primary and highest authority organization for data governance in an organization. Includes senior managers serving as executive data stewards, along with the DM Leader and the CIO. A business executive (Chief Data Steward) may formally chair the council, in partnership with the DM Executive and Data Stewardship Facilitators responsible for council participation, communication, meeting preparation, meeting agendas, issues, etc.
Data Stewardship Steering Committee(s)	One or more cross-functional groups of coordinating data stewards responsible for support and oversight of a particular data management initiative launched by the Data Governance Council, such as Enterprise Data Architecture, Master Data Management, or Meta-data Management. The Data Governance Council may delegate responsibilities to one or more Data Stewardship Committees.
Data Stewardship Team(s)	One or more temporary or permanent focused groups of business data stewards collaborating on data modeling, data definition, data quality requirement specification and data quality improvement, reference and master data management, and meta-data management, typically within an assigned subject area, led by a coordinating data steward in partnership with a data architect and a data stewardship facilitator.
Data Governance Office (DGO)	A staff organization in larger enterprises supporting the efforts of the Data Governance Council, Data Stewardship Steering Committees, and Data Stewardship Teams. The DGO may be within or outside of the IT organization. The DGO staff includes Data Stewardship Facilitators who enable stewardship activities performed by business data stewards.

Table 2.2 Types of Data Management Organizations

2.6.2 Types of Individual Roles

Table 2.3 contains a summary of many individual roles that may participate in data management activities.

2.7 Technology

The Technology section identifies and defines the categories of technology related to data management. Technology is covered in each chapter where tools are specifically mentioned.

© 2010 DAMA International

2.7.1 Software Product Classes

The metrics are the measurable things that each function is responsible for creating. Several Metrics measure multiple functions, and some functions do not (in this edition) have defined metrics. Metrics for data management include Data Value Metrics, Data Quality Metrics, and DM Program Metrics. The metrics for each data management function are listed in Appendix A7.

Types of Data Management Individual Roles	Description
Business Data Steward	A knowledge worker and business leader recognized as a subject matter expert who is assigned accountability for the data specifications and data quality of specifically assigned business entities, subject areas or databases, who will: 1. Participate on one or more Data Stewardship Teams. 2. Identify and define local and enterprise information needs. 3. Propose, draft, review, and refine business names, definitions, and other data model specifications for assigned entities and data attributes. 4. Ensure the validity and relevance of assigned data model subject areas. 5. Define and maintain data quality requirements and business rules for assigned data attributes. 6. Maintain assigned reference data values and meanings. 7. Assist in data quality test planning and design, test data creation, and data requirements verification. 8. Identify and help resolve data issues. 9. Assist in data quality analysis and improvement. 10. Provide input to data policies, standards, and procedures.
Coordinating Data Steward	A business data steward with additional responsibilities, who will: 1. Provide business leadership for a Data Stewardship Team. 2. Participate on a Data Stewardship Steering Committee. 3. Identify business data steward candidates. 4. Review and approve changes to reference data values and meanings. 5. Review and approve logical data models. 6. Ensure application data requirements are met. 7. Review data quality analysis and audits.

Types of Data Management Individual Roles	Description
Executive Data Steward	A role held by a senior manager sitting on the Data Governance Council, who will: 1. Serve as an active Data Governance Council member. 2. Represent departmental and enterprise data interests . 3. Appoint coordinating and business data stewards. 4. Review and approve data policies, standards, metrics, and procedures. 5. Review and approve data architecture, data models, and specifications. 6. Resolve data issues. 7. Sponsor and oversee data management projects and services. 8. Review and approve estimates of data asset value. 9. Communicate and promote the value of information. 10. Monitor and enforce data policies and practices within a department.
Data Stewardship Facilitator	A business analyst responsible for coordinating data governance and stewardship activities, who will:. 1. Help executives identify and appoint business data stewards 2. Schedule and announce meetings of the data governance council, data stewardship steering committees. and data stewardship teams. 3. Plan and publish meeting agendas. 4. Prepare and distribute meeting minutes. 5. Prepare meeting discussion materials and distribute for prior review. 6. Manage and coordinate resolution of data issues. 7. Assist in definition and framing of data issues and solution alternatives. 8. Assist in definition of data management policies and standards. 9. Assist in understanding business information needs. 10. Ensure business participation in data modeling and data architecture. 11. Assist in drafting business data names, definitions, and quality requirements.

Types of Data Management Individual Roles	Description
Data Management Executive	The highest-level manager of Data Management Services organizations in an IT department.. The DM Executive reports to the CIO and is the manager most directly responsible for data management, including coordinating data governance and data stewardship activities, overseeing data management projects, and supervising data management professionals. May be a manager, director, AVP or VP.
Data Architect	A senior data analyst responsible for data architecture and data integration.
Enterprise Data Architect	The senior data architect responsible for developing, maintaining, and leveraging the enterprise data model.
Data Warehouse Architect	A data architect responsible for data warehouses, data marts, and associated data integration processes.
Data Analyst / Data Modeler	An IT professional responsible for capturing and modeling data requirements, data definitions, business rules, data quality requirements, and logical and physical data models.
Data Model Administrator	Responsible for data model version control and change control.
Meta-data Specialist	Responsible for integration, control, and delivery of meta-data, including administration of meta-data repositories.
Data Quality Analyst	Responsible for determining the fitness of data for use.
Database Administrator	Responsible for the design, implementation, and support of structured data assets.
Data Security Administrator	Responsible for ensuring controlled access to classified data.
Data Integration Architect	A senior data integration developer responsible for designing technology to integrate and improve the quality of enterprise data assets.
Data Integration Specialist	A software designer and developer responsible for implementing systems to integrate (replicate, extract, transform, load) data assets in batch or near real time.
Business Intelligence Architect	A senior business intelligence analyst responsible for the design of the business intelligence user environment.
Business Intelligence Analyst / Administrator	Responsible for supporting effective use of business intelligence data by business professionals.
Business Intelligence Program Manager	Coordinates BI requirements and initiatives across the corporation and integrates them into a cohesive prioritized program and roadmap.
Analytics / Report Developer	A software developer responsible for creating reporting and analytical application solutions.

Types of Data Management Individual Roles	Description
Business Process Analyst	Responsible for understanding and optimizing business processes.
Enterprise Process Architect	Senior business process analyst responsible for overall quality of the enterprise process model and enterprise business model.
Application Architect	Senior developer responsible for integrating application systems.
Technical Architect	Senior technical engineer responsible for coordinating and integrating the IT infrastructure and the IT technology portfolio.
Technical Engineer	Senior technical analyst responsible for researching, implementing, administering, and supporting a portion of the information technology infrastructure.
Help Desk Administrator	Responsible for handling, tracking, and resolving issues related to use of information, information systems, or the IT infrastructure.
IT Auditor	An internal or external auditor of IT responsibilities, including data quality and / or data security.
Chief Knowledge Officer (CKO)	The executive with overall responsibility for knowledge management, including protection and control of intellectual property, enablement of professional development, collaboration, mentoring, and organizational learning.
Collaborators	Suppliers or consortium participants of an organization. These may engage in data sharing agreements.
Data Brokers	Suppliers of data and meta-data often by subscription for use in an organization.
Government and Regulatory Bodies	Data Management rules of engagement in the market are specified and enforced by various government and regulatory bodies. Privacy, confidential, proprietary data, and information are key areas.
Knowledge Workers	Business analyst consumers of data and information who add value to the data for the organization.

Table 2.3 Types of Individual Roles

2.7.2 Specialized Hardware

While most data technology is software running on general purpose hardware, occasionally specialized hardware is used to support unique data management requirements. Types of specialized hardware include:

- Parallel processing computers: Often used to support Very Large Databases (VLDB). There are two common parallel processing architectures, SMP (symmetrical multi-processing) and MPP (massive parallel processing).

- Data appliances: Servers built specifically for data transformation and distribution. These servers integrate with existing infrastructure either directly as a plug in, or peripherally as a network connection.

2.8 Recommended Reading

Adelman, Sid, Larissa Moss, and Majid Abai. <u>Data Strategy</u>. Addison-Wesley, 2005. ISBN 0-321-24099-5. 384 pages.

Boddie, John. <u>The Information Asset: Rational DP Funding and Other Radical Notions</u>. Prentice-Hall (Yourdon Press Computing Series), 1993. ISBN 0-134-57326-9. 174 pages.

Bryce, Milt and Tim Bryce. <u>The IRM Revolution: Blueprint for the 21st Century</u>. M. Bryce Associates Inc., 1988. ISBN 0-962-11890-7. 255 pages.

DAMA Chicago Chapter Standards Committee, editors. <u>Guidelines to Implementing Data Resource Management, 4th Edition</u>. Bellevue, WA: The Data Management Association (DAMA International), 2002. ISBN 0-9676674-1-0. 359 pages.

Durell, William R. <u>Data Administration: A Practical Guide to Successful Data Management</u>. New York: McGraw-Hill, 1985. ISBN 0-070-18391-0. 202 pages.

Horrocks, Brian and Judy Moss. <u>Practical Data Administration</u>. Prentice-Hall International, 1993. ISBN 0-13-689696-0.

Kent, William. <u>Data and Reality: Basic Assumptions in Data Processing Reconsidered</u>. Authorhouse, 2000. ISBN 1-585-00970-9. 276 pages.

Kerr, James M. <u>The IRM Imperative</u>. John Wiley & Sons, 1991. ISBN 0-471-52434-4.

Newton, Judith J. and Daniel Wahl, editors. <u>Manual For Data Administration</u>. Washington, DC: GPO, NIST Special Publications 500-208, Diane Publishing Co., 1993. ISBN 1-568-06362-8.

Purba, Sanjiv, editor. <u>Data Management Handbook, 3rd Edition</u>. Auerbach, 1999. ISBN 0-849-39832-0. 1048 pages.

3 Data Governance

Data Governance is the core function of the Data Management Framework shown in Figures 1.3. and 1.4. It interacts with and influences each of the surrounding ten data management functions. Chapter 3 defines the data governance function and explains the concepts and activities involved in data governance.

3.1 Introduction

Data governance is the exercise of authority and control (planning, monitoring, and enforcement) over the management of data assets. The data governance function guides how all other data management functions are performed. Data governance is high-level, executive data stewardship.

The context diagram for the data governance function is shown in Figure 3.1.

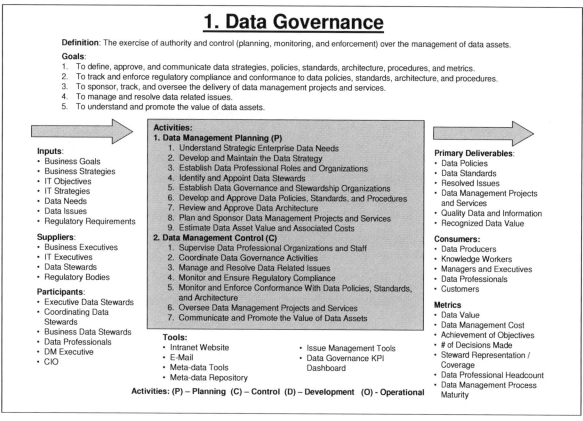

Figure 3.1 Data Governance Context Diagram

3.2 Concepts and Activities

Chapters 1 and 2 state that data management is a shared responsibility between business data stewards, representing stakeholders across the organization, and data professionals, who work on their behalf. Business data stewards are the trustees of enterprise data assets; data management professionals are the expert custodians of these assets. Effective data management depends on an effective partnership between business data stewards and data management professionals, especially in data governance.

Shared decision making is the hallmark of data governance, as shown in Figure 3.2. Effective data management requires working across organizational and system boundaries. Data Governance enables shared responsibility for selected decisions, crossing these boundaries and supporting an integrated view of data. Some decisions are primarily business decisions made with input and guidance from IT, others are primarily technical decisions made with input and guidance from business data stewards at all levels.

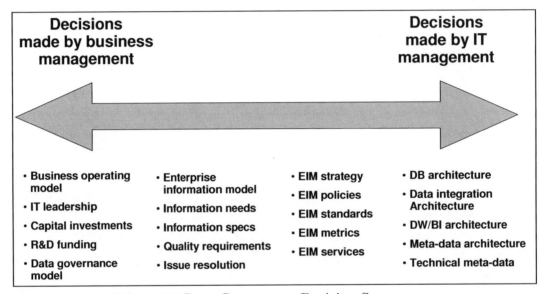

Figure 3.2 Data Governance Decision Spectrum

3.2.1 Data Governance

Data governance is accomplished most effectively as an on-going program and a continual improvement process.

Every effective data governance program is unique, taking into account distinctive organizational and cultural issues, and the immediate data management challenges and opportunities. Data governance is a relatively new term, and many organizations continue to pioneer new approaches. Nevertheless, effective data governance programs share many common characteristics, based on basic concepts and principles.

Data governance is not the same thing as IT governance. IT governance makes decisions about IT investments, the IT application portfolio, and the IT project portfolio. IT governance aligns the IT strategies and investments with enterprise goals and strategies. CobiT (Control Objectives for Information and related Technology) provides standards for IT governance, but only a small portion of the CobiT framework addresses managing information. Some critical issues, such as Sarbanes-Oxley compliance, span the concerns of corporate governance, IT governance, and data governance. Data governance is focused exclusively on the management of data assets.

Data governance is at the heart of managing data assets. In the circular depiction of the ten data management functions introduced in Chapter One, data governance is shown in the center.

Another way of depicting the controlling position of data governance is as "the management roof" over other data management functions, as shown in Figure 3.3.

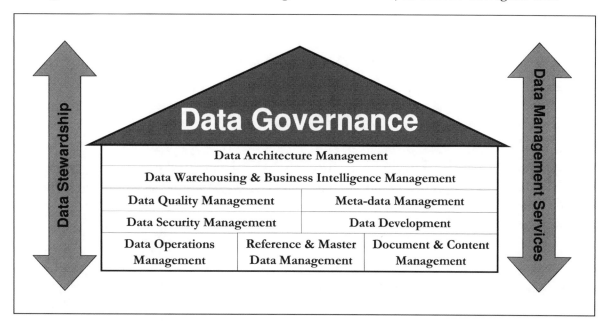

Figure 3.3 Data Governance, Stewardship, and Services

3.2.2 Data Stewardship

Data stewardship is the formal accountability for business responsibilities ensuring effective control and use of data assets. Some of these responsibilities are data governance responsibilities, but there are also significant data stewardship responsibilities within each of the other major data management functions.

A data steward is a business leader and / or recognized subject matter expert designated as accountable for these responsibilities. As in other endeavors, a good steward carefully protects, manages, and leverages the resources for which he / she is entrusted.

The best data stewards are found, not made. Many of these activities are performed by business professionals even before a formal data stewardship program is implemented. To that extent, data stewardship responsibilities are not new and additional responsibilities for these people. Whenever possible, appoint the people already interested and involved. Their appointment to a data stewardship role is a recognition and confirmation of the work they are already performing. Appointing data stewards formalizes their accountability.

Data stewards manage data assets on behalf of others and in the best interests of the organization. Data stewards are appointed to represent the data interests of all stakeholders, including but not limited to, the interests of their own functional departments and divisions. Data stewards must take an enterprise perspective to ensure the quality and effective use of enterprise data.

Organizations often differentiate between executive, coordinating, and business data stewards:

- *Executive data stewards* are senior managers who serve on a Data Governance Council.

- *Coordinating data stewards* lead and represent teams of business data stewards in discussions across teams and with executive data stewards. Coordinating data stewards are particularly important in large organizations.

- *Business data stewards* are recognized subject matter experts working with data management professionals on an ongoing basis to define and control data.

Data governance is high-level, executive data stewardship. In other words, data governance is the making of high-level data stewardship decisions, primarily by executive and coordinating data stewards.

Data stewardship responsibilities exist in data management functions beyond data governance:

- Data Architecture Management: Data stewards review, validate, approve, and refine data architecture. Business data stewards define data requirements specifications that data architects organize into the enterprise's data architecture. Coordinating data stewards help data architects integrate these specifications, resolving differences in names and meanings. Executive data stewards review and approve the enterprise data architecture. Data stewards of all levels and data architects collaborate to maintain data architecture.

- Data Development: Business data stewards define data requirements and the specifications that data analysts and architects organize into logical data models. Data stewards also validate physical data models and database designs, participate in database testing and conversion, and ensure consistent use of terms in user documentation and training. Data stewards identify data issues as they arise and escalate when necessary.

- Data Operations Management: Business data stewards define requirements for data recovery, retention and performance, and help negotiate service levels in these areas. Business data stewards also help identify, acquire, and control externally sourced data.

- Data Security Management: Business data stewards provide security, privacy and confidentiality requirements, identify and resolve data security issues, assist in data security audits, and classify the confidentiality of information in documents and other information products.

- Reference and Master Data Management: Business data stewards control the creation, update, and retirement of code values and other reference data, define master data management requirements, identify and help resolve master data management issues.

- Data Warehousing and Business Intelligence Management: Business data stewards provide business intelligence requirements and management metrics, and they identify and help resolve business intelligence issues.

- Document and Content Management: Business data stewards help define enterprise taxonomies and resolve content management issues.

- Meta-data Management: Data stewards at all levels create and maintain business meta-data (names, meanings, business rules), define meta-data access and integration needs, and use meta-data to make effective data stewardship and governance decisions. Defining and maintaining business meta-data is at the heart of data stewardship.

- Data Quality Management: Improving data quality is an essential part of data stewardship. Business data stewards define data quality requirements and business rules, test application edits and validations, assist in the analysis, certification, and auditing of data quality, lead data clean-up efforts, identify proactive ways to solve root causes of poor data quality, promote data quality awareness, and ensure data quality requirements are met. Data stewards actively profile and analyze data quality in partnership with data professionals.

3.2.3 Data Governance and Stewardship Organizations

Data governance guides each of the other data management functions. Every data governance program has a slightly different scope, but that scope may include:

- Data Strategy and Policies: Defining, communicating, monitoring.

- Data Standards and Architecture: Reviewing, approving, monitoring.

- Regulatory Compliance: Communicating, monitoring, enforcing.

- Issue Management: Identifying, defining, escalating, resolving.

- Data Management Projects: Sponsoring, overseeing.

- Data Asset Valuation: Estimating, approving, monitoring.

- Communication: Promoting, building awareness and appreciation.

Data governance is essentially "the government of data" within the enterprise. Like other governments, there are many different models of data governance – anarchy, dictatorship, and everything in between. Some decisions can be made without risk by individual managers. But the need for shared decision making and risk control drives most organizations to a representative form of data governance, so that all stakeholders and constituencies can be heard.

Data management professionals have responsibility for administering data policies, standards, and procedures, for managing and implementing data architecture, for protecting data assets and stakeholder interests, and for providing data management services.

In particular, three principles can be drawn from the representative government analogy:

1. Data governance includes responsibility for legislative functions (policies and standards), judicial functions (issue management) and executive functions (administration, services, and compliance).

   o Data stewardship and governance organizations have responsibility for setting policies, standards, architecture, and procedures, and for resolving data related issues.

   o Data management professional organizations have responsibility for administering data policies, standards, and procedures, for managing and implementing data architecture, for protecting data assets and stakeholder interests, and for providing data management services.

2. Data governance typically operates at both enterprise and local levels. In large organizations, data governance may also be required at levels in between, depending on the size of the enterprise.

3. Separation of duties between Data Stewardship (Legislative and Judicial) and Data Management Services (Executive) provides a degree of checks and balances for the management of data.

Typically, three cross-functional data stewardship and governance organizations have legislative and judicial responsibilities:

- The Data Governance Council has enterprise-wide authority over data management. Executive data stewards sitting on the council are senior managers representing both departmental and enterprise perspectives.

- The Data Stewardship Program Steering Committees support the Data Governance Council, much like congressional committees, drafting policies and standards for review and approval by the Data Governance Council regarding specific initiatives, and overseeing these sponsored initiatives.

- Data stewardship teams are focused groups of business data stewards collaborating on data stewardship activities within a defined subject area. Data stewardship teams bring together subject matter experts from across the enterprise to determine which data names, definitions, data quality requirements, and business rules should be consistent and what must remain locally unique. Data stewardship teams should be standing, permanent groups that meet regularly, working closely with data architects.

The rules defined by data governance organizations include the overall data strategy, data policies, data standards, data management procedures, data management metrics, the business data names, business definitions and business rules found in the enterprise data model, additional data requirement specifications, and data quality business rules.

The issues adjudicated by data governance organizations include data security issues, data access issues, data quality issues, regulatory compliance issues, policy and standards conformance issues, name and definition conflicts, and data governance procedural issues.

Data management professionals perform executive branch responsibilities much like governmental departments and agencies. They administer, monitor and enforce data policies, standards, and procedures. They coordinate, maintain, and implement data architecture. Data management professionals gather and review requirements, facilitate data modeling to serve stakeholder interests, and enable data delivery by implementing databases and applications. They acquire and protect data assets, monitor data quality, and audit data quality and security.

In addition to their other professional duties, some data management professionals provide staff support for data governance organizations. Business data stewards are business professionals and managers with part-time stewardship responsibilities. Data management professionals must respect their time and coordinate data governance activity—scheduling meetings, planning and publishing agendas, providing documents for review prior to each meeting, facilitating the meetings, tracking issues, following up on decisions, and publishing meeting minutes. Data architects facilitate each data stewardship team. The Data Management Executive and / or the enterprise data architect may staff Data Stewardship Program Steering Committees. The Data Management Executive and the Chief Information Officer (CIO) guide the Data Governance Council, often with assistance from a Data Governance Office (see 3.2.6 below).

At the same time, each organization should be chaired by a business representative. Coordinating data stewards chair their data stewardship teams. An executive data steward from the Data Governance Council should chair each Data Stewardship Coordinating Committee. A Chief Data Steward, selected from among the executive data stewards, chairs the Data Governance Council.

Large organizations may have divisional or departmental data governance councils working under the auspices of the Enterprise Data Governance Council. Smaller organizations should try to avoid such complexity.

3.2.4 Data Management Services Organizations

Data management professionals within the IT department report to one or more Data Management Services (DMS) organizations. In many enterprises, there may be a centralized DMS organization, while in others there are multiple decentralized groups. Some enterprises have both local DMS organizations as well as a centralized organization. A centralized DMS organization is sometimes known as a Data Management Center of Excellence (COE).

Data management professionals within DMS organizations may include data architects, data analysts, data modelers, data quality analysts, database administrators, data security administrators, meta-data administrators, data model administrators, data warehouse architects, data integration architects, and business intelligence analysts. These organizations may also include data integration developers and analytics / report developers, although often they remain in the Application Development organization with other developers. Decentralized organizations may include only a few of these roles. The data management professionals across all organizations constitute a data management professional community, and together with data stewards, they unite in a Data Management Community of Interest (COI).

3.2.5 The Data Management Executive

There is no substitute for the leadership of a CIO and a dedicated Data Management Executive, guiding the data management function and promoting the data management program. Visionary and active leadership is a critical success factor for effective data management.

The Data Management Executive leads the data management function, serving as the CIO's right hand for information. The Data Management Executive should report directly to the CIO, responsible for coordinating data management, data stewardship, and data governance. Given the broad scope of the CIO's responsibilities, the CIO needs one person accountable for managing data and information assets.

Data Management Services organizations and their staff should report to the Data Management Executive, directly or indirectly. The Data Management Executive is responsible for data management professional staffing, skills development, contractor management, budgeting and resource allocation, management metrics, data steward recruitment, collaboration across business and IT organizations, and management of the organizational and cultural changes required to support data management. The Data Management Executive works closely with peer leaders of Application Development, Infrastructure / Operations and other IT functions.

The Data Management Executive is responsible for implementing the decisions of the Data Governance Council. He or she serves as the operational coordinator for the Data Governance Council, working in close partnership with the Chief Data Steward, by maintaining the data strategy and overseeing data management projects.

3.2.6 The Data Governance Office

In larger enterprises, The Data Governance Office is a staff organization of data stewardship facilitators who support the activities and decision making of business data stewards at all levels. The purpose of the Data Governance Office is to provide full-time support for part-time business data stewardship responsibilities.

Much as a congressional committee is supported by staff professionals, the data stewardship facilitators perform the legwork required to obtain the information that enables business data stewards to make informed and effective decisions. In larger enterprises, the addition of staff responsibilities to data management responsibilities may be overwhelming. The Data Management Executive, data architects, and data quality analysts may not be able to find the necessary time to effectively coordinate the communicating, information gathering, and decision making required for data governance and stewardship. When this happens, organizations should consider creating a Data Governance Office.

It is critical that full-time data stewardship facilitators do not assume responsibility for data stewardship. Their role is to support the Data Governance Council, Data Stewardship Committees, and Data Stewardship Teams. The Data Governance Office may report to the Data Management Executive, or it may report outside of IT entirely. The diagram in Figure 3.4 depicts these organizations and their relationships.

3.3 Data Governance Activities

The activities comprising the data governance function are explained below. Each of the activities is important for fully implementing the data governance function within an organization.

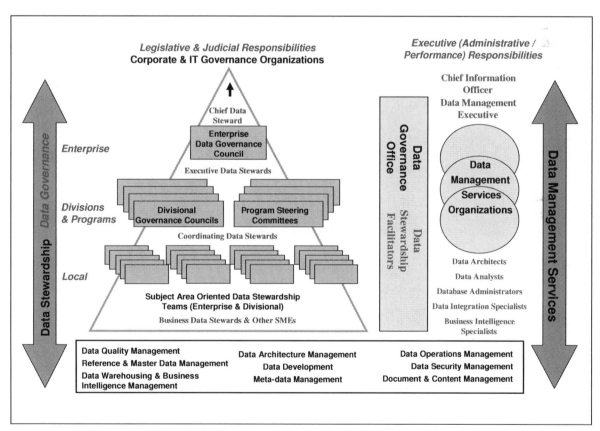

Figure 3.4 Data Management Organizations–Governance, Stewardship, Services

3.3.1 Data Strategy

A strategy is a set of choices and decisions that together chart a high-level course of action to achieve high-level goals. In the game of chess, a strategy is a sequenced set of moves to win by checkmate or to survive by stalemate. A strategic plan is a high-level course of action to achieve high-level goals.

Typically, a data strategy is a data management program strategy—a plan for maintaining and improving data quality, integrity, security, and access. However, a data strategy may also include business plans to use information to competitive advantage and support enterprise goals. Data strategy must come from an understanding of the data needs inherent in the business strategies. These data needs drive the data strategy.

Data strategy is not the same thing as data architecture. The decision to define data architecture may be part of a strategy, and the decisions to implement components of data architecture are strategic decisions. The strategy may influence the architecture, which, in turn, supports the strategy, guiding other decisions.

In many organizations, the data strategy is owned and maintained by the Data Governance Council, with guidance from the Chief Information Officer and the Data Management Executive. In other organizations, these executives may retain ownership and control of the data strategy; however, sharing ownership builds a data management partnership with the business. Often, the Data Management Executive will draft an initial data strategy even before a Data Governance Council is formed, in order to gain senior management commitment for establishing data stewardship and governance.

The components of a data strategy might include:

- A compelling vision for data management.

- A summary business case for data management, with selected examples.

- Guiding principles, values, and management perspectives.

- The mission and long-term directional goals of data management.

- Management measures of data management success.

- Short-term (12-24 months) SMART (specific / measurable / actionable / realistic / time-bound) data management program objectives.

- Descriptions of data management roles and organizations, along with a summary of their responsibilities and decision rights.

- Descriptions of data management program components and initiatives.

- An outline of the data management implementation roadmap (projects and action items).

- Scope boundaries and decisions to postpone investments and table certain issues.

The data strategy is often packaged into three separate deliverables, including:

- A Data Management Program Charter: Overall vision, business case, goals, guiding principles, measures of success, critical success factors, recognized risks, etc.

- A Data Management Scope Statement: Goals and objectives for some planning horizon, usually 3 years, and the roles, organizations, and individual leaders accountable for achieving these objectives.

- A Data Management Implementation Roadmap: Identifying specific programs, projects, task assignments, and delivery milestones.

These deliverables are often published as part of a Data Management Program intranet website.

The data strategy should address all data management functions relevant to the organization. For instance, the data strategy should include the meta-data management strategy. See Figure 2.1 for the complete list of data management functions.

3.3.2 Data Policies

Data policies are short statements of management intent and fundamental rules governing the creation, acquisition, integrity, security, quality, and use of data and information. Data policies are more fundamental, global, and business critical than detailed data standards. Data policies vary widely across organizations. Data policies describe "what" to do and what not to do, while standards and procedures describe "how" to do something. There should be relatively few data policies, and they should be stated briefly and directly.

Data policies are typically drafted by data management professionals. Next, data stewards and management review and refine the policies. The Data Governance Council conducts the final review, revision, and adoption of the data policies. The Data Governance Council may delegate this authority to the Data Stewardship Committee or the Data Management Services Organization.

Data policies must be effectively communicated, monitored, enforced, and periodically re-evaluated. Data policies may cover topics such as:

- Data modeling and other data development activities within the SDLC.

- Development and use of data architecture.

- Data quality expectations, roles, and responsibilities (including meta-data quality).

- Data security, including confidentiality classification policies, intellectual property policies, personal data privacy policies, general data access and usage policies, and data access by external parties.

- Database recovery and data retention.

- Access and use of externally sourced data.

- Sharing data internally and externally.

- Data warehousing and business intelligence policies.

- Unstructured data policies (electronic files and physical records).

3.3.3 Data Architecture

The Data Governance Council sponsors and approves the enterprise data model and other related aspects of data architecture. The Data Governance Council may appoint an Enterprise Data Architecture Steering Committee to oversee the program and its iterative projects. The enterprise data model should be developed and maintained jointly by data architects and data stewards working together in data stewardship teams oriented by subject area, and coordinated by the enterprise data architect.

As data stewardship teams propose changes and develop extensions to the enterprise data model, the Data Architecture Steering Committee oversees the project and reviews changes. The enterprise data model should ultimately be reviewed, approved, and formally adopted by the Data Governance Council. Executive data stewards on the Council should pay particular attention to the alignment of the enterprise data model with key business strategies, processes, organizations, and systems.

Similarly, the general approach, business case, and less technical aspects of related data architecture should also be reviewed, approved, and adopted by the Data Governance Council. This includes the data technology architecture, the data integration architecture, the data warehousing and business intelligence architecture, and the meta-data architecture. It may also include information content management architecture and enterprise taxonomies. The Council may delegate this responsibility to the Data Architecture Steering Committee.

3.3.4 Data Standards and Procedures

Data standards and guidelines include naming standards, requirement specification standards, data modeling standards, database design standards, architecture standards, and procedural standards for each data management function. Standards and guidelines vary widely within and across organizations. Data standards are usually drafted by data management professionals. Data standards should be reviewed, approved and adopted by the Data Governance Council, unless this authority is delegated to a Data Standards Steering Committee. Data standards and guidelines must be effectively communicated, monitored, enforced, and periodically re-evaluated.

Data management procedures are the documented methods, techniques, and steps followed to accomplish a specific activity or task. Like policies and standards, procedures vary widely across organizations. Procedural documentation is usually drafted by data management professionals, and may be reviewed by a Data Standards Steering Committee.

Data standards and procedural guidelines may include:

- Data modeling and architecture standards, including data naming conventions, definition standards, standard domains, and standard abbreviations.

- Standard business and technical meta-data to be captured, maintained, and integrated.

- Data model management guidelines and procedures.

- Meta-data integration and usage procedures.

- Standards for database recovery and business continuity, database performance, data retention, and external data acquisition.

- Data security standards and procedures.

- Reference data management control procedures.

- Match / merge and data cleansing standards and procedures.

- Business intelligence standards and procedures.

- Enterprise content management standards and procedures, including use of enterprise taxonomies, support for legal discovery and document and e-mail retention, electronic signatures, report formatting standards, and report distribution approaches.

3.3.5 Regulatory Compliance

Every enterprise is impacted by governmental and industry regulations. Many of these regulations dictate how data and information is to be managed. Generally, compliance with these regulations is not optional. Part of the data governance function is to monitor and ensure regulatory compliance. In fact, regulatory compliance is often the initial reason for implementing data governance. Data governance guides the implementation of adequate controls to ensure, document, and monitor compliance with data-related regulations.

For companies publicly traded in the United States, the Sarbanes-Oxley Act of 2002 established stringent financial reporting and auditing requirements. It was designed to make executives more responsible and accountable for oversight of their companies. There are several other regulations with significant implications on how information assets are managed. For example:

- HIPPA: The Health Information Protection and Portability Act (HIPPA) is a United States federal law enacted in 1996 requiring employers, medical providers, and insurance companies to respect the privacy and security of patient health information. Title II of HIPPA also established national standards for electronic health care transactions and national identifiers for providers, health insurance plans, and employers, encouraging electronic data interchange in US healthcare.

- Basel II New Accord: Since 2006, financial institutions doing business in European Union countries are required to report standard information proving liquidity.

- Solvency II: The European Union has similar regulations for the insurance industry.

- PCI-DSS: The Payment Card Industry Data Security Standards (PCI-DSS).

- The Government Accounting Standards Board (GASB) and the Financial Accounting Standards Board (FASB) accounting standards also have significant implications on how information assets are managed.

Data governance organizations work with other business and technical leadership to find the best answers to the following regulatory compliance questions:

- How relevant is a regulation? Why is it important for us?

- How do we interpret it? What policies and procedures does it require?

- Do we comply now? How do we comply now?

- How should we comply in the future? What will it take? When will we comply?

- How do we demonstrate and prove compliance?

- How do we monitor compliance? How often do we review compliance?

- How do we identify and report non-compliance?

- How do we manage and rectify non-compliance?

3.3.6 Issue Management

Data governance is the vehicle for identifying, managing, and resolving several different types of data related issues, including:

- Data quality issues.

- Data naming and definition conflicts.

- Business rule conflicts and clarifications.

- Data security, privacy, and confidentiality issues.

- Regulatory non-compliance issues.

- Non-conformance issues (policies, standards, architecture, and procedures).

- Conflicting policies, standards, architecture, and procedures.

- Conflicting stakeholder interests in data and information.

- Organizational and cultural change management issues.

- Issues regarding data governance procedures and decision rights.

- Negotiation and review of data sharing agreements.

Most issues can be resolved locally in Data Stewardship Teams. Issues requiring communication and / or escalation must be logged. Issues may be escalated to the Data Stewardship Committee, or higher to the Data Governance Council, as shown in Figure 3.5. Issues that cannot be resolved by the Data Governance Council should be escalated to corporate management and / or governance.

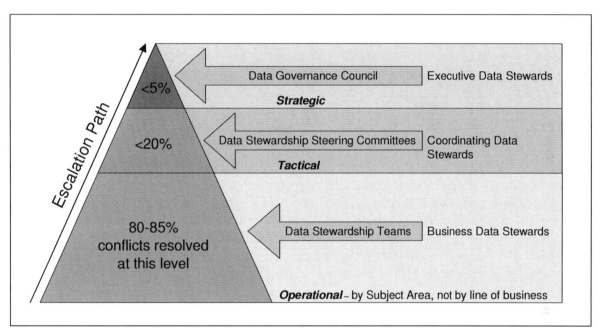

Figure 3.5 Data Issue Escalation Path

Data governance requires control mechanisms and procedures for:

- Identifying, capturing, logging, and updating issues.

- Tracking the status of issues.

- Documenting stakeholder viewpoints and resolution alternatives.

- Objective, neutral discussions where all viewpoints are heard.

- Escalating issues to higher levels of authority.

- Determining, documenting, and communicating issue resolutions.

Do not underestimate the importance and value of data issue management; and the need for these control mechanisms and procedures should not be underestimated, either. The judicial branch, which has responsibility for issue management, is an equal third partner with the legislative branch, which has responsibility for defining policies, standards, and the enterprise data architecture, and with the executive branch, which has responsibility for protecting and serving administrative responsibilities.

3.3.7 Data Management Projects

Data management initiatives usually provide enterprise-wide benefits requiring cross-functional sponsorship from the Data Governance Council. Some of these projects and programs are designed to implement or improve the overall data management function. Other projects and programs focus on one particular data management function, such as:

- Data Architecture Management.

- Data Warehousing and Business Intelligence Management.

- Reference and Master Data Management.

- Meta-data Management.

- Data Quality Management.

Significant organizational change is often required to implement more effective data management. Implementing a data strategy usually requires making some organizational and cultural changes to support that strategy. A data management roadmap sets out a course of action for initiating and / or improving data management functions. The roadmap typically consists of an assessment of current functions, definition of a target environment and target objectives, and a transition plan outlining the steps required to reach these targets, including an approach to organizational change management.

Every data management project should follow the project management standards of the organization. At a minimum, every project should begin with a clearly defined and documented project charter, outlining the mission, objectives, scope, resources, and delivery expectations of the sponsors, which in these cases, is the Data Governance Council. The Council helps define the business case for data management projects and oversees project status and progress. The Council coordinates its efforts with a Project Management Office (PMO), where one exists. Data management projects may be considered part of the overall IT project portfolio.

The Data Governance Council may also coordinate data management efforts with the sponsors of related projects, particularly large programs with enterprise-wide scope. These include enterprise resource planning (ERP) and customer relationship management (CRM) projects, or in the public sector, citizen relationship management projects. Such large programs benefit from formal data management, because:

1. Information quality is essential to the success of these projects, and

2. A key project objective is to integrate information across the enterprise.

Data management provides these projects with:

- A master blueprint for enterprise-wide information integration (a data architecture).

- Approaches to managing data quality and master data management.

- Strategies, tools, structures, and support to enable business intelligence.

- A proven approach to partnering with business leaders in governing enterprise integration.

3.3.8 Data Management Services

As the expert custodians and curators for data and information assets, data professionals provide many different services for the enterprise. Data Management Services organizations may formalize the definition and delivery of these service, in order to be more focused on meeting enterprise needs. These services range from high level governance coordination, enterprise architectural definition and coordination, information requirements analysis, data modeling facilitation, and data quality analysis to traditional database design, implementation, and production support services.

By offering the full range of data management activities as services, IT management can involve the Data Governance Council in the estimation of enterprise needs for these services and the justification of staffing and funding to provide these services. As sponsors of these on-going services, the Data Governance Council can oversee their effectiveness from a business perspective, vouch for data valuation assumptions, and confirm assessments of data value and data management business value contribution.

3.3.9 Data Asset Valuation

Data and information are truly assets because they have business value, tangible or intangible. Today's accounting practices consider data and information as intangible assets, much like software, documentation, expert knowledge, trade secrets, and other intellectual property. Goodwill is the accounting term for the additional amount of money a company is worth beyond the value of its tangible assets and any specifically referenced other intangible assets.

Organizations use many different approaches to estimate the value of their data assets. One way is to identify the direct and indirect business benefits derived from use of the data. Another way is to identify the cost of its loss, identifying the impacts of not having the current amount and quality level of data:

- What percentage change to revenue would occur?

- What percentage change to costs would occur?

- What risk exposures might occur, and what would be the potential financial impact?

Seen in this light, the impacts are often estimated to be quite large, but because there are so many other contributing factors, of which the loss of any might result in similar negative impacts, these impacts are understood to be somewhat disproportional. Typically, business leaders negotiate and agree on a conservative percentage of the total potential impact, which might be considered as the contribution to revenue (for instance) made by data assets in relative proportion to other contributing resources and factors.

Another way to determine data asset value is to estimate what competitors might pay for these assets, if offered exclusive of any other assets. Making these estimates and earning their acceptance requires a significant and on-going dialog with accountants and financial executives. These conversations are typically new and somewhat foreign to most IT managers.

Sometimes business stewards find it easier to estimate the value of business losses due to inadequate information. Information gaps—the difference between what information is needed and whatever trustworthy information is currently available—represent business liabilities. Closing and preventing these gaps represent opportunities for data management programs to provide some estimate of business value.

3.3.10 Communication and Promotion

Data stewards at all levels and data management professionals must continually communicate, educate, and promote the importance and value of data and information assets and the business contribution of data management functions. Raising stakeholder awareness and appreciation of data management issues and benefits is an on-going responsibility of everyone in the data management community.

All data producers and information consumers must understand data policies and their organization's commitment to data quality, data security, data protection, data delivery, and data support. All stakeholders should be aware of data stewardship and governance programs, organizations, roles, and responsibilities. All stakeholders should also be aware of organizational investments in data management projects, and the objectives and expectations for these projects. All stakeholders must understand whatever responsibilities they have to conform to data standards and comply with external regulations.

Every individual data management role and organization is responsible for communicating these key messages. However, organizations should specifically assign responsibility for communication planning to one or two individuals.

Organizations typically use several approaches to communicating these key messages. These approaches include:

- Maintaining an intranet website for a data management program.

- Posting announcements on other websites within the enterprise.

- Posting hardcopy announcements on actual bulletin boards at locations.

- Publishing a newsletter distributed in hardcopy or via e-mail.

- Taking advantage of opportunities to make short information and promotion announcements at department meetings.

- Presenting topics of interest to appropriate audiences.

- Promoting participation in a Data Management Community of Interest.

- Crafting ahead of time, the key messages that can be said succinctly whenever opportunities arise, helping individuals communicate these key messages consistently.

A data management intranet website is a particularly effective vehicle for communicating:

- Executive messages regarding significant data management issues.

- The data management strategy and program charter, including vision, benefits, goals, and principles.

- The data management implementation roadmap.

- Data policies and data standards.

- Descriptions of data stewardship roles and responsibilities.

- Procedures for issue identification and escalation.

- Documents and presentations describing key concepts, available for download.

- Data governance organization descriptions, members, and contact information.

- Data Management Services organization rosters and contact information.

- Individual profiles on data stewards and data management professionals.

- Program news announcements.

- Descriptions and links to related online resources.

- Entry points to request services or capture issues.

3.3.11 Related Governance Frameworks

At the time of this writing, there are no standard or commonly used frameworks for data governance, although some proprietary frameworks have been developed by a few consulting firms. Several frameworks do exist for related governance topics, including:

- Corporate Governance (COSO ERM).

- IT Governance (COBIT).

- Enterprise Architecture (Zachman Framework, TOGAF).

- System Development Lifecycle (Rational Unified Process, for example).

- System Development Process Improvement (SEI CMMI).

- Project Management (PRINCE II, PMI PMBOK).

- IT Service Management (ITIL, ISO 2000).

3.4 Summary

The guiding principles for implementing data governance into an organization, a summary table of the roles for each data governance activity, and organizational and cultural issues that may arise during implementation of a data governance function are summarized below.

3.4.1 Guiding Principles

The implementation of data governance into an organization follows eleven guiding principles:

1. Data management is a shared responsibility between business data stewards (trustees) and data management professionals (expert custodians).

2. Data stewards have responsibilities in all 10 data management functions.

3. Every data governance / data stewardship program is unique, taking into account the unique characteristics of the organization and its culture.

4. The best data stewards are found, not made. Whenever possible, appoint the people already interested and involved.

5. Shared decision making is the hallmark of data governance.

6. Data governance councils, and data stewardship committees and teams perform "legislative" and "judicial" responsibilities, while data management services organizations perform "executive branch" responsibilities (administer, coordinate, serve, protect).

7. Data governance occurs at both the enterprise and local levels and often at levels in between.

8. There is no substitute for visionary and active IT leadership in data management. The Data Management Executive is the CIO's right hand for managing data and information.

9. Some form of centralized organization of data management professionals is essential to enterprise-wide data integration.

10. Organizations should define a formal charter for the Data Governance Council, approved by the Board of Directors or Executive Committee, with specific authorities granted to that group.

11. Every enterprise should have a data strategy, driven by the enterprise business strategy, and used to guide all data management activities.

3.4.2 Process Summary

The process summary for the data governance function is shown in Table 3.1. The deliverables, responsible roles, approving roles, and contributing roles are shown for each activity in the data governance function. The Table is also shown in Appendix A9.

Activities	Deliverables	Responsible Roles	Approving Roles	Contributing Roles
1.1.1 Understand Strategic Enterprise Data Needs (P)	Strategic Enterprise Data Needs	DM Executive	Data Governance Council, CIO	Data Stewards, Data management professionals
1.1.2 Develop and Maintain the Data Strategy (P)	Data Strategy – Vision, Mission, Bus. Case, Goals, Objectives, Principles, Components, Metrics, Implementation Roadmap	DM Executive	Data Governance Council, CIO	Data Stewards, Data management professionals
1.1.3 Establish Data Management Professional Roles and Organizations (P)	Data Management Services organizations and staff	CIO	Data Governance Council	DM Executive
1.1.4 Establish Data Governance and Stewardship Organizations (P)	Data Governance Council, Data Stewardship Committee, Data Stewardship Teams	DM Executive, CIO, Data Governance Council	Senior Mgmt	Data Stewards, Data management professionals
1.1.5 Identify and Appoint Data Stewards (P)	Business Data Stewards, Coordinating Data Stewards, Executive Data Stewards	DM Executive, Executive Data Stewards	Data Governance Council	Coordinating Data Stewards, Data management professionals

Activities	Deliverables	Responsible Roles	Approving Roles	Contributing Roles
1.1.6 Develop, Review and Approve Data Policies, Standards, and Procedures (P)	Data Policies, Data Standards, Data Management Procedures	DM Executive	Data Governance Council, CIO	Data Stewardship Committee, Data Stewardship Teams, Data management professionals
1.1.7 Review and Approve Data Architecture (P)	Adopted Enterprise Data Model, Related Data Architecture	Data Governance Council	Data Governance Council, CIO	Enterprise Data Architect, Data Stewardship Committee, Data Stewards, Data Architects, DM Executive
1.1.8 Plan and Sponsor Data Management Projects and Services (P)	Data Management Projects, Data Management Services	Data Governance Council	Data Governance Council, CIO, IT Steering Committee	DM Executive, Data management professionals, Data Stewards
1.1.9 Estimate Data Asset Value and Associated Costs (P)	Data Asset Value Estimates, Data Mgmt. Cost Estimates	Data Stewards	Data Governance Council	DM Executive, Data management professionals
1.2.1 Supervise Data Professional Organizations and Staff (C)	Data Management Services organization(s) and staff	DM Executive(s)	CIO	Data management professionals
1.2.2 Coordinate Data Governance Activities (C)	Data Governance Organization Schedules, Meetings, Agendas, Documents, Minutes	DM Executive, Enterprise Data Architect, Data Architects	Data Governance Council, Data Stewardship Committee, Data Stewardship Teams, CIO	Data management professionals

Activities	Deliverables	Responsible Roles	Approving Roles	Contributing Roles
1.2.3 Manage and Resolve Data Related Issues (C)	Issue Log, Issue Resolutions	Data Stewardship Teams, Data Stewardship Committee, Data Governance Council	Data Stewardship Teams, Data Stewardship Committee, Data Governance Council	DM Executive, Data management professionals
1.2.4 Monitor and Ensure Regulatory Compliance (C)	Compliance Reporting, Non-compliance Issues	Data management professionals	Data Governance Council	DM Executive, CIO
1.2.5 Communicate, Monitor and Enforce Conformance with Data Policies, Standards, Procedures, and Architecture (C)	Policy / Standards / Arch / Procedure Communication, Non-conformance Issues	Data management professionals, Data Stewards	Data Governance Council, Data Stewardship Committee	DM Executive
1.2.6 Oversee Data Management Projects and Services (C)		DM Executive	Data Governance Council	Data management professionals
1.2.7 Communicate and Promote the Value of Data and Data Management (C)	Data Management Website, Data Management Newsletter, Understanding and Recognition	DM Executive, Data management professionals, Data Stewards, CIO	Data Governance Council	Data Stewards

Table 3.1 Data Governance Process Summary Table

3.4.3 Organizational and Cultural Issues

Questions may arise when an organization is planning to implement the data governance function. A few of the common questions are listed below with a general answer.

Q1: Why is every governance program unique?

A1: Each organization is unique in structure, culture, and circumstances. Each data governance program should be unique to address the needs of the organization, while at the same time sharing some common characteristics and basic principles. Each data governance program has different sponsoring individuals, business drivers, scope boundaries, regional and departmental organizations, approaches to business and IT liaison, relationships with other governance programs and major projects, collaboration and teamwork challenges, organizational heritage, shared values and beliefs, common expectations and attitudes, and unique meaning to organizational rites, rituals, and symbols. As the organization changes, the challenges posed for data governance also change. Good data governance programs address these challenges and take advantage of the opportunities they present.

Q2: Should data stewardship be a part-time or full-time responsibility?

A2: Experts generally recommend data stewards be given part-time responsibility for data stewardship. Data stewardship is a role, not a job. Data stewards need to be involved with the business to maintain business knowledge, peer respect, and credibility as subject matter experts and practical leaders.

Q3: Can full-time IT / business liaisons be data stewards?

A3: Yes, and their roles vary widely across organizations. However, true business leaders should also participate as data stewards, unless the scope and focus is technical. Problems occur when liaisons represent the business or IT exclusively, excluding either of their internal customers. Stewardship and governance are mechanisms for liaisons to be more effective by bringing all parties to the table.

Q4: What qualifications and skills are required of data steward role candidates?

A4: First and foremost, business knowledge and understanding of the data is required. People can be taught data management concepts and techniques, such as how to read a data model. Soft skills are also very important in data stewardship, including:

- Respected subject area expertise–information, processes, and rules.

- Organizational / cultural knowledge and industry perspective.

- Strong verbal and written communication skills.

- Clarity and precision in thinking and communication.

- Teamwork, diplomacy, and negotiation skills.

- Adaptability, objectivity, creativity, practicality, and openness to change.

- Ability to balance local and functional needs with enterprise needs.

Q5: How are individual data stewards and data governance organizations empowered? How do stewards earn respect?

A5: Maintaining the importance of data governance and data stewardship to the organization can be shown in several ways:

- Ensure there is strong and continued executive sponsorship and support–and that everybody knows about it. Where they lead, others will follow.

- When there is conflict, stay objective. Even better, really understand and appreciate both points of view. Then find a common goal and reframe the issue to drive attainment of that goal.

- Make sure there is something in it for them! Show how they will they benefit, personally and / or in the eyes of their boss. Make it easy to say yes by crafting win-win solutions.

- Information is more powerful than force. Impress people with facts and reasoning presented effectively, rather than pound on them saying, "Because you have to!"

- Earn not just respect, but also trust. Trust is essential to collaborative success. Earn trust over time by demonstrating sincere interest in others and by being open with information.

3.5 Recommended Reading

The references listed below provide additional reading that supports the material presented in Chapter 3. These recommended readings are also included in the Bibliography at the end of the Guide.

3.5.1 Websites

The Data Administration Newsletter (TDAN)–*http://www.TDAN.com*

DM Review Magazine–www.dmreview.com. Note: www.dmreview.com is now www.information-management.com.

EIM Insight, published by The Enterprise Information Management Institute–
http://eiminstitute.org

SearchDataManagement.com white paper library–
http://go.techtarget.com/r/3762877/5626178

3.5.2 Prominent Books

There are very few books specifically devoted to data governance. Perhaps the most pertinent book published to date is:

Thomas, Gwen. Alpha Males and Data Disasters: The Case for Data Governance. Brass Cannon Press, 2006. ISBN-10: 0-978-6579-0-X. 221 pages.

3.5.3 Regulatory and Compliance Books

Compliance is an important data governance issue. The following book is particularly focused on regulatory compliance:

Bloem, Jaap, Menno van Doorn, and Piyush Mittal. <u>Making IT Governance Work in a Sarbanes-Oxley World</u>. John Wiley & Sons, 2005. ISBN 0-471-74359-3. 304 pages.

3.5.4 General Books

The books and other materials listed below describe IT governance in general, which as noted above, is not at all the same thing as data governance. Nevertheless, they are closely related concepts, and these publications can be helpful:

Benson, Robert J., Tom Bugnitz, and Bill Walton. <u>From Business Strategy to IT Action: Right Decisions for a Better Bottom Line</u>. John Wiley & Sons, 2004. ISBN 0-471-49191-8. 309 pages.

IT Governance Institute. <u>Control Objectives for Information and related Technology (CobiT©)</u>. <u>www.isaca.org/cobit</u>

Lutchen, Mark. <u>Managing IT as a Business: A Survival Guide for CEOs</u>. John Wiley & Sons, 2003. ISBN 0-471-47104-6. 256 pages.

Maizlish, Bryan and Robert Handler. <u>IT Portfolio Management Step-By-Step: Unlocking the Business Value of Technology</u>. John Wiley & Sons, 2005. ISBN 0-471-64984-8. 400 pages.

Van Grembergen, Wim and Steven Dehaes. <u>Enterprise Governance of Information Technology: Achieving Strategic Alignment and Value</u>. Springer, 2009. ISBN 0-387-84881-5, 360 pages.

Van Grembergen, Wim and Steven Dehaes. <u>Implementing Information Technology Governance: Models, Practices and Cases</u>. IGI Publishing, 2007. ISBN 1-599-04924-3, 255 pages.

Van Grembergen, Wim and Steven Dehaes. <u>Strategies for Information Technology Governance</u>. IGI Publishing, 2003. ISBN 1-591-40284-0. 406 pages.

Weill, Peter and Jeanne Ross. <u>IT Governance: How Top Performers Manage IT Decision Rights for Superior Results</u>. Harvard Business School Press, 2004. ISBN 1-291-39253-5. 288 pages.

4 Data Architecture Management

Data Architecture Management is the second data management function in the Data Management Framework shown in Figures 1.3 and 1.4. It is the first data management function that interacts with and is influenced by the data governance function. Chapter 4 defines the data architecture management function and explains the concepts and activities involved in data architecture management.

4.1 Introduction

Data Architecture Management is the process of defining and maintaining specifications that:

- Provide a standard common business vocabulary,

- Express strategic data requirements,

- Outline high level integrated designs to meet these requirements, and

- Align with enterprise strategy and related business architecture.

Data architecture is an integrated set of specification artifacts used to define data requirements, guide integration and control of data assets, and align data investments with business strategy. It is also an integrated collection of master blueprints at different levels of abstraction. Data architecture includes formal data names, comprehensive data definitions, effective data structures, precise data integrity rules, and robust data documentation.

Data architecture is most valuable when it supports the information needs of the entire enterprise. Enterprise data architecture enables data standardization and integration across the enterprise. This chapter will focus on enterprise data architecture, although the same techniques apply to the more limited scope of a specific function or department within an organization.

Enterprise data architecture is part of the larger enterprise architecture, where data architecture integrates with other business and technology architecture. Enterprise architecture integrates data, process, organization, application, and technology architecture. It helps organizations manage change and improve effectiveness, agility, and accountability.

The context of the Data Architecture Management function is shown in the diagram in Figure 4.1.

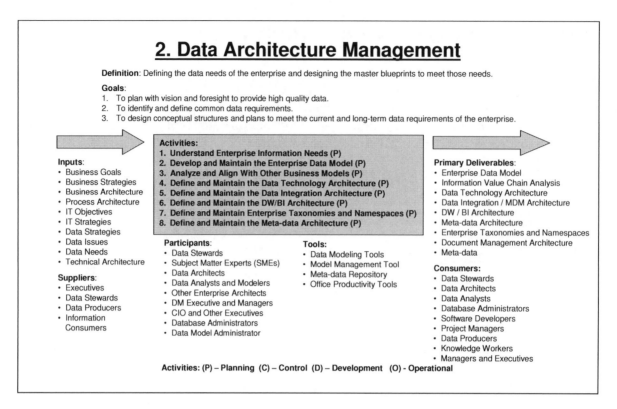

Figure 4.1 Data Architecture Management Diagram

Enterprise data architecture is an integrated set of specifications and documents. It includes three major categories of specifications:

1. The enterprise data model: The heart and soul of enterprise data architecture,

2. The information value chain analysis: Aligns data with business processes and other enterprise architecture components, and

3. Related data delivery architecture: Including database architecture, data integration architecture, data warehousing / business intelligence architecture, document content architecture, and meta-data architecture.

Enterprise data architecture is really a misnomer. It is about more than just data; it is also about terminology. Enterprise data architecture defines standard terms for the things that are important to the organization–things important enough to the business that data about these things is necessary to run the business. These things are *business entities*. Perhaps the most important and beneficial aspect of enterprise data architecture is establishing a common business vocabulary of business entities and the data attributes (characteristics) that matter about these entities. Enterprise data architecture defines the semantics of an enterprise.

4.2 Concepts and Activities

Chapter 1 stated that data architecture management is the function of defining the blueprint for managing data assets. Data architects play a key role in the critical function of data architecture management. The concepts and activities related to data architecture management and the roles of data architects are presented in this section.

4.2.1 Architecture Overview

Architecture is an organized arrangement of component elements, which optimizes the function, performance, feasibility, cost, and / or aesthetics of the overall structure or system. The word "architecture" is one of the most widely used terms in the information technology field. "Architecture" is a very evocative word–the analogy between designing buildings and designing information systems is extremely useful. Architecture is an integrated set of closely related views reflecting the issues and perspectives of different stakeholders. Understanding the architecture of something enables people to make some limited sense of something very complex, whether they are natural things (geological formations, mathematics, living organisms) or human-made things (including buildings, music, machines, organizations, processes, software, and databases).

Understanding building blueprints helps contractors build safe, functional, and aesthetically pleasing buildings within cost and time constraints. Studying anatomy (the architecture of living things) helps medical students learn how to provide medical care. People and organizations benefit from architecture when structures and systems become complex. The more complex the system, the greater the benefit derived from architecture.

Architecture may exist at different levels, from the macro-level of urban planning to the micro-level of creating machine parts. At each level, standards and protocols help ensure components function together as a whole. Architecture includes standards and their application to specific design needs.

In the context of information systems, architecture is "the design of any complex technical object or system".

Technology is certainly complex. The field of information technology greatly benefits from architectural designs that help manage complexity in hardware and software products. Technology architecture includes both "closed" design standards specific to a particular technology vendor and "open" standards available to any vendor.

Organizations are also complex. Integrating the disparate parts of an organization to meet strategic enterprise goals often requires an overall business architecture, which may include common designs and standards for business processes, business objectives, organizational structures, and organizational roles. For organizations, architecture is all about integration. Organizations that grow by acquisition face significant integration challenges and so greatly benefit from effective architecture.

Information systems are certainly very complex. Adding more and more relatively simple isolated applications, and building tactical approaches to moving and sharing data between these "silo" applications has made the application system portfolio of most organizations resemble a plate of spaghetti. The cost of understanding and maintaining this complexity grows, and the benefits of restructuring applications and databases according to an overall architecture become more and more attractive.

4.2.1.1 Enterprise Architecture

Enterprise Architecture is an integrated set of business and IT specification models and artifacts reflecting enterprise integration and standardization requirements. Enterprise architecture defines the context for business integration of data, process, organization, and technology, and the alignment of enterprise resources with enterprise goals. Enterprise architecture encompasses both business architecture and information systems architecture.

Enterprise architecture provides a systematic approach to managing information and systems assets, addressing strategic business requirements, and enabling informed portfolio management of the organization's projects. Enterprise architecture supports strategic decision-making by helping manage change, tracing the impact of organizational change on systems, and the business impact of changes to systems.

Enterprise architecture includes many related models and artifacts:

- Information architecture: Business entities, relationships, attributes, definitions, reference values.

- Process architecture: Functions, activities, workflow, events, cycles, products, procedures.

- Business architecture: Goals, strategies, roles, organization structures, locations.

- Systems architecture: Applications, software components, interfaces, projects.

- Technology architecture: Networks, hardware, software platforms, standards, protocols.

- Information value chain analysis artifacts: Mapping the relationships between data, process, business, systems, and technology.

Enterprise models generate most of the related artifacts from integrated specifications. Artifacts include graphical diagrams, tables, analysis matrices, and textual documents. These artifacts describe how the organization operates and what resources are required, in varying degrees of detail. Specifications should be traceable to the goals and objectives they support, and should conform to content and presentation standards. Few, if any, organizations have a comprehensive enterprise architecture including every potential component model and artifact.

Enterprise Architecture often distinguishes between the current "as-is" and the target "to be" perspectives, and sometimes includes intermediate stages and migration plans. Some enterprise architecture attempts to identify an ideal state as a reference model, and the target model is defined as a pragmatic, attainable step towards the ideal state. Keep enterprise architecture specifications of present state and future state current, in order to stay relevant and useful. No organization is ever completely done maintaining and enriching their enterprise architecture.

Each organization invests in developing and maintaining enterprise architecture based on their understanding of business need and business risk. Some organizations elect to define enterprise architecture in detail in order to manage risks better.

Enterprise architecture is a significant knowledge asset providing several benefits. It is a tool for planning, IT governance, and portfolio management. Enterprise architecture can:

- Enable integration of data, processes, technologies, and efforts.

- Align information systems with business strategy.

- Enable effective use and coordination of resources.

- Improve communication and understanding across the organization.

- Reduce the cost of managing the IT infrastructure.

- Guide business process improvement.

- Enable organizations to respond effectively to changing market opportunities, industry challenges, and technological advances. Enterprise architecture helps evaluate business risk, manage change, and improve business effectiveness, agility, and accountability.

Methods for defining enterprise architecture include IBM's Business Systems Planning (BSP) method and the Information Systems Planning (ISP) from James Martin's information engineering method.[1]

4.2.1.2 Architectural Frameworks

Architectural frameworks provide a way of thinking about and understanding architecture, and the structures or systems requiring architecture. Architecture is complex, and architectural frameworks provide an overall "architecture for architecture."

There are two different kinds of architectural frameworks:

- Classification frameworks organize the structure and views that encompass enterprise architecture. Frameworks define the standard syntax for the artifacts describing these views and the relationships between these views. Most artifacts are diagrams, tables, and matrices.

- Process frameworks specify methods for business and systems planning, analysis, and design processes. Some IT planning and software development lifecycle (SDLC) methods include their own composite classifications. Not all process frameworks specify the same set of things, and some are highly specialized.

---

[1] Information Engineering Book II: Planning and Analysis.

The scope of architectural frameworks is not limited to information systems architecture. Architectural frameworks help define the logical, physical, and technical artifacts produced in software analysis and design, which guide the solution design for specific information systems. Organizations adopt architectural frameworks for IT governance and architecture quality control. Organizations may mandate delivery of certain artifacts before approval of a system design.

Many frameworks are in existence, such as:

- TOGAF : The Open Group Architectural Framework is a process framework and standard software development lifecycle (SDLC) method developed by The Open Group, a vendor and technology neutral consortium for defining and promoting open standards for global interoperability. TOGAF Version 8 Enterprise Edition (TOGAF 8) may be licensed by any organization, whether members or non-members of The Open Group.

- ANSI / IEEE 1471-2000: A Recommended Practice for Architecture Description of Software-Intensive Systems, on track to become the ISO / IEC 25961 standard, defines solution design artifacts.

Some consulting firms have developed useful proprietary architectural frameworks. Several governments and defense departments have also developed architectural frameworks, including:

- Federal Enterprise Architecture (FEA): Produced by the Office of Management and Budget for use within the U.S. Government

- Government Enterprise Architecture (GEA): Legislated for use by departments of the Queensland (Australia) provincial government.

- DODAF: The US Department of Defense Architecture Framework.

- MODAF: The UK Ministry of Defense Architecture Framework.

- AGATE: The France DGA Architecture Framework.

4.2.1.3 The Zachman Framework for Enterprise Architecture

The Zachman Enterprise Framework[2] ™ is the most widely known and adopted architectural framework. Enterprise data architects, in particular, have accepted and used this framework since Zachman's first published description of the Framework in an IBM Systems Journal article in 1987.

The Zachman Enterprise Framework[2] ™, shown in Figure 4.2, has oriented the terminology towards business management, while retaining the elaborations used by the data and information systems communities. The terms for the perspective contributors (right hand row labels), the affirmation of the perspective content (left hand row labels), and the identification of the generic answers to each of the Questions (column footer labels) bring a level of clarification and understanding for each simple classification.

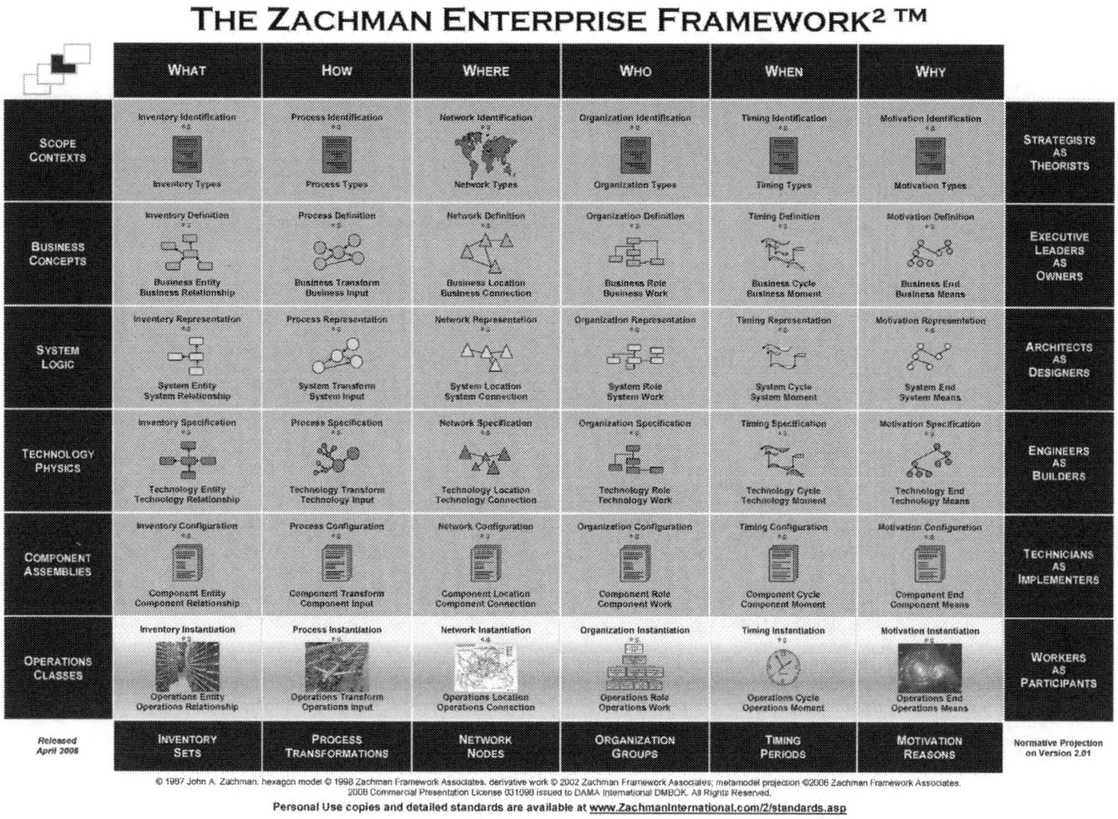

THE ZACHMAN ENTERPRISE FRAMEWORK² ™

	WHAT	HOW	WHERE	WHO	WHEN	WHY	
SCOPE CONTEXTS	Inventory Identification / Inventory Types	Process Identification / Process Types	Network Identification / Network Types	Organization Identification / Organization Types	Timing Identification / Timing Types	Motivation Identification / Motivation Types	STRATEGISTS AS THEORISTS
BUSINESS CONCEPTS	Inventory Definition / Business Entity Business Relationship	Process Definition / Business Transform Business Input	Network Definition / Business Location Business Connection	Organization Definition / Business Role Business Work	Timing Definition / Business Cycle Business Moment	Motivation Definition / Business End Business Means	EXECUTIVE LEADERS AS OWNERS
SYSTEM LOGIC	Inventory Representation / System Entity System Relationship	Process Representation / System Transform System Input	Network Representation / System Location System Connection	Organization Representation / System Role System Work	Timing Representation / System Cycle System Moment	Motivation Representation / System End System Means	ARCHITECTS AS DESIGNERS
TECHNOLOGY PHYSICS	Inventory Specification / Technology Entity Technology Relationship	Process Specification / Technology Transform Technology Input	Network Specification / Technology Location Technology Connection	Organization Specification / Technology Role Technology Work	Timing Specification / Technology Cycle Technology Moment	Motivation Specification / Technology End Technology Means	ENGINEERS AS BUILDERS
COMPONENT ASSEMBLIES	Inventory Configuration / Component Entity Component Relationship	Process Configuration / Component Transform Component Input	Network Configuration / Component Location Component Connection	Organization Configuration / Component Role Component Work	Timing Configuration / Component Cycle Component Moment	Motivation Configuration / Component End Component Means	TECHNICIANS AS IMPLEMENTERS
OPERATIONS CLASSES	Inventory Instantiation / Operations Entity Operations Relationship	Process Instantiation / Operations Transform Operations Input	Network Instantiation / Operations Location Operations Connection	Organization Instantiation / Operations Role Operations Work	Timing Instantiation / Operations Cycle Operations Moment	Motivation Instantiation / Operations End Operations Means	WORKERS AS PARTICIPANTS
Released April 2008	INVENTORY SETS	PROCESS TRANSFORMATIONS	NETWORK NODES	ORGANIZATION GROUPS	TIMING PERIODS	MOTIVATION REASONS	Normative Projection on Version 2.01

© 1987 John A. Zachman. hexagon model © 1998 Zachman Framework Associates. derivative work © 2002 Zachman Framework Associates; metamodel projection ©2008 Zachman Framework Associates. 2008 Commercial Presentation License 031098 issued to DAMA International DMBOK. All Rights Reserved.

Personal Use copies and detailed standards are available at www.ZachmanInternational.com/2/standards.asp

Figure 4.2 The Zachman Enterprise Framework² ™
(Licensed for use by DAMA International in the DAMA-DMBOK Guide)

Modeling the enterprise architecture is a common practice within the U.S. Federal Government to inform its Capital Planning and Investment Control (CPIC) process. The Clinger-Cohen Act (CCA, or the Information Technology Management Reform Act of 1996) requires all U.S. federal agencies to have and use formal enterprise architecture.

Access to the new Enterprise Architecture Standards and the Zachman Enterprise Framework² ™ graphics is available at no cost via registration at www.ZachmanInternational.com. A Concise Definition of the Framework, written by John Zachman, is also on that site.

According to its creator, John Zachman, the Framework is a logical structure for identifying and organizing descriptive representations (models) used to manage enterprises and develop systems. In fact, the Zachman Framework is a generic classification schema of design artifacts for any complex system. The Zachman Framework is not a method defining how to create the representations of any cell. It is a structure for describing enterprises and architectural models.

To understand systems architecture, Zachman studied how the fields of building construction and aerospace engineering define complex systems, and mapped information systems artifacts against these examples. The Zachman Framework is a 6 by 6 matrix representing the intersection of two classification schemas–two dimensions of systems architecture.

In the first dimension, Zachman recognized that in creating buildings, airplanes, or systems, there are many stakeholders, and each has different perspectives about "architecture". The planner, owner, designer, builder, implementer, and participant each have different issues to identify, understand, and resolve. Zachman depicted these perspectives as rows.

- The planner perspective (Scope Contexts): Lists of business elements defining scope identified by Strategists as Theorists.

- The owner perspective (Business Concepts): Semantic models of the business relationships between business elements defined by Executive Leaders as Owners.

- The designer perspective (System Logic): Logical models detailing system requirements and unconstrained design represented by Architects as Designers.

- The builder perspective (Technology Physics): Physical models optimizing the design for implementation for specific use under the constraints of specific technology, people, costs, and timeframes specified by Engineers as Builders.

- The implementer perspective (Component Assemblies): A technology-specific, out-of-context view of how components are assembled and operate configured by Technicians as Implementers.

- The participant perspective (Operations Classes): Actual functioning system instances used by Workers as Participants.

For the second dimension, each perspective's issues required different ways to answer the fundamental questions posed by the basic interrogatives of communication: who, what, why, when, where and how. Each question required answers in different formats. Zachman depicted each fundamental question as a column.

The revised labels for each column are in parentheses:

- What (the data column): Materials used to build the system (Inventory Sets).

- How (the function column): Activities performed (Process Transformations).

- Where (the network column): Locations, topography, and technology (Network Nodes).

- Who (the people column): Roles and organizations (Organization Groups).

- When (the time column): Events, cycles, and schedules (Time Periods).

- Why (the goal column): Goals, strategies, and initiatives (Motivation Reasons).

Each cell in the Zachman Framework represents a unique type of design artifact, defined by the intersection of its row and column.

While the columns in the Framework are not in any order of importance, the order of the rows is significant. Within each column, the contents of each cell constrain the contents of the cells below it. The transformation from perspective to perspective ensures alignment between the intentions of enterprise owners and subsequent decisions.

Each cell describes a primitive model, limited in focus to the column's single perspective. The granularity of detail in the Zachman Framework is a property of any individual cell regardless of the row. Depending on the need, each cell model may contain relatively little detail or an "excruciating" level of detail. The greater the integration needs, the more detail is needed in order to remove ambiguity.

No architectural framework is inherently correct or complete, and adopting any architectural framework is no guarantee of success. Some organizations and individuals adopt the Zachman Framework as a "thinking tool", while others use it as the Engineering Quality Assurance mechanism for solutions implementation.

There are several reasons why the Zachman Framework has been so widely adopted:

- It is relatively simple since it has only two dimensions and is easy to understand.

- It both addresses the enterprise in a comprehensive manner, and manages architecture for individual divisions and departments.

- It uses non-technical language to help people think and communicate more precisely.

- It can be used to frame and help understand a wide array of issues.

- It helps solve design problems, focusing on details without losing track of the whole.

- It helps teach many different information systems topics.

- It is a helpful planning tool, providing the context to guide better decisions.

- It is independent of specific tools or methods. Any design tool or method can map to the Framework to see what the tool or method does and does NOT do.

4.2.1.4 The Zachman Framework and Enterprise Data Architecture

The enterprise data architecture is an important part of the larger enterprise architecture that includes process, business, systems, and technology architecture. Data architects focus on the enterprise data architecture, working with other enterprise architects to integrate data architecture into a comprehensive enterprise architecture.

Enterprise data architecture typically consists of three major sets of design components:

1. An enterprise data model, identifying subject areas, business entities, the business rules governing the relationships between business entities, and at least some of the essential business data attributes.

2. The information value chain analysis, aligning data model components (subject areas and / or business entities) with business processes and other enterprise

architecture components, which may include organizations, roles, applications, goals, strategies, projects, and / or technology platforms.

3. Related data delivery architecture, including data technology architecture, data integration architecture, data warehousing / business intelligence architecture, enterprise taxonomies for content management, and meta-data architecture.

The cells in the first "data" column—now known as "Inventory Sets", represent familiar data modeling and database design artifacts (see Chapter 5 for more detail).

- Planner View (Scope Contexts): A list of subject areas and business entities.

- Owner View (Business Concepts): Conceptual data models showing the relationships between entities.

- Designer View (System Logic): Fully attributed and normalized logical data models.

- Builder View (Technology Physics): Physical data models optimized for constraining technology.

- Implementer View (Component Assemblies): Detailed representations of data structures, typically in SQL Data Definition Language (DDL).

- Functioning Enterprise: actual implemented instances.

The Zachman Framework enables concentration on selected cells without losing sight of the "big picture." It helps designers focus on details while still seeing the overall context, thereby building the "big picture" piece by piece.

4.2.2 Activities

The data architecture management function contains several activities related to defining the blueprint for managing data assets. An overview of each of these activities is presented in the following sections.

4.2.2.1 Understanding Enterprise Information Needs

In order to create an enterprise data architecture, the enterprise needs to first define its information needs. An enterprise data model is a way of capturing and defining enterprise information needs and data requirements. It represents a master blueprint for enterprise-wide data integration. The enterprise data model is therefore a critical input to all future systems development projects and the baseline for additional data requirements analysis and data modeling efforts undertaken at the project level.

Project conceptual and logical data models are based on the applicable portions of the enterprise data model. Some projects will benefit more from the enterprise data model than others will, depending on the project scope. Virtually every important project will benefit from, and affect, the enterprise data model.

One way of determining enterprise information needs is to evaluate the current inputs and outputs required by the organization, both from and to internal and external targets. Use actual system documentation and reports, and interview the participants. This material provides a list of important data entities, data attributes, and calculations. Organize these items by business unit and subject area. Review the list with the participants to ensure proper categorization and completeness. The list then becomes the basic requirements for an enterprise data model.

4.2.2.2 Develop and Maintain the Enterprise Data Model

Business entities are classes of real business things and concepts. Data is the set of facts we collect about business entities. Data models define these business entities and the kinds of facts (data attributes) needed about these entities to operate and guide the business. Data modeling is an analysis and design method used to:

1. Define and analyze data requirements, and

2. Design logical and physical data structures that support these requirements.

A data model is a set of data specifications and related diagrams that reflect data requirements and designs. An enterprise data model (EDM) is an *integrated, subject-oriented* data model defining the *essential* data produced and consumed across an entire organization.

- *Integrated* means that all of the data and rules in an organization are depicted once, and fit together seamlessly. The concepts in the model fit together as the CEO sees the enterprise, not reflecting separate and limited functional or departmental views. There is only one version of the Customer entity, one Order entity, etc. Every data attribute also has a single name and definition. The data model may additionally identify common synonyms and important distinctions between different sub-types of the same common business entity.

- *Subject-oriented* means the model is divided into commonly recognized subject areas that span across multiple business processes and application systems. Subject areas focus on the most essential business entities.

- *Essential* means the data critical to the effective operation and decision-making of the organization. Few, if any, enterprise data models define all the data within an enterprise. Essential data requirements may or may not be common to multiple applications and projects. Multiple systems may share some data defined in the enterprise data models, but other data may be critically important, yet created and used within a single system. Over time, the enterprise data model should define all data of importance to the enterprise. The definition of essential data will change over time as the business changes; the EDM must stay up-to-date with those changes.

Data modeling is an important technique used in Data Architecture Management and Data Development. Data Development implements data architecture, extending and adapting enterprise data models to meet specific business application needs and project requirements.

4.2.2.2.1 The Enterprise Data Model

The enterprise data model is an integrated set of closely related deliverables. Most of these deliverables are generated using a data modeling tool, but no data modeling tool can create all of the potential component deliverables of a complete enterprise data model. The central repository of the enterprise data model is either a data model file or a data model repository, both created and maintained by the data-modeling tool. This model artifact is included in meta-data and is discussed in depth in Chapter 11 on Meta-data Management. Few organizations create all the component artifacts of a comprehensive enterprise data model.

An enterprise data model is a significant investment in defining and documenting an organization's vocabulary, business rules, and business knowledge. Creating, maintaining, and enriching it require continuing investments of time and effort, even if starting with a purchased industry data model. Enterprise data modeling is the development and refinement of a common, consistent view, and an understanding of data entities, data attributes, and their relationships across the enterprise.

Organizations can purchase an enterprise data model, or build it from scratch. There are several vendors with industry standard logical data models. Most large database vendors include them as additional products. However, no purchased logical data model will be perfect out-of-the-box. Some customization is always involved.

Enterprise data models differ widely in terms of level of detail. When an organization first recognizes the need for an enterprise data model, it must make decisions regarding the time and effort that can be devoted to building it. Over time, as the needs of the enterprise demand, the scope and level of detail captured within an enterprise data model typically expands. Most successful enterprise data models are built incrementally and iteratively.

Build an enterprise data model in layers, as shown in Figure 4.3, focusing initially on the most critical business subject areas. The higher layers are the most fundamental, with lower layers dependent on the higher layers. In this respect, the enterprise data model is built top-down, although the contents of the model often benefit from bottom-up input. Such input is the result of analyzing and synthesizing the perspectives and details of existing logical and physical data models. Integrate such input into the enterprise perspective; the influence of existing models must not compromise the development of a common, shared enterprise viewpoint.

4.2.2.2.2 The Subject Area Model

The highest layer in an enterprise data model is a subject area model (SAM). The subject area model is a list of major subject areas that collectively express the essential scope of the enterprise. This list is one form of the "scope" view of data (Row 1, Column 1) in the Zachman Framework. At a more detailed level, business entities and object classes can also be depicted as lists.

There are two main ways to communicate a subject area model:

- An outline, which organizes smaller subject areas within larger subject areas.

- A diagram that presents and organizes the subject areas visually for easy reference.

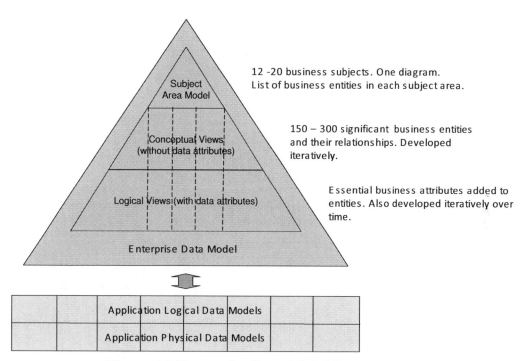

Figure 4.3 Enterprise Data Model Layers

The selection and naming of the enterprise's essential subject areas is critically important to the success of the entire enterprise data model. The list of enterprise subject areas becomes one of the most significant enterprise taxonomies. Organize other layers within the enterprise data model by subject area. Subject area-oriented iterations will organize the scope and priority of further incremental model development. The subject area model is "right" when it is both *acceptable* across all enterprise stakeholders and constituents, and *useful* in a practical sense as the organizing construct for data governance, data stewardship, and further enterprise data modeling.

Subject areas typically share the same name as a central business entity. Some subject areas align closely with very high-level business functions that focus on managing the information about the core business entity. Other subject areas revolve around a super-type business entity and its family of sub-types. Each subject area should have a short, one or two word name and a brief definition.

Subject areas are also important tools for data stewardship and governance. They define the scope of responsibilities for subject area-oriented data stewardship teams.

4.2.2.2.3 The Conceptual Data Model

The next lower level of the enterprise data model is the set of conceptual data model diagrams for each subject area. A conceptual data model defines business entities and the relationships between these business entities.

Business entities are the primary organizational structures in a conceptual data model. Business entities are the concepts and classes of things, people, and places that are familiar and of interest to the enterprise. The business needs data about these entities. Business entities are not named in IT language; they are named using business terms. A single example of a business entity is an instance. Keep data about instances of business entities, and make them easily recognizable.

Many business entities will appear within the scope of several subject areas. The scope boundaries of subject areas normally overlap, with some business entities included in both subject areas. For data governance and stewardship purposes, every business entity should have one primary subject area which 'owns' the master version of that entity.

Conceptual data model diagrams do not depict the data attributes of business entities. Conceptual data models may include many-to-many business relationships between entities. Since there are no attributes shown, conceptual data models do not attempt to normalize data.

The enterprise conceptual data model must include a glossary containing the business definitions and other meta-data associated with all business entities and their relationships. Other meta-data might include entity synonyms, instance examples, and security classifications.

A conceptual data model can foster improved business understanding and semantic reconciliation. It can serve as the framework for developing integrated information systems to support both transactional processing and business intelligence. It depicts how the enterprise sees information. See Chapter 5 for more about conceptual data modeling.

4.2.2.2.4 Enterprise Logical Data Models

Some enterprise data models also include logical data model diagrams for each subject area, adding a level of detail below the conceptual data model by depicting the essential data attributes for each entity. The enterprise logical data model identifies the data needed about each instance of a business entity. The essential data attributes included in such an enterprise data model represent common data requirements and standardized definitions for widely shared data attributes. Essential data attributes are those data attributes without which the enterprise cannot function. Determining which data attributes to include in the enterprise data model is a very subjective decision.

The enterprise logical data model diagrams continue to reflect an enterprise perspective. They are neutral and independent from any particular need, usage, and application context. Other more traditional "solution" logical data models reflect specific usage and application requirements.

Enterprise logical data models are only partially attributed. No enterprise logical data model can identify all possible data entities and data attributes. Enterprise logical data models may be normalized to some extent, but need not be as normalized as "solution" logical data models.

Enterprise logical data models should include a glossary of all business definitions and other associated meta-data about business entities and their data attributes, including data attribute domains. See Chapter 5 on Data Development for more about logical data modeling.

4.2.2.2.5 Other Enterprise Data Model Components

Some enterprise data models also include other components. These optional components might include:

- Individual data steward responsibility assignments for subject areas, entities, attributes, and / or reference data value sets. Chapter 3 on Data Governance covers this topic in more depth.

- Valid reference data values: controlled value sets for codes and / or labels and their business meaning. These enterprise-wide value sets are sometimes cross-referenced with departmental, divisional, or regional equivalents. Chapter 8 on Reference and Master Data Management covers this topic in more depth.

- Additional data quality specifications and rules for essential data attributes, such as accuracy / precision requirements, currency (timeliness), integrity rules, nullability, formatting, match / merge rules, and / or audit requirements. Chapter 12 on Data Quality Management covers this topic in more depth.

- Entity life cycles are state transition diagrams depicting the different lifecycle states of the most important entities and the trigger events that change an entity from one state to another. Entity life cycles are very useful in determining a rational set of status values (codes and / or labels) for a business entity. Section 4.2.2.5 expands on this topic.

4.2.2.3 Analyze and Align with Other Business Models

Information value-chain analysis maps the relationships between enterprise model elements and other business models. The term derives from the concept of the business value chain, introduced by Michael Porter in several books and articles on business strategy. The business value chain identifies the functions of an organization that contribute directly and indirectly to the organization's ultimate purpose, such as commercial profit, education, etc., and arranges the directly contributing functions from left to right in a diagram based on their dependencies and event sequence. Indirect support functions appear below this arrangement. The diagram in Figure 4.4 depicts a business value chain for an insurance company.

Information value-chain matrices are composite models. While information value-chain analysis is an output of data architecture, each matrix is also part of one of business process, organization, or application architecture. In this regard, information value-chain analysis is the glue binding together the various forms of "primitive models" in enterprise architecture. Data architects, data stewards, and other enterprise architects and subject matter experts share responsibility for each matrix's content.

4.2.2.4 Define and Maintain the Data Technology Architecture

Data technology architecture guides the selection and integration of data-related technology. Data technology architecture is both a part of the enterprise's overall technology architecture, as well as part of its data architecture. Data technology architecture defines standard tool categories, preferred tools in each category, and technology standards and protocols for technology integration.

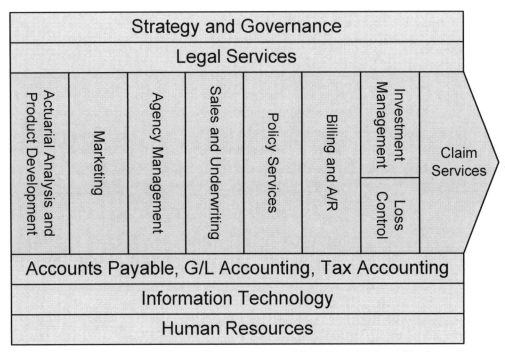

Figure 4.4 Example Insurance Business Value Chain

Technology categories in the data technology architecture include:

- Database management systems (DBMS).

- Database management utilities.

- Data modeling and model management tools.

- Business intelligence software for reporting and analysis.

- Extract-transform-load (ETL), changed data capture (CDC), and other data integration tools.

- Data quality analysis and data cleansing tools.

- Meta-data management software, including meta-data repositories.

Technology architecture components are included in different categories:

- *Current:* Products currently supported and used.

- *Deployment Period:* Products deployed for use in the next 1-2 years.

- *Strategic Period:* Products expected to be available for use in the next 2+ years.

- *Retirement:* Products the organization has retired or intends to retire this year.

- *Preferred:* Products preferred for use by most applications.

- *Containment:* Products limited to use by certain applications.

- *Emerging:* Products being researched and piloted for possible future deployment.

See Chapter 6 for more about managing data technologies.

4.2.2.5 Define and Maintain the Data Integration Architecture

Data integration architecture defines how data flows through all systems from beginning to end. Data integration architecture is both data architecture and application architecture, because it includes both databases and the applications that control the data flow into the system, between databases, and back out of the system. Data lineage and data flows are also names for this concept.

The relationships between the elements in each model are every bit as important as the relationships between the elements themselves. A series of two-dimensional matrices can map and document relationships between different kinds of enterprise model elements. Matrices can define the relationships to other aspects of the enterprise architecture besides business processes, such as:

- Data related to business roles, depicting which roles have responsibility for creating, updating, deleting, and using data about which business entities (CRUD).

- Data related to specific business organizations with these responsibilities.

- Data related to applications that may cross business functions.

- Data related to locations where local differences occur.

Building such matrices is a long-standing practice in enterprise modeling. IBM, in its Business Systems Planning (BSP) method, first introduced this practice. James Martin later popularized it in his Information Systems Planning (ISP) method. The practice is still valid and useful today.

The corporate information factory (CIF) concept is an example of data integration architecture. Data integration architecture generally divides data warehouses, staging databases, and data marts supporting business intelligence from the source databases, operational data stores (ODS),, master data management, and reference data / code management systems supporting online transaction processing and operational reporting. Chapter 8 on Reference and Master Data Management covers data integration architecture for reference and master data.

Data / process relationship matrices can have different levels of detail. Subject areas, business entities, or even essential data attributes can all represent data at different levels. High-level functions, mid-level activities, or low-level tasks all represent business processes.

4.2.2.6 Define and Maintain the DW / BI Architecture

Data warehouse architecture focuses on how data changes and snapshots are stored in data warehouse systems for maximum usefulness and performance. Data integration architecture shows how data moves from source systems through staging databases into data warehouses and data marts. Business intelligence architecture defines how decision support makes data available, including the selection and use of business intelligence tools. This topic is discussed in more detail in Chapter 9 on Data Warehousing and Business Intelligence Management.

4.2.2.7 Define and Maintain Enterprise Taxonomies and Namespaces

Taxonomy is the hierarchical structure used for outlining topics. The best-known example of taxonomy is the classification system for all living things developed originally by the biologist Linnaeus. The Dewey Decimal System is an example of a taxonomy for organizing and finding books in a library. Formal taxonomies are class hierarchies, while informal taxonomies are topical outlines that may not imply inheritance of characteristics from super-types.

Organizations develop their own taxonomies to organize collective thinking about topics. Taxonomies have proven particularly important in presenting and finding information on websites. Overall enterprise data architecture includes organizational taxonomies. The definition of terms used in such taxonomies should be consistent with the enterprise data model, as well as other models and ontologies.

4.2.2.8 Define and Maintain the Meta-data Architecture

Just as the data integration architecture defines how data flows across applications, the meta-data architecture defines the managed flow of meta-data. It defines how meta-data is created, integrated, controlled, and accessed. The meta-data repository is the core of any meta-data architecture. Meta-data architecture is the design for integration of meta-data across software tools, repositories, directories, glossaries, and data dictionaries. The focus of data integration architecture is to ensure the quality, integration, and effective use of reference, master, and business intelligence data. The focus of meta-data architecture is to ensure the quality, integration, and effective use of meta-data. Chapter 11 on Meta-data Management covers this topic in more detail.

4.3 Summary

Defining and maintaining data architecture is a collaborative effort requiring the active participation of data stewards and other subject matter experts, facilitated and supported by data architects and other data analysts. Data architects and analysts must work to optimize the highly valued time contributed by data stewards. The Data Management Executive must secure adequate commitment of time from the right people. Securing this commitment usually requires continual communication of the business case for data architecture and the effort required to define it.

Data architecture is a living thing that is never complete nor static. Business changes naturally drive changes to data architecture. Maintaining data architecture requires regular periodic review by data stewards. Reference to existing data architecture and relatively easy updates to data architecture can resolve many issues quickly. More significant issue resolution often requires new projects to be proposed, evaluated, approved, and performed. The outputs of these projects include updates to data architecture.

The value of data architecture is limited until data stewards participate, review, and refine data architecture, and management approves data architecture as a guiding force for systems implementation. The Data Governance Council is the ultimate sponsor and approving body for enterprise data architecture. Many organizations also form an Enterprise Architecture Council to coordinate data, process, business, system, and technology architecture.

Data architecture is just one part of overall enterprise architecture. Data architecture serves as a guide for integration. Refer to the data architecture when:

- Defining and evaluating new information systems projects: The enterprise data architecture serves as a zoning plan for long-term integration of information systems. The enterprise data architecture affects the goals and objectives of projects, and influences the priority of the projects in the project portfolio. Enterprise data architecture also influences the scope boundaries of projects and system releases.

- Defining project data requirements: The enterprise data architecture provides enterprise data requirements for individual projects, accelerating the identification and definition of these requirements.

- Reviewing project data designs: Design reviews ensure that conceptual, logical, and physical data models are consistent with and contribute to the long-term implementation of the enterprise data architecture.

4.3.1 Guiding Principles

The implementation of the data architecture management function into an organization follows eight guiding principles:

1. Data architecture is an integrated set of specification artifacts (master blueprints) used to define data requirements, guide data integration, control data assets, and align data investments with business strategy.

2. Enterprise data architecture is part of the overall enterprise architecture, along with process architecture, business architecture, systems architecture, and technology architecture.

3. Enterprise data architecture includes three major categories of specifications: the enterprise data model, information value chain analysis, and data delivery architecture.

4. Enterprise data architecture is about more than just data. It helps establish the semantics of an enterprise, using a common business vocabulary.

5. An enterprise data model is an integrated subject-oriented data model defining the essential data used across an entire organization. Build an enterprise data model in layers: a subject area overview, conceptual views of entities and relationships for each subject area, and more detailed, partially attributed views of these same subject areas.

6. Information value-chain analysis defines the critical relationships between data, processes, roles and organizations, and other enterprise elements.

7. Data delivery architecture defines the master blueprint for how data flows across databases and applications. This ensures data quality and integrity to support both transactional business processes and business intelligence reporting and analysis.

8. Architectural frameworks like TOGAF and The Zachman Framework help organize collective thinking about architecture. This allows different people with different objectives and perspectives to work together to meet common interests.

4.3.2 Process Summary

The process summary for the data architecture management function is shown in Table 4.1. The deliverables, responsible roles, approving roles, and contributing roles are shown for each activity in the architecture management function. The Table is also shown in Appendix A9.

Activities	Deliverables	Responsible Roles	Approving Roles	Contributing Roles
2.1 Understand Enterprise Information Needs (P)	Lists of essential information requirements	Enterprise Data Architect, Business SME's	Data Governance Council, Data Architecture Steering Committee, DM Executive, CIO	

Activities	Deliverables	Responsible Roles	Approving Roles	Contributing Roles
2.2 Develop and Maintain the Enterprise Data Model (P)	Enterprise Data Model: • Subject Area Model • Conceptual Model • Logical Model • Glossary	Enterprise Data Architect	Data Governance Council, Data Architecture Steering Committee, DM Executive, CIO	Data Architects, Data Stewards / Teams
2.3 Analyze and Align With Other Business Models (P)	Information Value Chain Analysis Matrices • Entity / Function • Entity / Org and Role • Entity / Application	Enterprise Data Architect	Data Governance Council, Data Architecture Steering Committee, DM Executive, CIO	Data Architects, Data Stewards / Teams, Enterprise Architects
2.4 Define and Maintain the Data Technology Architecture (P)	Data Technology Architecture (Technology, Distribution, Usage)	Enterprise Data Architect	DM Executive, CIO,Data Architecture Steering Committee, Data Governance Council	Database Administrators, Other Data Management. Professionals
2.5 Define and Maintain the Data Integration Architecture (P)	Data Integration Architecture • Data Lineage / Flows • Entity Lifecycles	Enterprise Data Architect	DM Executive, CIO,Data Architecture Steering Committee, Data Governance Council	Database Administrators, Data Integration Specialists, Other Data Management Professionals

Activities	Deliverables	Responsible Roles	Approving Roles	Contributing Roles
2.6 Define and Maintain the Data Warehouse / BI Architecture (P)	Data Warehouse / Business Intelligence Architecture	Data Warehouse Architect	Enterprise Data Architect, DM Executive, CIO, Data Architecture Steering Committee, Data Governance Council	Business Intelligence Specialists, Data Integration Specialists, Database Administrators, Other Data Management. Professionals
2.7 Define and Maintain Enterprise Taxonomies and Namespaces	Enterprise Taxonomies, XML Namespaces, Content Management Standards	Enterprise Data Architect	DM Executive, CIO, Data Architecture Steering Committee, Data Governance Council	Other Data Architects, Other Data Management Professionals
2.8 Define and Maintain the Meta-data Architecture (P)	Meta-data Architecture	Meta-data Architect	Enterprise Data Architect, DM Executive, CIO, Data Architecture Steering Committee, Data Governance Council	Meta-data Specialists, Other Data Management. Professionals

Table 4.1 Data Architecture Management Process Summary

4.3.3 Organizational and Cultural Issues

Q1: Are there any ramifications to implementing an enterprise data architecture?

A1: Implementation of enterprise data architecture can have many ramifications to an organization. First, everyone in the organization has to see the value of the overall data architecture. There will be some discovery of redundant systems and processes that may require changes to roles and responsibilities of some organization teams and individuals, so take care to discourage fear of workforce reduction. People who have been working on redundant systems become free to do interesting work on other systems. Second, everyone in the organization has to be committed to making sure that the data architecture remains current when the business needs or technology landscape change.

Implementation of an enterprise data architecture can have many ramifications to an organization's culture. Application-centric IT shops will have to make changes to their culture to become more data-aware, and pay more attention to what is moving through their applications, rather than just to what the application does. Data awareness is a way of making IT more knowledgeable about business needs and practices, so IT then becomes more of a partner with the business, rather than just a service provider.

4.4 Recommended Reading

The references listed below provide additional reading that support the material presented in Chapter 4. These recommended readings are also included in the Bibliography at the end of the Guide.

4.4.1 Books

Bernard, Scott A. An Introduction to Enterprise Architecture, 2nd Edition. Authorhouse, 2005. ISBN 1-420-88050-0. 351 pages.

Brackett, Michael. Data Sharing Using A Common Data Architecture. New York: John Wiley & Sons, 1994. ISBN 0-471-30993-1. 478 pages.

Carbone, Jane. IT Architecture Toolkit. Prentice Hall, 2004. ISBN 0-131-47379-4. 256 pages.

Cook, Melissa. Building Enterprise Information Architectures: Re-Engineering Information Systems. Prentice Hall, 1996. ISBN 0-134-40256-1. 224 pages.

Hagan, Paula J., ed. EABOK: Guide to the (Evolving) Enterprise Architecture Body of Knowledge. MITRE Corporation, 2004. 141 pages. A U.S. federally-funded guide to enterprise architecture in the context of legislative and strategic requirements. Available for free download at
http://www.mitre.org/work/tech_papers/tech_papers_04/04_0104/04_0104.pdf

Inmon, W. H., John A. Zachman, and Jonathan G. Geiger. Data Stores, Data Warehousing and the Zachman Framework: Managing Enterprise Knowledge. McGraw-Hill, 1997. ISBN 0-070-31429-2. 358 pages.

Lankhorst, Marc. Enterprise Architecture at Work: Modeling, Communication and Analysis. Springer, 2005. ISBN 3-540-24371-2. 334 pages.

Martin, James and Joe Leben. Strategic Data Planning Methodologies, 2nd Edition. Prentice Hall, 1989. ISBN 0-13-850538-1. 328 pages.

Perks, Col and Tony Beveridge. <u>Guide to Enterprise IT Architecture</u>. Springer, 2002. ISBN 0-387-95132-6. 480 pages.

Ross, Jeanne W., Peter Weill, and David Robertson. <u>Enterprise Architecture As Strategy: Creating a Foundation For Business Execution</u>. Harvard Business School Press, 2006. ISBN 1-591-39839-8. 288 pages.

Schekkerman, Jaap. <u>How to Survive in the Jungle of Enterprise Architecture Frameworks: Creating or Choosing an Enterprise Architecture Framework</u>. Trafford, 2006. 224 pages. ISBN 1-412-01607-X.

Spewak, Steven and Steven C. Hill, <u>Enterprise Architecture Planning</u>. John Wiley & Sons -QED, 1993. ISBN 0-471-59985-9. 367 pages.

The Open Group, <u>TOGAF: The Open Group Architecture Framework, Version 8.1 Enterprise Edition</u>. The Open Group. (<u>www.opengroup.org</u>). ISBN 1-93-16245-6. 491 pages.

Zachman, John A. <u>The Zachman Framework: A Primer for Enterprise Engineering and Manufacturing</u>. Metadata Systems Software Inc., Toronto, Canada. eBook available only in electronic form from <u>www.ZachmanInternational.com</u>.

4.4.2 Articles and Websites

Zachman, John. "A Concise Definition of the Enterprise Framework." Zachman International, 2008. Article in electronic form available for free download at <u>http://www.zachmaninternational.com/index.php/home-article/13#thezf</u>.

Zachman, John A. "A Framework for Information Systems Architecture", IBM_Systems Journal, Vol. 26 No. 3 1987, pages 276 to 292. IBM Publication G321-5298. Also available in a special issue of the IBM Systems Journal, "Turning Points in Computing: 1962-1999", IBM Publication G321-0135, pages 454 to 470
http://researchweb.watson.ibm.com/journal/sj/382/zachman.pdf.

Zachman, John A. and John F. Sowa,. "Extending and Formalizing the Framework for Information Systems Architecture", IBM Systems Journal. Vol. 31 No. 3 1992, pages 590 – 616. IBM Publication G321-5488.

5 Data Development

Data development is the third Data Management Function in the data management framework shown in Figures 1.3 and 1.4. It is the second data management function that interacts with and is influenced by the Data Governance function. Chapter 5 defines the data development function and explains the concepts and activities involved in data development.

5.1 Introduction

Data development is the analysis, design, implementation, deployment, and maintenance of data solutions to maximize the value of the data resources to the enterprise. Data development is the subset of project activities within the system development lifecycle (SDLC) focused on defining data requirements, designing the data solution components, and implementing these components. The primary data solution components are databases and other data structures. Other data solution components include information products (screens and reports) and data access interfaces.

The context of the Data Development Function is shown in the context diagram in Figure 5.1

Project team members must collaborate with each other for effective solution design.

- Business data stewards and subject matter experts (SMEs) provide *business requirements* for data and information, including business rules and data quality expectations, and then validate that these requirements have been met.

- Data architects, analysts, and database administrators have primary responsibility for *database design*. Database administrators collaborate with software developers to define data access services in layered service-oriented architecture (SOA) implementations.

- Software architects and developers (both application and data integration specialists) take primary responsibility for *data capture and usage design* within programs, as well as the *user interface design* for information products (screens and printed reports).

5.2 Concepts and Activities

The activities necessary to carry out the data development function are described below.

5.2.1 System Development Lifecycle (SDLC)

Data development activities occur in the context of systems development and maintenance efforts, known as the system development life cycle (SDLC). Projects manage most of these efforts. A project is an organized effort to accomplish something. A very small maintenance effort may be completed in a day. Very large multi-phase projects can take years to complete.

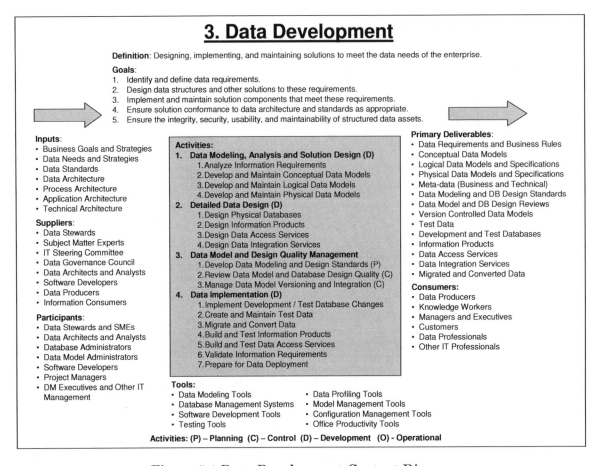

Figure 5.1 Data Development Context Diagram

System development and maintenance projects perform selected activities within the systems development lifecycle. The stages of the SDLC represent very high-level steps commonly taken to implement systems, as shown in Figure 5.2. There is no standardized outline of these stages, but in general, the SDLC includes the following specification and implementation activities:

- Project Planning , including scope definition and business case justification.

- Requirements Analysis.

- Solution Design.

- Detailed Design.

- Component Building.

- Testing, including unit, integration, system, performance, and acceptance testing.

- Deployment Preparation, including documentation development and training.

- Installation and Deployment, including piloting and rollout.

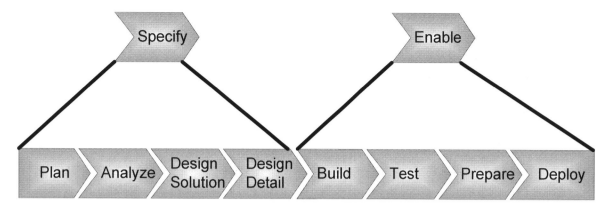

Figure 5.2 The System Development Lifecycle (SDLC)

System maintenance efforts also generally follow the same high-level SDLC processes in very rapid sequence, performing some small amounts of analysis, design, coding, testing, and deployment.

Many organizations have adopted SDLC methods that integrate systems development methods and techniques into a comprehensive approach to systems development. Methods guide system development project planning and performance. Most methods recommend detailed tasks and specific techniques to perform activities within each SDLC stage. These tasks and techniques create a data modeling series of deliverables leading ultimately to an implemented system. The outputs from early tasks serve as the inputs guiding subsequent tasks.

Different methods portray the SDLC in different ways, each with its own distinctive use of terms. Some methods define a waterfall approach to performing SDLC stages. Some methods define a spiral, iterative approach. These methods deliver complete solutions in increments by performing SDLC stages in multiple project phases, guided by some high-level planning, analysis, and design.

Information systems capture and deliver information (data in context with relevance and a time frame) to support business functions. These functions range from strategic planning to operational performance. Data stores and information products are integral components of every information system. An effective systems development project will maintain a balanced emphasis on data, process, and technology.

5.2.2 Styles of Data Modeling

Several different data modeling methods are available, each using different diagramming conventions or styles. The syntax for each of these styles differs slightly. While all data models use boxes and lines, each style uses different symbols and box contents to communicate detailed specifications. The DAMA-DMBOK Guide offers only a very brief introduction to these styles.

- IE: The most common data modeling diagramming style is the "information engineering" (IE) syntax, so named because it was popularized by James Martin in his influential books and training on Information Engineering. The IE notation uses tridents or "crow's feet", along with other symbols, to depict cardinality.

- IDEF1X: This is an alternate data modeling syntax developed originally for use by the U.S. Air Force, using circles (some darkened, some empty) and lines (some solid, some dotted) instead of "crow's feet" to communicate similar meanings. IDEF0 process diagrams often use IDEF1X notation.

- ORM: Object Role Modeling is an alternate modeling style with a syntax that enables very detailed specification of business data relationships and rules. ORM diagrams present so much information that effective consumption usually requires smaller subject area views, with fewer business entities on a single diagram. ORM is not widely used, but its proponents strongly advocate its benefits. ORM is particularly useful for modeling complex business relationships.

- UML: The Unified Modeling Language is an integrated set of diagramming conventions for several different forms of modeling. Grady Booch, Ivar Jacobsen, and James Rumbaugh developed UML to standardize object-oriented analysis and design. UML has become widely adopted, effectively achieving this purpose. UML is now widely used in many SDLC methods and has been adopted by many standards organizations.

UML defines several different types of models and diagrams. Class diagrams closely resemble other data model styles. In addition to modeling object-oriented software, semantic models for XML-based web services commonly use UML class diagrams. In fact, conceptual, logical, and even physical data modeling can use UML class diagrams.

Some practitioners see no need or value to modeling objects and data separately. Conceptual object class models are equivalent to conceptual data models. However, logical and physical data models usually differ substantially from logical and physical object-oriented program designs. Logical data models normalize data attributes, while object models do not. The attributes of an object represent data in program memory, while the attributes of a physical data model represent the data stored in a database, usually as columns in relational database tables. Recognizing these differences, most data professionals prefer to model data and / or databases in separate models with different diagramming styles.

When used consistently, the different diagramming conventions can quickly differentiate and communicate the purpose of each model. For example, some practitioners use IE notation for logical data modeling and use IDEF1X for physical data modeling, especially dimensional modeling. However, this is confusing for business data stewards reviewing different kinds of models. Data stewards do not need to become data modelers, but they should be fluent in reading and interpreting one primary diagramming convention.

5.2.3 Data Modeling, Analysis, and Solution Design

Data modeling is an analysis and design method used to 1) define and analyze data requirements, and 2) design data structures that support these requirements. A data model is a set of data specifications and related diagrams that reflect data requirements and designs. For the most part, conceptual data modeling and logical data modeling are requirements analysis activities, while physical data modeling is a design activity.

A model is a representation of something in our environment. It makes use of standard symbols that allow one quickly to grasp its content. Maps, organization charts, and building blueprints are examples of models in use every day. Think of a data model as a diagram that uses text and symbols to represent data elements and relationships between them. In fact, a single diagram may be one of several views provided for a single integrated data model. More formally, a data model is the integrated collection of specifications and related diagrams that represent data requirements and designs.

Although there are well-defined techniques and processes, there is an art to making data available in usable forms to a variety of different applications, as well as visually understandable. Data modeling is a complex process involving interactions between people and with technology, which do not compromise the integrity or security of the data. Good data models accurately express and effectively communicate data requirements and quality solution design. Some model diagrams try to communicate too much detail, reducing their effectiveness.

Two formulas guide a modeling approach:

- Purpose + audience = deliverables.

- Deliverables + resources + time = approach.

The purpose of a data model is to facilitate:

- Communication: A data model is a bridge to understanding data between people with different levels and types of experience. Data models help us understand a business area, an existing application, or the impact of modifying an existing structure. Data models may also facilitate training new business and / or technical staff.

- Formalization: A data model documents a single, precise definition of data requirements and data related business rules.

- Scope: A data model can help explain the data context and scope of purchased application packages.

Data models that include the same data may differ by:

- Scope: Expressing a perspective about data in terms of function (business view or application view), realm (process, department, division, enterprise, or industry view), and time (current state, short-term future, long-term future).

- Focus: Basic and critical concepts (conceptual view), detailed but independent of context (logical view), or optimized for a specific technology and use (physical view).

Use data models to specify the data required to meet information needs. Data flows through business processes packaged in information products. The data contained in these information products must meet business requirements. Data modeling is, in that sense, an analysis activity, reflecting business requirements. However, data modeling presents creative opportunities at every step, making it, at the same time, a design activity. Generally, there is more analysis involved in conceptual data modeling, and more design involved in physical data modeling, with a more balanced mixture of both in logical data modeling.

5.2.3.1 Analyze Information Requirements

Information is data in context that has relevance, and is timely. To identify information requirements, we need to first identify business information needs, often in the context of one or more business processes. Business processes consume as input, information products output from other business processes. The names of these information products often identify an essential business vocabulary that serves as the basis for data modeling. Regardless of whether processes or data are modeled sequentially (in either order), or concurrently, effective analysis and design should ensure a relatively balanced view of data (nouns) and processes (verbs), with equal emphasis on both process and data modeling.

Projects typically begin with a project request and the definition of a project charter that defines project objectives, deliverables, and scope boundaries. Initial project plans estimate the resources, effort, time, and cost required to accomplish project objectives. Every project charter should include data-specific objectives and identify the data within its scope. Reference to an enterprise data model provides the vocabulary to define the data scope of the project effectively.

Requirements analysis includes the elicitation, organization, documentation, review, refinement, approval, and change control of business requirements. Some of these requirements identify business needs for data and information. Express requirement specifications in both words and diagrams.

Logical data modeling is an important means of expressing business data requirements. For many people, as the old saying goes, "a picture is worth a thousand words." However, some people do not relate easily to pictures; they relate better to reports and tables created by data modeling tools. Many organizations have formal requirements - management disciplines to guide drafting and refining formal requirement statements, such as, "The system shall ...". Written data requirement specification documents may be maintained using requirements management tools. Carefully synchronize the contents of any such documentation with the specifications captured within data models.

Some methods include enterprise planning activities that define the enterprise data model, using techniques such as business systems planning (BSP) or information systems planning. Methods may also include the definition of related enterprise-wide data delivery architecture in the planning phase. Chapter 4 on Data Architecture Management covers these activities.

5.2.3.2 Develop and Maintain Conceptual Data Models

A conceptual data model is a visual, high-level perspective on a subject area of importance to the business. It contains only the basic and critical business entities within a given realm and function, with a description of each entity and the relationships between entities. Conceptual data models define the semantics (nouns and verbs) of the essential business vocabulary. Conceptual data model subject areas may reflect the data associated with a business process or application function. A conceptual data model is independent of technology (database, files, etc.) and usage context (whether the entity is in a billing system or a data warehouse).

Included in a conceptual data model is a glossary that defines each object within the conceptual data model. The definitions include business terms, relationship terms, entity synonyms, and security classifications. An example of a conceptual data model is shown in Figure 5.3.

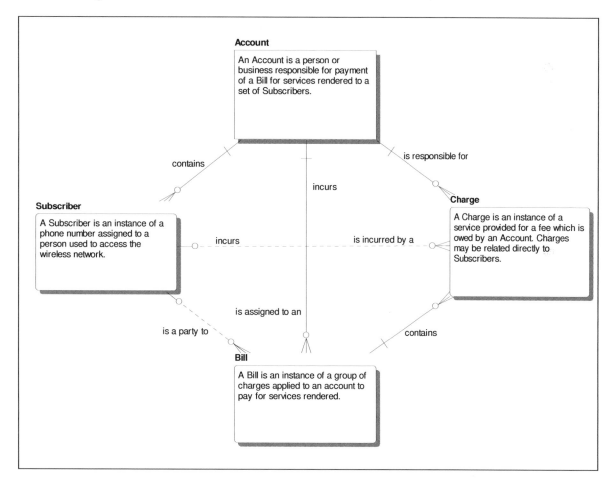

Figure 5.3 Conceptual Data Model Example

To create a conceptual data model, start with one subject area from the subject area model. Determine what objects are included within that subject area, and how they relate to each other. For example, a Customer subject area may contain the following entities: Account Owner, Sub Account, Contact Preferences, and Contact Information.

One Account Owner relates to one or more Sub Accounts. Each Account Owner has one set of Contact Preferences and one set of Contact Information at any time.

To maintain a conceptual data model, adopt a process to check any proposed changes to the production system against the conceptual model. If a project will involve changes, create an intermediate conceptual model and make the changes there. Copy the model changes to the production version of the conceptual model when implementing changes to the production system as part of the release process, to ensure that the model keeps in synch with current reality.

5.2.3.2.1 Entities

A business entity is something of interest to the organization, an object, or an event. A data entity is a collection of data about something that the business deems important and worthy of capture. An entity is a noun:

- A *who:* Person, organization, role, employee, customer, vendor, student, party, department, regulatory body, competitor, partner, subsidiary, team, family, household.

- A *what:* Product, service, resource, raw material, finished good, course, class.

- A *when:* Event, fiscal period.

- A *where:* Location, address, site, network node.

- A *why:* Policy, rule, request, complaint, return, inquiry.

- A *how:* Mechanism, tool, document, invoice, contract, agreement, standard, account.

An entity occurrence is the instantiation of a particular business entity. The entity *Customer* can have instances named Bob, Joe, Jane, and so forth. The entity *Account* can have instances of Bob's checking account, Bob's savings account, Joe's brokerage account, and so on.

An entity can appear in a conceptual or logical data model. Conceptual business entities describe the things about which we collect data, such as Customer, Product, and Account. Logical data entities follow the rules of normalization and abstraction, and therefore the concept Customer becomes numerous components such as Customer, Customer Type, and Customer Preference. Physical data models define tables that may or may not relate directly to entities in a comparable logical model.

Entities are either independent or dependent entities. An independent entity (or kernel entity) does not depend on any other entity for its existence. Each occurrence of an independent entity exists without referring to any other entity in the data model. A dependent entity depends on one or more other entities for its existence. There are three main types of dependent entity:

- Attributive / characteristic entity: An entity that depends on only one other parent entity, such as Employee Beneficiary depending on Employee.

- Associative / mapping entity: An entity that depends on two or more entities, such as Registration depending on a particular Student and Course.

- Category / sub-type or super-type entity: An entity that is "a kind of" another entity. Sub-types and super-types are examples of generalization and inheritance. A super-type entity is a generalization of all its subtypes, and each sub-type inherits the attributes of their super-type. For example, a Party super-type links to Person and Organization sub-types. Subtypes may be over-lapping (non-exclusive) or non-overlapping (exclusive). A non-overlapping sub-type entity instance must be either one sub-type or another, but not both.

5.2.3.2.2 Relationships

Business rules define constraints on what can and cannot be done. Business rules divide into two major categories:

- Data rules constrain how data relates to other data. For example, "Freshman students can register for at most 18 credits a semester." Data models focus on data business rules.

- Action rules are instructions on what to do when data elements contain certain values. Action rules are difficult to define in a data model. Business rules for data quality are action rules, and applications implement them as data entry edits and validations.

Data models express two primary types of data rules:

- Cardinality rules define the quantity of each entity instance that can participate in a relationship between two entities. For example, "Each company can employ many persons."

- Referential integrity rules ensure valid values. For example, "A person can exist without working for a company, but a company cannot exist unless at least one person is employed by the company."

Express cardinality and referential integrity business rules as relationships between entities in data models. Combine the examples above to express the relationship between Company and Person as follows:

- Each person can work for zero to many companies.

- Each company must employ one or many persons.

Relationship labels are verb phrases describing the business rules in each direction between two entities, along with the words that describe the "many" aspect of each relationship (cardinality) and the "zero or one" side of each relationship (referential integrity).

A relationship between two entities may be one of three relationship types:

- A *one-to-one relationship* says that a parent entity may have one and only one child entity.

- A *one-to-many relationship* says that a parent entity may have one or more child entities. One-to-many relationships are the most common relationships. In some one-to-many relationships, a child entity must have a parent, but in other relationships, the relationship to a parent is optional. In some one-to-many relationships, a parent entity must have at least one child entity, while in other one-to-many relationships, the relationship to any child is optional.

- A *many-to-many relationship* says that an instance of each entity may be associated with zero to many instances of the other entity, and vice versa.

A *recursive relationship* relates instances of an entity to other instances of the same entity. Recursive relationships may be one-to-one, one-to-many, or many-to-many.

5.2.3.3 Develop and Maintain Logical Data Models

A logical data model is a detailed representation of data requirements and the business rules that govern data quality, usually in support of a specific usage context (application requirements). Logical data models are still independent of any technology or specific implementation technical constraints. A logical data model often begins as an extension of a conceptual data model, adding data attributes to each entity. Organizations should have naming standards to guide the naming of logical data objects. Logical data models transform conceptual data model structures by applying two techniques: normalization and abstraction. An example of a logical data model is shown in Figure 5.4.

Normalization is the process of applying rules to organize business complexity into stable data structures. A deeper understanding of each data element is required, to see each data element in relationship to every other data element. The basic goal of normalization is to keep each data element in only one place.

Normalization rules sort data elements according to primary and foreign keys. Normalization rules sort into levels, with each level applying more granularity and specificity in search of the correct primary and foreign keys. Each level comprises a separate normal form, and each successive level includes previous levels. Normalization levels include:

- First normal form (1NF): Ensures each entity has a valid primary key, every data element depends on the primary key, and removes repeating groups, and ensuring each data element is atomic (not multi-valued).

- Second normal form (2NF): Ensures each entity has the minimal primary key and that every data element depends on the complete primary key.

- Third normal form (3NF): Ensures each entity has no hidden primary keys and that each data element depends on no data element outside the key ("the key, the whole key and nothing but the key").

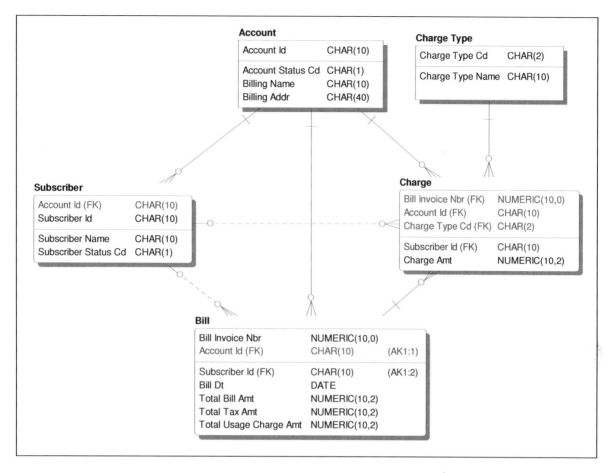

Figure 5.4 Logical Data Model Example

- Boyce / Codd normal form (BCNF): Resolves overlapping composite candidate keys. A candidate key is either a primary or an alternate key. 'Composite' means more than one (e.g. two data elements in an entity's primary key), and 'overlapping' means there are hidden business rules between the keys.

- Fourth normal form (4NF): Resolves all many-to-many-to-many relationships (and beyond) in pairs until they cannot be broken down into any smaller pieces.

- Fifth normal form (5NF): Resolves inter-entity dependencies into basic pairs, and all join dependencies use parts of primary keys.

- Sixth normal form (6NF): Adds temporal objects to primary keys, in order to allow for historical reporting and analysis over timeframes.

The term *normalized model* usually means the data is in 3NF. Situations requiring BCNF, 4NF, 5NF, and 6NF occur rarely; these forms are considered advanced topics in data modeling.

Abstraction is the redefinition of data entities, elements, and relationships by removing details to broaden the applicability of data structures to a wider class of situations, often by implementing super-types rather than sub-types. Using the generic Party Role super-type to represent the Customer, Employee, and Supplier sub-types is an example of applying abstraction.

Use normalization to show known details of entities. Use abstraction when some details of entities are missing or not yet discovered, or when the generic version of entities is more important or useful than the subtypes.

5.2.3.3.1 Attributes

An attribute is a property of an entity; a type of fact important to the business whose values help identify or describe an entity instance. For example, the attribute *Student Last Name* describes the last name of each student. Attributes translate in a physical data model to a field in a file or a column in a database table. Attributes use business names, while fields and columns use technical names that frequently include technical abbreviations. In a logical data model, business entities represent the essential nouns in the organization's vocabulary, and attributes represent adjectives.

An attribute in a logical model should be atomic. It should contain one and only one piece of data (fact) that cannot be divided into smaller pieces. For example, a conceptual data element called phone number divides into several logical data elements for phone type code (home, office, fax, mobile, etc.), country code, (1 for US and Canada), area code, prefix, base phone number, and extension.

An instance of an attribute is the value of the attribute for a particular entity instance. An occurrence of a data value is its appearance as an attribute instance for an entity instance. The data element instance 60106 for example, belongs to the Customer Employee Zip Code data element, which exists for the Customer instance Bob.

Entity and attribute definitions are essential contributors to the business value of any data model. High-quality definitions clarify the meaning of business vocabulary and provide rigor to the business rules governing entity relationships. High-quality definitions assist business professionals in making intelligent business decisions, and they assist IT professionals in making intelligent application design decisions. High-quality data definitions exhibit three essential characteristics: clarity, accuracy, and completeness.

5.2.3.3.2 Domains

The complete set of all possible values for an attribute is a domain. An attribute can never contain values outside of its assigned domain. Some domains have a limited number of specific defined values, or minimum or maximum limits for numbers. Business rules can also restrict domains.

Attributes often share the same domain. For example, an employee hire date and a purchase order date must be:

- A valid calendar date (for example, not February 31st).

- A date that falls on a weekday.

- A date that does not fall on a holiday.

A data dictionary contains a collection of domains and the attributes that relate to each domain, among other things.

5.2.3.3.3 Keys

Attributes assigned to entities are either key or non-key attributes. A key data element helps identify one unique entity instance from all others, either fully (by itself) or partially (in combination with other key elements). Non-key data elements describe the entity instance but do not help uniquely identify it.

A key (or candidate key) represents the one or more attributes whose values uniquely identify an entity instance. A composite key is a key containing two or more attributes. One of these candidate keys becomes the primary key. There should be only one primary key. All other candidate keys become alternate keys.

To avoid using composite primary keys, or key attributes with values that change over time, use a surrogate key. A surrogate key contains a randomly generated value uniquely assigned to an entity instance. 'Surrogate' means 'substitute'. Use a surrogate key when a truly unique data element or set of data elements exists within the entity. Other names for surrogate keys are anonymous keys, or non-intelligent keys. Note that simply having a key generated by sequence number actually still has some intelligence. A person can tell in which order the rows were inserted into the table by the sequence, similar to a row number. True surrogate keys are random, not sequential.

A foreign key is an attribute that provides a link to another entity. Simply put, a foreign key is an attribute that appears in both entities in a relationship, and partially or fully identifies either one or both of the entities. When a one-to-many relationship exists between two entities, the entity on the child side of the relationship inherits the primary key attributes from the entity on the parent side of the relationship. The foreign key enables navigation between data structures.

An identifying relationship occurs when the foreign key attribute(s) of a parent entity appears as part of the composite primary key of a child entity. A non-identifying relationship occurs when the foreign key of a parent entity is a non-key attribute(s) describing the child entity.

5.2.3.4 Develop and Maintain Physical Data Models

A physical data model optimizes the implementation of detailed data requirements and business rules in light of technology constraints, application usage, performance requirements, and modeling standards. Design relational databases with the specific capabilities of a database management system in mind (IBM DB2 or UDB, Oracle, Teradata, Sybase, or Microsoft SQL Server or Access). Organizations should have naming standards to guide the naming of physical data objects. An example of a physical data model is shown in Figure 5.5.

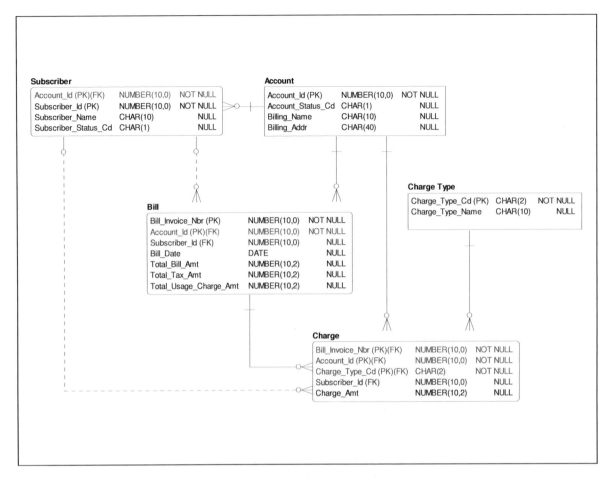

Figure 5.5 Physical Data Model Example

Physical data model design includes making decisions about:

- The technical name of each table and column (relational databases), or file and field (non-relational databases), or schema and element (XML databases).

- The logical domain, physical data type, length, and nullability of each column or field.

- Any default values for columns or fields, especially for NOT NULL constraints.

- Primary and alternate unique keys and indexes, including how to assign keys.

- Implementation of small reference data value sets in the logical model, such as a) separate code tables, b) a master shared code table, or c) simply as rules or constraints.

- Implementation of minor supertype / subtype logical model entities in the physical database design where the sub-type entities' attributes are merged into a table representing the super-type entity as nullable columns, or collapsing the super-type entity's attributes in a table for each sub-type.

Going forward, we will use the term 'tables' to refer to tables, files, and schemas; the term 'columns' to refer to columns, fields, and elements; and the term 'rows' to refer to rows, records, or instances.

Physical data modeling transforms the logical data model using several techniques, including:

- Denormalization: Selectively and justifiably violating normalization rules, re-introducing redundancy into the data model to reduce retrieval time, potentially at the expense of additional space, additional insert / update time, and reduced data quality.

- Surrogate keys: Substitute keys not visible to the business.

- Indexing: Create additional index files to optimize specific types of queries.

- Partitioning: Break a table or file vertically (separating groups of columns) or horizontally (separating groups of rows).

- Views: Virtual tables used to simplify queries, control data access, and rename columns, without the redundancy and loss of referential integrity due to de-normalization.

- Dimensionality: Creation of fact tables with associated dimension tables, structured as star schemas and snowflake schemas, for business intelligence (see Chapter 9).

5.2.4 Detailed Data Design

Detailed data design activities include:

- Detailed physical database design, including views, functions, triggers, and stored procedures.

- Other supporting data structures, such as XML schemas and object classes.

- Information products, such as the use of data in screens and reports.

- Data access solutions, including data access objects, integration services, and reporting and analysis services.

Database administrators (DBAs) take the lead role in database design, and a collaborative role in designing information products (XML schemas, messages, screens, and reports) and related data services (data access services, data integration services, and business intelligence services). Data analysts take the lead role in designing information products and related data services, and a collaborative role in database design.

5.2.4.1 Design Physical Databases

Detailed design includes database implementation specifications. A physical database design may take advantage of the unique functions and capabilities of a specific database management system, which may or may not be included in the data model itself.

For relational databases, the primary design deliverables are the Data Definition Language (DDL) specifications. DDL is a subset of Structured Query Language (SQL) used to create tables, indexes, views, and other physical database objects. For XML databases, the primary design deliverable is the namespace.

A complete, high-quality database design document is more than just DDL statements. Section 5.2.4.1.3 describes a complete physical design document.

Whether or not the DBA collaborates in physical data modeling, the DBA has primary responsibility for detailed database design, including:

- Ensuring the design meets data integrity requirements.

- Determining the most appropriate physical structure to house and organize the data, such as relational or other type of DBMS, files, OLAP cubes, XML, etc.

- Determining database resource requirements, such as server size and location, disk space requirements, CPU and memory requirements, and network requirements.

- Creating detailed design specifications for data structures, such as relational database tables, indexes, views, OLAP data cubes, XML schemas, etc.

- Ensuring performance requirements are met, including batch and online response time requirements for queries, inserts, updates, and deletes.

- Designing for backup, recovery, archiving, and purge processing, ensuring availability requirements are met, and database maintenance operations can be performed within the window(s) of time available (see Chapter 6).

- Designing data security implementation, including authentication, encryption needs, application roles, and the data access and update permissions they should be assigned. The general rule is never to grant permissions on database objects to individual users, only to roles. Users can then be moved into and out of roles as needed; this greatly reduces maintenance and enhances data security (see Chapter 7).

- Determine partitioning and hashing schemes, where appropriate.

- Requiring SQL code review to ensure that the code meets coding standards and will run efficiently.

5.2.4.1.1 Physical Database Design

Choose a database design based on both a choice of architecture and a choice of technology. Base the choice of architecture (for example, relational, hierarchical, network, object, star schema, snowflake, cube, etc.) on several considerations:

- Whether (and how often) the data is updated.

- The natural organization of the data.

- How the data is viewed and used.

The choice of implementation technology (for example, relational, XML, OLAP, or Object technology) may be governed by many different factors, including how long the data needs to be kept, whether it must be integrated with other data or passed across system or application boundaries, and on requirements of data security, integrity, recoverability, accessibility, and reusability.

There may also be organizational or political factors, including organizational biases and developer skill sets, that lean toward a particular technology or vendor. Other factors influencing physical database design include:

- Purchase and licensing requirements, including the DBMS, the database server, and any client-side data access and reporting tools.

- Auditing and privacy requirements (e.g., Sarbanes-Oxley, PCI, HIPAA, etc.).

- Application requirements; for example, whether the database must support a web application or web service, or a particular analysis or reporting tool.

- Database service level agreements (SLAs).

Database designers must find the answers to several questions, including:

- What are the performance requirements? What is the maximum permissible time for a query to return results, or for a critical set of updates to occur?

- What are the availability requirements for the database? What are the window(s) of time for performing database operations? How often should database backups and transaction log backups be done (i.e., what is the longest period of time we can risk non-recoverability of the data)?

- What is the expected size of the database? What is the expected rate of growth of the data? At what point can old or unused data be archived or deleted? How many concurrent users are anticipated?

- What sorts of data virtualization are needed to support application requirements in a way that does not tightly couple the application to the database schema?

- Will other applications need the data? If so, what data and how?

- Will users expect to be able to do ad-hoc querying and reporting of the data? If so, how and with which tools?

- What, if any, business or application processes does the database need to implement? (e.g., trigger code that does cross-database integrity checking or updating, application classes encapsulated in database procedures or functions, database views that provide table recombination for ease of use or security purposes, etc.).

- Are there application or developer concerns regarding the database, or the database development process, that need to be addressed?

- Is the application code efficient? Can a code change relieve a performance issue?

In designing and building the database, the DBA should keep the following design principles firmly in mind (remember the acronym PRISM):

- Performance and Ease of Use: Ensure quick and easy access to data by approved users in a usable and business-relevant form, maximizing the business value of both applications and data.

- Reusability: The database structure should ensure that, where appropriate, multiple applications would be able to use the data. The database structure should also ensure that multiple business purposes, (such as business analysis, quality improvement, strategic planning, customer relationship management, and process improvement) could use the data. Avoid coupling a database, data structure, or data object to a single application. Do not tightly couple an application to a database! Data should reflect the real entities and attributes of the business, not the requirements of a single application.

- Integrity: The data should always have a valid business meaning and value, regardless of context, and should always reflect a valid state of the business. Enforce data integrity as close to the data as possible, and immediately detect and report violations of data integrity constraints.

- Security: True and accurate data should always be immediately available to authorized users, but only to authorized users. The privacy concerns of all stakeholders, including customers, business partners, and government regulators, must be met. Enforce data security, like data integrity, as close to the data as possible, and immediately detect and report security violations.

- Maintainability: Perform all data work at a cost that yields value by ensuring that the cost of creating, storing, maintaining, using, and disposing of data does not exceed its value to the organization. Ensure the fastest possible response to changes in business processes and new business requirements.

Here are some recommended best practices for physical database design:

1. For relational databases supporting transaction processing (OLTP) applications, use a normalized design to promote data integrity, reusability, good update performance, and data extensibility.

2. At the same time, use views, functions, and stored procedures to create non-normalized, application-specific, object-friendly, conceptual (virtual) views of data. Do not force developers to work at the physical database level, nor tightly couple database schemas to applications. The goal is to abstract the functionality of the data from its physical structure and make it as easy as possible to work with.

3. Use standard naming conventions and meaningful, descriptive names across all databases and database objects for ease of maintenance, especially if abbreviations are necessary.

4. Enforce data security and integrity at the database level, not in the application. This enables the easy reuse of data, while saving developers the work of having to write and test code-level constraints in every application that uses a given piece of data.

5. Try to keep database processing on the database server as much as possible, for maximum performance, ease of maintenance, security, scalability, reduced network traffic, and lower cost of development. For example, implement all database updates and complex SQL queries as stored procedures in the database, instead of embedding them in the application code, and use server-side (rather than client-side) cursors. Using stored procedures makes it easy to isolate and fix errors and performance problems, enhances performance, and greatly reduces network traffic.

6. Grant permissions on database objects (tables, views, stored procedures, functions, and so on) only to application groups or roles, not to individuals. This improves both security and ease of maintenance.

7. Do not permit any direct, ad-hoc updating of the database; do all updates in a controlled manner, through pre-defined procedures.

5.2.4.1.2 Performance Modifications

When implementing a physical database, consider how the database will perform when applications make requests to access and modify data. There are several techniques used to optimize database performance.

Indexing can improve query performance in many cases. The database designer must select and define appropriate indexes for database tables. An index is an alternate path for accessing data in the database to optimize query (data retrieval) performance. Major RDBMS products support many types of indexes. Indexes can be unique or non-unique, clustered or non-clustered, partitioned or non-partitioned, single column or multi-column, b-tree or bitmap or hashed. Without an appropriate index, the DBMS will revert to reading every row in the table (table scan) to retrieve any data. On large tables, this is very costly. Try to build indexes on large tables to support the most frequently run queries, using the most frequently referenced columns, particularly keys (primary, alternate, and foreign).

Denormalization is the deliberate transformation of a normalized logical data model into tables with redundant data. In other words, it intentionally puts one data element in multiple places. This process does introduce risk of data errors due to duplication. Implement data quality checks to ensure that the copies of the data elements stay correctly stored. Only denormalized specifically to improve database query performance, by either segregating or combining data to reduce query set sizes, combining data to reduce joins, or performing and storing costly data calculations. Denormalization techniques include (among others):

- Collapse hierarchies (roll-up): To reduce joins, combine direct-path parent / child relationships into one table, repeating the parent columns in each row. This is a major tool in dimensional modeling (discussed in Chapter 9 on Data Warehousing and Business Intelligence).

- Divide hierarchies (push down): To reduce query sets, where parent tables are divided into multiple child tables by type. For example, create customer tables that each contain a different type of customer, such as checking, mortgage, investment, etc.

- Vertically split: To reduce query sets, create subset tables which contain subsets of columns. For example, split a customer table into two based on whether the fields are mostly static or mostly volatile (to improve load / index performance), or based on whether the fields are commonly or uncommonly included in queries (to improve table scan performance).

- Horizontally split: To reduce query sets, create subset tables using the value of a column as the differentiator. For example, create regional customer tables that contain only customers in a specific region.

- Combine and pre-join tables: To reduce joins where two tables are joined in a significant number of queries, consider creating a table which already has the result set of a join of both tables.

- Repeat columns in one row: To reduce row counts or to enable row-to-row comparisons, create a table with repeated rows. For example, rather than 12 rows for 12 months, have 12 columns, one for each month.

- Derive data from stored data: To reduce calculation expense at query time, especially calculations that require data from multiple tables, pre-calculate columns and store the results in a table, either a new table or one of the participants in the calculation.

- Create reporting copies: To improve report performance, create a table which contains all the elements needed for reporting, already calculated and joined, and update that periodically.

- Create duplicates (mirrors): To improve performance where certain data sets are frequently used and are often in contention, create duplicate versions for separate user groups, or for loading vs. querying.

5.2.4.1.3 Physical Database Design Documentation

The physical database design document guides implementation and maintenance. It is reviewable to catch and correct errors in the design before creating or updating the database. It is modifiable for ease of implementation of future iterations of the design. A physical database design document consists of the following components:

- An introductory description of the business function of the database design; for example, what aspect or subset of the business data does this database design encompass?

- A graphical model of the design, done in ER format for a relational design, or in UML for an object-oriented design.

- Database-language specification statements. In Structured Query Language (SQL), these are the Data Definition Language (DDL) specifications for all database objects (tablespaces, tables, indexes, indexspaces, views, sequences, etc., and XML Namespaces).

- Documentation of the technical meta-data, including data type, length, domain, source, and usage of each column, and the structure of keys and indexes related to each table.

- Use cases or sample data, showing what the actual data will look like.

- Short descriptions, as needed, to explain:
    o The database architecture and technology chosen, and why they were chosen.
    o Constraints that affected the selection of the DBMS, including cost constraints, policy constraints, performance constraints, reliability or scalability constraints, security constraints, application constraints, expected data volumes, etc.
    o The database design process, including the methods and tools used.
    o The differences between the physical database design and the logical data model, and the reasons for these differences.
    o The update mechanism chosen for the database, and its implementation.
    o Security requirements for the database, and their implementation.
    o The service-level agreement (SLA) for the database and its implementation.
    o User and / or application requirements for the database and their implementation.

5.2.4.2 Design Information Products

While database design is the primary focus of data development, data professionals should also participate in the design of related data deliverables.

Data analysts may assist software designers and developers in the design of information products, including screens and reports, to meet business data requirements. Data analysts should ensure consistent use of business data terminology, and should ensure that presentation formats add appropriate context to the data for data producers and information consumers.

The DBA will often assist in the development of applications that make data more readily available, in a more usable form, to business users and managers. Many exciting new technologies exist for this purpose, and the DBA should be familiar with them:

- Reporting services: Reporting services give business users the ability to execute both canned and ad-hoc reports, and have the data made available to them in a number of different ways, such as delivered (published) via email or RSS feed, accessible via web browser or portal, extracted to an Excel spreadsheet, and so on.

- Analysis services: Analysis services give business users to ability to "slice and dice" data across multiple business dimensions, such as to analyze sales trends for products or product categories across multiple geographic areas and / or dates / times. This also includes "predictive analytics", which is the analysis of data to identify future trends and potential business opportunities.

- Dashboards: A dashboard is a type of user interface designed to display a wide array of analytics indicators, such as charts and graphs, efficiently. The user can "drill down" through these indicators to view the data beneath.

- Scorecards: A scorecard is a specialized type of analytics display that indicates scores or calculated evaluations of performance. Scorecards often have an actual value (the measure), a goal or forecast (the baseline), a score (measure compared to baseline), and an indicator (a visual representation of how favorable or unfavorable the score may be).

- Portals: Portals are web interfaces that present links to multiple applications and sources of information on a single, well-designed, easily accessible web page. Portals provide a means of bringing together a large number of diverse users, with different information needs, and creating a "community" based on common interests. Portals provide users with the ability to share documents, search through document libraries, hold discussions, and collaborate on projects.

- XML Delivery: To enable the effective use of XML within databases and applications, it is often necessary to create schema definitions. These definitions validate XML documents, XML transforms (using XSLT to convert XML to HTML, or some other presentation form), and database objects. Database objects needing validation include views, stored procedures, and functions that can search through XML documents, convert XML data to relational form (or vice-versa), and merge relational and XML data.

- Business Process Automation: Use data integrated from multiple databases as input to software for business process automation that coordinates multiple business processes across disparate platforms.

- Application Integration: Similarly, data integration (along with its core components, data transformation, and cleansing) is a key component of Enterprise Application Integration (EAI) software, enabling data to be easily passed from application to application across disparate platforms.

The DBA's involvement with the development of these products may include data analysis, the creation of data structures (such as XML schemas, OLAP cubes, or data marts) and database objects to support these products, enabling access to data, and assisting with data integration and delivery.

DBAs may assist software developers by creating and maintaining database access statements. In SQL, these statements are known as Data Manipulation Language (DML) and include SELECT, INSERT, UPDATE, and DELETE statements. DBAs often review these statements and recommend alternate approaches and performance tuning modifications.

DBAs may collaborate with software designers and developers on designing data access-layer services in a service-oriented architecture (SOA). Data access services standardize data access and insulate programs from database changes.

5.2.4.3 Design Data Access Services

It will oftentimes be necessary (and desirable) to access data in remote databases, and to combine that data with data in the local database. Several mechanisms exist for doing this, and the DBA should be familiar with the strengths and weaknesses of each. Some of the most common methods of accessing and reusing remote data are as follows:

- "Linked Server" type connections: Some DBMSs permit you to define remote database servers as "linked servers", and access them over an ODBC or OLE / DB connection. This approach has the advantage of being quick, easy, and inexpensive; however, there are some caveats to keep in mind:
  - Such connections have limited functionality; generally limited to executing a hard-coded query defined as a string literal, or a stored procedure.
  - They can present security concerns. Do not use hard-coded user identifiers and passwords in defining such connections, and restrict permissions on the target server to a read-only subset of only the required data.
  - They do not scale well. Use them only for relatively small amounts of data).
  - They are synchronous, requiring the calling procedure to wait for all the data to be returned.
  - They are dependent on the quality of the vendor-supplied ODBC or OLE / DB drivers (which is sometimes abysmal).

  However, this method has one major advantage: it is easily implementable in the database, allowing access to remote data from views, triggers, functions, and stored procedures in the database.

- SOA Web Services: Encapsulate remote data access in the form of web services and call them from applications. Implement these either synchronously or asynchronously, depending on the requirements of the application. This approach greatly increases the reusability of data to applications, and generally performs and scales quite well. However, there are a couple of drawbacks:
  - o Web services are harder and more costly to write, test, and deploy.
  - o The organization runs the risk of creating an "SOA Nightmare" of numerous point-to-point, application-specific, non-reusable web services, all of which need to be maintained in response to changing database schemas and locations.
  - o It is difficult for database objects to consume web services. They must usually be consumed by applications. Some of the newer DBMSs permit you to encapsulate application classes as stored procedures or functions; however, this method will not work for views.

- Message Brokers: Some DBMSs (e.g., Microsoft SQL Server 2005) allow you to implement messaging services in the database. A stored procedure or function in one database can send a message resulting in the execution of a query, stored procedure, or function in another database, with the results returned asynchronously to the calling procedure. This approach is relatively easy to implement, reliable, scalable, and performs well. However, it only works with instances of the same DBMS.

- Data Access Classes: Write application classes that use ODBC or OLE / DB connections to access data on remote, disparate servers and make it available to applications. In the .NET environment, this data can be stored internally as an ADO.NET dataset object (a sort of in-memory database) for ease of access and better performance. Similar third party and open-source technology exists for Unix / Linux and Java applications.

- ETL: In cases where it is not technologically feasible to access data at its source, or where performance considerations make this access untenable, various DBMS and third-party ETL tools can bridge the gap. These tools extract data from the source, transform it as necessary (e.g., reformatting and cleansing it), and either load it into a read-only table in the database, or stream the result set to the calling procedure or application. Execute a DBMS ETL package from a stored procedure or function, and schedule it to execute at periodic intervals. Major drawbacks are that it may not scale or perform well for large numbers of records, and may be difficult and expensive to maintain over time.

- Replication: Another option for getting data from one database environment to another is replication. Most DBMSs support some type of replication technology (e.g., mirroring and log shipping), although this replication requires that the source and target servers be the same DBMS. For replication across disparate platforms or DBMSs, more "home grown" solutions are possible. For example, a batch process on one platform can extract data to a flat file on disk. The file can be copied (using FTP or some similar mechanism) to the target server, and then loaded via another batch process. The challenge is to get the timing right (i.e., ensure that the data gets to the target server before it is needed), and to make sure that any failures in the replication process are promptly detected and reported. Note that if the replicated data is going to be updated on the target server (try to avoid this if possible!), a secure and reliable mechanism must be put into place to replicate those updates back to the source server, ideally through some sort of two-phase commit process.

- Co-location: As a last resort, it may be necessary to co-locate the source and target databases (or DBMS instances) on the same database server. Obviously, this is not an ideal solution, since it tightly-couples the two databases. It should be used only in situations where the data is similar in business meaning and use, and where the volumes of data required (or the frequency of access) precludes any other solution.

Remember that the end goal is to enable the easy and inexpensive reuse of data across the enterprise, the avoidance, wherever possible, of costly data replication schemes, and the prevention, wherever possible, of redundant and inconsistent data.

5.2.4.4 Design Data Integration Services

A database transaction is an atomic unit of recoverable work. A transaction can include multiple database instructions. Upon completion of all the steps within the transaction, issue a database COMMIT to make all changes together. Up to that point, the changes can be rolled back. A transaction is atomic, meaning either "all or nothing". It performs either all the instructions, or none. Application developers define database transactions by determining when to COMMIT changes.

A critical aspect of database design is determining appropriate update mechanisms. Whenever multiple users can concurrently update tables, implement some concurrency control mechanism to ensure that two users cannot update the same record at the same time. This usually involves adding a data element of type "timestamp" or "datetime" to each of these tables, making sure that the value of this field is checked before the record is modified, and updating whenever the record is changed.

Use locks to ensure the integrity of data, permitting only one user to change a database row at any one time. Lock data at different levels, known as lock granularity. DBAs determine the appropriate level of locking for each database object, such as column, row, page, table, file, or database.

Data analysts and data integration specialists define source-to-target mappings and data transformation designs for extract-transform-load (ETL) programs and other technology for on-going data movement, cleansing, and integration. DBAs may collaborate in this design activity.

Data analysts, data integration specialists, and DBAs also design programs and utilities for data migration and conversion from old data structures to new data structures.

Several methods are available, but any method chosen must satisfy the following criteria:

1. Do all updates in a controlled manner. Do not allow direct, ad-hoc updating of the database.

2. Manage all updates relating to a particular business process as a single unit of work, and either commit or completely roll back the transaction, known as transactional integrity. Do not allow partial updates of the database to occur.

3. Do not allow two or more users to update the same record at the same time, without the other's knowledge, known as concurrency control.

4. Immediately abort the current transaction and roll back errors in updating, and immediately report the error to the calling process or application.

5. Restrict the ability to update a particular database table to a set of users (contained in one or more user roles) authorized to do so.

6. Restrict updates to a small number of records at a time, to prevent excessive locking of tables and "hanging" of an application when rolling back a large update.

Consider the following possible update mechanisms:

- Fundamental stored procedures *(FSPs)*: Each FSP implements one operation (Insert, Update, Delete, or Select) on a limited number of records, usually designated by one or more key values, for a single database table. Automatically generate FSPs, if used, either from the physical model or from the database schema. This greatly reduces the time required to implement a database, and makes it easier to change the schema in response to new requirements.

- Application data layer: Write an application component that calls stored procedures in the database to perform updates across multiple tables, or that calls multiple FSPs. Stored procedures are recommended because they perform better since the SQL code is precompiled and pre-optimized. They are more secure since only designated users or roles can execute them, and the tables are not opened up to SQL injection attacks. They are easier to maintain and errors or performance problems can be easily detected and corrected.

- Dataset updating: Update records in an application dataset or data table through a DataAdapter object, which can, in turn, be associated with a set of stored procedures that perform Insert, Update, Delete, and Select operations.

- Updateable views: In some relational DBMSs, views can be associated with a set of "Instead Of" triggers that can handle updates of the underlying tables in a controlled manner. As with FSPs, it is preferable to generate the code in an automated fashion to reduce or eliminate time spent in coding, testing, and maintenance.

5.2.5 Data Model and Design Quality Management

Data analysts and designers act as an intermediary between information consumers (the people with business requirements for data) and the data producers who capture the data in usable form. Data professionals must juggle the business data requirements of the information consumers, including executives, and the application requirements of data producers. Systems requirements document application data requirements in the form of use cases, an application class model, and service level agreements (SLAs).

Data professionals must also balance the short-term versus long-term business interests. Information consumers need data in a timely fashion to meet short-term business obligations and to take advantage of current business opportunities. System-development project teams must meet time and budget constraints. However, they must also meet the long-term interests of all stakeholders by ensuring that an organization's data resides in data structures that are secure, recoverable, sharable, and reusable, and that this data is as correct, timely, relevant, and usable as possible. Therefore, data models and database designs should be a reasonable balance between the short-term needs and the long-term needs of the enterprise.

5.2.5.1 Develop Data Modeling and Design Standards

Data modeling and database design standards serve as the guiding principles to effectively meet business data needs, conform to data architecture, and ensure data quality. Data architects, data analysts, and database administrators must jointly develop these standards. They must complement and not conflict with related IT standards.

Publish data model and database naming standards for each type of modeling object and database object. Naming standards are particularly important for entities, tables, attributes, keys, views, and indexes. Names should be unique and as descriptive as possible.

Logical names should be meaningful to business users, using full words as much as possible and avoiding all but the most familiar abbreviations. Physical names must conform to the maximum length allowed by the DBMS and use abbreviations where necessary. While logical names use blank spaces as separators between words, physical names typically use underscores as word separators.

Naming standards should minimize name changes across environments. Names should not reflect their specific environment, such as test, QA, or production. Class words can be useful to distinguish attributes from entities, and column names from table names. They can also show which attributes and columns are quantitative rather than qualitative, which can be important when analyzing the contents of those columns.

Data modeling and database design standards should include:

- A list and description of standard data modeling and database design deliverables.

- A list of standard names, acceptable abbreviations, and abbreviation rules for uncommon words, that apply to all data model objects.

- A list of standard naming formats for all data model objects, including attribute and column class words.

- A list and description of standard methods for creating and maintaining these deliverables.

- A list and description of data modeling and database design roles and responsibilities.

- A list and description of all meta-data properties captured in data modeling and database design, including both business meta-data and technical meta-data, with guidelines defining meta-data quality expectations and requirements.

- Guidelines for how to use data modeling tools.

- Guidelines for preparing for and leading design reviews.

5.2.5.2 Review Data Model and Database Design Quality

Project teams should conduct requirements reviews and design reviews as appropriate. These reviews should include a conceptual data model review, a logical data model review, and a physical database design review.

Conduct design reviews with a group of subject matter experts representing different backgrounds, skills, expectations, and opinions. Participants must be able to discuss different viewpoints and reach group consensus without personal conflict, as all participants share the common goal of promoting the most practical, best performing and most usable design. Chair each design review with one leader who facilitates the meeting. The leader creates and follows an agenda, ensures all required documentation is available and distributed, solicits input from all participants, maintains order and keeps the meeting moving, and summarizes the group's consensus findings. Many design reviews also utilize a scribe to capture points of discussion.

5.2.5.2.1 Conceptual and Logical Data Model Reviews

Conceptual data model and logical data model design reviews should ensure that:

1. Business data requirements are completely captured and clearly expressed in the model, including the business rules governing entity relationships.

2. Business (logical) names and business definitions for entities and attributes (business semantics) are clear, practical, consistent, and complementary. The same term must be used in both names and descriptions.

3. Data modeling standards, including naming standards, have been followed.

4. The conceptual and logical data models have been validated.

5.2.5.2.2 Physical Database Design Review

Physical database design reviews should ensure that:

1. The design meets business, technology, usage, and performance requirements.

2. Database design standards, including naming and abbreviation standards, have been followed.

3. Availability, recovery, archiving, and purging procedures are defined according to standards.

4. Meta-data quality expectations and requirements are met in order to properly update any meta-data repository.

5. The physical data model has been validated.

All concerned stakeholders, including the DBA group, the data analyst / architect, the business data owners and / or stewards, the application developers, and the project managers, should review and approve the physical database design document. The complete design document should be ready as part of the production turnover of the database.

5.2.5.2.3 Data Model Validation

Validate data models against modeling standards, business requirements, and database requirements. Here are some sample validation questions:

- Does the model match applicable modeling standards? Does the model use standard data dictionary terms? Does the model use standard domains? Does the model use class word suffixes on all applicable columns? Does the model include descriptions of all objects and relationships? Does the model use abbreviation standards where applicable?

- Does the model match the business requirements? Does the model contain all the relevant data items? Can you execute the required transactions against the database? Can you retrieve the transaction contents correctly? Can you execute any required queries against the model?

- Does the model match the database requirements? Are there no objects named the same as database-reserved words? Do all objects have unique names? Does the model assign owners to all objects?

5.2.5.3 Manage Data Model Versioning and Integration

Data models and other design specifications require careful change control, just like requirements specifications and other SDLC deliverables. Note each change to a data model to preserve the lineage of changes over time. If a change involves the logical model, such as a new or changed business data requirement, the data analyst or architect must review and approve the change.

Each change should note:

- *Why* the project or situation required the change.

- *What and How* the object(s) changed, including which tables had columns added, modified, or removed, etc.

- *When* the change was approved and when the change was made to the model. This is not necessarily when the change was implemented in a system.

- *Who* made the change.

- *Where the change was made;* in which models.

Changes may be made to multiple parts of Enterprise models simultaneously, as part of the normal process. It is important to integrate any changes to a model part back into the enterprise model, especially the enterprise logical model, to prevent errors in data and databases during future development.

Some data modeling tools include repositories that provide data model versioning and integration functionality. Otherwise, preserve data models in DDL exports or XML files, checking them in and out of a standard source code management (SCM) system just like application code.

5.2.6 Data Implementation

Data implementation consists of data management activities that support system building, testing, and deployment, including:

- Database implementation and change management in the development and test environments.

- Test data creation, including any security procedures, such as obfuscation.

- Development of data migration and conversion programs, both for project development through the SDLC and for business situations like consolidations or divestitures.

- Validation of data quality requirements.

- Creation and delivery of user training.

- Contribution to the development of effective documentation.

After design, the DBA is responsible for implementing the designed data structures in the development and test environments. These structures include database tables or files, views, stored procedures, and functions, OLAP data cubes, XSLT schemas, and other similar objects. The DBA is responsible for change control of the development database environment and its configuration. Change control procedures for development and test environments should be similar or the same as those used to control production environments. The DBA should manage configuration changes to database design specification (DDL) files using the same change and configuration management tools and practices used for other information system deliverables.

5.2.6.1 Implement Development / Test Database Changes

As changes to the database are required during the course of application development, the DBA either implements or oversees them. These changes usually come from the developer. Implementation happens depending on roles and responsibilities:

- Developers may have the ability to create and update database objects directly , such as views, functions, and stored procedures, and then update the DBAs and data modelers for review and update of the data model.

- The development team may have their own "developer DBA" who is given permission to make schema changes, with the proviso that these changes be reviewed with the DBA and data modeler.

- Developers may work with the data modelers, who make the change to the model in the data modeling tool, and then generate 'change DDL" for the DBAs to review and implement.

- Developers may work with the data modelers, who interactively 'push' changes to the development environment, using functionality in the data-modeling tool, after review and approval by the DBAs.

If an iterative development method is being used (for example, Agile Development), then some of the work of reviewing and approving changes, and updating the logical and physical models, may need to be done asynchronously. Consider giving approvals verbally so that development can proceed without undue interruption, and do the update of the models as a follow-on task. However, take care to ensure that the database does not get "out-of-synch" with the logical model, and that the database does not become "stove-piped" by being tightly coupled to a single application. Implement application-specific database requirements as much as possible, using views, stored procedures, functions, and other forms of data virtualization.

DBAs should carefully monitor all database code to ensure that it is written to the same standards as application code. All database code should be well documented, testable (ideally, containing built-in diagnostic code that can be triggered via a passed parameter), understandable, consistent with the agreed-upon standards, and easily maintainable. The DBA should also identify, as early as possible, poor SQL coding practices that could lead to errors or performance problems, and bring them to the attention of the developers before multiple stored procedures or functions replicate poor SQL code. A little extra attention at the beginning of a project can save everyone a great deal of grief later on.

5.2.6.2 Create and Maintain Test Data

The DBA and software developers and testers may collaborate to populate databases in the development environment with test data. Either generate test data, or extract a representative subset of production data. Strictly observe privacy and confidentiality requirements and practices for test data. Delete obsolete, unusable, and no longer needed test data.

The DBA may also assist the developers with the creation of SQL scripts and data integration "packages", such as DTS or SSIS packages, used to create and maintain test data. Usually, this work is the primary responsibility of the development team, but oftentimes they need and appreciate the expertise of the DBA. This is another way that DBAs can add value to the development effort.

5.2.6.3 Migrate and Convert Data

A key component of many projects is the migration of legacy data to a new database environment, including any necessary data cleansing and reformatting. This is a significant effort. The time and cost required should not be (but probably will be) under-estimated. It will require the collaborative effort of the data architect / analyst(s) familiar with the legacy data model(s) and the target data model, the DBA, business users, and developers familiar with the legacy application(s). Depending on where the legacy data is stored, this effort may involve the use of many different technologies, including SQL, COBOL, Unix scripting, DBMS integration packages such as DTS or SSIS, non-relational DBMSs, third-party ETL applications, data integration web services, FTP, RPC, ODBC, OLE / DB, and so on. Data migration efforts can easily consume thousands of hours of effort.

5.2.6.4 Build and Test Information Products

Data professionals, including the DBA, should collaborate with software developers on development and testing of information products created by the system, including:

- Implementing mechanisms for integrating data from multiple sources, along with the appropriate meta-data to ensure meaningful integration of the data.

- Implementing mechanisms for reporting and analyzing the data, including online and web-based reporting, ad-hoc querying, BI scorecards, OLAP, portals, and the like.

- Implementing mechanisms for replication of the data, if network latency or other concerns make it impractical to service all users from a single data source.

Software developers are responsible for coding and testing programs, including database access calls. Software developers are also responsible for creating, testing, and maintaining information products, including screens and reports. Testing includes unit, integration, and performance testing.

5.2.6.5 Build and Test Data Access Services

DBAs are responsible for developing data access services. The DBA collaborates with software developers in developing, testing, and executing data access services, first for development and test environments, and later for production deployment.

Data requirements should include business rules for data access to guide the implementation of data access services, collaborating with software developers.

Business data stewards and other subject matter experts (SMEs) should validate the correct implementation of data access requirements and performance through user acceptance testing.

5.2.6.6 Build and Test Data Integration Services

Data integration specialists are responsible for developing ETL programs and technology for data integration, as well as data migration and conversion from old data structures into new structures. The DBA collaborates with software developers in developing, testing, and executing data migration and conversion programs and procedures, first for development and test data, and later for production deployment.

Data requirements should include business rules for data quality to guide the implementation of application edits and database referential integrity constraints. Business data stewards and other subject matter experts (SMEs) should validate the correct implementation of data requirements through user acceptance testing.

5.2.6.7 Validate Information Requirements

The responsibilities of data professionals within the SDLC do not end with design. They continue to interact as part of project teams for system development through the implementation of these designs. Database administrators are particularly active in these SDLC stages. Business data stewards may also remain involved after analysis and design, or a separate independent quality assurance team may control the test process. The primary work will be in testing and validating that the solution meets the requirements, but also in planning deployment, developing training, and documentation.

In any application development project, especially those using iterative ("Agile") methods, data (and database) requirements may change abruptly, in response to either new or changed business requirements, invalidated assumptions regarding the data, or re-prioritization of existing requirements. The data modeler may serve as the intermediary between the developers and the data analyst / architect, reviewing any additions or changes to business data requirements. The data modeler would also properly reflect them in the logical and physical data models. The DBA would implement any changes in the most effective manner in the database. The DBA then works with the developers to test the implementation of the data requirements, and make sure that the application requirements are satisfied.

5.2.6.8 Prepare for Data Deployment

While database administrators resolve technical implementation and testing issues, data analysts can leverage the business knowledge captured in data modeling to define clear and consistent language in user training and documentation. Business concepts, terminology, definitions, and rules depicted in data models are an important part of application user training, even if data models themselves are not useful as teaching illustrations. The data stewards that contribute business knowledge to the definition of the data models, and who are accountable for system data quality, are often also the process and application owners responsible for user acceptance of both the system and related training and documentation. Use their nomenclature consistently.

Data stewards and data analysts should participate in deployment preparation, including development and review of training materials and system documentation, especially to ensure consistent use of defined business data terminology. Help desk support staff also requires orientation and training in how system users appropriately access, manipulate, and interpret data.

The DBA is primarily responsible for implementing new and changed database objects into the production environment (see Chapter 6 on Data Operations Management). Database administrators should carefully control the installation of new databases and changes to existing databases in the production environment. Once installed, business data stewards and data analysts should monitor the early use of the system to see that business data requirements are indeed met.

5.3 Summary

The guiding principles for implementing data development into an organization, a summary table of the roles for each data development activity, and organization and cultural issues that may arise during data development are summarized below.

5.3.1 Guiding Principles

The implementation of the data development function into an organization follows nine guiding principles:

1. Data development activities are an integral part of the software development lifecycle (SDLC).

2. Data modeling is an essential technique for effective data management and system design.

3. Conceptual and logical data modeling express business and application requirements, while physical data modeling represents solution design. Data modeling and database design define detail solution component specifications.

4. Data modeling and database design balances tradeoffs and needs.

5. Data professionals should collaborate with other project team members to design information products and data access and integration interfaces.

6. Data modeling and database design should follow documented standards.

7. Design reviews should review all data models and designs, in order to ensure they meet business requirements and follow design standards.

8. Data models represent valuable knowledge resources (meta-data). Carefully manage and control them through library, configuration, and change management to ensure data model quality and availability.

9. Database administrators (DBAs) and other data professionals play important roles in the construction, testing, and deployment of databases and related application systems.

5.3.2 Data Development Process Summary

The process summary for the data development function is shown in Table 5.1. The deliverables, responsible roles, approving roles, and contributing roles are shown for each activity in the data development function. The Table is also shown in Appendix A9.

Activities	Deliverables	Responsible Roles	Approving Roles	Contributing Roles
3.1.1 Analyze Information Requirements (D)	Information Requirement Specification Statements	Data Architects, Data Analysts	Data Stewards	Data Stewards, Other SMEs
3.1.2 Develop and Maintain Conceptual Data Models (D)	Conceptual Data Model Diagrams and Reports	Data Architects, Data Analysts	Data Stewards, Data Architects	Data Stewards, Other SMEs
3.1.3 Develop and Maintain Logical Data Models (D)	Logical Data Model Diagrams and Reports	Data Architects, Data Analysts, Data Modelers	Data Stewards, Data Architects	Data Stewards, Other SMEs
3.1.4 Develop and Maintain Physical Data Models (D)	Physical Data Model Diagrams and Reports	Data Architects, Data Modelers, DBAs	DBAs, Data Architects	Software Developers
3.2.1 Design Physical Databases (D)	DDL Specifications, OLAP Cube Specs, XML schemas	DBAs, Application Architects, Software Developers	Data Architects, DBAs, Application Architects	Data Analysts, Data Modelers, Software Developers
3.2.2 Design Information Products (D)	Application Screens, Reports	Software Developers	Application Architects	Data Analysts, DBAs
3.2.3 Design Data Access Services (D)	Data Access Service Design Specifications	Software Developers, DBAs	Application Architects, Data Architects	Data Analysts, DBAs
3.2.4 Design Data Integration Services (D)	Source-to-Target Maps, ETL Design Specs, Conversion Designs	Data Integration Specialists, DBAs, Data Analysts	DBAs, Data Architects, Application Architects	Data Analysts, Data Stewards, DBAs
3.3.1 Develop Data Modeling and Database Design Standards (P)	Data Modeling Standards Documents, Database Design Standards Documents	Data Architects, Data Analysts, Data Modelers, DBAs	DM Executive, Data Governance Council	Data Stewards, Application Architects, Software Developers

Activities	Deliverables	Responsible Roles	Approving Roles	Contributing Roles
3.3.2 Review Data Model and Database Design Quality (C)	Design Review Findings	Data Architects, Data Analysts, Data Modelers, DBAs	DM Executive, Project Manager	Application Architects, Software Developers
3.3.3 Manage Data Model Versioning and Integration (C)	Model Management Libraries and Contents	Data Model Administrators, Data Modelers	Data Architects, DM Executive	Data Analysts, DBAs
3.4.1 Implement Development and Test Database Changes (D)	Dev and Test DB Environments, Database Tables, Other DB Objects	DBAs	DM Executive	Data Architects, Data Analysts, Software Developers
3.4.2 Create and Maintain Test Data (D)	Test Databases, Test Data	DBAs, Data Analysts, Software Developers, Test Analysts	Data Architects, Application Architects, Data Stewards	Data Stewards, Software Developers, Data Analysts
3.4.3 Migrate and Convert Data (D)	Migrated and Converted Data	DBAs, Software Developers	Data Stewards, Data Architects	Data Analysts
3.4.4 Build and Test Information Products (D)	Information Products: Screens, Reports	Software Developers	Data Stewards, Application Architects, Data Architects	DBAs, Data Analysts
3.4.5 Build and Test Data Access Services (D)	Data Access Services (interfaces)	Software Developers	Data Architects, Application Architects	DBAs
3.4.6 Build and Test Data Integration Services (D)	Data Integration Services (ETL, etc.)	Data Integration Specialists	Data Stewards, Data Architects	DBAs, Data Analysts
3.4.7 Validate Information Requirements (D)	Validated Requirements, User Acceptance Signoff	Data Stewards, Testing Specialists	Data Stewards	Data Analysts, Data Architects, DBAs

Activities	Deliverables	Responsible Roles	Approving Roles	Contributing Roles
3.4.8 Prepare for Data Deployment (D)	User Training, User Documentation	Data Stewards, Business SMEs, Training Specialists, Data Analysts	Data Stewards, Data Architects	Data Stewards, Data Architects, DBAs

Table 5.1 Data Development Process Summary

5.3.3 Organizational and Cultural Issues

Q1: What is the biggest issue with data delivery?

A1: The biggest organizational and cultural issue regarding data delivery is simply recognizing the need for it and taking advantage of what data development offers. Many organizations focus on application development, overlooking the importance of the data itself. Simply discovering the importance and usefulness of data analysis and data modeling can be transformational to an organization. Both the Business and IT start considering the impact to data when considering system changes, sometimes realizing that they already have similar data and functionality in another application, or that they don't really need what they thought they had or wanted.

Q2: How does one begin formal data development?

A2: In order to start the transformation, it is necessary to start documenting systems from a data point of view. Data flows, data models, and data quality analyses all factor into this documentation. Start with one system, and move to systems that either give or receive data directly from the first system. Network diagrams from infrastructure can help with this.

Next, distribute pictures of the systems' data flows and data models to the stakeholders of that system, both business and IT. Sit down with them to verify that what the pictures show is what they understand the system to do, or what they see the system does. Make sure that all stakeholders believe that the documentation shows the current reality of the system.

Then, publicize the existence of these new documents. Create a master version of the documents and implement changes to them as part of the SDLC. When a project goes into production, part of the production release is to distribute the updated data flows and data models.

Once the word gets out, data analysts and data modelers will be very busy both documenting additional systems and helping software engineers to use these new documents during project work. Additional headcount for that team will probably become necessary.

It will be an iterative process to get access to all systems in order to analyze them. Be persistent. The money saved from reduced system redundancy, reduced redundancy of data storage, and more efficient development can save the organization millions of dollars.

The last step is to change the culture of the organization, moving toward automatically referring to these documents during requirements and design of projects as standard operating procedure. Once data development is part of the culture, the organization devoted to maintaining it will grow to fit the organization's need.

5.4 Recommended Reading

The references listed below provide additional reading that support the material presented in Chapter 5. These recommended readings are also included in the Bibliography at the end of the Guide.

5.4.1 Data Modeling and Database Design

Ambler, Scott. Agile Database Techniques: Effective Strategies for the Agile Software Developer. Wiley & Sons, 2003. ISBN 0-471-20283-5.

Ambler, Scott W. and Pramodkumar J. Sadalage. Refactoring Databases: Evolutionary Database Design. Addison-Wesley, 2006. ISBN 0-321-29353-3.

Avison, David and Christine Cuthbertson. A Management Approach to Database Applications. McGraw Hill, 2002. ISBN 0-077-09782-3.

Brackett, Michael H. Practical Data Design. Prentice Hall, 1990. ISBN 0-136-90827-6.

Bruce, Thomas A. Designing Quality Databases with IDEF1X Information Models. Dorset House, 1991. ISBN 10:0932633188. 584 pages.

Carlis, John and Joseph Maguire. Mastering Data Modeling - A User-Driven Approach. Addison Wesley, 2000. ISBN 0-201-70045-X.

Date, C. J. An Introduction to Database Systems, 8th Edition. Addison-Wesley, 2003. ISBN 0-321-19784-4.

Date, C. J. and Hugh Darwen. Databases, Types and the Relational Model: The Third Manifesto, 3rd Edition. Addison Wesley, 2006. ISBN 0-321-39942-0.

DeAngelis, Carla. Data Modeling with Erwin. Indiana: Sams Publishing, 2000. ISBN 0-672-31868-7.

Dorsey, Paul. Enterprise Data Modeling Using UML. McGraw-Hill Osborne Media, 2007. ISBN 0-072-26374-1.

Fleming, Candace C. and Barbara Von Halle. The Handbook of Relational Database Design. Addison Wesley, 1989. ISBN 0-201-11434-8.

Halpin, Terry. Information Modeling and Relational Databases: From Conceptual Analysis to Logical Design. Morgan Kaufmann, 2001. ISBN 1-558-60672-6.

Halpin, Terry, Ken Evans, Pat Hallock, and Bill McLean. <u>Database Modeling with Microsoft Visio for Enterprise Architects</u>. Morgan Kaufmann, 2003. ISBN 1-558-60919-9.

Harrington, Jan L. <u>Relational Database Design Clearly Explained, 2nd Edition</u>. Morgan Kaufmann, 2002. ISBN 1-558-60820-6.

Hay, David C. <u>Data Model Patterns: A Metadata Map</u>. Morgan Kaufmann, 2006. ISBN 0-120-88798-3.

Hay, David C. <u>Data Model Patterns: Conventions of Thought</u>. Dorset House Publishing, 1996. ISBN 0-932633-29-3.

Hay, David C. <u>Requirements Analysis From Business Views to Architecture</u>. Prentice Hall, 2003. ISBN 0-120-28228-6.

Hernandez, Michael J. <u>Database Design for Mere Mortals: A Hands-On Guide to Relational Database Design, 2nd Edition</u>. Addison-Wesley, 2003. ISBN 0-201-75284-0.

Hoberman, Steve. <u>The Data Modeler's Workbench. Tools and Techniques for Analysis and Design</u>. John Wiley & Sons, 2001. ISBN 0-471-11175-9.

Hoberman, Steve. <u>Data Modeling Made Simple: A Practical Guide for Business & Information Technology Professionals</u>. Technics Publications, LLC, 2005. ISBN 0-977-14000-8.

Hoffer, Jeffrey A., Joey F.. George, and Joseph S. Valacich. <u>Modern Systems Analysis and Design, 4th Edition.</u> Prentice Hall, 2004. ISBN 0-131-45461-7.

Krogstie, John, Terry Halpin, and Keng Siau, editors. <u>Information Modeling Methods and Methodologies: Advanced Topics in Database Research</u>. Idea Group Publishing, 2005. ISBN 1-591-40375-8.

Muller, Robert. J. <u>Database Design for Smarties: Using UML for Data Modeling</u>. San Francisco, CA, USA, Morgan Kaufmann, 1999. ISBN 1-558-60515-0.

Newton, Judith J. and Daniel Wahl,, editors. <u>Manual For Data Administration</u>. Washington, DC: GPO, NIST Special Publications 500-208, 1993.

Pascal, Fabian. <u>Practical Issues In Database Management: A Reference For The Thinking Practitioner</u>. Addison-Wesley, 2000. ISBN 0-201-48555-9.

Reingruber, Michael. C. and William W. Gregory. <u>The Data Modeling Handbook: A Best-Practice Approach to Building Quality Data Models</u>. John Wiley & Sons, 1994. ISBN 0-471-05290-6.

Riordan, Rebecca M. <u>Designing Effective Database Systems</u>. Addison-Wesley, 2005. ISBN 0-321-20903-3.

Rob, Peter and Carlos Coronel. <u>Database Systems: Design, Implementation, and Management, 7th Edition</u>. Course Technology, 2006. ISBN 1-418-83593-5.

Schmidt, Bob. Data Modeling for Information Professionals. Prentice Hall, 1999. ISBN 0-13-080450-9.

Silverston, Len. The Data Model Resource Book, Volume 1: A Library of Universal Data Models for All Enterprises, 2nd Edition, John Wiley & Sons, 2001. ISBN 0-471-38023-7.

Silverston, Len. The Data Model Resource Book, Volume 2: A Library of Data Models for Specific Industries, 2nd Edition. John Wiley & Sons, 2001. ISBN 0-471-35348-5.

Simsion, Graeme C. and Graham C. Witt. Data Modeling Essentials, 3rd Edition. Morgan Kaufmann, 2005. ISBN 0-126-44551-6.

Teorey, Toby , Sam Lightstone, and Tom Nadeau. Database Modeling and Design, 4th Edition. Morgan Kaufmann, 2006. ISBN 1-558-60500-2.

Thalheim, Bernhard. Entity-Relationship Modeling: Foundations of Database Technology. Springer, 2000. ISBN 3-540-65470-4.

Van der Lans, Rick F. Introduction to SQL: Mastering the Relational Database Language, 4th Edition. Addison-Wesley, 2006. ISBN 0-321-30596-5.

Watson, Richard T. Data Management: Databases And Organization, 5th Edition. John Wiley & Sons, 2005. ISBN 0-471-71536-0.

5.4.2 Business Rules

Chisholm, Malcolm. How to Build a Business Rules Engine: Extending Application Functionality Through Metadata Engineering. Morgan Kaufmann, 2003. ISBN 1-558-60918-0.

Date, C. J., What Not How: The Business Rules Approach To Application Development. Addison-Wesley, 2000. ISBN 0-201-70850-7.

Morgan, Tony. Business Rules and Information Systems: Aligning IT with Business Goals. Addison-Wesley, 2002. ISBN 0-201-74391-4.

Ross, Ronald G. Business Rules Concepts, 2nd Edition. Business Rule Solutions, 2005. ISBN 0-941-04906-X.

Ross, Ronald G. Principles of the Business Rule Approach. Addison-Wesley, 2003. ISBN 0-201-78893-4.

Von Halle, Barbara. Business Rules Applied: Building Better Systems Using the Business Rules Approach. John Wiley & Sons, 2001. ISBN 0-471-41293-7.

5.4.3 Information Engineering

Finkelstein, Clive. An Introduction to Information Engineering: From Strategic Planning to Information Systems. Addison-Wesley, 1990. ISBN 0-201-41654-9.

Finkelstein, Clive. Information Engineering: Strategic Systems Development. Addison-Wesley, 1993. ASIN B000XUA41C.

Inmon, W. H. <u>Advanced Topics in Information Engineering</u>. John Wiley & Sons - QED, 1989. ISBN 0-894-35269-5.

Inmon, W. H. <u>Information Engineering For The Practitioner</u>. Prentice-Hall (Yourdon Press), 1988. ISBN 0-13-464579-0.

Martin, James. <u>Information Engineering Book 1: Introduction</u>. Prentice-Hall, 1989. ISBN 0-13-464462-X. Also see <u>Book 2: Analysis and Design</u> and <u>Book 3: Design and Construction</u>.

5.4.4 Agile Development

Ambler, Scott. <u>Agile Database Techniques: Effective Strategies for the Agile Software Developer</u>. Wiley & Sons, 2003. ISBN 0-471-20283-5.

5.4.5 Object Orientation and Object-Oriented Design

Wirfs-Brock, Rebecca, Brian Wilkerson, and Lauren Wiener. <u>Designing Object-Oriented Software</u>. NJ: Prentice Hall, 1990. ISBN 0-13-629825-7.

Coad, Peter. <u>Object Models: Strategies, Patterns And Applications, 2nd Edition</u>. Prentice Hall PTR, 1996. ISBN 0-13-840117-9.

Entsminger, Gary. <u>The Tao Of Objects</u>. M & T Books, 1990. ISBN 1-55851-155-5.

Goldberg, Adele and Kenneth S, Rubin. <u>Succeeding With Objects</u>. Addison-Wesley, 1995. ISBN 0-201-62878-3.

Graham, Ian, <u>Migrating To Object Technology</u>. Addison-Wesley, 1995. ISBN 0-201-59389-0.

Jacobson, Ivar, Maria Ericsson, and Agneta Jacobson. <u>The Object Advantage</u>. Addison-Wesley, 1995. ISBN 0-201-42289-1.

Taylor, David. <u>Business Engineering With Object Technology</u>. New York: John Wiley, 1995. ISBN 0-471-04521-7

Taylor, David. <u>Object Oriented Technology: A Manager's Guide</u>. Reading, MA: Addison-Wesley, 1990. ISBN 0-201-56358-4

5.4.6 Service-oriented architecture (SOA)

Barry, Douglas K. <u>Web Services and Service-Oriented Architectures: The Savvy Manager's Guide</u>. Morgan Kaufmann, 2003. ISBN 1-55860-906-7.

Erl, Thomas. <u>Service-Oriented Architecture: A Field Guide to Integrating XML and Web Services</u>. Prentice Hall, 2004. ISBN 0-131-42898-5.

Erl, Thomas. <u>Service-Oriented Architecture: Concepts, Technology and Design</u>. Prentice Hall, 2004. ISBN 0-131-85858-0.

5.4.7 SQL

Celko, Joe. <u>Joe Celko's SQL for Smarties: Advanced SQL Programming, 3rd Edition</u>. ISBN 10: 0123693799. 840 pages.

Celko, Joe. <u>Joe Celko's Trees and Hierarchies in SQL for Smarties</u>. Morgan Kaufmann, 2004. ISBN 1-558-60920-2.

Date, C. J., with Hugh Darwen. <u>A Guide to the SQL Standard, 4th Edition</u>. Addison-Wesley, 1997. ISBN 0-201-96426-0.

Kline, Kevin, with Daniel Kline. <u>SQL in a Nutshell.</u> O'Reilly, 2001. ISBN 0-471-16518-2.

Van der Lans, Rick F. <u>Introduction to SQL: Mastering the Relational Database Language, 4th Edition</u>. Addison-Wesley, 2006. ISBN 0-321-30596-5.

5.4.8 Software Process Improvement

Humphrey, Watts S. <u>Managing The Software Process</u>. Addison Wesley, 1989. ISBN 0-201-18095-2.

5.4.9 XML

Aiken, Peter and M. David Allen. <u>XML in Data Management: Understanding and Applying Them Together</u>. Morgan Kaufmann, 2004. ISBN 0-12-45599-4.

Bean, James. <u>XML for Data Architects: Designing for Reuse and Integration</u>. Morgan Kaufmann, 2003. ISBN 1-558-60907-5.

Finkelstein, Clive and Peter Aiken. <u>Building Corporate Portals with XML</u>. McGraw-Hill, 1999. ISBN 10: 0079137059. 512 pages.

Melton, Jim and Stephen Buxton. <u>Querying XML: XQuery, XPath and SQL/XML in Context</u>. Morgan Kaufmann, 2006. ISBN 1-558-60711-0.

6 Data Operations Management

Data Operations Management is the fourth Data Management Function in the data management framework shown in Figures 1.3 and 1.4. It is the third data management function that interacts with and is influenced by the Data Governance function. Chapter 6 defines the data operations management function and explains the concepts and activities involved in data operations management.

6.1 Introduction

Data operations management is the development, maintenance, and support of structured data to maximize the value of the data resources to the enterprise. Data operations management includes two sub-functions: database support and data technology management.

The goals of data operations management include:

1. Protect and ensure the integrity of structured data assets.

2. Manage the availability of data throughout its lifecycle.

3. Optimize performance of database transactions.

The context diagram for data operations management is shown in Figure 6.1.

6.2 Concepts and Activities

Chapter 1 stated that data operations management is the function of providing support from data acquisition to data purging. Database administrators (DBAs) play a key role in this critical function. The concepts and activities related to data operations management and the roles of database administrators are presented in this section.

6.2.1 Database Support

Database support is at the heart of data management, and is provided by DBAs. The role of DBA is the most established and most widely adopted data professional role, and database administration practices are perhaps the most mature of all data management practices. DBAs play the dominant role in data operations management, as well as in Data Security Management (see Chapter 7). As discussed in Chapter 5, DBAs also play critical roles in Data Development, particularly in physical data modeling and database design, as well as support for development and test database environments.

In fact, many DBAs specialize as Development DBAs or Production DBAs. Development DBAs focus on data development activities, while Production DBAs perform data operations management activities. In some organizations, each specialized role reports to different organizations within IT. Production DBAs may be part of a production infrastructure and operations support group. Development DBAs and / or production DBAs are sometimes integrated into application development organizations.

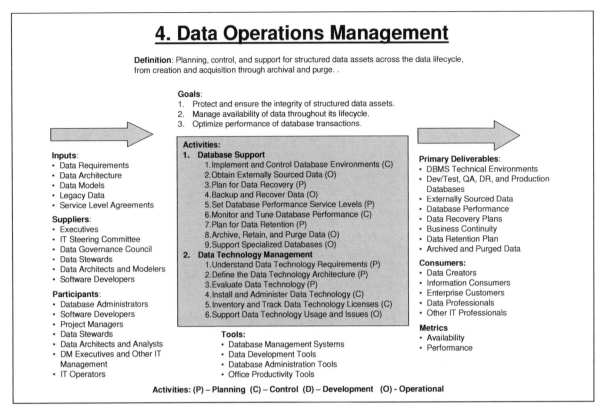

Figure 6.1 Data Operations Management Context Diagram

Production DBAs take primary responsibility for data operations management, including:

- Ensuring the performance and reliability of the database, including performance tuning, monitoring, and error reporting.

- Implementing appropriate backup and recovery mechanisms to guarantee the recoverability of the data in any circumstance.

- Implementing mechanisms for clustering and failover of the database, if continual data availability data is a requirement.

- Implementing mechanisms for archiving data operations management.

The Production DBA is responsible for the following primary deliverables:

1. A production database environment, including an instance of the DBMS and its supporting server, of a sufficient size and capacity to ensure adequate performance, configured for the appropriate level of security, reliability, and availability. Database System Administration is responsible for the DBMS environment.

2. Mechanisms and processes for controlled implementation and changes to databases into the production environment.

3. Appropriate mechanisms for ensuring the availability, integrity, and recoverability of the data in response to all possible circumstances that could result in loss or corruption of data.

4. Appropriate mechanisms for detecting and reporting any error that occurs in the database, the DBMS, or the data server.

5. Database availability, recovery, and performance in accordance with service level agreements.

DBAs do not perform all the activities of data operations management exclusively. Data stewards, data architects, and data analysts participate in planning for recovery, retention, and performance. Data stewards, data architects, and data analysts may also participate in obtaining and processing data from external sources

6.2.1.1 Implement and Control Database Environments

Database systems administration includes the following tasks:

- Updating DBMS software – DBAs install new versions of the DBMS software and apply maintenance fixes supplied by the DBMS vendor in all environments, from development to production.

- Maintaining multiple installations, including different DBMS versions – DBAs install and maintain multiple instances of the DBMS software in development, testing, and production environments, and manage migration of the DBMS software versions through environments.

- Installing and administering related data technology, including data integration software and third party data administration tools.

- Setting and tuning DBMS system parameters.

- Managing database connectivity – In addition to data security issues (see Chapter 7), accessing databases across the enterprise requires technical expertise. DBAs provide technical guidance and support for IT and business users requiring database connectivity.

- Working with system programmers and network administrators to tune operating systems, networks, and transaction processing middleware to work with the DBMS.

- Dedicating appropriate storage for the DBMS, and enabling the DBMS to work with storage devices and storage management software. Storage management optimizes the use of different storage technology for cost-effective storage of older, less frequently referenced data. Storage management software migrates less frequently referenced data to less expensive storage devices, resulting in slower retrieval time. Some databases work with storage management software so that partitioned database tables can be migrated to slower, less expensive storage. DBAs work with storage administrators to set up and monitor effective storage management procedures.

Prepare checklists to ensure these tasks are performed at a high level of quality. These checklists lay out the steps involved. The work of one DBA should be audited by another DBA before the changes go into production.

The DBA is the custodian of all database changes. While many parties may request changes, the DBA defines the precise changes to make to the database, implements the changes, and controls the changes. DBAs should use a controlled, documented, and auditable process for moving application database changes to the Quality Assurance or Certification (QA) and Production environments, in part due to Sarbanes-Oxley and other regulatory requirements. A manager-approved service request or change request usually initiates the process. In most cases, the DBA should have a back out plan to reverse changes in case of problems.

Test all changes to the QA environment in the development / test environment, first, and test all changes to production, except for emergency changes, in the QA environment. While Development DBAs control changes to development / test environments, Production DBAs control changes to production environments, as well as usually controlling QA environments.

6.2.1.2 Obtain Externally Sourced Data

Most organizations obtain some data from external third-party sources, such as lists of potential customers purchased from an information broker, or product data provided by a supplier. The data is either licensed or provided free of charge; is provided in a number of different formats (CD, DVD, EDI, XML, RSS feeds, text files); and is a one-time-only or regularly updated via a subscription service. Some acquisitions require legal agreements.

A managed approach to data acquisition centralizes responsibility for data subscription services with data analysts. The data analyst will need to document the external data source in the logical data model and data dictionary. A developer may design and create scripts or programs to read the data and load it into a database. The DBA will be responsible for implementing the necessary processes to load the data into the database and / or make it available to the application.

6.2.1.3 Plan for Data Recovery

Data governance councils should establish service level agreements (SLAs) with IT data management services organizations for data availability and recovery. SLAs set availability expectations, allowing time for database maintenance and backup, and set recovery time expectations for different recovery scenarios, including potential disasters.

DBAs must make sure a recovery plan exists for all databases and database servers, covering all possible scenarios that could result in loss or corruption of data. This includes, but is not limited to:

- Loss of the physical database server.

- Loss of one or more disk storage devices.

- Loss of a database, including the DBMS master database, temporary storage database, transaction log segment, etc.

- Corruption of database index or data pages.

- Loss of the database or log segment file system.

- Loss of database or transaction log backup files.

Management and the organization's business continuity group, if one exists, should review and approve the data recovery plan. The DBA group must have easy access to all data recovery plans.

Keep a copy of the plan, along with all necessary software, such as the software needed to install and configure the DBMS, instructions, and security codes, such as the administrator password, in a secure, off-site location in the event of a disaster. Backups of all databases should be kept in a secure, off-site location.

6.2.1.4 Backup and Recover Data

Make regular backups of databases and, for OLTP databases, the database transaction logs. The SLA for the database should include an agreement with the data owners as to how frequently to make these backups. Balance the importance of the data against the cost of protecting it. For large databases, frequent backups can consume large amounts of disk storage and server resources. At least once a day, make a complete backup of each database.

Furthermore, databases should reside on some sort of managed storage area, ideally a RAID array on a storage area network or SAN, with daily back up to tape. For OLTP databases, the frequency of transaction log backups will depend on the frequency of updating, and the amount of data involved. For frequently updated databases, more frequent log dumps will not only provide greater protection, but will also reduce the impact of the backups on server resources and applications. Backup files should be kept on a separate file system from the databases, and should be backed up to tape, or some separate storage medium, daily. Store copies of the daily backups in a secure off-site facility.

For extremely critical data, the DBA will need to implement some sort of replication scheme in which data moves to another database on a remote server. In the event of database failure, applications can then "fail over" to the remote database and continue processing. Several different replication schemes exist, including mirroring and log shipping. In mirroring, updates to the primary database are replicated immediately (relatively speaking) to the secondary database, as part of a two-phase commit process. In log shipping, a secondary server receives and loads copies of the primary database's transaction logs at regular intervals. The choice of replication method depends on how critical the data is, and how important it is that failover to the secondary server be immediate. Mirroring is usually a more expensive option than log shipping. For one secondary server, use mirroring; use log shipping to update additional secondary servers.

Other data protection options include server clustering, in which databases on a shared disk array can failover from one physical server to another, and server virtualization, where the failover occurs between virtual server instances residing on two or more physical machines.

Most DBMSs support hot backups of the database - backups taken while applications are running. When some updates occur in transit, they will roll either forward to completion, or roll back when the backup reloads. The alternative is a cold backup taken when the database is off-line. However, this may not be a viable option if applications need to be continuously available.

The DBA will also, when necessary, recover lost or damaged databases by reloading them from the necessary database and transaction log backups to recover as much of the data as possible.

6.2.1.5 Set Database Performance Service Levels

Database performance has two facets - availability and performance. Performance cannot be measured without availability. An unavailable database has a performance measure of zero.

SLAs between data management services organizations and data owners define expectations for database performance. Typically, the agreement will identify an expected timeframe of database availability, and a select few application transactions (a mix of complex queries and updates), each with a specified maximum allowable execution time during identified availability periods. If process execution times consistently exceed the SLA, or database availability is not consistently compliant with the SLA, the data owners will ask the DBA to identify the source of the problem and take appropriate remedial action.

Availability is the percentage of time that a system or database can be used for productive work. Availability requirements are constantly increasing, raising the business risks and costs of unavailable data. Activities to ensure availability are increasingly performed in shrinking maintenance windows.

Four related factors affect availability:

- Manageability: The ability to create and maintain an effective environment.

- Recoverability: The ability to reestablish service after interruption, and correct errors caused by unforeseen events or component failures.

- Reliability: The ability to deliver service at specified levels for a stated period.

- Serviceability: The ability to determine the existence of problems, diagnose their causes, and repair / solve the problems.

Many things may cause a loss of database availability, including:

- Planned and unplanned outages.

- Loss of the server hardware.

- Disk hardware failure.

- Operating system failure.

- DBMS software failure.

- Application problems.

- Network failure.

- Data center site loss.

- Security and authorization problems.

- Corruption of data (due to bugs, poor design, or user error).

- Loss of database objects.

- Loss of data.

- Data replication failure.

- Severe performance problems.

- Recovery failures.

- Human error.

DBAs are responsible for doing everything possible to ensure databases stay online and operational, including:

- Running database backup utilities.

- Running database reorganization utilities.

- Running statistics gathering utilities.

- Running integrity checking utilities.

- Automating the execution of these utilities.

- Exploiting table space clustering and partitioning.

- Replicating data across mirror databases to ensure high availability.

6.2.1.6 Monitor and Tune Database Performance

DBAs optimize database performance both proactively and reactively, by monitoring performance and by responding to problems quickly and competently. Most DBMSs provide the capability of monitoring performance, allowing DBAs to generate analysis reports. Most server operating systems have similar monitoring and reporting capabilities. DBAs should run activity and performance reports against both the DBMS and the server on a regular basis, including during periods of heavy activity. They should compare these reports to previous reports to identify any negative trends and save them to help analyze problems over time.

Data movement may occur in real time through online transactions. However, many data movement and transformation activities are performed through batch programs, which may be Extract-Transform-Load (ETL) programs or limited to one system internally. These batch jobs must complete within specified windows in the operating schedule. DBAs and data integration specialists monitor the performance of batch data jobs, noting exceptional completion times and errors, determining the root cause of errors, and resolving these issues.

When performance problems occur, the DBA should use the monitoring and administration tools of the DBMS to help identify the source of the problem. A few of the most common possible reasons for poor database performance are:

- Memory allocation (buffer / cache for data).

- Locking and blocking: In some cases, a process running in the database may lock up database resources, such as tables or data pages, and block another process that needs them. If the problem persists over too long an interval of time, the DBA can kill the blocking process. In some cases, two processes may "deadlock", with each process locking resources needed by the other. Most DBMSs will automatically terminate one of these processes after a certain interval of time. These types of problems are often the result of poor coding, either in the database or in the application.

- Failure to update database statistics: Most relational DBMSs have a built-in query optimizer, which relies on stored statistics about the data and indexes to make decisions about how to execute a given query most effectively. Update these statistics regularly and frequently, especially in databases that are very active. Failure to do so will result in poorly performing queries.

- Poor SQL coding: Perhaps the most common cause of poor database performance is poorly coded SQL. Query coders need a basic understanding of how the SQL query optimizer works, and should code SQL in a way that takes maximum advantage of the optimizer's capabilities. Encapsulate complex SQL in stored procedures, which can be pre-compiled and pre-optimized, rather than embed it in application code. Use views to pre-define complex table joins. In addition, avoid using complex SQL, including table joins, in database functions, which, unlike stored procedures, are opaque to the query optimizer.

- Insufficient indexing: Code complex queries and queries involving large tables to use indexes built on the tables. Create the indexes necessary to support these queries. Be careful about creating too many indexes on heavily updated tables, as this will slow down update processing.

- Application activity: Ideally, applications should be running on a separate server from the DBMS, so that they are not competing for resources. Configure and tune database servers for maximum performance. In addition, the new DBMSs allow application objects, such as Java and .NET classes, to be encapsulated in database objects and executed in the DBMS. Be careful about making use of this capability. It can be very useful in certain cases, but executing application code on the database server can affect the performance of database processes.

- Increase in the number, size, or use of databases: For DBMSs that support multiple databases, and multiple applications, there may be a "breaking point" where the addition of more databases has an adverse effect on the performance of existing databases. In this case, create a new database server. In addition, relocate databases that have grown very large, or that are being used more heavily than before, to a different server. In some cases, address problems with large databases by archiving less-used data to another location, or by deleting expired or obsolete data.

- Database volatility: In some cases, large numbers of table inserts and deletes over a short while can create inaccurate database distribution statistics. In these cases, turn off updating database statistics for these tables, as the incorrect statistics will adversely affect the query optimizer.

After the cause of the problem is identified, the DBA will take whatever action is needed to resolve the problem, including working with application developers to improve and optimize the database code, and archiving or deleting data that is no longer actively needed by application processes.

In exceptional cases, the DBA may consider working with the data modeler to de-normalize the affected portion of the database. Do this only after other measures, such as the creation of views and indexes, and the rewriting of SQL code, have been tried; and only after careful consideration of the possible consequences, such as loss of data integrity and the increase in complexity of SQL queries against de-normalized tables. This caveat applies only to OLTP databases. For read-only reporting and analytical databases, de-normalization for performance and ease of access is the rule rather than the exception, and poses no threat or risk.

6.2.1.7 Plan for Data Retention

One important part of the physical database design is the data retention plan. Discuss data retention with the data owners at design time, and reach agreement on how to treat data over its useful life. It is incorrect to assume that all data will reside forever in primary storage. Data that is not actively needed to support application processes should be archived to some sort of secondary storage on less-expensive disk, or tape, or a CD / DVD jukebox, perhaps on a separate server. Purge data that is obsolete and unnecessary, even for regulatory purposes. Some data may become a liability if kept longer than necessary. Remember that one of the principal goals of data management is that the cost of maintaining data should not exceed its value to the organization.

6.2.1.8 Archive, Retain, and Purge Data

The DBAs will work with application developers and other operations staff, including server and storage administrators, to implement the approved data retention plan. This may require creating a secondary storage area, building a secondary database server, replicating less-needed data to a separate database, partitioning existing database tables, arranging for tape or disk backups, and creating database jobs which periodically purge unneeded data.

6.2.1.9 Support Specialized Databases

Do not assume that a single type of database architecture or DBMS works for every need. Some specialized situations require specialized types of databases. Manage these specialized databases differently from traditional relational databases. For example, most Computer Assisted Design and Manufacturing (CAD / CAM) applications will require an Object database, as will most embedded real-time applications. Geospatial applications, such as MapQuest, make use of specialized geospatial databases. Other applications, such as the shopping-cart applications found on most online retail web sites, make use of XML databases to initially store the customer order data. This data is then copied into one or more traditional OLTP databases or data warehouses. In addition, many off-the-shelf vendor applications may use their own proprietary databases. At the very least, their schemas will be proprietary and mostly concealed, even if they sit on top of traditional relational DBMSs.

Administration of databases used only to support a particular application should not present any great difficulty. The DBA will mostly be responsible for ensuring regular backups of the databases and performing recovery tests. However, if data from these databases needs to be merged with other existing data, say in one or more relational databases, it may present a data integration challenge. These considerations should be discussed and resolved whenever such databases are proposed or brought into the organization.

6.2.2 Data Technology Management

DBAs and other data professionals manage the technology related to their field. Managing data technology should follow the same principles and standards for managing any technology.

The leading reference model for technology management is the Information Technology Infrastructure Library (ITIL), a technology management process model developed in the United Kingdom. ITIL principles apply to managing data technology. For more information, refer to the ITIL website, http://www.itil-officialsite.com.

6.2.2.1 Understand Data Technology Requirements

It is important to understand not only how technology works, but also how it can provide value in the context of a particular business. The DBA, along with the rest of the data services organization, should work closely with business users and managers to understand the data and information needs of the business. This will enable them to suggest the best possible applications of technology to solve business problems and take advantage of new business opportunities.

Data professionals must first understand the requirements of a data technology before determining what technical solution to choose for a particular situation. These questions are a starting point for understanding suitability of a data technology and are not all-inclusive.

1. What problem does this data technology mean to solve?

2. What does this data technology do that is unavailable in other data technologies?

3. What does this data technology not do that is available in other data technologies?

4. Are there any specific hardware requirements for this data technology?

5. Are there any specific Operating System requirements for this data technology?

6. Are there any specific software requirements or additional applications required for this data technology to perform as advertised?

7. Are there any specific storage requirements for this data technology?

8. Are there any specific network or connectivity requirements for this data technology?

9. Does this data technology include data security functionality? If not, what other tools does this technology work with that provides for data security functionality?

10. Are there any specific skills required to be able support this data technology? Do we have those skills in-house or must we acquire them?

6.2.2.2 Define the Data Technology Architecture

Data technology is part of the enterprise's overall technology architecture, but it is also often considered part of its data architecture.

Data technology architecture addresses three basic questions:

1. What technologies are standard (which are required, preferred, or acceptable)?

2. Which technologies apply to which purposes and circumstances?

3. In a distributed environment, which technologies exist where, and how does data move from one node to another?

Data technologies to be included in the technology architecture include:

- Database management systems (DBMS) software.

- Related database management utilities.

- Data modeling and model management software.

- Business intelligence software for reporting and analysis.

- Extract-transform-load (ETL) and other data integration tools.

- Data quality analysis and data cleansing tools.

- Meta-data management software, including meta-data repositories.

Technology architecture components are sometimes referred to as "bricks". Several categories or views representing facets of data technology bricks are:

- Current: Products currently supported and used.

- Deployment Period: Products to be deployed for use in the next 1-2 years.

- Strategic Period: Products expected to be available for use in the next 2+ years.

- Retirement: Products the organization has retired or intends to retire this year.

- Preferred: Products preferred for use by most applications.

- Containment: Products limited to use by certain applications.

- Emerging: Products being researched and piloted for possible future deployment.

The technology road map for the organization consists of these reviewed, approved, and published bricks, and this helps govern future technology decisions.

It is important to understand several things about technology:

- It is never free. Even open-source technology requires care and feeding.

- It should always be regarded as the means to an end, rather than the end itself.

- Most importantly, buying the same technology that everyone else is using, and using it in the same way, does not create business value or competitive advantage for the enterprise.

After the necessary discussions with the business users and managers, the data services group can summarize the data technology objectives for the business in the form of a strategic roadmap that can be used to inform and direct future data technology research and project work.

6.2.2.3 Evaluate Data Technology

Selecting appropriate data related technology, particularly the appropriate database management technology, is an important data management responsibility. Management selects data technology to meet business needs, including total cost, reliability, and integration.

Selecting data technology involves business data stewards, DBAs, data architects, data analysts, other data management professionals, and other IT professionals. Data technologies to be researched and evaluated include:

- Database management systems (DBMS) software.

- Database utilities, such as backup and recovery tools, and performance monitors.

- Data modeling and model management software.

- Database management tools, such as editors, schema generators, and database object generators.

- Business intelligence software for reporting and analysis.

- Extract-transfer-load (ETL) and other data integration tools.

- Data quality analysis and data cleansing tools.

- Data virtualization technology.

- Meta-data management software, including meta-data repositories.

In addition, data professionals may have unique requirements for tools used in other fields, including:

- Change management (source code library and configuration) tools.

- Problem and issue management tools.

- Test management tools.

- Test data generators.

Make selection decisions using a standard technology evaluation process and applying the decision analysis concepts defined by Kepner and Tregoe in <u>The Rational Manager</u>. List alternatives and compare them against a defined set of weighted decision criteria, including feature requirements and functional objectives. The basic method includes the following steps:

1. Understand user needs, objectives, and related requirements.

2. Understand the technology in general.

3. Identify available technology alternatives.

4. Identify the features required.

5. Weigh the importance of each feature.

6. Understand each technology alternative.

7. Evaluate and score each technology alternative's ability to meet requirements.

8. Calculate total scores and rank technology alternatives by score.

9. Evaluate the results, including the weighted criteria.

10. Present the case for selecting the highest ranking alternative.

Selecting strategic DBMS software is particularly important. DBMS software has a major impact on data integration, application performance, and DBA productivity. Some of the factors to consider when selecting DBMS software include:

- Product architecture and complexity.

- Application profile, such as transaction processing, business intelligence, and personal profiles.

- Organizational appetite for technical risk.

- Hardware platform and operating system support.

- Availability of supporting software tools.

- Performance benchmarks.

- Scalability.

- Software, memory, and storage requirements.

- Available supply of trained technical professionals.

- Cost of ownership, such as licensing, maintenance, and computing resources.

- Vendor reputation.

- Vendor support policy and release schedule.

- Customer references.

The DBA will need to assist in evaluating technology alternatives. A number of factors come into play here:

- The availability, stability, maturity, and cost of current products.

- The suitability of a given product to meet the current business need / problem.

- The extensibility of a given product to meet other business needs.

- The product's "fit" with the organization's technology and architecture roadmap (see section 4.2.2.4).

- The product's "fit" with other products and technology used by the organization.

- The vendor's reputation, stability, and expected longevity – Is this a vendor that the company will want to, and be able to, do business with over an extended period?

- The degree of support expected from the vendor – Will upgrades be made available frequently and at minimal cost? Will help from the vendor be available when needed?

The DBA will need to carefully test each candidate product to determine its strengths and weaknesses, ease of implementation and use, applicability to current and future business needs and problems, and whether it lives up to the vendor's hype.

6.2.2.4 Install and Administer Data Technology

The DBAs face the work of deploying new technology products in development / test, QA / certification, and production environments. They will need to create and document processes and procedures for administering the product with the least amount of effort and expense. Remember that the expense of the product, including administration, licensing, and support must not exceed the product's value to the business. Remember also that the purchase of new products, and the implementation of new technology, will probably *not* be accompanied by an increase in staffing, so the technology will need to be, as much as possible, self-monitoring and self-administering.

Also, remember that the cost and complexity of implementing new technology is usually under-estimated, and the features and benefits are usually over-estimated. It is a good idea to start with small pilot projects and proof-of-concept (POC) implementations, to get a good idea of the true costs and benefits before proceeding with a full-blown production implementation.

6.2.2.5 Inventory and Track Data Technology Licenses

Organizations must comply with all licensing agreements and regulatory requirements. Carefully track and conduct yearly audits of software license and annual support costs, as well as server lease agreements and other fixed costs. Being out-of-compliance with licensing agreements poses serious financial and legal risks for an organization.

This data can also determine the total cost-of-ownership (TCO) for each type of technology and technology product. Regularly evaluate technologies and products that are becoming obsolete, unsupported, less useful, or too expensive.

6.2.2.6 Support Data Technology Usage and Issues

When a business need requires new technology, the DBAs will work with business users and application developers to ensure the most effective use of the technology, to explore new applications of the technology, and to address any problems or issues that surface from its use.

DBAs and other data professionals serve as Level 2 technical support, working with help desks and technology vendor support to understand, analyze, and resolve user problems.

The key to effective understanding and use of any technology is training. Organizations should make sure they have an effective training plan and budget in place for everyone involved in implementing, supporting, and using data and database technology. Training plans should include appropriate levels of cross training to better support application development, especially Agile development. DBAs should have, and take the opportunity to learn, application development skills such as class modeling, use-case analysis, and application data access. Developers should learn some database skills, especially SQL coding!

6.3 Summary

The guiding principles for implementing data operations management into an organization, a summary table of the roles for each data operations management activity, and organization and cultural issues that may arise during data operations management are summarized below.

6.3.1 Guiding Principles

In his book <u>Database Administration</u>, Craig Mullins offers DBAs the following rules of thumb for data operations management:

1. Write everything down.

2. Keep everything.

3. Whenever possible, automate a procedure.

4. Focus to understand the purpose of each task, manage scope, simplify, do one thing at a time.

5. Measure twice, cut once.

6. Don't panic; react calmly and rationally, because panic causes more errors.

7. Understand the business, not just the technology.

8. Work together to collaborate, be accessible, audit each other's work, share your knowledge.

9. Use all of the resources at your disposal.

10. Keep up to date.

6.3.2 Process Summary

The process summary for the data operations management function is shown in Table 6.1. The deliverables, responsible roles, approving roles, and contributing roles are shown for each activity in the data operations management function. The Table is also shown in Appendix A9.

Activities	Deliverables	Responsible Roles	Approving Roles	Contributing Roles
4.1.1 Implement and Control Database Environments	Production database environment maintenance, managed changes to production databases, releases	DBAs	DM Executive	System programmers, data stewards, data analysts, software developers, project managers
4.1.2 Acquire Externally Sourced Data (O)	Externally sourced data	DBAs, data analysts, data stewards	Data Governance Council	Data stewards, data analysts
4.1.3 Plan for Data Recovery (P)	Data availability SLAs, data recovery plans	DBAs	DM Executive, Data Governance Council	
4.1.4 Backup and Recover Data (O)	Database backups and logs,restored databases,business continuity	DBAs	DM Executive	
4.1.5 Set Database Performance Service Levels (P)	Database performance SLAs	DBAs	DM Executive, Data Governance Council	
4.1.6 Monitor and Tune Database Performance (O)	Database performance reporting, Database performance	DBAs		
4.1.7 Plan for Data Retention (P)	Data retention plan, storage management procedures	DBAs	DM Executive	Storage management specialists
4.1.8 Archive, Retrieve and Purge Data (O)	Archived data, retrieved data, purged data	DBAs	DM Executive	

Activities	Deliverables	Responsible Roles	Approving Roles	Contributing Roles
4.1.9 Manage Specialized Databases (O)	Geospatial databases, CAD / CAM databases, XML databases, object databases	DBAs	DM Executive	Data stewards, Subject matter experts
4.2.1 Understand Data Technology Requirements (P)	Data technology requirements	Data architect, DBAs	DM Executive	Data stewards, other IT professionals
4.2.2 Define the Database Architecture (P) (same as 2.3)	Data technology architecture	Data architect	DM Executive, Data Governance Council	DBAs, data analysts, data stewards
4.2.3 Evaluate Data Technology (P)	Tool evaluation findings, tool selection decisions	Data analysts, DBAs	DM Executive, Data Governance Council	Data stewards, other IT professionals
4.2.4 Install and Administer Data Technology (O)	Installed technology	DBAs	DM Executive	Data analysts, other data professionals
4.2.5 Inventory and Track Data Technology Licenses (C)	License inventory	DBAs	DM Executive	Other data professionals
4.2.6 Support Data Technology Usage and Issues (O)	Identified and resolved technology issues	DBAs	DM Executive	Other data professionals

Table 6.1 Data Operations Management Process Summary

6.3.3 Organizational and Cultural Issues

Q1: What are common organizational and cultural obstacles to database administration?

A1: DBAs often do not effectively promote the value of their work to the organization. They need to recognize the legitimate concerns of data owners and data consumers, balance short-term and long-term data needs, educate others in the organization about the importance of good data management practices, and optimize data development practices to ensure maximum benefit to the organization and minimal impact on data consumers. By regarding data work as an abstract set of principles and practices, and disregarding the human elements involved, DBAs risk propagating an "us versus them" mentality, and being regarded as dogmatic, impractical, unhelpful, and obstructionist.

Many disconnects, mostly clashes in frames of reference, contribute to this problem. Organizations generally regard information technology in terms of specific applications, not data, and usually see data from an application-centric point of view. The long-term value to organizations of secure, reusable, high-quality data, such as data as a corporate resource, is not as easily recognized or appreciated.

Application development often sees data management as an impediment to application development, as something that makes development projects take longer and cost more without providing additional benefit. DBAs have been slow to adapt to changes in technology, such as XML, objects, and service-oriented architectures, and new methods of application development, such as Agile Development, XP, and Scrum. Developers, on the other hand, often fail to recognize how good data management practices can help them achieve their long-term goals of object and application reuse, and true service-oriented application architecture.

There are several things that DBAs and other data-management practitioners can do to help overcome these organizational and cultural obstacles, and promote a more helpful and collaborative approach to meeting the organization's data and information needs:

- Automate database development processes, developing tools and processes that shorten each development cycle, reduce errors and rework, and minimize the impact on the development team. In this way, DBAs can adapt to more iterative (agile) approaches to application development.

- Develop, and promote the use of, abstracted and reusable data objects that free applications from being tightly coupled to database schemas; the so-called object-relational impedance mismatch. A number of mechanisms exist for doing this, including database views, triggers, functions and stored procedures, application data objects and data-access layers, XML and XSLT, ADO.NET typed datasets, and web services. The DBA should be familiar with all available means of virtualizing data and be able to recommend the best approach for any situation. The end goal is to make using the database as quick, easy, and painless as possible.

- Promote database standards and best practices as requirements, but be flexible enough to deviate from them if given acceptable reasons for these deviations. Database standards should never be a threat to the success of a project.

- Link database standards to various levels of support in the SLA. For example, the SLA can reflect DBA-recommended and developer-accepted methods of ensuring data integrity and data security. The SLA should reflect the transfer of responsibility from the DBAs to the development team if the development team will be coding their own database update procedures or data access layer. This prevents an "all or nothing" approach to standards.

- Establish project needs and support requirements up-front, to reduce misunderstandings about what the project team wants, and does not want, from the data group. Make sure that everyone is clear about what work the DBAs will, and won't, be doing - the way in which the work will be done, the standards that will, or won't, be followed, the timeline for the project, the number of hours and resources involved, and the level of support that will be required during development and after implementation. This will help forestall unpleasant surprises midway through the development process.

- Communicate constantly with the project team, both during development and after implementation, to detect and resolve any issues as early as possible. This includes reviewing data access code, stored procedures, views, and database functions written by the development team. This will also help surface any problems with or misunderstandings about the database design.

- Stay business-focused. The objective is meeting the business requirements and deriving the maximum business value from the project. It does not help to win the battles and lose the war.

- Adopt a "can do" attitude and be as helpful as possible. If you are always telling people "no", don't be surprised when they choose to ignore you and find another path. Recognize that people need to do whatever they need to do, and if you don't help them succeed, they may help you fail.

- Accept any defeats and failures encountered during a project as "lessons learned", and apply that to future projects. You do not have to win every battle. If problems arise from having done things wrong, you can always point to them later as reasons for doing things right in the future.

- Communicate with people on their level and in their terms. It is better to talk with business people in terms of business needs and ROI, and with developers in terms of object-orientation, loose coupling, and ease of development.

- Concentrate on solving other people's problems, not your own.

To sum up, we need to understand who our stakeholders are, and what their needs and concerns are. We need to develop a set of clear, concise, practical, business-focused standards for doing the best possible work in the best possible way. Moreover, we need to teach and implement those standards in a way that provides maximum value to our stakeholders, and earns their respect for us as facilitators, contributors, and solution providers.

Q2: How many DBAs does an organization need?

A2: The answer to this question varies by organization. There is no standard staffing rule of thumb. However, there may be a significant business cost to understaffing. An overworked DBA staff can make mistakes that cost much more in downtime and operational problems than might be saved in salary cost avoidance by minimizing the DBA staff. Many factors need to be considered when determining the optimal number of DBAs for the organization. These factors include:

- The number of databases.

- The size and complexity of the databases.

- The number of DBMS platforms and environments.

- The number of users.

- The number of supported applications.

- The type and complexity of applications.

- Availability requirements.

- The business risk and impact of downtime.

- Performance requirements.

- Service level agreements and related customer expectations.

- The number of database change requests made.

- DBA staff experience.

- Software developer experience with databases.

- End user experience.

- The maturity of DBA tools.

- The extent of DBA responsibilities for database logic (stored procedures, triggers, user-defined functions), integration, access interfaces, and information products.

Q3: What is an application DBA?

A3: An application DBA is responsible for one or more databases in all environments (development / test, QA, and production), as opposed to database systems administration for any of these environments. Sometimes, application DBAs report to the organizational units responsible for development and maintenance of the applications supported by their databases. There are pros and cons to staffing application DBAs. Application DBAs are viewed as integral members of an application support team, and by focusing on a specific database, they can provide better service to application developers. However, application DBAs can easily become isolated and lose sight of the organization's overall data needs and common DBA practices. Constant collaboration between DBAs and data analysts, modelers, and architects is necessary to prevent DBA isolation and disengagement.

Q4: What is a procedural DBA?

A4: A procedural DBA specializes in development and support of procedural logic controlled and execute by the DBMS: stored procedures, triggers, and user defined functions (UDFs). The procedural DBA ensures this procedural logic is planned, implemented, tested, and shared (reused). Procedural DBAs lead the review and administration of procedural database objects.

6.4 Recommended Reading

The references listed below provide additional reading that support the material presented in Chapter 6. These recommended readings are also included in the Bibliography at the end of the Guide.

Dunham, Jeff. Database Performance Tuning Handbook. McGraw-Hill, 1998. ISBN 0-07-018244-2.

Hackathorn, Richard D. Enterprise Database Connectivity. Wiley Professional Computing, 1993. ISBN 0-4761-57802-9. 352 pages.

Hoffer, Jeffrey, Mary Prescott, and Fred McFadden. Modern Database Management, 7th Edition. Prentice Hall, 2004. ISBN 0-131-45320-3. 736 pages.

Kepner, Charles H. and Benjamin B. Tregoe. The New Rational Manager. Princeton Research Press, 1981. 224 pages.

Kroenke, D. M. Database Processing: Fundamentals, Design, and Implementation, 10th Edition. Pearson Prentice Hall, 2005. ISBN 0-131-67626-3. 696 pages.

Martin, James. Information Engineering Book II: Planning and Analysis. Prentice-Hall, Inc., 1990. Englewoood Cliffs, New Jersey.

Mattison, Rob. Understanding Database Management Systems, 2nd Edition. McGraw-Hill, 1998. ISBN 0-07-049999-3. 665 pages.

Mullins, Craig S. Database Administration: The Complete Guide to Practices and Procedures. Addison-Wesley, 2002. ISBN 0-201-74129-6. 736 pages.

Parsaye, Kamran and Mark Chignell. Intelligent Database Tools and Applications: Hyperinformation Access, Data Quality, Visualization, Automatic Discovery. John Wiley & Sons, 1993. ISBN 0-471-57066-4. 560 pages.

Pascal, Fabian, Practical Issues In Database Management: A Reference For The Thinking Practitioner. Addison-Wesley, 2000. ISBN 0-201-48555-9. 288 pages.

Piedad, Floyd, and Michael Hawkins. High Availability: Design, Techniques and Processes. Prentice Hall, 2001. ISBN 0-13-096288-0.

Rob, Peter, and Carlos Coronel. Database Systems: Design, Implementation, and Management, 7th Edition. Course Technology, 2006. ISBN 1-418-83593-5. 688 pages.

7 Data Security Management

Data Security Management is the fifth Data Management Function in the data management framework shown in Figures 1.3 and 1.4. It is the fourth data management function that interacts with and is influenced by the Data Governance function. Chapter 7 defines the data security management function and explains the concepts and activities involved in data operations management.

7.1 Introduction

Data Security Management is the planning, development, and execution of security policies and procedures to provide proper authentication, authorization, access, and auditing of data and information assets.

Effective data security policies and procedures ensure that the right people can use and update data in the right way, and that all inappropriate access and update is restricted. Understanding and complying with the privacy and confidentiality interests and needs of all stakeholders is in the best interest of any organization. Client, supplier, and constituent relationships all trust in, and depend on, the responsible use of data. Time invested in better understanding stakeholder interests and concerns generally proves to be a wise investment.

An effective data security management function establishes judicious governance mechanisms that are easy enough to abide by on a daily operational basis by all stakeholders. The context for Data Security Management is shown in Figure 7.1.

7.2 Concepts and Activities

The ultimate goal of data security management is to protect information assets in alignment with privacy and confidentiality regulations and business requirements. These requirements come from several different, very important sources:

- Stakeholder Concerns: Organizations must recognize the privacy and confidentiality needs of their stakeholders, including clients, patients, students, citizens, suppliers, or business partners. Stakeholders are the ultimate owners of the data about them, and everyone in the organization must be a responsible trustee of this data.

- Government Regulations: Government regulations protect some of the stakeholder security interests. Some regulations restrict access to information, while other regulations ensure openness, transparency, and accountability.

- Proprietary Business Concerns: Each organization has its own proprietary data to protect; ensuring competitive advantage provided by intellectual property and intimate knowledge of customer needs and business partner relationships is a cornerstone in any business plan.

- Legitimate Access Needs: Data security implementers must also understand the legitimate needs for data access. Business strategy, rules, and processes require individuals in certain roles to take responsibility for access to and maintenance of certain data.

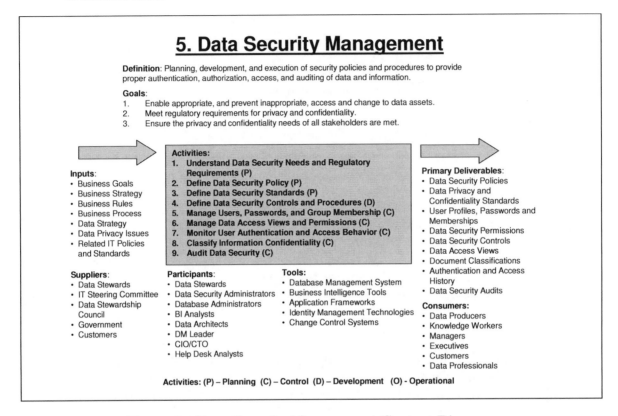

5. Data Security Management

Definition: Planning, development, and execution of security policies and procedures to provide proper authentication, authorization, access, and auditing of data and information.

Goals:
1. Enable appropriate, and prevent inappropriate, access and change to data assets.
2. Meet regulatory requirements for privacy and confidentiality.
3. Ensure the privacy and confidentiality needs of all stakeholders are met.

Inputs:
• Business Goals
• Business Strategy
• Business Rules
• Business Process
• Data Strategy
• Data Privacy Issues
• Related IT Policies and Standards

Activities:
1. Understand Data Security Needs and Regulatory Requirements (P)
2. Define Data Security Policy (P)
3. Define Data Security Standards (P)
4. Define Data Security Controls and Procedures (D)
5. Manage Users, Passwords, and Group Membership (C)
6. Manage Data Access Views and Permissions (C)
7. Monitor User Authentication and Access Behavior (C)
8. Classify Information Confidentiality (C)
9. Audit Data Security (C)

Primary Deliverables:
• Data Security Policies
• Data Privacy and Confidentiality Standards
• User Profiles, Passwords and Memberships
• Data Security Permissions
• Data Security Controls
• Data Access Views
• Document Classifications
• Authentication and Access History
• Data Security Audits

Suppliers:
• Data Stewards
• IT Steering Committee
• Data Stewardship Council
• Government
• Customers

Participants:
• Data Stewards
• Data Security Administrators
• Database Administrators
• BI Analysts
• Data Architects
• DM Leader
• CIO/CTO
• Help Desk Analysts

Tools:
• Database Management System
• Business Intelligence Tools
• Application Frameworks
• Identity Management Technologies
• Change Control Systems

Consumers:
• Data Producers
• Knowledge Workers
• Managers
• Executives
• Customers
• Data Professionals

Activities: (P) – Planning (C) – Control (D) – Development (O) - Operational

Figure 7.1 Data Security Management Context Diagram

Data security requirements and the procedures to meet these requirements can be categorized into four basic groups (the four A's):

- Authentication: Validate users are who they say they are.

- Authorization: Identify the right individuals and grant them the right privileges to specific, appropriate views of data.

- Access: Enable these individuals and their privileges in a timely manner.

- Audit: Review security actions and user activity to ensure compliance with regulations and conformance with policy and standards.

7.2.1 Understand Data Security Needs and Regulatory Requirements

It is important to distinguish between business rules and procedures, and the rules imposed by application software products. While application systems serve as vehicles to enforce business rules and procedures, it is common for these systems to have their own unique set of data security requirements over and above those required for business processes. These unique requirements are becoming more common with packaged and off-the-shelf systems.

7.2.1.1 Business Requirements

Implementing data security within an enterprise begins with a thorough understanding of business requirements. The business mission and strategy that percolates through the data strategy must be the guiding factor in planning data security policy. Address short-term and long-term goals to achieve a balanced and effective data security function.

The business needs of an enterprise define the degree of rigidity required for data security. The size of the enterprise and the industry to which it belongs greatly influence this degree. For example, a financial or a securities enterprise in the United States is highly regulated and, irrespective of the size, is required to maintain stringent data security standards. On the other hand, a small scale retail enterprise may not choose to have an extended data security management function compared to a large size retailer, even though both of them may be involved with similar core business activities.

Business rules and processes define the security touch points. Every event in the business workflow has its own security requirements. Data-to-process and data-to-role relationship matrices are useful tools to map these needs and guide definition of data security role-groups, parameters, and permissions. In addition, data security administrators must also assess the administrative requirements of software tools, application packages, and IT systems used by the enterprise.

Identify detailed application security requirements in the analysis phase of every systems development project.

7.2.1.2 Regulatory Requirements

Today's fast changing and global environment requires organizations to comply with a growing set of regulations. The ethical and legal issues facing organizations in the Information Age are leading governments to establish new laws and standards.

Requirements of several newer regulations, like the United States Sarbanes-Oxley Act of 2002, Canadian Bill 198, and the CLERP Act of Australia, have all imposed strict security controls on information management. The European Union's Basel II Accord imposes information controls for all financial institutions doing business in its related countries. A list of major privacy and security regulations appears in section 7.5.1.

7.2.2 Define Data Security Policy

Definition of data security policy based on data security requirements is a collaborative effort involving IT security administrators, data stewards, internal and external audit teams, and the legal department. Data security professionals sometimes take an ironclad approach to security, and in the process may cause inconvenient impediments for data consumers. Develop data security policies so that compliance is easier than non-compliance. The data governance council should review and approve high-level data security policy.

The enterprise IT strategy and standards typically dictate high-level policies for access to enterprise data assets. It is common to have the IT Security Policy and Data Security

Policy be part of a combined security policy. The preference, however, should be to separate them out. Data security policies are more granular in nature and take a very data-centric approach compared to an IT security policy. Defining directory structures and an identity management framework can be the IT Security Policy component, whereas defining the individual application, database roles, user groups, and password standards can be part of the Data Security Policy.

7.2.3 Define Data Security Standards

There is no one prescribed way of implementing data security to meet privacy and confidentiality requirements. Regulations generally focus on ensuring achievement of the 'end', yet rarely define the 'means' for achieving it. Organizations should design their own security controls, demonstrate that the controls meet the requirements of the law or regulations, and document the implementation of those controls.

Information technology strategy and standards can also influence:

- Tools used to manage data security.

- Data encryption standards and mechanisms.

- Access guidelines to external vendors and contractors.

- Data transmission protocols over the internet.

- Documentation requirements.

- Remote access standards.

- Security breach incident reporting procedures.

Consider physical security, especially with the explosion of portable devices and media, to formulate an effective data security strategy. Physical security standards, as part of enterprise IT policies, provide guidelines including:

- Access to data using mobile devices.

- Storage of data on portable devices such as laptops, DVDs, CDs or USB drives.

- Disposal of these devices in compliance with records management policies.

An organization, its stakeholders, and its regulators have needs regarding data access, privacy, and confidentiality. Using these as requirements, an organization can develop a practical, implementable security policy, including data security guiding principles. The focus should be on quality and consistency, not creating a voluminous body of guidelines. The data security policy should be in a format that is easily accessible by the suppliers, consumers and stakeholders. An organization could post this policy on their company intranet or a similar collaboration portal. The Data Governance Council reviews and approves the policy. Ownership and maintenance responsibility for the data security policy resides with the Data Management Executive and IT security administrators.

Execution of the policy requires satisfying the four A's of securing information assets: authentication, authorization, access, and audit. Information classification, access rights, role groups, users, and passwords are the means to implementing policy and satisfying the four A's.

7.2.4 Define Data Security Controls and Procedures

Implementation and administration of data security policy is primarily the responsibility of security administrators. Database security is often one responsibility of database administrators (DBAs).

Organizations must implement proper controls to meet the objectives of pertinent laws. For instance, a control objective might read, *'Review DBA and User rights and privileges on a monthly basis'*. The organization's control to satisfy this objective might be implementing a process to validate assigned permissions against a change management system used for tracking all user permission requests. Further, the control may also require a workflow approval process or signed paper form to record and document each request.

7.2.5 Manage Users, Passwords, and Group Membership

Access and update privileges can be granted to individual user accounts, but this approach results in a great deal of redundant effort. Role groups enable security administrators to define privileges by role, and to grant these privileges to users by enrolling them in the appropriate role group. While it may be technically possible to enroll users in more than one group, this practice may make it difficult to understand the specific privileges granted to a specific user. Whenever possible, try to assign each user to only one role group.

Construct group definitions at a workgroup or business unit level. Organize roles in a hierarchy, so that child roles further restrict the privileges of parent roles. The ongoing maintenance of these hierarchies is a complex operation requiring reporting systems capable of granular drill down to individual user privileges. Security role hierarchy examples are shown in Figure 7.2.

Security administrators create, modify, and delete user accounts and groups. Changes made to the group taxonomy and membership should require some level of approval, and tracking using a change management system.

Data consistency in user and group management is a challenge in a heterogeneous environment. User information such as name, title, and number must be stored redundantly in several locations. These islands of data often conflict, representing multiple versions of the 'truth'. To avoid data integrity issues, manage user identity data and role-group membership data centrally.

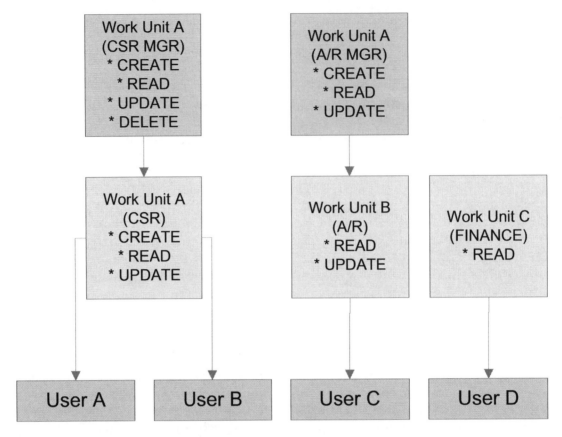

Figure 7.2 Security Role Hierarchy Example Diagram

7.2.5.1 Password Standards and Procedures

Passwords are the first line of defense in protecting access to data. Every user account should be required to have a password set by the user (account owner) with a sufficient level of password complexity defined in the security standards, commonly referred to as 'strong' passwords. Do not permit blank passwords. Typical password complexity requirements require a password to:

- Contain at least 8 characters.

- Contain an uppercase letter and a numeral.

- Not be the same as the username.

- Not be the same as the previous 5 passwords used.

- Not contain complete dictionary words in any language.

- Not be incremental (Password1, Password2, etc).

- Not have two characters repeated sequentially.

- Avoid using adjacent characters from the keyboard.

- If the system supports a space in passwords, then a 'pass phrase' can be used.

Traditionally, users have had different accounts and passwords for each individual resource, platform, application system, and / or workstation. This approach requires users to manage several passwords and accounts. Organizations with enterprise user directories may have a synchronization mechanism established between the heterogeneous resources to ease user password management. In such cases, the user is required to enter the password only once, usually when logging into the workstation, after which all authentication and authorization is done through a reference to the enterprise user directory. An identity management system implements this capability, commonly referred to as the 'single-sign-on'.

Ongoing maintenance of passwords is normally a user responsibility, requiring users to change their passwords every 45 to 60 days. When creating a new user account, the generated password should be set to expire immediately so users can set their passwords for subsequent use. Security administrators and help desk analysts assist in troubleshooting and resolving password related issues.

7.2.6 Manage Data Access Views and Permissions

Data security management involves not just preventing inappropriate access, but also enabling valid and appropriate access to data. Most sets of data do not have any restricted access requirements. Control sensitive data access by granting permissions (opt-in). Without permission, a user can do nothing.

Control data access at an individual or group level. Smaller organizations may find it acceptable to manage data access at the individual level. Larger organizations will benefit greatly from role-based access control, granting permissions to role groups and thereby to each group member. Regardless of approach, granting privileges requires careful analysis of data needs and stewardship responsibilities.

Relational database views provide another important mechanism for data security, enabling restrictions to data in tables to certain rows based on data values. Views can also restrict access to certain columns, allowing wider access to some columns and limited access to more confidential fields.

Access control degrades when achieved through shared or service accounts. Designed as a convenience for administrators, these accounts often come with enhanced privileges and are untraceable to any particular user or administrator. Enterprises using shared or service accounts run the risk of data security breaches. Some organizations configure monitoring systems to ignore any alerts related to these accounts, further enhancing this risk. Evaluate use of such accounts carefully, and never use them frequently or by default.

7.2.7 Monitor User Authentication and Access Behavior

Monitoring authentication and access behavior is critical because:

- It provides information about who is connecting and accessing information assets, which is a basic requirement for compliance auditing.

- It alerts security administrators to unforeseen situations, compensating for oversights in data security planning, design, and implementation.

Monitoring helps detect unusual or suspicious transactions that may warrant further investigation and issue resolution. Perform monitoring either actively or passively. Automated systems with human checks and balances in place best accomplish both methods.

Systems containing confidential information such as salary, financial data, etc. commonly implement active, real-time monitoring. In such cases, real-time monitoring can alert the security administrator or data steward when the system observes a suspicious activity or inappropriate access. The system sends notification to the data steward, usually in the form of email alerts or other configurable notification mechanisms.

Passive monitoring tracks changes over time by taking snapshots of the current state of a system at regular intervals, and comparing trends against a benchmark or defined set of criteria. The system sends reports to the data stewards accountable for the data. While active monitoring is more of a detection mechanism, consider passive monitoring to be an assessment mechanism.

Automated monitoring does impose an overhead on the underlying systems. While advances in technology have reduced resource consumption concerns in recent years, monitoring may still affect system performance. Deciding what needs to be monitored, for how long, and what actions should be taken in the event of an alert, requires careful analysis. Iterative configuration changes may be required to achieve the optimal parameters for proper monitoring.

Enforce monitoring at several layers or data touch points. Monitoring can be:

- Application specific.

- Implemented for certain users and / or role groups.

- Implemented for certain privileges.

- Used for data integrity validation.

- Implemented for configuration and core meta-data validation.

- Implemented across heterogeneous systems for checking dependencies.

7.2.8 Classify Information Confidentially

Classify an enterprise's data and information products using a simple confidentiality classification schema. Most organizations classify the level of confidentiality for information found within documents, including reports. A typical classification schema might include the following five confidentiality classification levels:

- For General Audiences: Information available to anyone, including the general public. General audiences is the assumed default classification.

- Internal Use Only: Information limited to employees or members, but with minimal risk if shared. Internal use only may be shown or discussed, but not copied outside the organization.

- Confidential: Information which should not be shared outside the organization. Client Confidential information may not be shared with other clients.

- Restricted Confidential: Information limited to individuals performing certain roles with the "need to know". Restricted confidential may require individuals to qualify through clearance.

- Registered Confidential: Information so confidential that anyone accessing the information must sign a legal agreement to access the data and assume responsibility for its secrecy.

Classify documents and reports based on the highest level of confidentiality for any information found within the document. Label each page or screen with the classification in the header or footer. Information products classified "For General Audiences" do not need labels. Assume any unlabeled products to be for General Audiences. Document authors and information product designers are responsible for evaluating, correctly classifying, and labeling the appropriate confidentiality level for each document.

Also, classify databases, relational tables, columns, and views. Information confidentiality classification is an important meta-data characteristic, guiding how users are granted access privileges. Data stewards are responsible for evaluating and determining the appropriate confidentiality level for data.

7.2.9 Audit Data Security

Auditing data security is a recurring control activity with responsibility to analyze, validate, counsel, and recommend policies, standards, and activities related to data security management. Auditing is a managerial activity performed with the help of analysts working on the actual implementation and details. Internal or external auditors may perform audits; however, auditors must be independent of the data and / or process involved in the audit. Data security auditors should not have direct responsibility for the activities being audited, to help ensure the integrity of the auditing activity and results. Auditing is not a faultfinding mission. The goal of auditing is to provide management and the data governance council with objective, unbiased assessments, and rational, practical recommendations.

Data security policy statements, standards documents, implementation guides, change requests, access monitoring logs, report outputs, and other records (electronic or hard copy) form the basis of auditing. In addition to examining existing evidence, audits may also include performing tests and checks.

Auditing data security includes:

- Analyzing data security policy and standards against best practices and needs.

- Analyzing implementation procedures and actual practices to ensure consistency with data security goals, policies, standards, guidelines, and desired outcomes.

- Assessing whether existing standards and procedures are adequate and in alignment with business and technology requirements.

- Verifying the organization is in compliance with regulatory requirements.

- Reviewing the reliability and accuracy of data security audit data.

- Evaluating escalation procedures and notification mechanisms in the event of a data security breach.

- Reviewing contracts, data sharing agreements, and data security obligations of outsourced and external vendors, ensuring they meet their obligations, and ensuring the organization meets its obligations for externally sourced data.

- Reporting to senior management, data stewards, and other stakeholders on the 'State of Data Security' within the organization and the maturity of its practices.

- Recommending data security design, operational, and compliance improvements.

Auditing data security is no substitute for effective management of data security. Auditing is a supportive, repeatable process, which should occur regularly, efficiently, and consistently.

7.3 Data Security in an Outsourced World

Organizations may choose to outsource certain IT functions, such as batch operations, application development, and / or database administration. Some may even outsource data security administration. You can outsource almost anything, but not your liability.

Outsourcing IT operations introduces additional data security challenges and responsibilities. Outsourcing increases the number of people who share accountability for data across organizational and geographic boundaries. Previously informal roles and responsibilities must now be explicitly defined as contractual obligations. Outsourcing contracts must specify the responsibilities and expectations of each role.

Any form of outsourcing increases risk to the organization, including some loss of control over the technical environment and the people working with the organization's data. Data security risk is escalated to include the outsource vendor, so any data security measures and processes must look at the risk from the outsource vendor not only as an external risk, but also as an internal risk.

Transferring control, but not accountability, requires tighter risk management and control mechanisms. Some of these mechanisms include:

- Service level agreements.

- Limited liability provisions in the outsourcing contract.

- Right-to-audit clauses in the contract.

- Clearly defined consequences to breaching contractual obligations.

- Frequent data security reports from the service vendor.

- Independent monitoring of vendor system activity.

- More frequent and thorough data security auditing.

- Constant communication with the service vendor.

In an outsourced environment, it is critical to maintain and track the lineage, or flow, of data across systems and individuals to maintain a 'chain of custody'. Outsourcing organizations especially benefit from developing CRUD (Create, Read, Update, and Delete) matrices that map data responsibilities across business processes, applications, roles, and organizations, tracing the transformation, lineage, and chain of custody for data.

Responsible, Accountable, Consulted, and Informed (RACI) matrices also help clarify roles, the separation of duties and responsibilities of different roles and their data security requirements.

The RACI matrix can also become part of the contractual documents, agreements, and data security policies. Defining responsibility matrices like RACI will establish clear accountability and ownership among the parties involved in the outsourcing engagement, leading to support of the overall data security policies and their implementation.

In outsourcing information technology operations, the accountability for maintaining data still lies with the organization. It is critical to have appropriate compliance mechanisms in place and have realistic expectations from parties entering into the outsourcing agreements.

7.4 Summary

The guiding principles for implementing data security management into an organization, a summary table of the roles for each data security management activity, and organization and cultural issues that may arise during data security management are summarized below.

7.4.1 Guiding Principles

The implementation of the data security management function into an organization follows fifteen guiding principles:

1. Be a responsible trustee of data about all parties. They own the data. Understand and respect the privacy and confidentiality needs of all stakeholders, be they clients, patients, students, citizens, suppliers, or business partners.

2. Understand and comply with all pertinent regulations and guidelines.

3. Data-to-process and data-to-role relationship (CRUD–Create, Read, Update, Delete) matrices help map data access needs and guide definition of data security role groups, parameters, and permissions.

4. Definition of data security requirements and data security policy is a collaborative effort involving IT security administrators, data stewards, internal and external audit teams, and the legal department. The data governance council should review and approve high-level data security policy.

5. Identify detailed application security requirements in the analysis phase of every systems development project.

6. Classify all enterprise data and information products against a simple confidentiality classification schema.

7. Every user account should have a password set by the user following a set of password complexity guidelines, and expiring every 45 to 60 days.

8. Create role groups; define privileges by role; and grant privileges to users by assigning them to the appropriate role group. Whenever possible, assign each user to only one role group.

9. Some level of management must formally request, track, and approve all initial authorizations and subsequent changes to user and group authorizations.

10. To avoid data integrity issues with security access information, centrally manage user identity data and group membership data.

11. Use relational database views to restrict access to sensitive columns and / or specific rows.

12. Strictly limit and carefully consider every use of shared or service user accounts.

13. Monitor data access to certain information actively, and take periodic snapshots of data access activity to understand trends and compare against standards criteria.

14. Periodically conduct objective, independent, data security audits to verify regulatory compliance and standards conformance, and to analyze the effectiveness and maturity of data security policy and practice.

15. In an outsourced environment, be sure to clearly define the roles and responsibilities for data security, and understand the "chain of custody" for data across organizations and roles.

7.4.2 Process Summary

The process summary for the data security management function is shown in Table 7.1. The deliverables, responsible roles, approving roles, and contributing roles are shown for each activity in the data security management function. The Table is also shown in Appendix A9.

Activities	Deliverables	Responsible Roles	Approving Roles	Contributing Roles
5.1 Understand Data Security Needs and Regulatory Requirements (P)	Data Security Requirements and Regulations	Data Stewards, DM Executive, Security Administrators	Data Governance Council	Data Stewards, Legal Department, IT Security
5.2 Define Data Security Policy (P)	Data Security Policy	Data Stewards, DM Executive, Security Administrators	Data Governance Council	Data Stewards, Legal Department, IT Security
5.3 Define Data Security Standards (P)	Data Security Standards	Data Stewards, DM Executive, Security Administrators	Data Governance Council	Data Stewards, Legal Department, IT Security
5.4 Define Data Security Controls and Procedures (D)	Data Security Controls and Procedures	Security Administrators	DM Executive	Data Stewards, IT Security
5.5 Manage Users, Passwords and Group Membership (C)	User Accounts, Passwords, Role Groups	Security Administrators, DBAs	Management	Data Producers, Data Consumers, Help Desk
5.6 Manage Data Access Views and Permissions (C)	Data Access Views Data Resource Permissions	Security Administrators, DBAs	Management	Data Producers, Data Consumers, Software Developers, Management, Help Desk

Activities	Deliverables	Responsible Roles	Approving Roles	Contributing Roles
5.7 Monitor User Authentication and Access Behavior (C)	Data Access Logs, Security Notification Alerts, Data Security Reports	Security Administrators, DBAs	DM Executive	Data Stewards, Help Desk
5.8 Classify Information Confidentiality (C)	Classified Documents, Classified Databases	Document Authors, Report Designers, Data Stewards	Management	Data Stewards
5.9 Audit Data Security (C)	Data Security Audit Reports	Data Security Auditors	Data Governance Council, DM Executive	Security Administrators, DBAs, Data Stewards

Table 7.1 Data Security Management Process Summary

7.4.3 Organizational and Cultural Issues

Q1: How can data security really be successful?

A1: Successful data security is deeply incorporated into the corporate culture, but this is not the case in many companies. Organizations often end up being reactive on data security management instead of being proactive. The maturity level in data security management has increased over the years, but there is still opportunity for improvement. Data security breaches have shown that companies are still struggling and faltering in becoming organized. On the positive side, recently introduced regulations are increasing accountability, auditability, and awareness of the importance of data security.

Q2: Can there be good security while still allowing access?

A2: Protecting and securing data without stifling user access to data is a daunting task. Organizations with a process management culture will find it relatively less challenging to have a formidable framework for data security management in place. Regularly evaluate data security policies, procedures, and activities to strike the best possible balance between the data security requirements of all stakeholders.

Q3: What does data security really mean?

A3: Data security means different things to different people. Certain data elements may be considered sensitive in some organizations and cultures, but not in others. Certain individuals or roles may have additional rights and responsibilities that do not even exist in other organizations.

Q4: Do data security measures apply to everyone?

A4: Applying data security measures inconsistently or improperly within an organization can lead to employee dissatisfaction and risk to the organization. Role-based security depends on the organization to define and assign the roles, and apply them consistently.

Q5: Do customers and employees need to be involved in data security?

A5: Implementing data security measures without regard for the expectations of customers and employees can result in employee dissatisfaction, customer dissatisfaction, and organizational risk. Any data security measure or process must take into account the viewpoint of those who will be working with those measures and processes, in order to ensure the highest compliance.

Q6: How do you really avoid security breaches?

A6: People need to understand and appreciate the need for data security. The best way to avoid data security breaches is to build awareness and understanding of security requirements, policies, and procedures. Organizations can build awareness and increase compliance through:

- *Promotion of standards through training on security initiatives at all levels of the organization.* Follow training with evaluation mechanisms such as online tests focused on improving employee awareness. Such training and testing should be made mandatory and made a pre-requisite for employee performance evaluation.

- *Definition of data security policies for workgroups and departments that complement and align with enterprise policies.* Adopting an 'act local' mindset helps engage people more actively.

- *Links to data security within organizational initiatives.* Organizations should include objective metrics for data security activities in their balanced scorecard measurements and project evaluations.

- *Inclusion of data security requirements in service level agreements and outsourcing contractual obligations.*

- *Emphasis on the legal, contractual, and regulatory requirements applicable to their industry to build a sense of urgency and an internal framework for data security management.*

Q7: What is the one primary guiding principle for data security?

A7: Success in data security management depends on being proactive about engaging people, managing change, and overcoming cultural bottlenecks.

7.5 Recommended Reading

The references listed below provide additional reading that support the material presented in Chapter 7. These recommended readings are also included in the Bibliography at the end of the Guide.

7.5.1 Texts and Articles

Afyouni, Hassan A. Database Security and Auditing: Protecting Data Integrity and Accessibility. Course Technology, 2005. ISBN 0-619-21559-3.

Anderson, Ross J. Security Engineering: A Guide to Building Dependable Distributed Systems. Wiley, 2008. ISBN 0-470-06852-6.

Axelrod, C. Warren. Outsourcing Information Security. Artech House, 2004. ISBN 0-58053-531-3.

Calder, Alan and Steve Watkins. IT Governance: A Manager's Guide to Data Security and BS 7799/ISO 17799, 3rd Edition. Kogan Page, 2005. ISBN 0-749-44414-2.

Castano, Silvana, Maria Grazia Fugini, Giancarlo Martella, and Pierangela Samarati. Database Security. Addison-Wesley, 1995. ISBN 0-201-59375-0.

Dennis, Jill Callahan. Privacy and Confidentiality of Health Information. Jossey-Bass, 2000. ISBN 0-787-95278-8.

Gertz, Michael and Sushil Jajodia. Handbook of Database Security: Applications and Trends. Springer, 2007. ISBN 0-387-48532-5.

Jaquith, Andrew. Security Metrics: Replacing Fear, Uncertainty and Doubt. Addison-Wesley, 2007. ISBN 0-321-349998-9.

Landoll, Douglas J. The Security Risk Assessment Handbook: A Complete Guide for Performing Security Risk Assessments. CRC, 2005. ISBN 0-849-32998-1.

Litchfield, David, Chris Anley, John Heasman, and Bill Frindlay. The Database Hacker's Handbook: Defending Database Servers. Wiley, 2005. ISBN 0-764-57801-4.

Mullins, Craig S. Database Administration: The Complete Guide to Practices and Procedures. Addison-Wesley, 2002. ISBN 0-201-74129-6.

Peltier, Thomas R. Information Security Policies and Procedures: A Practitioner's Reference, 2nd Edition. Auerbach, 2004. ISBN 0-849-31958-7.

Shostack, Adam and Andrew Stewart. The New School of Information Security. Addison-Wesley, 2008. ISBN 0-321-50278-7.

Thuraisingham, Bhavani. Database and Applications Security: Integrating Information Security and Data Management. Auerbac Publications, 2005. ISN 0-849-32224-3.

Whitman, Michael R. and Herbert H. Mattord. <u>Principles of Information Security, Third Edition.</u> Course Technology, 2007. ISBN 1-423-90177-0.

7.5.2 Major Privacy and Security Regulations

The major privacy and security regulations affecting Data Security standards are listed below.

7.5.2.1 Non-United States Privacy Laws:

- **Argentina**: Personal Data Protection Act of 2000 (aka Habeas Data).
- **Austria**: Data Protection Act 2000, Austrian Federal Law Gazette Part I No. 165/1999 (DSG 2000).
- **Australia**: Privacy Act of 1988.
- **Brazil**: Privacy currently governed by Article 5 of the 1988 Constitution.
- **Canada**: The Privacy Act - July 1983, Personal Information Protection and Electronic Data Act (PIPEDA) of 2000 (Bill C-6).
- **Chile**: Act on the Protection of Personal Data, August 1998.
- **Columbia**: No specific privacy law, but the Columbian constitution provides any person the right to update and access their personal information.
- **Czech Republic**: Act on Protection of Personal Data (April 2000) No. 101.
- **Denmark**: Act on Processing of Personal Data, Act No. 429, May 2000.
- **Estonia**: Personal Data Protection Act, June 1996, Consolidated July 2002.
- **European Union**: Data Protection Directive of 1998.
- **European Union**: Internet Privacy Law of 2002 (DIRECTIVE 2002/58/EC).
- **Finland**: Act on the Amendment of the Personal Data Act (986) 2000.
- **France**: Data Protection Act of 1978 (revised in 2004).
- **Germany**: Federal Data Protection Act of 2001.
- **Greece**: Law No.2472 on the Protection of Individuals with Regard to the Processing of Personal Data, April 1997.
- **Hong Kong**: Personal Data Ordinance (The "Ordinance").
- **Hungary**: Act LXIII of 1992 on the Protection of Personal Data and the Publicity of Data of Public Interests.
- **Iceland**: Act of Protection of Individual; Processing Personal Data (Jan 2000).
- **Ireland**: Data Protection (Amendment) Act, Number 6 of 2003.
- **India**: Information Technology Act of 2000.
- **Italy**: Data Protection Code of 2003 Italy: Processing of Personal Data Act, Jan. 1997.
- **Japan**: Personal Information Protection Law (Act).
- **Japan**: Law for the Protection of Computer Processed Data Held by Administrative Organizations, December 1988.
- **Korea**: Act on Personal Information Protection of Public Agencies Act on Information and Communication Network Usage.
- **Latvia**: Personal Data Protection Law, March 23, 2000.
- **Lithuania**: Law on Legal Protection of Personal Data (June 1996).
- **Luxembourg**: Law of 2 August 2002 on the Protection of Persons with Regard to the Processing of Personal Data.

- **Malaysia**: Common Law principle of confidentiality Draft Personal data Protection Bill Banking and Financial Institutions Act of 1989 privacy provisions.
- **Malta**: Data Protection Act (Act XXVI of 2001), Amended March 22, 2002, November 15, 2002 and July 15, 2003.
- **New Zealand**: Privacy Act, May 1993; Privacy Amendment Act, 1993; Privacy Amendment Act, 1994.
- **Norway**: Personal Data Act (April 2000) - Act of 14 April 2000 No. 31 Relating to the Processing of Personal Data (Personal Data Act).
- **Philippines**: No general data protection law, but there is a recognized right of privacy in civil law.
- **Poland**: Act of the Protection of Personal Data (August 1997).
- **Singapore**: The E-commerce Code for the Protection of Personal Information and Communications of Consumers of Internet Commerce.
- **Slovak** Republic: Act No. 428 of 3 July 2002 on Personal Data Protection.
- **Slovenia**: Personal Data Protection Act , RS No. 55/99.
- **South Korea**: The Act on Promotion of Information and Communications Network Utilization and Data Protection of 2000.
- **Spain**: ORGANIC LAW 15/1999 of 13 December on the Protection of Personal Data.
- **Switzerland**: The Federal Law on Data Protection of 1992.
- **Sweden**: Personal Data Protection Act (1998:204), October 24, 1998.
- **Taiwan**: Computer Processed Personal data Protection Law - applies only to public institutions.
- **Thailand**: Official Information Act (1997) for state agencies (Personal data Protection bill under consideration).
- **Vietnam**: The Law on Electronic Transactions (Draft: Finalized in 2006).

7.5.2.2 United States Privacy Laws:

- Americans with Disabilities Act (ADA).
- Cable Communications Policy Act of 1984 (Cable Act).
- California Senate Bill 1386 (SB 1386).
- Children's Internet Protection Act of 2001 (CIPA).
- Children's Online Privacy Protection Act of 1998 (COPPA).
- Communications Assistance for Law Enforcement Act of 1994 (CALEA).
- Computer Fraud and Abuse Act of 1986 (CFAA).
- Computer Security Act of 1987 - (Superseded by the Federal Information Security Management Act (FISMA).
- Consumer Credit Reporting Reform Act of 1996 (CCRRA) - Modifies the Fair Credit Reporting Act (FCRA).
- Controlling the Assault of Non-Solicited Pornography and Marketing (CAN-SPAM) Act of 2003.
- Electronic Funds Transfer Act (EFTA).
- Fair and Accurate Credit Transactions Act (FACTA) of 2003.
- Fair Credit Reporting Act.
- Federal Information Security Management Act (FISMA).
- Federal Trade Commission Act (FTCA).

- Driver's Privacy Protection Act of 1994.
- Electronic Communications Privacy Act of 1986 (ECPA).
- Electronic Freedom of Information Act of 1996 (E-FOIA).
- Fair Credit Reporting Act of 1999 (FCRA).
- Family Education Rights and Privacy Act of 1974 (FERPA; also known as the Buckley Amendment).
- Gramm-Leach-Bliley Financial Services Modernization Act of 1999 (GLBA).
- Privacy Act of 1974.
- Privacy Protection Act of 1980 (PPA).
- Right to Financial Privacy Act of 1978 (RFPA).
- Telecommunications Act of 1996.
- Telephone Consumer Protection Act of 1991 (TCPA).
- Uniting and Strengthening America by Providing Appropriate Tools Required to Intercept and Obstruct Terrorism Act of 2001 (USA PATRIOT Act).
- Video Privacy Protection Act of 1988.

7.5.2.3 Industry-Specific Security and Privacy Regulations:

- **Financial Services**: Gramm-Leach-Bliley Act (GLBA), PCI Data Security Standard.
- **Healthcare and Pharmaceuticals**: HIPAA (Health Insurance Portability and Accountability Act of 1996) and FDA 21 CFR Part 11.
- **Infrastructure and Energy**: FERC and NERC Cybersecurity Standards, the Chemical Sector Cyber Security Program and Customs-Trade Partnership against Terrorism (C-TPAT).
- **U.S. Federal Government**: FISMA and related NSA Guidelines and NIST Standard.
  CAN-SPAM - Federal law regarding unsolicited electronic mail.

8 Reference and Master Data Management

Reference and Master Data Management is the sixth Data Management Function in the data management framework shown in Figures 1.3 and 1.4. It is the fifth data management function that interacts with and is influenced by the Data Governance function. Chapter 8 defines the reference and master data management function and explains the concepts and activities involved in reference and master data management.

8.1 Introduction

In any organization, different groups, processes, and systems need the same information. Data created in early processes should provide the context for data created in later processes. However, different groups use the same data for different purposes. Sales, Finance, and Manufacturing departments all care about product sales, but each department has different data quality expectations. Such purpose-specific requirements lead organizations to create purpose-specific applications, each with similar but inconsistent data values in differing formats. These inconsistencies have a dramatically negative impact on overall data quality.

Reference and Master Data Management is the ongoing reconciliation and maintenance of reference data and master data.

- *Reference Data Management* is control over defined domain values (also known as vocabularies), including control over standardized terms, code values and other unique identifiers, business definitions for each value, business relationships within and across domain value lists, and the consistent, shared use of accurate, timely and relevant reference data values to classify and categorize data.

- *Master Data Management* is control over master data values to enable consistent, shared, contextual use across systems, of the most accurate, timely, and relevant version of truth about essential business entities.

Reference data and master data provide the context for transaction data. For example, a customer sales transaction identifies customer, the employee making the sale, and the product or service sold, as well as additional reference data such as the transaction status and any applicable accounting codes. Other reference data elements are derived, such as product type and the sales quarter.

As of publication of this guide, no single unique term has been popularized that encompasses both reference and master data management. Sometimes one or the other term refers to both reference and master data management. In any conversation using these terms, it is wise to clarify what each participant means by their use of each term.

The context diagram for Reference and Master Data Management is shown in Figure 8.1 The quality of transaction data is very dependent on the quality of reference and master data. Improving the quality of reference and master data improves the quality of all data and has a dramatic impact on business confidence about its own data.

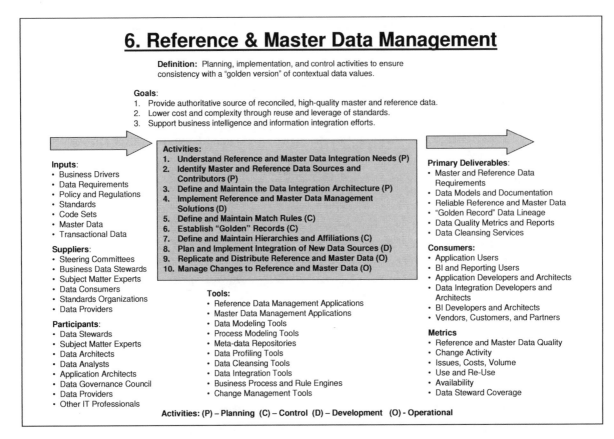

6. Reference & Master Data Management

Definition: Planning, implementation, and control activities to ensure consistency with a "golden version" of contextual data values.

Goals:
1. Provide authoritative source of reconciled, high-quality master and reference data.
2. Lower cost and complexity through reuse and leverage of standards.
3. Support business intelligence and information integration efforts.

Inputs:
• Business Drivers
• Data Requirements
• Policy and Regulations
• Standards
• Code Sets
• Master Data
• Transactional Data

Suppliers:
• Steering Committees
• Business Data Stewards
• Subject Matter Experts
• Data Consumers
• Standards Organizations
• Data Providers

Participants:
• Data Stewards
• Subject Matter Experts
• Data Architects
• Data Analysts
• Application Architects
• Data Governance Council
• Data Providers
• Other IT Professionals

Activities:
1. Understand Reference and Master Data Integration Needs (P)
2. Identify Master and Reference Data Sources and Contributors (P)
3. Define and Maintain the Data Integration Architecture (P)
4. Implement Reference and Master Data Management Solutions (D)
5. Define and Maintain Match Rules (C)
6. Establish "Golden" Records (C)
7. Define and Maintain Hierarchies and Affiliations (C)
8. Plan and Implement Integration of New Data Sources (D)
9. Replicate and Distribute Reference and Master Data (O)
10. Manage Changes to Reference and Master Data (O)

Tools:
• Reference Data Management Applications
• Master Data Management Applications
• Data Modeling Tools
• Process Modeling Tools
• Meta-data Repositories
• Data Profiling Tools
• Data Cleansing Tools
• Data Integration Tools
• Business Process and Rule Engines
• Change Management Tools

Primary Deliverables:
• Master and Reference Data Requirements
• Data Models and Documentation
• Reliable Reference and Master Data
• "Golden Record" Data Lineage
• Data Quality Metrics and Reports
• Data Cleansing Services

Consumers:
• Application Users
• BI and Reporting Users
• Application Developers and Architects
• Data Integration Developers and Architects
• BI Developers and Architects
• Vendors, Customers, and Partners

Metrics:
• Reference and Master Data Quality
• Change Activity
• Issues, Costs, Volume
• Use and Re-Use
• Availability
• Data Steward Coverage

Activities: (P) – Planning (C) – Control (D) – Development (O) - Operational

Figure 8.1 Reference and Master Data Management Context Diagram

Hence, all reference and master data management programs are specialized data quality improvement programs, requiring all the data quality management activities described in Chapter 12. These programs are also dependent on active data stewardship and the data governance activities described in Chapter 3. Reference and master data management is most successful when funded as an on-going data quality improvement program, not a single, one-time-only project effort.

The cost and complexity of each program is determined by the business drivers requiring the effort. The two most common drivers for Reference and Master Data Management are:

• Improving data quality and integration across data sources, applications, and technologies

• Providing a consolidated, 360-degree view of information about important business parties, roles and products, particularly for more effective reporting and analytics.

Given the cost and complexity of the effort, implement any overall solution iteratively, with clear understanding of the business drivers, supported by existing standards as well as prior lessons learned, in close partnership with business data stewards.

8.2 Concepts and Activities

While both reference data management and master data management share similar purposes and many common activities and techniques, there are some distinct differences between the two functions. In reference data management, business data stewards maintain lists of valid data values (codes, and so on) and their business meanings, through internal definition or external sourcing. Business data stewards also manage the relationships between reference data values, particularly in hierarchies.

Master data management requires identifying and / or developing a "golden" record of truth for each product, place, person, or organization. In some cases, a "system of record" provides the definitive data about an instance. However, even one system may accidentally produce more than one record about the same instance. A variety of techniques are used to determine, as best possible, the most accurate and timely data about the instance.

Once the most accurate, current, relevant values are established, reference and master data is made available for consistent shared use across both transactional application systems and data warehouse / business intelligence environments. Sometimes data replicates and propagates from a master database to one or more other databases. Other applications may read reference and master data directly from the master database.

Reference and master data management occurs in both online transaction processing (OLTP) and in data warehousing and business intelligence environments. Ideally, all transaction-processing databases use the same golden records and values. Unfortunately, most organizations have inconsistent reference and master data across their transaction systems, requiring data warehousing systems to identify not only the most truthful system of record, but the most accurate, golden reference and master data values. Much of the cost of data warehousing is in the cleansing and reconciliation of reference and master data from disparate sources. Sometimes, organizations even maintain slowly changing reference data in dimensional tables, such as organizational and product hierarchies, within the data warehousing and business intelligence environment, rather than maintaining the data in a master operational database and replicating to other operational databases and to data warehouses.

To share consistent reference and master data across applications effectively, organizations need to understand:

- Who needs what information?

- What data is available from different sources?

- How does data from different sources differ? Which values are the most valid (the most accurate, timely, and relevant)?

- How can inconsistencies in such information be reconciled?

- How to share the most valid values effectively and efficiently?

8.2.1 Reference Data

Reference data is data used to classify or categorize other data. Business rules usually dictate that reference data values conform to one of several allowed values. The set of allowable data values is a *value domain*. Some organizations define reference data value domains internally, such as Order Status: New, In Progress, Closed, Cancelled, and so on. Other reference data value domains are defined externally as government or industry standards, such as the two-letter United States Postal Service standard postal code abbreviations for U.S. states, such as CA for California.

More than one set of reference data value domains may refer to the same conceptual domain. Each value is unique within its own value domain. For example, each state may have:

- An official name ("California").

- A legal name ("State of California").

- A standard postal code abbreviation ("CA").

- An International Standards Organization (ISO) standard code ("US-CA").

- A United States Federal Information Processing Standards (FIPS) code ("06").

In all organizations, reference data exists in virtually every database across the organization. Reference tables (sometimes called code tables) link via foreign keys into other relational database tables, and the referential integrity functions within the database management system ensure only valid values from the reference tables are used in other tables.

Some reference data sets are just simple two-column value lists, pairing a code value with a code description, as shown in Table 8.1. The code value, taken from the ISO 3166-1993 Country Code List, is the primary identifier, the short form reference value that appears in other contexts. The code description is the more meaningful name or label displayed in place of the code on screens, drop-down lists, and reports.

Code Value	Description
US	United States of America
GB	United Kingdom (Great Britain)

Table 8.1 Sample ISO Country Code Reference Data

Note that in this example, the code value for United Kingdom is GB according to international standards, and not UK, even though UK is a common short form using in many forms of communication.

Some reference data sets cross-reference multiple code values representing the same things. Different application databases may use different code sets to represent the same conceptual attribute. A master cross-reference data set enables translation from one code to another. Note that numeric codes, such as the FIPS state numeric codes shown in Table 8.2, are limited to numeric values, but arithmetic functions cannot be performed on these numbers.

USPS State Code	ISO State Code	FIPS Numeric State Code	State Abbreviation	State Name	Formal State Name
CA	US-CA	06	Calif.	California	State of California
KY	US-KY	21	Ky.	Kentucky	Commonwealth of Kentucky
WI	US-WI	55	Wis.	Wisconsin	State of Wisconsin

Table 8.2 Sample State Code Cross-Reference Data

Some reference data sets also include business definitions for each value. Definitions provide differentiating information that the label alone does not provide. Definitions rarely display on reports or drop-down lists, but they may appear in the Help function for applications, guiding the appropriate use of codes in context.

Using the example of help desk ticket status in Table 8.3, without a definition of what the code value indicates, ticket status tracking cannot occur effectively and accurately. This type of differentiation is especially necessary for classifications driving performance metrics or other business intelligence analytics.

Code	Description	Definition
1	New	Indicates a newly created ticket without an assigned resource
2	Assigned	Indicates a ticket that has a named resource assigned
3	Work In Progress	Indicates the assigned resource started working on the ticket
4	Resolved	Indicates request is assumed to be fulfilled per the assigned resource
5	Cancelled	Indicates request was cancelled based on requester interaction
6	Pending	Indicates request cannot proceed without additional information.
7	Fulfilled	Indicates request was fulfilled and verified by the requester

Table 8.3 Sample Help Desk Reference Data

Some reference data sets define a taxonomy of data values, specifying the hierarchical relationships between data values using the Universal Standard Products and Services Classification (UNSPSC), as shown in Table 8.4. Using taxonomic reference data, capture information at different levels of specificity, while each level provides an accurate view of the information.

Taxonomic reference data can be important in many contexts, most significantly for content classification, multi-faceted navigation, and business intelligence. In traditional relational databases, taxonomic reference data would be stored in a recursive relationship. Taxonomy management tools usually maintain hierarchical information, among other things.

Code Value	Description	Parent Code
10161600	Floral plants	10160000
10161601	Rose plants	10161600
10161602	Poinsettias plants	10161600
10161603	Orchids plants	10161600
10161700	Cut flowers	10160000
10161705	Cut roses	10161700

Table 8.4 Sample Hierarchical Reference Data

Meta-data about reference data sets may document:

- The meaning and purpose of each reference data value domain.

- The reference tables and databases where the reference data appears.

- The source of the data in each table.

- The version currently available.

- When the data was last updated.

- How the data in each table is maintained.

- Who is accountable for the quality of the data and meta-data.

Reference data value domains change slowly. Business data stewards should maintain reference data values and associated meta-data, including code values, standard descriptions, and business definitions. Communicate to consumers any additions and changes to reference data sets.

Business data stewards serve not only as the accountable authority for internally defined reference data sets, but also as the accountable authority on externally defined standard reference data sets, monitoring changes and working with data professionals to update externally defined reference data when it changes.

8.2.2 Master Data

Master data is data about the business entities that provide context for business transactions. Unlike reference data, master data values are usually not limited to pre-defined domain values. However, business rules typically dictate the format and allowable ranges of master data values. Common organizational master data includes data about:

- Parties include individuals, organizations, and their roles, such as customers, citizens, patients, vendors, suppliers, business partners, competitors, employees, students, and so on.

- Products, both internal and external.

- Financial structures, such as general ledger accounts, cost centers, profit centers, and so on.

- Locations, such as addresses.

Master data is the authoritative, most accurate data available about key business entities, used to establish the context for transactional data. Master data values are considered golden.

The term *master data management* has its roots in the term *master file*, a phrase coined before databases became commonplace. Some believe master data management (MDM) to be a fashionable buzzword, soon to be replaced by some other new buzzword. However, the need for high quality reference and master data is timeless and the techniques and activities of reference and master data management will be valuable for many years to come.

Master Data Management is the process of defining and maintaining how master data will be created, integrated, maintained, and used throughout the enterprise. The challenges of MDM are 1) to determine the most accurate, golden data values from among potentially conflicting data values, and 2) to use the golden values instead of other less accurate data. Master data management systems attempt to determine the golden data values and then make that data available wherever needed.

MDM can be implemented through data integration tools (such as ETL), data cleansing tools, operational data stores (ODS) that serve as master data hubs, or specialized MDM applications. There are three primary MDM focus areas:

1. Identification of duplicate records within and across data sources to build and maintain global IDs and associated cross-references to enable information integration.

2. Reconciliation across data sources and providing the "golden record" or the best version of the truth. These consolidated records provide a merged view of the information across systems and seek to address name and address inconsistencies.

3. Provision of access to the golden data across applications, either through direct reads, or by replication feeds to OLTP and DW / BI databases.

MDM challenges organizations to discover:

- What are the important roles, organizations, places, and things referenced repeatedly?

- What data is describing the same person, organization, place, or thing?

- Where is this data stored? What is the source for the data?

- Which data is more accurate? Which data source is more reliable and credible? Which data is most current?

- What data is relevant for specific needs? How do these needs overlap or conflict?

- What data from multiple sources can be integrated to create a more complete view and provide a more comprehensive understanding of the person, organization, place, or thing?

- What business rules can be established to automate master data quality improvement by accurately matching and merging data about the same person, organization, place, or thing?

- How do we identify and restore data that was inappropriately matched and merged?

- How do we provide our golden data values to other systems across the enterprise?

- How do we identify where and when data other than the golden values is used?

Different groups that interact with different parties have different data quality needs and expectations. Many data inconsistencies cannot be resolved through automated programs and need to be resolved through data governance.

MDM solution requirements may be different, depending on the type of master data (party, financial, product, location, and so on) and the type of support transactions need. Implement different solution architectures based on the solution needs, structure of the organization, and business drivers for MDM. MDM data hubs and applications may specialize in managing particular master data subject areas.

8.2.2.1 Party Master Data

Party master data includes data about individuals, organizations, and the roles they play in business relationships. In the commercial environment, this includes customer, employee, vendor, partner, and competitor data. In the public sector, the focus is on data about citizens. In law enforcement, the focus is on suspects, witnesses, and victims. In not-for-profit organizations, the focus is on members and donors. In healthcare, the focus is on patients and providers, while in education, the focus in on students and faculty.

Customer relationship management (CRM) systems perform MDM for customer data, in addition to other business functions. MDM for customer data is also called Customer Data Integration (CDI). CRM databases attempt to provide the most complete and accurate information about each and every customer. CRM systems compare customer data from multiple sources. An essential aspect of CRM is identifying duplicate, redundant, and conflicting data about the same customer.

- Is this data about the same customer or two different customers?

- If the data is about the same customer, which data values conflict, and which are more accurate? Which data sources are more trustworthy?

Other systems may perform similar MDM functions for individuals, organizations and their roles. For example, human resource management (HRM) systems manage master data about employees and applicants. Vendor management systems manage master data about suppliers.

Regardless of industry, managing business party master data poses unique challenges due to:

- The complexity of roles and relationships played by individuals and organizations.

- Difficulties in unique identification.

- The high number of data sources.

- The business importance and potential impact of the data.

MDM is particularly challenging for parties playing multiple roles.

8.2.2.2 Financial Master Data

Financial master data includes data about business units, cost centers, profit centers, general ledger accounts, budgets, projections, and projects. Typically, an Enterprise Resource Planning (ERP) system serves as the central hub for financial master data (chart of accounts), with project details and transactions created and maintained in one or more spoke applications. This is especially common in organizations with distributed back-office functions.

Financial MDM solutions focus on not only creating, maintaining, and sharing information, but also simulating how changes to existing financial data may affect the organization's bottom line, such as budgeting and projections. Financial master data simulations are often part of business intelligence reporting, analysis, and planning modules with a focus on hierarchy management. Model different versions of financial structures to understand potential financial impacts. Once a decision is made, the agreed upon structural changes can be disseminated to all appropriate systems.

8.2.2.3 Product Master Data

Product master data can focus on an organization's internal products or services or the entire industry, including competitor products, and services. Product master data may exist in structured or unstructured formats. It may include information about bill-of-materials component assemblies, part / ingredient usage, versions, patch fixes, pricing, discount terms, auxiliary products, manuals, design documents and images (CAD drawings), recipes (manufacturing instructions), and standard operating procedures. Specialized systems or ERP applications can enable product master data management.

Product Lifecycle Management (PLM) focuses on managing the lifecycle of a product or service from its conception (such as research), through its development, manufacturing, sale / delivery, service, and disposal. Organizations implement PLM systems for a number of reasons. PLM can help reduce time to market by leveraging prior information while improving overall data quality. In industries with long product development cycles (as much as 8 to 12 years in the pharmaceutical industry), PLM systems enable cross-process cost and legal agreements tracking as product concepts evolve from one idea to many potential products under different names and potentially different licensing agreements.

8.2.2.4 Location Master Data

Location master data provides the ability to track and share reference information about different geographies, and create hierarchical relationships or territories based on geographic information to support other processes. The distinction between reference and master data particularly blurs between location reference data and location master data:

- Location reference data typically includes geopolitical data, such as countries, states / provinces, counties, cities / towns, postal codes, geographic regions, sales territories, and so on.

- Location master data includes business party addresses and business party location, and geographic positioning coordinates, such as latitude, longitude, and altitude.

Different industries require specialized earth science data (geographic data about seismic faults, flood plains, soil, annual rainfall, and severe weather risk areas) and related sociological data (population, ethnicity, income, and terrorism risk), usually supplied from external sources.

8.2.3 Understand Reference and Master Data Integration Needs

Reference and master data requirements are relatively easy to discover and understand for a single application. It is much more difficult to develop an understanding of these needs across applications, especially across the entire enterprise. Analyzing the root causes of a data quality problem usually uncovers requirements for reference and master data integration. Organizations that have successfully managed reference and master data have focused on one subject area at a time. They analyze all occurrences of a few business entities, across all physical databases and for differing usage patterns.

8.2.4 Identify Reference and Master Data Sources and Contributors

Successful organizations first understand the needs for reference and master data. Then they trace the lineage of this data to identify the original and interim source databases, files, applications, organizations, and even the individual roles that create and maintain the data. Understand both the up-stream sources and the down-stream needs to capture quality data at its source.

8.2.5 Define and Maintain the Data integration Architecture

As discussed in Chapter 4, effective data integration architecture controls the shared access, replication, and flow of data to ensure data quality and consistency, particularly for reference and master data. Without data integration architecture, local reference and master data management occurs in application silos, inevitably resulting in redundant and inconsistent data.

There are several basic architectural approaches to reference and master data integration. Sometimes an authoritative source is easily identifiable and officially established as the system of record.

A code management system may be the system of record for many reference data sets. Its database would be the database of record. In Figure 8.2, the database of record serves as a reference data "hub" supplying reference data to other "spoke" applications and databases. Some applications can read reference and master data directly from the database of record. Other applications subscribe to published, replicated data from the database of record. Applications reading directly from a hub database must manage their own referential integrity in application code, while application databases with replicated data can implement referential integrity through the DBMS.

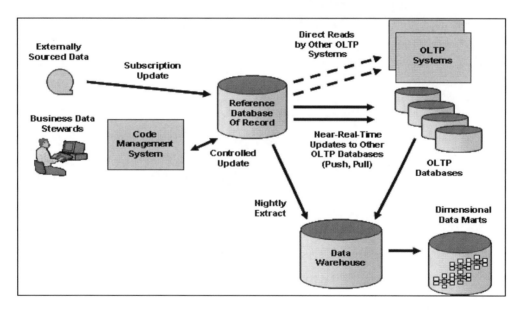

Figure 8.2 Reference Data Management Architecture Example

Replicated data updates other databases in real time (synchronous, coordinated updates). More commonly, replicated data is pushed to other application databases through a subscribe-and-publish approach in near-real time (asynchronous updates) as changes are made to the database of record. In other circumstances, snapshot data can be replicated as needed (pulled) from the database of record. For example, an insurance company's claims system might be a purchased application package with its own database, with policy data replicated from the policy database of record as related claims go through processing, reflecting the current state of the policy at that point in time.

Each master data subject area will likely have its own unique system of record. The human resource system usually serves as the system of record for employee data. A CRM system might serve as the system of record for customer data, while an ERP system might serve as the system of record for financial and product data. Each system's database may serve as the authoritative master data hub for the master data about its specialization.

Only the reference or master database of record should be the source system for replicated reference or master data supplied to data warehouses and data marts, as shown in Figure 8.3. Updates to the reference or master database of record should occur in data warehouses and data marts.

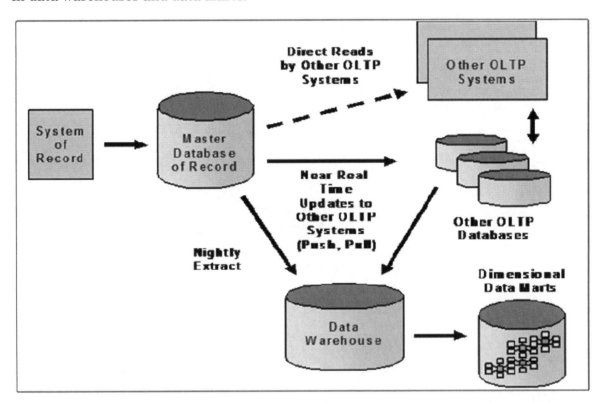

Figure 8.3 Master Data Management Architecture Example

Having many authoritative databases of record can create a very complex data integration environment An alternative implementation of the basic "hub and spokes" design is to have each database of record provide its authoritative reference and master data into a master data operational data store (ODS) that serves as the hub for all reference and master data for all OLTP applications. Some applications may even use the ODS as their driving database, while other applications have their own specialized application databases with replicated data supplied from the ODS data hub through a "subscribe and publish" approach.

In Figure 8.4, four different systems of record (A, B, C, and D) provide four different master subject areas. System A does not need data from Systems B, C, and D, and so provides direct updates to "A" master data without its own database. Systems B, C, and D have their own application databases. System B reads "A" master data directly from the ODS, and provides the ODS with master data about "B". System C provides the ODS with "C" master data. Like System B, it also reads "A" master data directly from the ODS, but it subscribes to replicated "B" master data from the ODS. System D supplies "D" master data to the ODS, and receives feeds from the ODS for master data about subject areas A, B and C.

The primary advantage of this design is the standardization of interfaces to the ODS and the elimination of point-to-point interfaces. This advantage simplifies maintenance changes.

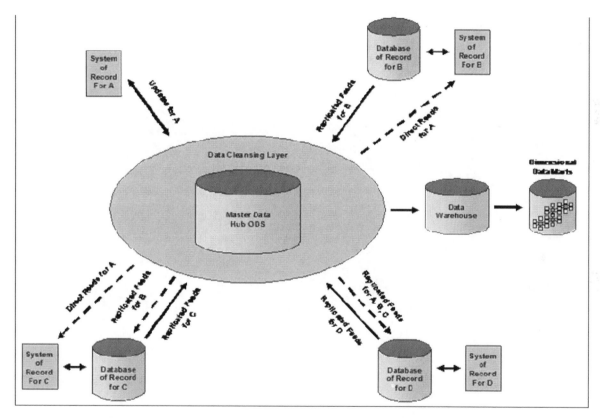

Figure 8.4 Reference and Master Data Hub Operational Data Store (ODS)

The data hub model is particularly useful when there is no clear system of record for the master data. In this case, multiple systems supply data. New data or updates from one system may need to be reconciled with data already supplied by another system. The ODS becomes the primary (if not sole) source of the data warehouse, reducing the complexity of extracts and the processing time for data transformation, cleansing and reconciliation. Of course, data warehouses must reflect historical changes made to the ODS, while the ODS may need to only reflect the current state.

The data integration architecture should also provide common data integration services, as shown in Figure 8.5. These services include:

- Change request processing, including review and approval.

- Data quality checks on externally acquired reference and master data.

- Consistent application of data quality rules and matching rules.

- Consistent patterns of processing.

- Consistent meta-data about mappings, transformations, programs and jobs.

- Consistent audit, error resolution and performance monitoring data.

- Consistent approaches to replicating data (including "subscribe and publish").

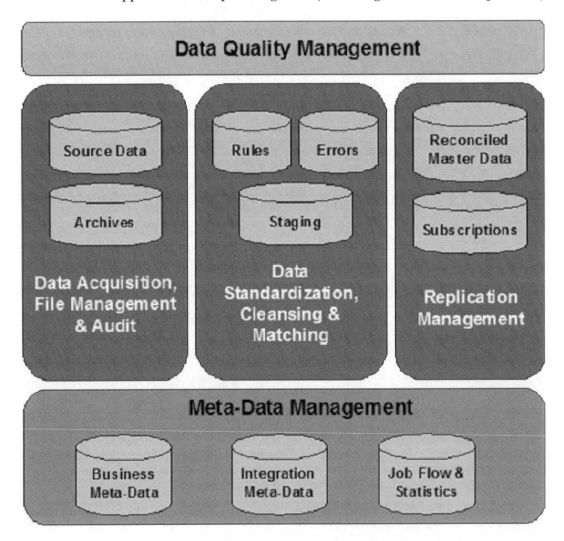

Figure 8.5 Data Integration Services Architecture

To reconcile inconsistent reference and master data effectively, it is important to both identify which data elements are represented inconsistently, and determine how best to represent the data. Establishing master data standards can be a time consuming task as it may involve multiple stakeholders. Training may also be required for those who have been used to seeing data in other formats. Apply the same data standards, regardless of integration technology, to enable effective standardization, sharing, and distribution of reference and master data.

8.2.6 Implement Reference and Master Data Management Solutions

Reference and master data management solutions cannot be implemented overnight. Given the variety, complexity, and instability of requirements, no single solution or implementation project is likely to meet all reference and master data management needs. Organizations should expect to implement reference and master data management solutions iteratively and incrementally through several related projects and phases, guided by their architecture, business priorities, and an implementation program roadmap.

Some organizations may have a centralized code management system that provides business data stewards with a common, consistent facility for maintaining golden, authoritative reference data values. The code management system serves as the system of record for reference data under its control. Other systems requiring access to reference data either read it directly from the code management database, or receive replicated data from the central code management database as it updates. These other systems include both transaction management systems and data warehouses. Despite best efforts, these systems are rarely complete in scope; somehow, pockets of unmanaged reference data persist.

Several vendors offer master data management applications. Typically, these applications are specialized for customer data integration (CDI), product data integration (PDI) or some other master data subject area, such as other parties, locations, and financial structures. Some also manage hierarchical relationships in business intelligence environments. Other vendors promote use of their data integration software products and implementation services to create custom master data management solutions for the organization.

8.2.7 Define and Maintain Match Rules

One of the greatest on-going challenges in master data management is the matching, merging, and linking of data from multiple systems about the same person, group, place, or thing. Matching is particularly challenging for data about people. Different identifiers in different systems relate to individuals (and organizations to a lesser extent), sometimes for different roles and sometimes for the same role. Matching attempts to remove redundancy, to improve data quality, and provide information that is more comprehensive.

Perform data matching by applying inference rules. Data cleansing tools and MDM applications often include matching inference engines used to match data. These tools are dependent on clearly defined matching rules, including the acceptability of matches at different confidence levels.

Some matches occur with great confidence, based on exact data matches across multiple fields. Other matches are suggested with less confidence due to conflicting values. For example:

- If two records share the same last name, first name, birth date, and social security number, but the street address differs, is it safe to assume they are about the same person who has changed their mailing address?

- If two records share the same social security number, street address, and first name, but the last name differs, is it safe to assume they are about the same person who has changed their last name? Would the likelihood be increased or decreased based on gender and age?

- How do these examples change if the social security number is unknown for one record? What other identifiers are useful to determine the likelihood of a match? How much confidence is required for the organization to assert a match?

Despite the best efforts, match decisions sometimes prove to be incorrect. It is essential to maintain the history of matches so that matches can be undone when discovered to be incorrect. Match rate metrics enable organizations to monitor the impact and effectiveness of their matching inference rules.

Establish match rules for three primary scenarios with their different associated workflows:

- *Duplicate identification match rules* focus on a specific set of fields that uniquely identify an entity and identify merge opportunities without taking automatic action. Business data stewards can review these occurrences and decide to take action on a case-by-case basis.

- *Match-merge rules* match records and merge the data from these records into a single, unified, reconciled, and comprehensive record. If the rules apply across data sources, create a single unique and comprehensive record in each database. Minimally, use trusted data from one database to supplement data in other databases, replacing missing values or values thought to be inaccurate.

- *Match-link rules* identify and cross-reference records that appear to relate to a master record without updating the content of the cross-referenced record. Match-link rules are easier to implement and much easier to reverse.

Match-merge rules are complex due to the need to identify so many possible circumstances, with different levels of confidence and trust placed on data values in different fields from different sources. The challenges with match-merge rules are 1) the operational complexity of reconciling the data, and 2) the cost of reversing the operation if there is a false merge.

Match-link, on the other hand, is a simple operation, as it acts on the cross-reference table and not the individual fields of the merged master data record, even though it may be more difficult to present comprehensive information from multiple records.

Periodically re-evaluate match-merge and match-link rules. because confidence levels change over time. Many data matching engines provide statistical correlations of data values to help establish confidence levels.

Assign Global IDs to link and reconcile matched records about the same person from different data sources. Generate Global IDs by only one authorized system, so that each value is unique. Then assign Global IDs to records across systems for cross-reference, matching data with different identifiers but thought to be about the same person.

8.2.8 Establish Golden Records

The techniques used to establish the most accurate and complete reference data are different from the techniques used to provide the most accurate and complete master data. Because reference data sets are value domains with distinct values, manage each reference data set as a controlled vocabulary. Establishing golden master data values requires more inference, application of matching rules, and review of the results.

8.2.8.1 Vocabulary Management and Reference Data

A *vocabulary* is a collection of terms / concepts and their relationships. Describe the terms / concepts at many levels of detail. The relationships may or may not be strictly hierarchical. Business data stewards maintain vocabularies and their associated reference data sets (codes, labels, meanings, associations). Vocabulary management is defining, sourcing, importing, and maintaining a vocabulary and its associated reference data.

ANSI / NISO Z39.19-2005, which provides the Guidelines for the Construction, Format, and Management of Monolingual Controlled Vocabularies, describes vocabulary management as a way *"to improve the effectiveness of information storage and retrieval systems, Web navigation systems, and other environments that seek to both identify and locate desired content via some sort of description using language. The primary purpose of vocabulary control is to achieve consistency in the description of content objects and to facilitate retrieval."*

Some of the key questions to ask to enable vocabulary management are:

- What information concepts (data attributes) will this vocabulary support?

- Who is the audience for this vocabulary? What processes do they support, and what roles do they play?

- Why is the vocabulary needed? Will it support applications, content management, analytics, and so on?

- Who identifies and approves the preferred vocabulary and vocabulary terms?

- What are the current vocabularies different groups use to classify this information? Where are they located? How were they created? Who are their subject matter experts? Are there any security or privacy concerns for any of them?

- Are there existing standards that can be leveraged to fulfill this need? Are there concerns about using an external standard vs. internal? How frequently is the standard updated and what is the degree of change of each update? Are standards accessible in an easy to import / maintain format in a cost efficient manner?

Understanding the answers to these questions will enable more effective data integration.

The most significant activity in vocabulary management is the identification of the standard list of preferred terms and their synonyms (equivalent terms). Data profiling can help assess term values and frequencies in order to assess potential risk and complexity in vocabulary management.

Vocabulary management requires data governance, enabling data stewards to assess stakeholder needs, and the impacts of proposed changes, before making collaborative and formally approved decisions.

8.2.8.2 Defining Golden Master Data Values

Golden data values are the data values thought to be the most accurate, current, and relevant for shared, consistent use across applications. Organizations determine golden values by analyzing data quality, applying data quality rules and matching rules, and incorporating data quality controls into the applications that acquire, create, and update data.

Applications can enforce data quality rules, including:

- Incorporating simple edit checks against referenced data and key business rules.

- Ensuring new records, such as addresses, that are being entered do not already exist in the system through applying data standardization and search-before-create automation.

- Creating prompts for the user if data does not meet accuracy (this address does not exist) expectations, while providing a way to submit exceptions that can be audited in the future.

Establish data quality measurements to set expectations, measure improvements, and help identify root causes of data quality problems. Assess data quality through a combination of data profiling activities and verification against adherence to business rules.

Term and abbreviation standardization is a type of data cleansing activity that ensures certain terms and short forms of those terms consistently appear in the standardized data set, as shown in Figure 8.5. Data cleansing tools typically provide address standardization dictionaries that translate different words and abbreviations to a standard word or abbreviation. For example, "St", "Str", "Street" may all map to "St.". Sometimes the same abbreviation will be used for more than one term, such as, "Saint" may also be abbreviated as "St.", making any automatic reverse translation from abbreviation to full word extremely difficult. Many other names may need standardization, such as organization names (U., Univ, University, and so on) and product names. All data consumers should have ready access to the definitions for standard abbreviations.

Source ID	Name	Address	Telephone
123	John Smith	123 Main, Dataland, SQ 98765	
234	J. Smith	123 Main, Dataland, SQ	2345678900

Source Data

Source ID	Name	Address	Telephone
123	John Smith	123 Main St., Dataland, SQ 98765	
234	J. Smith	123 Main St., Dataland, SQ 98765	+1 234 567 9800

Cleansed / Standardized Data

Table 8.5 Data Standardization Example

Exposing one set of data quality rules in the integration environment (ETL, web services, and so on) will allow any data source to leverage one set of validation and standardization rules.

Once the data is standardized and cleansed, the next step is to attempt reconciliation of redundant data through application of matching rules.

8.2.9 Define and Maintain Hierarchies and Affiliations

Vocabularies and their associated reference data sets are often more than lists of preferred terms and their synonyms. They may also include hierarchical relationships between the terms. These relationships may be general-to-specific classifications ("is a kind of" relationships) or whole-part assemblies ("is a part of" relationships). There may also be non-hierarchical relationships between terms that are worth identifying.

Affiliation management is the establishment and maintenance of relationships between master data records. Examples include ownership affiliations (such as Company X is a subsidiary of Company Y, a parent-child relationship) or other associations (such as Person XYZ works at Company X). Managing hierarchies specifically within a business intelligence environment is sometimes called dimension hierarchy management.

8.2.10 Plan and Implement Integration of New Data Sources

Integrating new reference data sources involves (among other tasks):

- Receiving and responding to new data acquisition requests from different groups.

- Performing data quality assessment services using data cleansing and data profiling tools.

- Assessing data integration complexity and cost.

- Piloting the acquisition of data and its impact on match rules.

- Determining who will be responsible for data quality.

- Finalizing data quality metrics.

8.2.11 Replicate and Distribute Reference and Master Data

Reference and master data may be read directly from a database of record, or may be replicated from the database of record to other application databases for transaction processing, and data warehouses for business intelligence. By replicating the data, the application database can more easily ensure referential integrity. In other words, the database can ensure that only valid reference data codes and master data identifiers are used as foreign key values in other tables, providing the context for related data. Data integration procedures must ensure timely replication and distribution of reference and master data to these application databases.

Reference data most commonly appears as pick list values in applications. Reference data values also commonly appear as search criteria in content management engines. Reference data values found in unstructured documents are often indexed to enable quick searches.

8.2.12 Manage Changes to Reference and Master Data

In a managed master data environment, specific individuals have the role of a business data steward. They have the authority to create, update, and retire reference data values, and to a lesser extent, in some circumstances, master data values. Business data stewards work with data professionals to ensure the highest quality reference and master data. Many organizations define more specific roles and responsibilities, with individuals often performing more than one role.

Reference data sets change slowly. Formally control changes to controlled vocabularies and their reference data sets by following the basic change request process:

1. Create and receive a change request.

2. Identify the related stakeholders and understand their interests.

3. Identify and evaluate the impacts of the proposed change.

4. Decide to accept or reject the change, or recommend a decision to management or governance.

5. Review and approve or deny the recommendation, if needed.

6. Communicate the decision to stakeholders prior to making the change.

7. Update the data.

8. Inform stakeholders the change has been made.

Changes to internal or external reference data sets may be minor or major. For example, country code lists go through minor revisions as geopolitical space changes. When the Soviet Union broke into many independent states, the term for Soviet Union was deprecated with an end of life date, and new terms added for new countries. On the other hand, the ICD-9 Diagnostic Codes in use for many years are being superseded by a new set of ICD-10 Diagnostic Codes with substantially different data. Manage a major change like this as a small project, identifying stakeholders and system impacts, such as applications, integration, reporting, and so on.

Of course, any changes to reference data that was replicated elsewhere must also be applied to the replicated data.

Sometimes terms and codes are retired. The codes still appear in the context of transactional data, so the codes may not disappear due to referential integrity. The codes found in a data warehouse also represent historical truth. Code tables, therefore, require effective date and expiration date columns, and application logic must refer to the currently valid codes when establishing new foreign key relationships.

Sometimes codes are added to code tables prior to their effectiveness. For example, new codes that become effective January 1st may be added to their production code table in December, but not used by the application until the New Year.

By relating new codes to old codes, a data warehouse can depict not only how data aggregated historically, but also how the past might restate according to today's coding structures.

Carefully assess the impact of reference data changes. If the term is being retired, approach all consumers of this data to mitigate the impact of such a retirement. Changes to relationships may affect existing integration and data aggregation rules. Changes to reference meta-data (business definitions, data sources, business data steward assignments, and so on.) should also be controlled, and in some cases, reviewed for approval, depending on the impact.

The key to successful master data management is management support for relinquishing local control of shared data. To sustain this support, provide channels to receive and respond to requests for changes to reference and master data. These same channels should also receive and respond to other kinds of requests, including:

- *New data source requests* which ask to bring new information into the managed data environment.

- *Data content research requests* for when there is disagreement by an information consumer on the quality of the data. To respond to these requests, business data stewards and data professionals need to look at from where and whom the information came, then follow up with corrective action or clarification in a timely manner.

- *Data specification change requests* for change of business definitions or data structures. Such changes can have a cascading impact in application and business intelligence environments. Data architects, application architects, and business data stewards must review these requests, and the Data Governance Council may need to decide on a disposition of the request.

8.3 Summary

The guiding principles for implementing reference and master data management into an organization, a summary table of the roles for each reference and master data management activity, and organization and cultural issues that may arise during reference and master data management are summarized below.

8.3.1 Guiding Principles

The implementation of the reference and master data management function into an organization follows six guiding principles:

1. Shared reference and master data belongs to the organization, not to a particular application or department.

2. Reference and master data management is an on-going data quality improvement program; its goals cannot be achieved by one project alone.

3. Business data stewards are the authorities accountable for controlling reference data values. Business data stewards work with data professionals to improve the quality of reference and master data.

4. Golden data values represent the organization's best efforts at determining the most accurate, current, and relevant data values for contextual use. New data may prove earlier assumptions to be false. Therefore, apply matching rules with caution, and ensure that any changes that are made are reversible.

5. Replicate master data values only from the database of record.

6. Request, communicate, and, in some cases, approve of changes to reference data values before implementation.

8.3.2 Process Summary

The process summary for the reference and master data management function is shown in Table 8.6. The deliverables, responsible roles, approving roles, and contributing roles are shown for each activity in the reference and master data management function. The Table is also shown in Appendix A9.

Activities	Deliverables	Responsible Roles	Approving Roles	Contributing Roles
6.1 Understand Reference Data Integration Needs (P)	Reference and Master Data Requirements	Business Analysts	Stakeholders, Data Governance Council	Business Data Stewards, Subject Matter Experts
6.2 Identify Reference Data Sources and Contributors (P)	Description and Assessment of Sources and Contributors	Data Architects, Data Stewards	Data Governance Council	Data Analysts, Subject Matter Experts
6.3 Define and Maintain the Data Integration Architecture (P)	Reference and Master Data Integration Architecture and Roadmap	Data Architects	Data Governance Council	Application Architects, Data Stewards
	Data Integration Services Design Specifications	Data Architects, Application Architects	IT Management	Other IT Professionals, Stakeholders
6.4 Implement Reference and Master Data Management Solutions (D)	Reference Data Management Applications and Databases, Master Data Management Application and Databases	Application Architects, Data Architects	Data Governance Council	Other IT Professionals
	Data Quality Services	Application Architects, Data Architects	Data Governance Council	Data Analysts, Other IT Professionals
	Data Replication and Access Services for Applications	Data Architects, Application Architects, Integration Developers	Data Governance Council	Data Analysts, Other IT Professionals
	Data Replication Services for Data Warehousing			

Activities	Deliverables	Responsible Roles	Approving Roles	Contributing Roles
6.5 Define and Maintain Match Rules (P)	Record Matching Rules (Functional Specifications)	Business Analysts, Data Architects, Business Data Stewards	Data Governance Council	Application Architects, Subject Matter Experts
6.6 Establish Golden Records (C)	Reliable Reference and Master Data	Data Stewards	Stakeholders	Data Analysts, Data Architects, Subject Matter Experts, Other IT Professionals
	Cross-Reference Data	Data Stewards	Stakeholders	Data Analysts, Subject Matter Experts
	Data Lineage Reports	Data Architects	Data Stewards	Data Analysts
	Data Quality Reports	Data Analysts	Data Stewards, Stakeholders	Data Architects
6.7 Define and Maintain Hierarchies and Affiliations (C)	Defined Hierarchies and Affiliations	Data Stewards	Stakeholders	Data Analysts, Data Providers
6.8 Plan and Implement Integration of New Sources (D)	Data Source Quality and Integration Assessments	Data Analysts, Data Architects, Application Architects	Data Stewards, IT Management	Data Providers, Subject Matter Experts
	Integrated new data source	Data Architects, Application Architects	Data Stewards, Stakeholders	Data Analysts, Other IT Professionals
6.9 Replicate and Distribute Reference and Master Data (O)	Replicated Data	Data Architects, Application Architects	Data Stewards, Stakeholders,	Data Analysts, Other IT Professionals
6.10 Manage Changes to Reference and Master Data (C)	Change Request Procedures	Data Architects	Data Governance Council, Data Stewards	Other IT Professionals, Stakeholders
	Change Requests and Responses	Data Stewards	Data Governance Council	Stakeholders, Data Analysts, Data Architects, Application Architects

Activities	Deliverables	Responsible Roles	Approving Roles	Contributing Roles
	Change Request Metrics	Data Architects	Data Stewards, Data Governance Council	Data Analysts, Other IT Professionals

Table 8.6. Reference and Master Data Management Process Summary

8.3.3 Organizational and Cultural Considerations

Q1: What is the primary focus for Master Data Management?

A1: Effective MDM solutions require continuing focus on people. Different stakeholders have different needs, different expectations, different attitudes, and different assumptions about the data and the importance of improving data quality. Data professionals need to be exceptionally good listeners, noting both the explicit and implicit messages communicated by stakeholders. Data professionals also need to be great negotiators, forging small agreements that bring people together toward a deeper, shared understanding of enterprise needs and issues. Data professionals must respect and cannot minimize local perspectives and needs in this process.

Q2: Do procedures and practices need to be changed in order to improve the quality of reference and master data?

A2: Improving the quality of reference and master data will undoubtedly require changes to procedures and traditional practices. Every organization is unique, and there are few if any approaches that will work well everywhere. Solutions should be scoped and implemented based on both current organizational readiness and the evolutionary needs of the future.

Q3: What is the most challenging aspect of implementing reference and master data management?

A3: Perhaps the most challenging cultural change is determining which individuals are accountable for which decisions – business data stewards, architects, managers, and executives – and which decisions data stewardship teams, program steering committees and the Data Governance Council should make collaboratively. Data governance involves stakeholders in making and supporting decisions affecting them. Without effective data governance and data stewardship, MDM solutions will be another data integration utility within the IT organization, unable to deliver its full potential and the organization's expectations.

8.4 Recommended Reading

The references listed below provide additional reading that support the material presented in Chapter 8. These recommended readings are also included in the Bibliography at the end of the Guide.

Bean, James. XML for Data Architects: Designing for Reuse and Integration. Morgan Kaufmann, 2003. ISBN 1-558-60907-5. 250 pages.

Berson, Alex and Larry Dubov. Master Data Management and Customer Data Integration for a Global Enterprise. McGraw-Hill, 2007. ISBN 0-072-26349-0. 400 pages.

Brackett, Michael. Data Sharing Using A Common Data Architecture. New York: John Wiley & Sons, 1994. ISBN 0-471-30993-1. 478 pages.

Chisholm, Malcolm. Managing Reference Data in Enterprise Databases: Binding Corporate Data to the Wider World. Morgan Kaufmann, 2000. ISBN 1-558-60697-1. 389 pages.

Dreibelbis, Allen, Eberhard Hechler, Ivan Milman, Martin Oberhofer, Paul van Run, and Dan Wolfson. Enterprise Master Data Management: An SOA Approach to Managing Core Information. IBM Press, 2008. ISBN 978-0-13-236625-0. 617 pages.

Dyche, Jill and Evan Levy. Customer Data Integration: Reaching a Single Version of the Truth. John Wiley & Sons, 2006. ISBN 0-471-91697-8. 320 pages.

Finkelstein, Clive. Enterprise Architecture for Integration: Rapid Delivery Methods and Techniques. Artech House Mobile Communications Library, 2006. ISBN 1-580-53713-8. 546 pages.

Loshin, David. Master Data Management. Morgan Kaufmann, 2008. ISBN 98-0-12-374225-4. 274 pages.

Loshin, David. Enterprise Knowledge Management: The Data Quality Approach. Morgan Kaufmann, 2001. ISBN 0-124-55840-2. 494 pages.

National Information Standards Association (NISO), ANSI/NISO Z39.19-2005: Guidelines for the Construction, Format, and Management of Monolingual Controlled Vocabularies. 2005. 172 pages. www.niso.org

9 Data Warehousing and Business Intelligence Management

Data warehouse and business intelligence management is the seventh Data Management Function in the data management framework shown in Figures 1.3 and 1.4. It is the sixth data management function that interacts with and is influenced by the Data Governance function. Chapter 9 defines the data warehousing and business intelligence management function and explains the concepts and activities involved in data warehousing and business intelligence management.

9.1 Introduction

A *Data Warehouse* (DW) is a combination of two primary components. The first is an integrated decision support database. The second is the related software programs used to collect, cleanse, transform, and store data from a variety of operational and external sources. Both of these parts combine to support historical, analytical, and business intelligence (BI) requirements. A data warehouse may also include dependent data marts, which are subset copies of a data warehouse database. In its broadest context, a data warehouse includes any data stores or extracts used to support the delivery of data for BI purposes.

An *Enterprise Data Warehouse* (EDW) is a centralized data warehouse designed to service the business intelligence needs of the entire organization. An EDW adheres to an enterprise data model to ensure consistency of decision support activities across the enterprise.

Data Warehousing is the term used to describe the operational extract, cleansing, transformation, and load processes—and associated control processes—that maintain the data contained within a data warehouse. The data warehousing process focuses on enabling an integrated and historical business context on operational data by enforcing business rules and maintaining appropriate business data relationships. Data Warehousing also includes processes that interact with meta-data repositories.

Data warehousing is a technology solution supporting Business Intelligence (BI). *Business Intelligence* is a set of business capabilities. BI means many things, including:

1. Query, analysis, and reporting activity by knowledge workers to monitor and understand the financial operation health of, and make business decisions about, the enterprise.

2. Query, analysis, and reporting processes and procedures.

3. A synonym for the business intelligence environment.

4. The market segment for business intelligence software tools.

5. Strategic and operational analytics and reporting on corporate operational data to support business decisions, risk management, and compliance.

6. A synonym for Decision Support Systems (DSS).

Data Warehousing and Business Intelligence Management (DW-BIM) is the collection, integration, and presentation of data to knowledge workers for the purpose of business analysis and decision-making. DW-BIM is composed of activities supporting all phases of the decision support life cycle that provides context, moves and transforms data from sources to a common target data store, and then provides knowledge workers various means of access, manipulation, and reporting of the integrated target data.

Figure 9.1 outlines the context of Data Warehousing and Business Intelligence Management.

Figure 9.1 DW and BI Management Context Diagram

Objectives for DW-BIM include:

- Providing integrated storage of required current and historical data, organized by subject areas.

- Ensuring credible, quality data for all appropriate access capabilities.

　　　　　　　　　　　　　　　　　　　　　© 2010 DAMA International

- Ensuring a stable, high-performance, reliable environment for data acquisition, data management, and data access.

- Providing an easy-to-use, flexible, and comprehensive data access environment.

- Delivering both content and access to the content in increments appropriate to the organization's objectives.

- Leveraging, rather than duplicating, relevant data management component functions such as Reference and Master Data Management, Data Governance (DG), Data Quality (DQ), and Meta-data (MD).

- Providing an enterprise focal point for data delivery in support of the decisions, policies, procedures, definitions, and standards that arise from DG.

- Defining, building, and supporting all data stores, data processes, data infrastructure, and data tools that contain integrated, post-transactional, and refined data used for information viewing, analysis, or data request fulfillment.

- Integrating newly discovered data as a result of BI processes into the DW for further analytics and BI use.

9.2 Concepts and Activities

The purpose of this section is to provide some foundational DW-BIM concepts and definitions, before diving into the details of the specific DW-BIM activities. It presents a quick tour of the history of DW-BIM and an overview of typical DW-BIM components. An explanation of some general DW-BIM terminology follows, and a brief introduction and overview of dimensional modeling and its terminology leads into the activities identified in Figure 9.1.

9.2.1 Data Warehousing—A Brief Retrospective and Historical Tour

In a discussion of any length about data warehousing, two names will invariably come up—Bill Inmon and Ralph Kimball. Each has made significant contributions that have both advanced and shaped the practice of data warehousing. Here is a brief introduction to their major contributions along with some comparisons and contrasts of their approaches.

9.2.1.1 Classic Characteristics of a Data Warehouse—Inmon Version

In the early 1990's Bill Inmon defined the data warehouse as "a subject oriented, integrated, time variant, and non-volatile collection of summary and detailed historical data used to support the strategic decision-making processes for the corporation."

These key characteristics give a clear distinction of the nature of the data warehouse data compared to typical operational systems, and still hold largely true as distinctive characteristics of data warehouses.

- *Subject Oriented*: Subject orientation of the data warehouse refers to the organization of data along the lines of the major entities of the corporation. The data warehouse is neither functional nor application oriented. Design the data warehouse to meet the data needs of the corporation and not the specific analytical requirements of a particular department.

- *Integrated*: Integration refers to the unification and cohesiveness of the data stored in the data warehouse, and covers many aspects, including key structures, encoding and decoding of structures, definitions of the data, naming conventions, and so on. Implicit in this integration is establishing system(s) of record for all data to be included in the scope of the DW. Building the data warehouse is not merely copying data from the operational environment to the data warehouse. Simply consolidating data from multiple sources into a single data source results in a warehouse of data, and not a data warehouse.

- *Time Variant*: Time variance of the data warehouse refers to how every record in the data warehouse is accurate relative to a moment in time, and often shows up as an element of time in the key structure. As such, think of the data warehouse as a historical record of snapshots of data, where each snapshot has one moment in time when the record is accurate.

- *Non-Volatile*: Non-volatility of the data warehouse refers to the fact that updates to records during normal processing do not occur, and if updates occur at all, they occur on an exception basis. The blending of current operational data with deep, detailed historical data in the data warehouse challenges the non-volatile nature of the data warehouse. Blending is necessary to support both the tactical as well as the strategic decision-making processes. The historical trend and its impacts are covered in section 9.2.4.1, Active Data Warehousing.

- *Summarized and Detail Data*: The data in the data warehouse must contain detailed data, representing the atomic level transactions of the enterprise, as well as summarized data. Note: In early versions of the approach, cost and space considerations drove the need for summarized data. Today, performance considerations almost exclusively drive data summarization.

- *Historical*: Where operational systems rightfully focus on current-valued data, a hallmark of data warehouses is that they contain a vast amount of historical data (typically 5 to 10 years worth of data). The bulk of this data is typically at a summarized level. The older the data is, the more summarized it usually is.

9.2.1.2 Classic Characteristics of a Data Warehouse—Kimball Version

Ralph Kimball took a different approach, defining a data warehouse simply as "a copy of transaction data specifically structured for query and analysis." The copy, to differentiate it from the operational system, has a different structure (the dimensional data model) to enable business users to understand and use the data more successfully, and to address DW query performance. Data warehouses always contain more than just transactional data—reference data is necessary to give context to the transactions. However, transactional data is the vast majority of the data in a data warehouse.

Dimensional data models are relational data models. They just do not consistently comply with normalization rules. Dimensional data models reflect business processes more simply than normalized models.

9.2.2 DW / BI Architecture and Components

This section introduces the major components found in most DW / BI environments by providing an overview of the big picture views presented by both Inmon and Kimball. First is the Corporate Information Factory, from Inmon. Second is Kimball's approach, which he refers to as the "DW Chess Pieces". Both views and their components are described and contrasted.

9.2.2.1 Inmon's Corporate Information Factory

Inmon, along with Claudia Imhoff and Ryan Sousa, identified and wrote about components of a corporate data architecture for DW-BIM and called this the "Corporate Information Factory" (CIF). These components appear in tables following Figure 9.2.

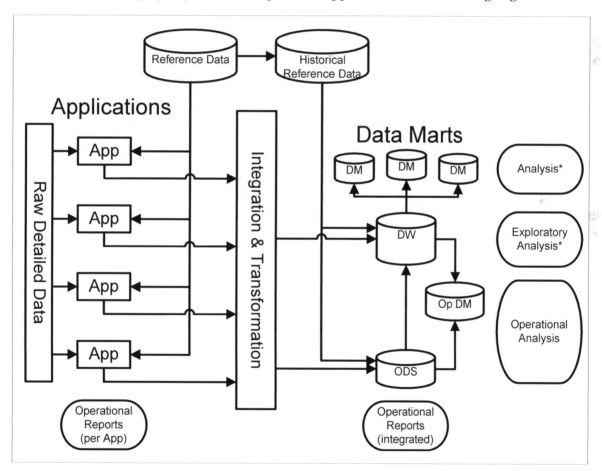

Figure 9.2 The Corporate Information Factory

Table 9.1 lists and describes the basic components of the Corporate Information Factory view of DW / BI architecture.

Label – Name	Description
Raw Detailed data	Operational / Transactional Application data of the enterprise. The raw detailed data provides the source data to be integrated into the Operational Data Store (ODS) and DW components. They can also be in database or other storage or file format.
Integration and Transformation	This layer of the architecture is where the un-integrated data from the various application sources stores is combined / integrated and transformed into the corporate representation in the DW.
Reference Data	Reference data was a precursor to what is currently referred to as Master Data Management. The purpose was to allow common storage and access for important and frequently used common data. Focus and shared understanding on data upstream of the Data Warehouse simplifies the integration task in the DW.
Historical Reference Data	When current valued reference data is necessary for transactional applications, and at the same time it is critical to have accurate integration and presentation of historical data, it is necessary to capture the reference data that was in place at any point in time. For more discussion on reference data, see Chapter 8 Master and Reference Data Management.
Operational Data Store (ODS)	The focus of data integration is meeting operating and classically operational reporting needs that require data from multiple operational systems. The main distinguishing data characteristics of an ODS compared to a DW include current-valued vs. DW historical data and volatile vs. DW non-volatile data. Note: ODS is an optional portion of the overall CIF architecture, dependent upon specific operational needs, and acknowledged as a component that many businesses omit.
Operational Data Mart (Oper-Mart)	A data mart focuses on tactical decision support. Distinguishing characteristics include current-valued vs. DW historical data, tactical vs. DW strategic analysis, and sourcing of data from an ODS rather than just the DW. The Oper-Mart was a later addition to the CIF architecture.
Data Warehouse (DW)	The DW is a large, comprehensive corporate resource, whose primary purpose is to provide a single integration point for corporate data in order to serve management decision, and strategic analysis and planning. The data flows into a DW from the application systems and ODS ,and flows out to the data marts, usually in one direction only. Data that needs correction is rejected, corrected at its source, and re-fed through the system.
Data Marts (DM)	The purpose of the data marts is to provide for DSS / information processing and access that is customized and tailored for the needs of a particular department or common analytic need.

Table 9.1 Corporate Information Factory Component Descriptions

Table 9.2 provides context for the reporting scope and purpose of each of the Corporate Information Factory components and some explanatory notes.

Component	Reporting Scope / Purpose	Notes
Applications	Isolated Operational Reports	Limited to data within one application instance
ODS	Integrated Operational Reports	Reports requiring data from multiple source systems. Typically, they have more operational than analytical orientation, with little historical data.
DW	Exploratory Analysis	The complete set of corporate data allows for discovery of new relationships and information. Many BI data mining tools work with flat-file extracts from the DW, which can also offload the processing burden from the DW.
Oper-Mart	Tactical Analytics	Analytic reporting based on current-values with a tactical focus. Dimensional data modeling techniques employed.
Data Mart	Analytics – classical management decision support, and Strategic Analytics	Inmon's early focus was on "departmental analysis", which was experientially true for real-world organizational issues, such as political and funding expediency. Later work expanded concepts to common-analytic needs crossing departmental boundaries.

Table 9.2 Corporate Information Factory Component Reporting Scope and Purpose

Table 9.3 provides a compare-and-contrast from a business and application perspective between the four major components of the Corporate Information Factory, such as between the Applications, ODS, DW and Data Marts.

Note the following general observations about the contrast between the information on the right hand side for DW and Data Marts, compared to the left hand side for applications, in particular:

- The purpose shifts from execution to analysis.

- End users are typically decision makers instead of doers (front line workers).

- System usage is more ad hoc than the fixed operations of the transactional operations.

- Response time requirements are relaxed because strategic decisions allow more time than daily operations.

- Much more data is involved in each operation / query or process

	Application Data	ODS	DW	Data Mart
Business Purpose	Specific Business Function	Corp Integrated Operational Needs	Central Data Repository Integration and Reuse	Analysis: Departmental (Inmon) Business Process (Kimball) Business Measures (Wells)
System Orientation	Operations (Execution)	Operations (Reports)	Infrastructure	Informational, Analytic (DSS)
Target Users	End Users: Clerical (Daily Operations)	Line Managers: Tactical Decision Makers	Systems: Data Marts, Data Mining	Executives: Performance Metrics / Enterprise Metrics Sr. Mgrs: Organization Metrics Mid Mgrs: Process Metrics Knowledge Workers: Activity
How System is Used	Fixed Ops	Operational Reporting	Stage, Store, Feed	Ad-Hoc
System Availability	High	Medium	Varies	Relaxed
Typical Response Time	Seconds	Seconds to Minutes	Longer (Batch)	Seconds to Hours

	Application Data	ODS	DW	Data Mart
# Records in an op.	Limited	Small to Med.	Large	Large
Amount of Data Per Process	Small	Medium	Large	Large
System Development Life Cycle (SDLC)	Classic	Classic	Classic	Modified

Table 9.3 Corporate Information Factory Components—Business / Application View

Table 9.4 provides a compare-and-contrast from a data perspective between the four major components of the Corporate Information Factory, such as between the applications, ODS, DW and Data Marts.

Table 9.4, especially the breakout rows for Amount of History and Latency, represents a classic framework where a majority of DW processes are for higher latency and, often, over-night batch processing. The combination of continued business pressure and requirements for more data faster, and the improvement in underlying technology, are blurring the lines and requiring advances in architectural design and approach. These topics are covered briefly in Section 9.2.4.1, Active Data Warehousing. Considered an advanced topic, it is not presented here as a separate architectural alternative.

	Application	ODS	DW	Data Mart
Orientation	Functional	Subject	Subject	Limited Subject
View	Application	Corporate (Ops)	Corporate (Historical)	Focused Analysis
Integration	Not Integrated - Application Specific	Integrated Corporate Data	Integrated Corporate Data	Integrated Subset
Volatility	High, Create / Read / Update / Destroy (CRUD)	Volatile	Non-Volatile	Non-Volatile
Time	Current Value	Current Value	Time Variant	Time Variant
Detail Level	Detail Only	Detail Only	Detail + Summary	Detail + Summary
Amount of History*	30 to 180 Days	30 to 180 days	5-10 years	1-5 years

	Application	ODS	DW	Data Mart
Latency*	Real Time to Near Real Time (NRT)	NRT	> 24 hours	1 day to 1 month
Normalized?	Yes	Yes	Yes	No
Modeling	Relational	Relational	Relational	Dimensional

Table 9.4 Corporate Information Factory Components—Data View

Note the following general observations about the contrast between the data perspective on the right hand side for DW and Data Marts, compared to the left hand side for applications, in particular:

- Data is Subject vs. functional orientation.

- Integrated data vs. stove-piped or siloed.

- Data is time-variant vs. current-valued only.

- Higher latency in the data.

- Significantly more history is available.

9.2.2.2 Kimball's Business Development Lifecycle and DW Chess Pieces

Ralph Kimball calls his approach the Business Dimensional Lifecycle; however, it is still commonly referred to as the Kimball Approach. From his Design Tip #49*, "We chose the Business Dimensional Lifecycle label instead, because it reinforced our core tenets about successful data warehousing based on our collective experiences since the mid-1980s."

The basis of the Business Dimensional Lifecycle is three tenets:

- *Business Focus*: Both immediate business requirements and more long-term broad data integration and consistency.

- *Atomic Dimensional Data Models*: Both for ease of business user understanding and query performance.

- *Iterative Evolution Management*: Manage changes and enhancements to the data warehouse as individual, finite projects, even though there never is an end to the number of these projects.

The Business Dimensional Lifecycle advocates using conformed dimensions and facts design. The conformation process enforces an enterprise taxonomy and consistent

---

* Margy Ross, "Design Tip #49 Off the Bench", Number 49, September 15, 2003. www.kimballgroup.com

business rules so that the parts of the data warehouse become re-usable components that are already integrated.

Figure 9.3 is a representation of what Kimball refers to as Data Warehouse Chess Pieces (Adapted from figures in <u>The Data Warehouse Toolkit</u>, 2nd Edition, Ralph Kimball and Margy Ross, John Wiley & Sons, 2002). Note that Kimball's use of the term "Data Warehouse" has been more inclusive and expansive than that of Inmon. In the diagram below, Kimball uses the term Data Warehouse to encompass everything in both the data staging and data presentation areas.

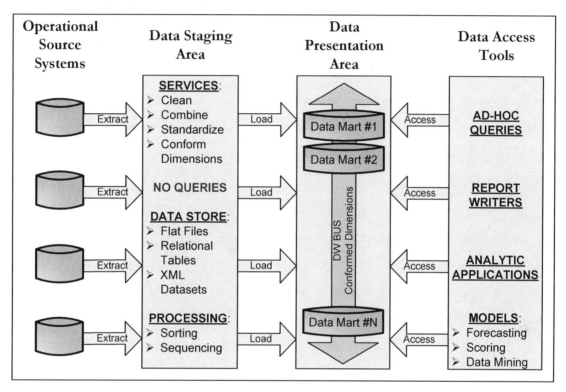

Figure 9.3 Kimball's Data Warehouse Chess Pieces

Table 9.5 describes the basic components of the Kimball's Data Warehouse Chess Pieces view of DW / BI architecture and notes how these components map to CIF components.

Name	Description
Operational Source Systems	Operational / Transactional Applications of the Enterprise. These provide the source data to be integrated into the ODS and DW components. Equivalent to the Application systems in the CIF diagram.

Name	Description
Data Staging Area	Kimball artfully uses the analogy of a "kitchen" to refer to this area as one where the data is prepared behind-the-scenes for presentation. He refers to it as the comprehensive set of all storage and ETL processes that stand between the source systems and the data presentation area.
	The key difference in the architectural approach here is that Kimball's focus has always been on the efficient end-delivery of the analytical data. With that scope, smaller than Inmon's corporate management of data, the data staging area becomes a potentially eclectic set of processes needed to integrate and transform data for presentation.
	Similar to combining two CIF components, such as Integration and Transformation, and DW.
	Note: In recent years, Kimball has acknowledged that an enterprise DW can fit into the architecture inside his Data Staging Area.
Data Presentation Area	Similar to the Data Marts in the CIF picture, with the key architectural difference being an integrating paradigm of a "DW Bus", such as shared or conformed dimensions unifying the multiple data marts.
Data Access Tools	Focus on the needs and requirements for the end customers / consumers of the data has been a hallmark of Kimball's approach. These needs translate into selection criteria from a broad range of data access tools to the right tools for the right task.
	In the CIF model, the access tools are outside of the DW architecture.

Table 9.5 Kimball's DW Chess Pieces—Component Descriptions

9.2.3 Tactical, Strategic and Operational BI

Tactical BI is the application of BI tools to analyze business trends by comparing a metric to the same metric from a previous month or year, etc. or to analyze historical data in order to discover trends that need attention. Use Tactical BI to support short-term business decisions.

Strategic BI has classically involved providing metrics to executives, often in conjunction with some formal method of business performance management, to help them determine if the corporation is on target for meeting its goals. Use Strategic BI to support long-term corporate goals and objectives.

Operational BI provides BI to the front lines of the business, where analytical capabilities guide operational decisions. Use Operational BI to manage and optimize business operations. Operational BI was the last of these three approaches to evolve in the industry. Operational BI entails the coupling of BI applications with operational functions and processes, with a requirement for very low tolerance for latency (near real-time data capture and data delivery). Therefore, more architectural approaches such as Service-oriented architectuure (SOA) become necessary to support operational BI fully. Some of these approaches are discussed in Section 9.2.4.1, Active Data Warehousing.

9.2.4 Types of Data Warehousing

The three major types of data warehousing are described in the following sections.

9.2.4.1 Active Data Warehousing

Data Warehouses serving tactical and strategic BI have existed for many years, often with a daily loading frequency, often serviced by a nightly batch window. These architectures were very dependent upon one of Inmon's original hallmarks of data in the data warehouse, such as non-volatile data.

With the onset of Operational BI (and other general requirements from the business) pushing for lower latency and more integration of real time or near real time data into the data warehouse, new architectural approaches are emerging to deal with the inclusion of volatile data. A common application of operational BI is the automated banking machine (ABM) data provisioning. When making a banking transaction, historical balances and new balances resulting from immediate banking actions, need to be presented to the banking customer real-time. Full treatment of those new approaches for this data provisioning is beyond the scope of this introduction, but it will suffice to introduce two of the key design concepts that are required—isolation of change, and alternatives to batch ETL.

The impact of the changes from new volatile data must be isolated from the bulk of the historical, non-volatile DW data. Typical architectural approaches for isolation include a combination of building partitions and using union queries for the different partitions, when necessary.

Many alternatives to batch ETL handle the shorter and shorter latency requirements for data availability in the DW; some of these include trickle-feeds, pipelining, and Service-oriented architectuure (SOA) where Data Services are designed and maintained.

9.2.4.2 Multi-dimensional Analysis – OLAP

Online Analytical Processing (OLAP) refers to an approach to providing fast performance for multi-dimensional analytic queries. The term OLAP originated, in part, to make a clear distinction from OLTP, Online Transactional Processing. The typical output of OLAP queries are in a matrix format. The dimensions form the rows and columns of the matrix; and the factors, or measures, are the values inside the matrix. Conceptually, this illustrates as a cube. Multi-dimensional analysis with cubes is particularly useful where there are well-known ways analysts want to look at summaries of data.

A common application is financial analysis, where analysts want to repeatedly traverse known hierarchies to analyze data; for example, date (such as Year, Quarter, Month, Week, Day), organization (such as Region, Country, Business Unit, Department), and product hierarchy (such as Product Category, Product Line, Product).

9.2.4.3 ROLAP, MOLAP, HOLAP and DOLAP

Three classic implementation approaches support Online Analytical Processing. The names of these relate to the respective underlying database implementation approach, such as Relational, Multi-dimensional, Hybrid, and Database.

- *Relational Online Analytical Processing (ROLAP)*: ROLAP supports OLAP by using techniques that implement multi-dimensionality in the two-dimensional tables of relational database managements systems (RDBMS). Star schema joins are a common database design technique used in ROLAP environments.

- *Multi-dimensional Online Analytical Processing (MOLAP)*: MOLAP supports OLAP by using proprietary and specialized multi-dimensional database technology.

- *Hybrid Online Analytical Processing (HOLAP)*: This is simply a combination of ROLAP and MOLAP. HOLAP implementations allow part of the data to be stored in MOLAP form and another part of the data to be stored in ROLAP. Implementations vary on the control a designer has to vary the mix of partitioning.

- *Database Online Analytical Processing (DOLAP)*: A virtual OLAP cube is available as a special proprietary function of a classic relational database.

9.2.5 Dimensional Data Modeling Concepts and Terminology

Dimensional data modeling is the preferred modeling technique for designing data marts. Dr. Ralph Kimball pioneered many of the terms and techniques of dimensional data modeling. The purpose of this section is to introduce the concepts and terms.

Kimball's focus has been on end-user presentation of the data, and dimensional data modeling, in general, focuses on making it simple for the end-user to understand and access the data. Inherent in the design technique is a conscious trade-off of preferring and choosing easy to understand and use structures from an end-user perspective, at the cost of more implementation work for the developers. This helps contribute to the fact that the majority of data mart design work ends up being in ETL processing.

Table 9.6 contrasts the typical differences in the characteristics of systems built from relational modeling for transactional applications versus those built with dimensional data modeling for data marts.

	Entity Relationship Modeling (Transactional Applications)	Dimensional Data Modeling (Data Marts)
Typical System	Operational	Informational, Analytic (BI)
# Records in an operation	A few	Many (millions +)
Typical Response Time	Seconds	Seconds, minutes to hours
Target users	Clerical – front line staff	Management and analysts
Orientation	Application – Run the business	Analysis – Analyze the business
Availability	High	Relaxed
Amount of Data Per Process	Small	Large
Time Horizon for data	60-180 days	One to many years
How System is Used	Fixed Operations	Fixed and Ad-Hoc

Table 9.6 System Characteristics for Transactional Applications and Data Marts

Dimensional data modeling is a subset of entity relationship data modeling, and has the basic building blocks of entities, attributes, and relationships. The entities come in two basic types: facts, which provide the measurements; and dimensions, which provide the context. Relationships in simple dimensional modeling are constrained to all go through the fact table, and all dimension-to-fact relationships are one-to-many (1:M).

9.2.5.1 Fact Tables

Fact tables represent and contain important business measures. The term "fact" is overloaded, as "fact tables" (entities) contain one or more "facts" (attributes representing measures). The rows of a fact table correspond to a particular measurement and are numeric, such as amounts, quantities, or counts. Some measurements are the results of algorithms so that meta-data becomes critical to proper understanding and usage. Fact tables take up the most space in the database (90% is a reasonable rule of thumb), and tend to have a large number of rows.

Fact tables express or resolve many-to-many relationships between the dimensions. Access to fact tables is usually through the dimension tables.

Fact tables often have a number of control columns that express when the row was loaded, by what program, or indicators for most current record, or other statuses. These fields help the programmers, the operators and the super-users navigate and validate the data.

9.2.5.2 Dimension Tables

Dimension tables, or dimensions for short, represent the important objects of the business and contain textual descriptions of the business. Dimensions serve as the primary source for "query by" or "report by" constraints. They act as the entry points or links into the fact tables, and their contents provide report groupings and report labels. Dimensions are typically highly de-normalized and account for about 10% of the total data, as a rule of thumb. The depth and quality of the detailed design of dimensions determine the analytic usefulness of the resulting systems.

All designs will likely have a Date dimension and an Organization or Party dimension at a minimum. Other dimensions depend on the type of analysis that supports the data in the fact table.

Dimension tables typically have a small number of rows and large number of columns. Main contents of a dimension table are:

- Surrogate or non-surrogate key.

- The primary key representing what is used to link to other tables in the DW.

- Descriptive elements, including codes, descriptions, names, statuses, and so on.

- Any hierarchy information, including multiple hierarchies and often 'types' breakdown.

- The business key that the business user uses to identify a unique row.

- The source system key identification fields for traceability.

- Control fields similar to the fact table control fields but geared to the type of dimension history capture that is designed, such as Types 1-3, 4 and 6 described below.

Dimensions must have unique identifiers for each row. The two main approaches to identifying keys for dimension tables are surrogate keys and natural keys.

9.2.5.2.1 Surrogate Keys

Kimball's approach gives each dimension a single primary key, populated by a number unrelated to the actual data. The number is a "surrogate key" or "anonymous key", and can be either a sequential number, or a truly random number. The advantages of using surrogate keys include:

- *Performance:* Numeric fields sometimes search faster than other types of fields.

- *Isolation:* It is a buffer from business key field changes. The surrogate key may not need changing if a field type or length changes on the source system.

- *Integration:* Enables combinations of data from different sources. The identifying key on the source systems usually do not have the same structure as other systems.

- *Enhancement:* Values, such as "Unknown" or "Not Applicable", have their own specific key value in addition to all of the keys for valid rows.

- *Interoperability:* Some data access libraries and GUI functions work better with surrogate keys, because they do not need additional knowledge about the underlying system to function properly.

- *Versioning:* Enables multiple instances of the same dimension value, which is necessary for tracking changes over time.

- *De-bugging:* Supports load issue analysis, and re-run capability.

In exchange for these advantages, there is extra ETL processing necessary to map the numeric key values to source key values, and maintain the mapping tables.

9.2.5.2.2 Natural Keys

For some systems, it is preferable not to create additional key fields, using, instead, the data that is already present to identify unique rows. The advantages of using natural keys include:

- *Lower overhead:* The key fields are already present, not requiring any additional modeling to create or processing to populate.

- *Ease of change:* In RDBMS where the concept of a domain exists, it is easy to make global changes due to changes on the source system.

- *Performance advantage:* Using the values in the unique keys may eliminate some joins entirely, improving performance.

- *Data lineage*: Easier to track across systems, especially where the data travels through more than two systems.

In exchange for these advantages, there can be a need to identify multiple fields in each query as part of the join, and possibly complex values for those non-numeric fields. Also, in some RDBMS, joins using long text strings may perform worse than those using numbers.

9.2.5.3 Dimension Attribute Types

The three main types of dimension attributes are differentiated by the need to retain historical copies. They are creatively named Type 1, Type 2 (and 2a), and Type 3. There are two other types that do not appear very often, also creatively named Type 4 and Type 6 (1+2+3). Types 1 through 3 can co-exist within the same table, and the actions during update depend on which fields with which types are having updates applied.

9.2.5.3.1 Type 1 Overwrite

Type 1 dimension attributes have no need for any historical records at all. The only interest is in the current value, so any updates completely overwrite the prior value in the field in that row. An example of Type 1 is 'hair color'. When an update occurs, there is no need to retain the current value.

9.2.5.3.2 Type 2 New Row

Type 2 dimension attributes need all historical records. Every time one of these Type 2 fields changes, a new row with the current information is appended to the table, and the previously current row's expiration date field is updated to expire it. An example is Billing Address. When the Billing Address changes, the row with the old address expires and a new row with the current Billing Address information is appended.

Note that managing Type 2 attributes requires that the table's key be able to handle multiple instances of the same natural key, either through the use of surrogate keys, by the addition of an index value to the primary key, or the addition of a date value (effective, expiration, insert, and so on) to the primary key.

9.2.5.3.3 Type 3 New Column

Type 3 dimension attributes need only a selected, known portion of history. Multiple fields in the same row contain the historical values. When an update occurs, the current value is moved to the next appropriate field, and the last, no longer necessary, value drops off. An example is a credit score, where only the original score when the account opened, the most current score, and the immediate prior score are valuable. An update would move the current score to the prior score.

Another example is monthly bill totals. There can be 12 fields, named Month01, Month02, etc., or January, February, etc. If the former, then the current month value updates Month01 and all other values move down one field. If the latter, then when the proper month is updated, the user knows that the month after the current month contains last year's data.

One useful purpose of Type 3 is for attribute value migrations. For example, a company decides to reorganize its product hierarchy, but wants to see sales figures for both the old hierarchy and the new for a year, to make sure that all sales are being recorded appropriately. Having both the old and the new available for a period of time allows this transition in the data.

9.2.5.3.4 Type 4 New Table

Type 4 dimension attributes initiate a move of the expired row into a 'history' table, and the row in the 'current' table is updated with the current information. An example would be a Supplier table, where expired Supplier rows roll off into the history table after an update, so that the main dimension table only contains current Supplier rows. The latter is sometimes called a Type 2a dimension.

Retrievals involving timelines are more complex in a Type 4 design, since current and history tables need to be joined before joining with the fact table. Therefore, it is optimal when the vast majority of access uses current dimension data and the historical table is maintained more for audit purposes than for active retrievals.

9.2.5.3.5 Type 6 1+2+3

Type 6 treats the dimension table as a Type 2, where any change to any value creates a new row, but the key value (surrogate or natural) does not change. One way to implement Type 6 is to add three fields to each row—effective date, expiration date, and a current row indicator. Queries looking for data as of any particular point in time check to see if the desired date is between the effective and end dates. Queries looking for only current data, add filters for the current row indicator. Adding filters has the drawback of requiring additional knowledge to create queries that correctly ask for the proper row by period value or indicator.

Another way to implement Type 6 is to add an index field instead of a current row indicator, with the current value of 0. Updated rows get the index value of zero, and all rows add 1 to their index values to move them down the line. Queries looking for the current values would set the filter for index value equal to zero, and queries looking for prior times would still use the effective and expiration dates. This technique has the drawback that all fact rows will link automatically to the index version 0 (the current row). Queries joining to the fact table will not find any prior values of the dimension unless the dimensional effective and expiration dates are included in the query.

9.2.5.4 Star Schema

A *star schema* is the representation of a dimensional data model with a single fact table in the center connecting to a number of surrounding dimension tables, as shown in Figure 9.4. It is also referred to as a star join schema, emphasizing that the joins from the central fact table are via single primary keys to each of the surrounding dimension tables. The central fact table has a compound key composed of the dimension keys.

9.2.5.5 Snowflaking

Snowflaking is the term given to de-normalizing the flat, single-table, dimensional structure in a star schema into the respective component hierarchical or network structures. Kimball's design methods discourage snowflaking on two main principals: 1) it dilutes the simplicity and end-user understandability of the star schema, and 2) the space savings are typically minimal.

Three types of snowflake tables are recognized: true snowflakes, outriggers, and bridges:

- *Snowflake tables*: Formed when a hierarchy is resolved into level tables. For example: a daily Period Dimension table resolves into the detail table for Date, and another table for Month or Year that is linked directly to the Date table.

- *Outrigger tables:* Formed when attributes in one dimension table links to rows in another dimension table. For example, a date field in one dimension (such as Employee Hire Date) links to the Period Dimension table to facilitate queries that want to sort Employees by Hire Date Fiscal Year.

- *Bridge tables:* Formed in two situations. The first is when a many-to-many relationship between two dimensions that is not or cannot be resolved through a fact table relationship. One example is a bank account with shared owners. The bridge table captures the list of owners in an 'owner group' bridge table. The second is when normalizing variable-depth or ragged hierarchies. The bridge table can capture each parent-child relationship in the hierarchy, enabling more efficient traversal.

9.2.5.6 Grain

Kimball coined the term *grain* to stand for the meaning or description of a single row of data in a fact table. Or, put another way, it refers to the atomic level of the data for a transaction. Defining the grain of a fact table is one of the key steps in Kimball's dimensional design method. For example, if the fact table has data for a store for all transactions for a month, we know the grain or limits of the data in the fact table will not include data for last year.

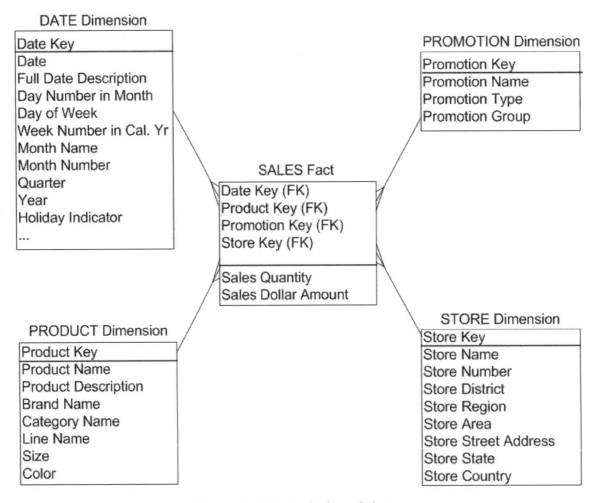

Figure 9.4 Example Star Schema

9.2.5.7 Conformed Dimensions

Conformed dimensions are the common or shared dimensions across multiple data marts in Kimball's design method. More precisely, Kimball defines dimensions to be conformed when they either match in terms of both data element names and their respective values, or contain a strict subset. The practical importance is that the row headers from any answer sets from conformed dimensions must be able to match exactly.

For example, think of multiple data marts or fact tables, all linking directly to the same dimension table, or a direct copy of that dimension table. Updates to that dimension table automatically show in all queries for those data marts.

Reuse of conformed dimensions in other star schemas allows for modular development of the DW. Stars can be clipped together through conformed dimensions as the design grows. A DW that starts with a fact table for the Accounts Payable Department can be clipped onto a fact on vendor performance in Supply Department through a Product dimension that they share in common. Ultimately, queries walk across subject areas to unify data access to the DW across the entire enterprise.

9.2.5.8 Conformed Facts

Conformed facts use standardized definitions of terms across individual marts. Different business users may use the same term in different ways. Does "customer additions" refer to "gross additions" or "adjusted additions"? Does "orders processed" refer to the entire order, or the sum of individual line items.

Developers need to be keenly aware of things that may be called the same but are different concepts across organizations, or conversely things that are called differently but are actually the same concept across organizations.

9.2.5.9 DW-Bus Architecture and Bus Matrix

The term *bus* came from Kimball's electrical engineering background, where a bus was something providing common power to a number of electrical components. Building on that analogy, the DW-bus architecture of conformed dimensions is what allows multiple data marts to co-exist and share by plugging into a bus of shared or conformed dimensions.

The DW-bus matrix is a tabular way of showing the intersection of data marts, data processes, or data subject areas with the shared conformed dimensions. Table 9.7 shows a sample tabular representation of bus architecture. The opportunity for conformed dimensions appears where a data mart is marked as using multiple dimensions (the row). The DW-bus appears where multiple data marts use the same dimensions (the column).

The DW-bus matrix is a very effective communication and planning tool. Its unifying concept is one of Kimball's most valuable contributions to the DW-BIM practice. The unifying concept becomes a key living design document in the DW-BIM. As new design pieces are added, the existing dimensions and facts, complete with their sources, update logic, and schedule, need to be reviewed for possible re-use.

Business Process (Marts)	Conformed Dimensions				
	Date	Product	Store	Vendor	Warehouse
Sales	X	X	X		
Inventory	X	X	X	X	X
Orders	X	X		X	

Table 9.7 DW-Bus Matrix Example

9.3 DW-BIM Activities

Data warehousing is concerned primarily with the part of the DW-BIM lifecycle from data source to a common data store across all relevant departments—in short, data content. BIM is concerned with the portion of lifecycle from common data store to targeted audience use—in short, data presentation.

DW and BIM naturally intertwine, as no DW can deliver value to the organization without some means of providing access to the collected data along with analytic and reporting capabilities. In turn, the effectiveness of a BIM capability is directly dependent upon the provision of data from the DW that is timely, relevant, integrated, and has other quality factors controlled for and documented as required.

DW-BIM activities overlap with many of the data management functions already covered in the Guide. The purpose of the DW-BIM Activities section is to articulate the activities involved in DW-BIM in a practical implementation based context. It includes references to other data management functions, with definitions elsewhere in the Guide, as well as providing practical insights into the various methods, tools, and techniques that are specific to the DW-BIM function.

9.3.1 Understand Business Intelligence Information Needs

Starting with and keeping a consistent business focus throughout the DW-BIM lifecycle is essential to success. Looking at the value chain of the enterprise is a good way to understand the business context. The specific business processes in a company's value chain provide a natural business-oriented context in which to frame areas of analysis. See Section 4.2.2.3 for further information on Value Chains and Figure 4.4 for a good example.

Gathering requirements for DW-BIM projects has both similarities to and differences from gathering requirements for other projects in typical IT development. In DW-BIM projects, it is generally more important to understand the broader business context of the business area targeted, as reporting is generalized and exploratory. The broader business context is in stark contrast to operational systems, where the development process defines, up-front, the precise specific details and requirements of operations and reports.

Analysis for DW-BIM projects is more ad-hoc by nature and involves asking questions, which, in turn, lead to new or different questions. Of course, querying will be limited by the nature and quality of the data available. And although the exact specifications of all reports will not be known, what can be known is the context for the questions—the ways the knowledge workers will most likely want to slice-and-dice the data.

Identify and scope the business area, then identify and interview the appropriate business people. Ask what they do and why. Capture specific questions they want to ask. Document how they distinguish between and categorize important aspects of the information. Ask the business people how they track and define success. Where possible, define and capture key performance metrics and formulae.

Capturing the actual business vocabulary and terminology is a key to success. The BI requirements-gathering activity is a great opportunity to partner with the Meta-data Management function (see Chapter 11), as it is critical to have a business-understandable context of data end-to-end; from the initial data sources, through all the transformations, to the end presentation. In summary, a DW-BIM project requirements write-up should frame the whole context of the business areas and / or processes that are in scope.

Document the business context, then explore the details of the actual source data. Typically, the ETL portion can consume 67% of a DW-BIM project's dollars and time. Data profiling is very helpful, and collaborating with the Data Quality function is essential (see Chapter 12). Evaluation of the state of the source data leads to more accurate up-front estimates for feasibility and scope of effort. The evaluation is also important for setting appropriate expectations.

Note that the DW is often the first place where the pain of poor quality data in source systems and / or data entry functions becomes apparent. Collaborating with the Data Governance function (see Chapter 3) is critical, as business input on how to handle all the unexpected variations that inevitably occur in the actual data is essential.

Creating an executive summary of the identified business intelligence needs is a best practice. The executive summary should include an overview of the business context, have a list of sample questions, provide commentary on the existing data quality and level-of-effort for cleansing and integration, and describe related organizations and business functions. It may also include a mock-up drawing for navigation of the solution showing the pathways for query and reporting in the selected presentation product. Review the executive summary with the business for prioritization in the DW-BIM program.

When starting a DW-BIM program, a good way to decide where to start is using a simple assessment of business impact and technical feasibility. Technical feasibility will take into consideration things like complexity, availability and state of the data, and the availability of subject matter experts. Projects that have high business impact and high technical feasibility are good candidates for starting.

Most importantly, assess the necessary business support, considering three critical success factors:

- *Business Sponsorship:* Is there appropriate executive sponsorship, i.e., an identified and engaged steering committee and commensurate funding? DW-BIM projects require strong executive sponsorship.

- *Business Goals and Scope:* Is there a clearly identified business need, purpose, and scope for the effort?

- *Business Resources:* Is there a commitment by business management to the availability and engagement of the appropriate business subject matter experts? The lack of commitment is a common point of failure and a good enough reason to halt a DW-BIM project until commitment is confirmed.

9.3.2 Define and Maintain the DW-BI Architecture

Chapter 4, on Data Architecture Management, provided excellent coverage of both data architecture in general, as well as many of the specific components of the DW-BIM architecture, including enterprise data models (subject area, conceptual, and logical), data technology architecture, and data integration architecture. Section 9.2.2 introduced the key components of DW-BIM architecture. The current section adds some practical considerations related to defining and maintaining the DW-BIM architecture.

Successful DW-BIM architecture requires the identification and bringing together of a number of key roles, potentially from other major functions, including:

- *Technical Architect*: Hardware, operating systems, databases, and DW-BIM architecture.

- *Data Architect*: Data analysis, systems of record, data modeling, and data mapping.

- *ETL Architect / Design Lead*: Staging and transform, data marts, and schedules.

- *Meta-data Specialist*: Meta-data interfaces, meta-data architecture, and contents.

- *BI Application Architect / Design Lead*: BI tool interfaces and report design, meta-data delivery, data and report navigation, and delivery (such as push, pull, canned, ad-hoc).

DW-BIM needs to leverage many of the disciplines and components of a company's IT department and business functions; thus, another key set of initial activities includes assessing and integrating the appropriate business processes, architectures, and technology standards, including ones for:

- Servers.

- Databases.

- Database gold copies (systems of record) identification and business sign-off.

- Security.

- Data retention.

- ETL tools.

- Data quality tools.

- Meta-data tools.

- BI tools.

- Monitoring and management tools and reports.

- Schedulers and schedules, including standard business and calendar key schedules.

- Error handling processes and procedures.

Technical requirements including performance, availability, and timing needs are key drivers in developing the DW-BIM architecture. The DW-BIM architecture should answer the basic questions about what data goes where, when, why and how. The 'how' needs to cover the hardware and software detail. It is the organizing framework to bring all the activities together.

The design decisions and principles for what data detail the DW contains is a key design priority for DW-BIM architecture. Publishing the clear rules for what data will only be available via operational reporting (such as in non-DW) is critical to the success of DW-BIM efforts. The best DW-BIM architectures will design a mechanism to connect back to transactional level and operational level reports from atomic DW data. Having this mechanism is part of the art of good DW design. It will protect the DW from having to carry every transactional detail.

An example is providing a viewing mechanism for key operational reports or forms based on a transactional key, such as Invoice Number. Customers will always want all the detail available, but some of the operational data has value only in the context of the original report, and does not provide analytic value, such as long description fields.

It is very important that the DW-BIM architecture integrate with the overall corporate reporting architecture. Many different design techniques exist, but one helpful technique is to focus on defining business-appropriate Service Level Agreements (SLAs). Often the response time, data retention, and availability requirements and needs differ greatly between classes of business needs and their respective supporting systems, such as operating reporting versus DW versus data marts. Several tables in Section 9.2.2 will be helpful in considering the varying aspects of different design components of the DW-BIM architecture.

Another critical success factor is to identify a plan for data re-use, sharing, and extension. The DW-Bus matrix introduced in Section 9.2.5.9 provides a good organizing paradigm.

Finally, no DW-BIM effort can be successful without business acceptance of data. Business acceptance includes the data being understandable, having verifiable quality, and having a demonstrable lineage. Sign-off by the Business on the data should be part of the User Acceptance Testing. Structured random testing of the data in the BIM tool against data in the source systems over the initial load and a few update load cycles should be performed to meet sign-off criteria. Meeting these requirements is paramount for every DW-BIM architecture. Consider, up-front, a few critically important architectural sub-components, along with their supporting activities:

- *Data quality feedback loop*: How easy is the integration of needed changes into operational systems?

- *End to-end meta-data*: Does the architecture support the integrated end-to-end flow of meta-data? In particular, is there transparency and availability of meaning and context designed in across the architecture? Does the architecture and design support easy access to answers when the business wants to know "What does this report, this data element, this metric, etc., mean?"

- *End-to-end verifiable data lineage*: To use modern, popular, TV parlance, is the evidence chain-of-custody for all DW-BIM data readily verifiable? Is a system of record for all data identified?

9.3.3 Implement Data Warehouses and Data Marts

Data warehouses and data marts are the two major classes of formal data stores in the DW-BIM landscape.

The purpose of a data warehouse is to integrate data from multiple sources and then serve up that integrated data for BI purposes. This consumption is typically through data marts or other systems (e.g. a flat file to a data-mining application). The design of a data warehouse is a relational database design with normalization techniques. Ideally, a single data warehouse will integrate data from multiple source systems, and serve data to multiple data marts.

The primary purpose of data marts is to provide data for analysis to knowledge workers. Successful data marts must provide access to this data in a simple, understandable, and well-performing manner. Dimensional modeling (using de-normalization techniques) and design, as introduced in Section 9.2.5, has largely been the technique of choice for designing user-oriented data marts. Create a data mart to meet specialized business analysis needs. Data marts often include aggregated and summarized information to support faster analysis. Kimball's vision has only data marts and no normalized DW layer.

Chapter 5 covers detailed data design, and database design, in particular. The references at the end of the chapter provide a number of excellent books on DW-BIM implementation methods.

In review, the use of data warehouses and data marts could be considered an application of one of Covey's famous Seven Habits[2], such as start with the end in mind. First, identify the business problem to solve, then identify the details and what would be used (end solution piece of the software and associated data mart). From there, continue to work back into the integrated data required (the data warehouse), and ultimately, all the way back to the data sources.

9.3.4 Implement Business Intelligence Tools and User Interfaces

The maturity of the BI market and a wide range of available BI tools makes it rare for companies to build their own BI tools.* The purpose of this section is to introduce the types of tools available in the BI marketplace, an overview of their chief characteristics, and some information to help match the tools to the appropriate customer-level capabilities.

Implementing the right BI tool or User Interface (UI) is about identifying the right tools for the right user set. Almost all BI tools also come with their own meta-data repositories to manage their internal data maps and statistics. Some vendors make these repositories open to the end user, while some allow business meta-data to be entered. Enterprise meta-data repositories must link to, or copy from, these repositories to get a complete view of the reporting and analysis activity that the tool is providing. Chapter 11 covers Meta-Data Management.

9.3.4.1 Query and Reporting Tools

Query and reporting is the process of querying a data source, then formatting it to create a report, either a production style report such as an invoice, or a management report.

The needs within business operations reporting are often different from the needs within business query and reporting. Yet sometimes, the needs blur and lines cross. Just as you can use a hammer to get a screw into the wall, you can use a business operations-reporting tool for management reporting. The converse, however, is not true; rarely can you use a business query and reporting tool to develop business operations reports. A business query tool may not support pixel-perfect layouts, normalized data sources, or the programmability that IT developers demand.

With business query and reporting, the data source is more often a data warehouse or data mart (though not always). While IT develops production reports, power users and casual business users develop their own reports with business query tools. Table 9.8 provides an excellent generalization of the mapping classes of BI tools to their respective primary classes of users. It compares some additional characteristics that

---

[2] Covey, Stephen R. The 7 Habits of Highly Effective People. Freedom Press, 2004.

* The material in this section is primarily from "The Business Intelligence Market" by Cindi Howson, BIScorecard®, http://www.biscorecard.com/SecureDownload.asp?qdocID=40; used by permission, with minor changes and additions.

help distinguish business operations-style reports from business query and reporting-style reports. These characteristics are by no means absolute, and you will not necessarily find vendor tools that fit precisely either. Business operations reports are not necessarily pixel-perfect, although some are. Use reports generated with business query tools individually, departmentally, or enterprise-wide.

Characteristics	Business Operations Reports	Business and Query Reporting
Primary Author	IT Developer	Power users or business user
Purpose	Document preparation	Decision making
Report Delivery	Paper or email, embedded in an application	Portal, spreadsheet, email
Print Quality	Pixel perfect	historically presentation quality, now pixel perfect
User Base	10s of 1000s	100s or 1000s
Data Source	OLTP – real time	Data warehouse or data mart, occasionally OLTP
Level of Data Detail	Atomic	Aggregated, filtered
Scope	Operational	Tactical, strategic
Usage	Often embedded within an OLTP application	BI as a separate application

Table 9.8 Production versus Business and Query Reporting

In the last few years, there has been a tremendous coalescing and collapsing of the marketplace with respect to reporting tools. All of the major BI vendors now offer classic pixel-perfect report capabilities that were once primarily in the domain of application reports. From a simple cost perspective, the delivery mechanism and infrastructure for reports or even information is agnostic to the content or type of information. In other words, it is prudent for companies to leverage common infrastructure and delivery mechanisms. These include the web, email, and applications for the delivery of all kinds of information and reports, of which DW-BIM is a subset.

Production reporting crosses the DW-BIM boundary and often queries transactional systems to produce operational items such as invoices or bank statements. The developers of production reports tend to be IT personnel.

Business query and reporting tools enable users who want to author their own reports, or create outputs for use by others. They are less concerned with the precise layout because they are not trying to generate an invoice or the like. However, they do want charts and tables quickly and intuitively. Some tools focus on innovative visualization of the data as a means to show meaning in the data with data maps, and moving landscapes of data over time. The formatting capabilities vary dramatically in this segment. Tools in this segment are referred to as ad hoc query tools. Often the reports created by business users become standard reports, not exclusively used for ad hoc business questions.

Figure 9.5 relates the classes of BI tools to the respective classes of BI users for those tools.

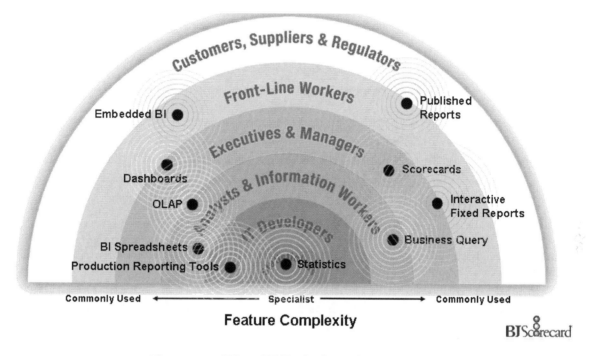

Figure 9.5 What BI Tools for What Users?

In defining the target user groups, there is a spectrum of BI needs. First, know your user groups and then match the tool to the user groups in your company. On one end, IT developers may be most concerned with extracting the data, and focus on advanced functionality. On the other end of the spectrum, information consumers may want fast access to previously developed and executed reports. These consumers may want some degree of interactivity such as drill, filter, sort, or may only want to see a static report.

Keep in mind that drilling is an OLAP functionality. So is this a need just for Analyst or Power Users, or is it something that customers / suppliers / casual users would also like, but that perhaps has not been possible in the past?

You need to understand how all classes of users expect to use the tool, including Web users. Will the Web just be a delivery mechanism, or also a report-authoring environment? Will you / how will you provide offline access for reports that are available over the Web?

Users may move from one class of users to another as their skills increase or as they perform different business functions. A supply chain manager, for example, may want to view a static financial report, but will want a highly interactive report for analyzing inventory. A financial analyst and a line manager responsible for expenses may be a power user when analyzing total expenses but a customer viewing a static report of one phone bill.

External users typically look at static reports, like a summary of their activity. Increasingly, however, companies are providing more interactive extranet reporting for their best customers and biggest suppliers. Front-line workers may use static, published reports, or a nugget of information embedded within an application. Executives and managers will use a combination of fixed reports, dashboards, and scorecards. Managers and power users tend to want to drill into these reports slice and dice the data to identify the root cause of problems.

9.3.4.2 On Line Analytical Processing (OLAP) Tools

OLAP provides interactive, multi-dimensional analysis with different dimensions and different levels of detail. Section 9.2.3.2, Multi-dimensional Analysis—MOLAP, briefly introduced this topic. This section covers OLAP tools, which provide for the arrangement of data into OLAP cubes for fast analysis.

Typically, cubes in the BI tools are generated from a star (or snowflake) database schema. The OLAP cubes consist of numeric facts, called *measures,* from the fact tables. These cubes can be virtual on-demand or batch jobbed. The dimensions categorize their facts in the respective schema (See Section 9.2.2).

The value of OLAP tools and cubes is reduction of the chance of confusion and erroneous interpretation, by aligning the data content with the analyst's mental model. The analyst can navigate through the database and screen for a particular subset of the data, changing the data's orientations and defining analytical calculations. Slice-and-dice is the user-initiated process of navigation by calling for page displays interactively, through the specification of slices via rotations and drill down / up. Common OLAP operations include slice and dice, drill down, drill up, roll up, and pivot.

- *Slice*: A slice is a subset of a multi-dimensional array corresponding to a single value for one or more members of the dimensions not in the subset.

- *Dice*: The dice operation is a slice on more than two dimensions of a data cube, or more than two consecutive slices.

- *Drill Down / Up*: Drilling down or up is a specific analytical technique whereby the user navigates among levels of data, ranging from the most summarized (up) to the most detailed (down).

- *Roll-up*: A roll-up involves computing all of the data relationships for one or more dimensions. To do this, define a computational relationship or formula.

- *Pivot*: To change the dimensional orientation of a report or page display.

9.3.4.3 Analytic Applications

Henry Morris of IDC first coined the term "analytic applications" in the mid 1990s, clarifying how they are different from OLAP and BI tools in general.[3] Analytic applications include the logic and processes to extract data from well-known source systems, such as vendor ERP systems, a data model for the data mart, and pre-built reports and dashboards. Analytic applications provide businesses with a pre-built solution to optimize a functional area (people management, for example) or industry vertical (retail analytics, for example).

Different types of analytic applications include customer, financial, supply chain, manufacturing, and human resource applications.

The buy versus build approach greatly influences the nuances within analytic applications. When you buy an analytic application, you buy the data model and pre-built cubes and reports with functional metrics. These buy applications tell you what is important, what you should be monitoring, and provide some of the technology to help you get to value faster. For example, with a general BI tool, you determine how and whether to calculate business measures, such as average sale per store visit, and in which reports you want it to appear. A pre-built analytic application provides this and other metrics for you. Some build analytic applications provide a development environment for assembling applications.

The value proposition of analytic applications is in the quick start, such as the shortened time-to-market and delivery. Some of the key questions for evaluation of analytic applications are:

1. Do we have the standard source systems for which ETL is supplied? If yes, how much have we modified it? Less modification equals more value and a better fit.

2. How many other source systems do we need to integrate? The fewer the sources, the better the value and fit.

3. How much do the canned industry standard queries, reports, and dashboards match our business? Involve your business analysts and customers and let them answer that!

4. How much of the analytic application's infrastructure matches your existing infrastructure? The better the match, the better the value and fit.

9.3.4.4 Implementing Management Dashboards and Scorecards

Dashboards and scorecards are both ways of efficiently presenting performance information. Typically, dashboards are oriented more toward dynamic presentation of operational information, while scorecards are more static representations of longer-term

---

[3] Morris, Henry. *Analytic Applications and Business Performance Management.* DM Review Magazine, March, 1999. www.dmreview.com. Note: www.dmreview.com is now www.information-management.com.

organizational, tactical, or strategic goals. Scorecards focus on a given metric and compare them to a target, often reflecting a simple status of red, yellow, and green for goals, based on business rules; dashboards typically present multiple numbers in many different ways.

Typically, scorecards are divided into 4 quadrants or views of the organization: Finance, Customer, Environment, and Employees, though there is flexibility, depending on the priorities of the Organization. Each will have a number of metrics that are reported and trended to various targets set by senior executives. Variance to targets is shown, usually with a root cause or comment accompanying each metric. Reporting is usually on a set interval, and ownership of each metric is assigned so that performance improvement expectations can be enforced.

In his book on Performance Dashboards, Wayne Eckerson provides in depth coverage of the types and the architectures of dashboards. The purpose of presenting this information is to provide an example of the way various BI techniques combine to create a rich integrated BI environment. Figure 9.6 is an adaptation of a related TDWI publication[*].

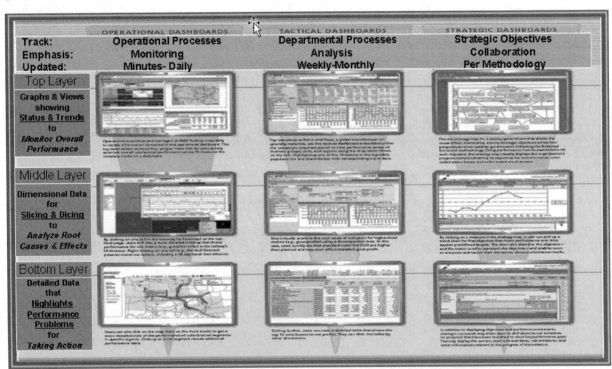

Figure 9.6 The Three Threes of Performance Dashboards

9.3.4.5 Performance Management Tools

Performance management applications include budgeting, planning, and financial consolidation. There have been a number of major acquisitions in this segment, as ERP

---

[*] Modified from "The Three Threes of Performance Dashboards" based on work by Wayne Eckerson

vendors and BI vendors see great growth opportunities here and believe BI and Performance Management are converging. On the customer buying side, the degree to which customers buy BI and performance management from the same vendor depends on product capabilities, but also on the degree to which the CFO and CIO co-operate. It is important to note that budgeting and planning does not apply only to financial metrics, but to workforce, capital, and so on, as well.

9.3.4.6 Predictive Analytics and Data Mining Tools

Data mining is a particular kind of analysis that reveals patterns in data using various algorithms. Whereas standard query and reporting tools require you to ask a specific question, a data mining tool will help users discover relationships or show patterns in a more exploratory fashion. Predictive analytics ('what-if' analysis) allow users to create a model, test the model based on actual data, and then project future results. Underlying engines may be neural networks or inference.

Use data mining in predictive analysis, fraud detection, root cause analysis (through clustering), customer segmentation and scoring, and market basket analysis. Although data mining is one segment of the BI market, it continues to be an application reserved for specialist users. In the past, statisticians have largely extracted data from source systems and data warehouses to perform analyses outside of the BI environment. Recent partnerships between BI and DB vendors are providing tighter coupling and integrating of analytic processing and DB capabilities. Typically flat file extracts are used to train the engine, and then a full run on a source database is performed, producing statistical reports and charts.

Note that a good strategy for interfacing with many data mining tools is to work with the business analysts to define the data set needed for analysis, and then arrange for a periodic file extract. This strategy offloads the intense multi-pass processing involved in data mining from the DW, and many data mining tools work with file-based input, as well.

9.3.4.7 Advanced Visualization and Discovery Tools

Advanced visualization and discovery tools often use an in-memory architecture to allow users to interact with the data in a highly visual, interactive way. Patterns in a large dataset can be difficult to recognize in a numbers display. A pattern can be picked up visually fairly quickly, when thousands of data points are loaded into a sophisticated display on a single page of display.

The difference in these tools versus most dashboard products is usually in:

1. The degree of sophisticated analysis and visualization types, such as small multiples, spark lines, heat maps, histograms, waterfall charts, bullet graphs, and so on.

2. Adherence to best practices according to the visualization community.

3. The degree of interactivity and visual discovery *versus* creating a chart on a tabular data display.

9.3.5 Process Data for Business Intelligence

The lion's share of the work in any DW-BIM effort is in the preparation and processing of the data. This section introduces some of the architectural components and sub-activities involved in processing data for BI.

9.3.5.1 Staging Areas

A staging area is the intermediate data store between an original data source and the centralized data repository. All required cleansing, transformation, reconciliation, and relationships happen in this area.

Advanced architectures implement these processes in a well-defined and progressive manner. Dividing the work reduces the overall complexity, and makes debugging much simpler. Having an initial staging area is a common, simple strategy to offload a complete set of data from the respective source system as-is, i.e., with no transforms.

A change-capture mechanism reduces the volume of transmitted data sets. Several months to a few years of data can be stored in this initial staging area. Benefits of this approach include:

- Improving performance on the source system by allowing limited history to be stored there.

- Pro-active capture of a full set of data, allowing for future needs.

- Minimizing the time and performance impact on the source system by having a single extract.

- Pro-active creation of a data store that is not subject to transactional system limitations.

Use subsequent design components to filter data only needed for business priorities, and do iterative, progressive, conforming and normalization. Designs that further allow separation of data conforming, such as conforming types and value sets, from merging and normalization will be simpler to maintain. Many architectures name this data integration and transformation to distinguish it from the simple copy-only staging area.

9.3.5.2 Mapping Sources and Targets

Source-to-target mapping is the documentation activity that defines data type details and transformation rules for all required entities and data elements, and from each individual source to each individual target. DW-BIM adds additional requirements to this classic source-to-target mapping process encountered as a component of any typical data migration. In particular, one of the goals of the DW-BIM effort should be to provide a complete lineage for each data element available in the BI environment all the way back to its respective source(s)

The most difficult part of any mapping effort is determining valid links between data elements in multiple equivalent systems. Consider the effort to consolidate data into an EDW from multiple billing or order management systems. Chances are that tables and fields that contain equivalent data do not have the same names or structures. A solid taxonomy is necessary to match the data elements in different systems into a consistent structure in the EDW. Gold sources or system of record source(s) must be signed off by the Business.

9.3.5.3 Data Cleansing and Transformations (Data Acquisition)

Data cleansing focuses on the activities that correct and enhance the domain values of individual data elements, including enforcement of standards. Cleansing is particularly necessary for initial loads where significant history is involved. The preferred strategy is to push data cleansing and correction activity back to the source systems, whenever possible.

Strategies must be developed for rows of data that are loaded but found to be incorrect. A policy for deleting old records may cause some havoc with related tables and surrogate keys, expiring a row and loading the new data as a whole new row may be a better option.

Data transformation focuses on activities that provide organizational context between data elements, entities, and subject areas. Organizational context includes cross-referencing, reference and master data management (see Chapter 8), and complete and correct relationships. Data transformation is an essential component of being able to integrate data from multiple sources. Data transformation development requires extensive involvement with Data Governance.

9.3.6 Monitor and Tune Data Warehousing Processes

Transparency and visibility are the key principles that should drive DW-BIM monitoring. The more one can expose the details of the DW-BIM activities, the more end-customers can see and understand what is going on (and have confidence in the BI) and less direct end-customer support will be required. Providing a dashboard that exposes the high-level status of data delivery activities, with drill-down capability, is a best practice that allows an on-demand-pull of information by both support personnel and customers. The addition of data quality measures will enhance the value of this dashboard where performance is more than just speed and timing.

Processing should be monitored across the system for bottlenecks and dependencies among processes. Database tuning techniques should be employed where and when needed, including partitioning, tuned backup and recovery strategies. Archiving is a difficult subject in data warehousing. Users often consider the data warehouse as an active archive due to the long histories that are built, and are unwilling, particularly if the OLAP sources have dropped records, to see the data warehouse engage in archiving.

Management by exception is a great policy to apply here. Sending success messages will typically result in ignored messages, but sending attention messages upon failure is a prudent addition to a monitoring dashboard.

9.3.7 Monitor and Tune BI Activity and Performance

A best practice for BI monitoring and tuning is to define and display a set of customer-facing satisfaction metrics. Average query response time and the number of users per day / week / month, are examples of useful metrics to display. In addition to displaying the statistical measures available from the systems, it is useful to survey DW-BIM customers regularly.

Regular review of usage statistics and patterns is essential. Reports providing frequency and resource usage of data, queries, and reports allow prudent enhancement. Tuning BI activity is analogous to the principle of profiling applications in order to know where the bottlenecks are and where to apply optimization efforts. The creation of indexes and aggregations is most effective when done according to usage patterns and statistics. Tremendous performance gains can come from simple solutions such as posting the completed daily results to a report that runs hundreds or thousands of times a day.

9.4 Summary

The guiding principles for implementing data warehousing and business intelligence management into an organization, a summary table of the roles for each data warehousing and business intelligence activity, and organization and cultural issues that may arise during data warehousing and business intelligence management are summarized below.

9.4.1 Guiding Principles

The implementation of the data warehousing and business intelligence management function into an organization follows eleven guiding principles:

1. Obtain executive commitment and support. These projects are labor intensive.

2. Secure business SME's. Support and high availability are necessary for getting the correct data and useful BI solution.

3. Be business focused and driven. Make sure DW / BI work is serving real priority business needs and solving burning business problems. Let the business drive the prioritization.

4. Demonstrable data quality is essential. Critical to DW / BI success is being able to answer basic questions like "Why is this sum X?" "How was that computed?" and "Where did the data come from?"

5. Provide incremental value. Ideally deliver in continual 2-3 month segments.

6. Transparency and self service. The more context (meta-data of all kinds) provided, the more value customers derive. Wisely exposing information about the process reduces calls and increases satisfaction.

7. One size does not fit all. Make sure you find the right tools and products for each of your customer segments.

8. Think and architect globally, act and build locally. Let the big-picture and end-vision guide the architecture, but build and deliver incrementally, with much shorter term and more project-based focus.

9. Collaborate with and integrate all other data initiatives, especially those for data governance, data quality, and meta-data.

10. Start with the end in mind. Let the business priority and scope of end-data-delivery in the BI space drive the creation of the DW content. The main purpose for the existence of the DW is to serve up data to the end business customers via the BI capabilities.

11. Summarize and optimize last, not first. Build on the atomic data and add aggregates or summaries as needed for performance, but not to replace the detail.

9.4.2 Process Summary

The process summary for the data warehousing and business intelligence management function is shown in Table 9.9. The deliverables, responsible roles, approving roles, and contributing roles are shown for each activity in the data warehousing and business intelligence management function. The Table is also shown in Appendix A9.

Activities	Deliverables	Responsible Roles	Approving Roles	Contributing Roles
7.1 Understand Business Intelligence Information Needs (P)	DW-BIM Project Requirements	Data / BI Analyst, BI Program Manager, SME	Data Steward, Business Executives and Managers	Meta-Data Specialist, Business Process Lead
7.2 Define the Data Warehouse / BI Architecture (P) (same as 2.1.5)	Data Warehouse / Business Intelligence Architecture	Data Warehouse Architect, Business Intelligence Architect	Enterprise Data Architect, DM Executive, CIO, Data Architecture Steering Committee, Data Governance Council	Business Intelligence Specialists, Data Integration Specialists, DBAs, Other Data Mgmt. Professionals, IT architects

Activities	Deliverables	Responsible Roles	Approving Roles	Contributing Roles
7.3 Implement Data Warehouses and Data Marts (D)	Data Warehouses, Data Marts, OLAP Cubes	Business Intelligence Specialists	Data Warehouse Architect, Data Stewardship Teams	Data Integration Specialists, DBAs, Other Data Mgmt. Professionals, Other IT Professionals
7.4 Implement Business Intelligence Tools and User Interfaces (D)	BI Tools and User Environments, Query and Reporting, Dashboards, Scorecards, Analytic Applications, etc.	Business Intelligence Specialists	Data Warehouse Architect, Data Stewardship Committee, Data Governance Council, Business Executives and Managers	Data Warehouse Architect, Other Data Mgmt. Professionals,, Other IT Professionals
7.5 Process Data for Business Intelligence (O)	Accessible Integrated Data, Data Quality Feedback Details	Data Integration Specialists	Data Stewards	Other Data Mgmt. Professionals, Other IT Professionals
7.6 Monitor and Tune Data Warehousing Processes (C)	DW Performance Reports	DBAs, Data Integration Specialists		IT Operators
7.7 Monitor and Tune BI Activity and Performance (C)	BI Performance Reports, New Indexes, New Aggregations	Business Intelligence Specialists, DBAs, Business Intelligence Analysts		Other Data Mgmt. Professionals, IT Operators, IT Auditors

Table 9.9 DW and BI Management Process Summary

9.4.3 Organizational and Cultural Issues

Q1: I can't get CEO / CIO support. What can I do?

A1: Try to discover what their burning business problems and issues are and align your project with providing solutions to those.

Q2: How do I balance the pressures of individual project delivery with DW / BI program goals of building out re-usable data and infrastructure?

A2a: Build out re-usable infrastructure and data a piece at a time.

A2b: Use the DW- bus matrix as a communication and marketing tool. On a project by project basis, negotiate a give-and-take – e.g., "Here are the conformed dimensions that other projects have developed that you get to benefit from."; and "Here are the ones we are asking this project to contribute to building so other future projects can benefit."

A2c: Don't apply the same rigor and overhead to all data sources. Relax the rules / overhead for single source, project-specific data. Use business priorities to determine where to apply extra rigor. In short, use the classic 80 / 20 rule: 80% of the value comes from 20% of the data. Determine what that 20% is and focus on it.

9.5 Recommended Reading

The references listed below provide additional reading that support the material presented in Chapter 9. These recommended readings are also included in the Bibliography at the end of the Guide.

9.5.1 Data Warehousing

Adamson, Christopher. <u>Mastering Data Warehouse Aggregates: Solutions for Star Schema Performance</u>. John Wiley & Sons, 2006. ISBN 0-471-77709-9. 345 pages.

Adamson, Christopher and Michael Venerable. <u>Data Warehouse Design Solutions</u>. John Wiley & Sons, 1998. ISBN 0-471-25195-X. 544 pages.

Adelman, Sid and Larissa T. Moss. <u>Data Warehouse Project Management</u>. Addison-Wesley Professional, 2000. ISBN 0-201-61635-1. 448 pages.

Adelman, Sid and others. <u>Impossible Data Warehouse Situations: Solutions from the Experts</u>. Addison-Wesley, 2002. ISBN 0-201-76033-9. 432 pages.

Brackett, Michael. <u>The Data Warehouse Challenge: Taming Data Chaos</u>. New York: John Wiley & Sons, 1996. ISBN 0-471-12744-2. 579 pages.

Caserta, Joe and Ralph Kimball. <u>The Data Warehouse ETL Toolkit: Practical Techniques for Extracting, Cleaning, Conforming and Delivering Data</u>. John Wiley & Sons, 2004. ISBN 0-764-56757-8. 525 pages.

Correy, Michael J. and Michael Abby. Oracle Data Warehousing: A Practical Guide to Successful Data Warehouse Analysis, Build and Roll-Out. TATA McGraw-Hill, 1997. ISBN 0-074-63069-5.

Covey, Stephen R. The 7 Habits of Highly Effective People. Free Press, 2004. ISBN 0743269519. 384 Pages.

Dyche, Jill. E-Data: Turning Data Into Information With Data Warehousing. Addison-Wesley, 2000. ISBN 0-201-65780-5. 384 pages.

Gill, Harjinder S. and Prekash C. Rao. The Official Guide To Data Warehousing. Que, 1996. ISBN 0-789-70714-4. 382 pages.

Hackney, Douglas. Understanding and Implementing Successful Data Marts. Addison Wesley, 1997. ISBN 0-201-18380-3. 464 pages.

Imhoff, Claudia, Nicholas Galemmo and Jonathan G. Geiger. Mastering Data Warehouse Design: Relational and Dimensional Techniques. John Wiley & Sons, 2003. ISBN 0-471-32421-3. 456 pages.

Imhoff, Claudia, Lisa Loftis and Jonathan G. Geiger. Building the Customer-Centric Enterprise: Data Warehousing Techniques for Supporting Customer Relationship Management. John Wiley & Sons, 2001. ISBN 0-471-31981-3. 512 pages.

Inmon, W. H. Building the Data Warehouse, 4th Edition. John Wiley & Sons, 2005. ISBN 0-764-59944-5. 543 pages.

Inmon, W. H. Building the Operational Data Store, 2nd edition. John Wiley & Sons, 1999. ISBN 0-471-32888-X. 336 pages.

Inmon, W. H., Claudia Imhoff and Ryan Sousa. The Corporate Information Factory, 2nd edition. John Wiley & Sons, 2000. ISBN 0-471-39961-2. 400 pages.

Inmon, W. H. and Richard D. Hackathorn. Using the Data Warehouse. Wiley-QED, 1994. ISBN 0-471-05966-8. 305 pages.

Inmon, William H., John A. Zachman and Jonathan G. Geiger. Data Stores, Data Warehousing and the Zachman Framework. McGraw-Hill, 1997. ISBN 0-070-31429-2. 358 pages.

Kimball, Ralph and Margy Ross. The Data Warehouse Toolkit: The Complete Guide to Dimensional Modeling, 2nd edition. New York: John Wiley & Sons, 2002. ISBN 0-471-20024-7. 464 pages.

Kimball, Ralph, Laura Reeves, Margy Ross and Warren Thornwaite. The Data Warehouse Lifecycle Toolkit: Expert Methods for Designing, Developing and Deploying Data Warehouses. John Wiley & Sons, 1998. ISBN 0-471-25547-5. 800 pages.

Kimball, Ralph and Richard Merz. The Data Webhouse Toolkit: Building the Web-Enabled Data Warehouse. John Wiley & Sons, 2000. ISBN 0-471-37680-9. 416 pages.

Mattison, Rob, <u>Web Warehousing & Knowledge Management</u>. McGraw Hill, 1999. ISBN 0-070-41103-4. 576 pages.

Morris, Henry. *Analytic Applications and Business Performance Management*. <u>DM Review Magazine</u>, March, 1999. <u>www.dmreview.com</u>. Note: www.dmreview.com is now <u>www.information-management.com</u>.

Moss, Larissa T. and Shaku Atre. <u>Business Intelligence Roadmap: The Complete Project Lifecycle for Decision-Support Applications</u>. Addison-Wesley, 2003. ISBN 0-201-78420-3. 576 pages.

Poe, Vidette, Patricia Klauer and Stephen Brobst. <u>Building A Data Warehouse for Decision Support, 2nd edition</u>. Prentice-Hall, 1997. ISBN 0-137-69639-6. 285 pages.

Ponniah, Paulraj. <u>Data Warehousing Fundamentals: A Comprehensive Guide for IT Professionals</u>. John Wiley & Sons – Interscience, 2001. ISBN 0-471-41254-6. 528 pages.

Westerman, Paul. <u>Data Warehousing: Using the Wal-Mart Model</u>. Morgan Kaufman, 2000. ISBN 155860684X. 297 pages.

9.5.2 Business Intelligence

Biere, Mike. <u>Business Intelligence for the Enterprise</u>. IBM Press, 2003. ISBN 0-131-41303-1. 240 pages.

Eckerson, Wayne W. Performance Dashboards: MEassuring, Monitoring, and Managing Your Business. Wiley, 2005. ISBN-10: 0471724173. 320 pages.

Bischoff, Joyce and Ted Alexander. <u>Data Warehouse: Practical Advice from the Experts</u>. Prentice-Hall, 1997. ISBN 0-135-77370-9. 428 pages.

Howson, Cindi. "The Business Intelligence Market". <u>http://www.biscorecard.com/</u>. Requires annual subscription to this website.

Malik, Shadan. Enterprise Dashboards: Design and Best Practices for IT. Wiley, 2005. ISBN 0471738069. 240 pages.

Moss, Larissa T., and Shaku Atre. <u>Business Intelligence Roadmap: The Complete Project Lifecycle for Decision-Support Applications</u>. Addison-Wesley, 2003. ISBN 0-201-78420-3. 576 pages.

Vitt, Elizabeth, Michael Luckevich and Stacia Misner. **Business Intelligence**. Microsoft Press, 2008. ISBN 073562660X. 220 pages.

9.5.3 Data Mining

Cabena, Peter, Hadjnian, Stadler, Verhees and Zanasi. <u>Discovering Data Mining: From Concept to Implementation</u>. Prentice Hall, 1997. ISBN-10: 0137439806

Delmater, Rhonda and Monte Hancock Jr. <u>Data Mining Explained, A Manager's Guide to Customer-Centric Business Intelligence</u>. Digital Press, Woburn, MA, 2001. ISBN 1-5555-8231-1.

Rud, Olivia Parr. <u>Data Mining Cookbook: Modeling Data for Marketing, Risk and Customer Relationship Management</u>. John Wiley & Sons, 2000. ISBN 0-471-38564-6. 367 pages.

9.5.4 OLAP

Thomsen, Erik. <u>OLAP Solutions: Building Multidimensional Information Systems, 2nd edition</u>. Wiley, 2002. ISBN-10: 0471400300. 688 pages.

Wremble, Robert and Christian Koncilia. <u>Data Warehouses and Olap: Concepts, Architectures and Solutions</u>. IGI Global, 2006. ISBN: 1599043645. 332 pages.

http://www.olapcouncil.org/research/resrchly.htm

10 Document and Content Management

Document and Content Management is the eighth Data Management Function in the data management framework shown in Figures 1.3 and 1.4. It is the seventh data management function that interacts with and is influenced by the Data Governance function. Chapter 10 defines the document and content management function and explains the concepts and activities involved in document and content management.

10.1 Introduction

Document and Content Management is the control over capture, storage, access, and use of data and information stored outside relational databases. Document and Content Management focuses on integrity and access.. Therefore, it is roughly equivalent to data operations management for relational databases. Since most unstructured data has a direct relationship to data stored in structured files and relational databases, the management decisions need to provide consistency across all three areas. However, Document and Content Management looks beyond the purely operational focus. Its strategic and tactical focus overlaps with other data management functions in addressing the need for data governance, architecture, security, managed meta-data, and data quality for unstructured data.

As its name implies, Document and Content Management includes two sub-functions:

- Document management is the storage, inventory, and control of electronic and paper documents. Consider any file or record a document; and document management includes records management[4]. Document management encompasses the processes, techniques, and technologies for controlling and organizing documents and records, whether stored electronically or on paper.

- Content management refers to the processes, techniques, and technologies for organizing, categorizing, and structuring access to information content, resulting in effective retrieval and reuse. Content management is particularly important in developing websites and portals, but the techniques of indexing based on keywords, and organizing based on taxonomies, can be applied across technology platforms. Sometimes, content management is referred to as Enterprise Content Management (ECM), implying the scope of content management is across the entire enterprise.

In general, document management concerns files with less awareness of file content. The information content within a file may guide how to manage that file, but document management treats the file as a single entity. Content management looks inside each file and tries to identify and use the concepts included in a file's information content.

---

[4] The ISO 15489: 2001 standard defines records management as "The field of management responsible for the efficient and systematic control of the creation, receipt, maintenance, use and disposition of records, including the processes for capturing and maintaining evidence of and information about business activities and transactions in the form of records."

The context diagram for Document and Content Management is shown in Figure 10.1.

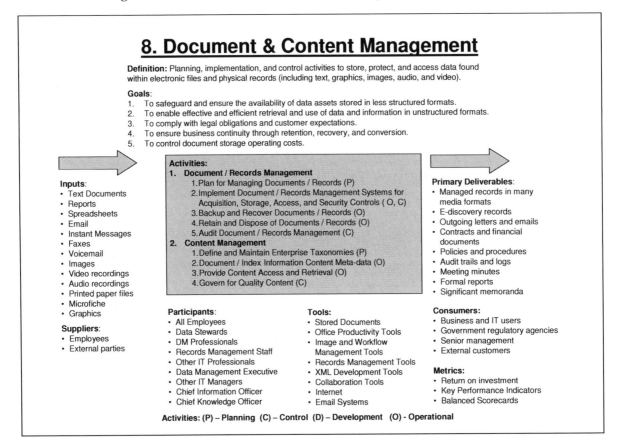

Figure 10.1 Document and Content Management Context Diagram

10.2 Concepts and Activities

The boundaries between document management and content management are blurring as business processes and roles intertwine, and vendors try to widen the markets for their technology products.

The fundamental principles of data management, as outlined in this Guide, apply to both structured and unstructured data. Unstructured data is a valuable corporate asset. Storage, integrity, security, content quality, access, and effective use guide the management of unstructured data. Unstructured data requires data governance, architecture, security meta-data, and data quality.

A document management system is an application used to track and store electronic documents and electronic images of paper documents. Document library systems, electronic mail systems and image management systems are specialized forms of a document management system. Document management systems commonly provide storage, versioning, security, meta-data management, content indexing, and retrieval capabilities.

A content management system is used to collect, organize, index, and retrieve information content; storing the content either as components or whole documents, while maintaining links between components. It may also provide controls for revising information content within documents. While a document management system may provide content management functionality over the documents under its control, a content management system is essentially independent of where and how the documents are stored.

10.2.1 Unstructured Data

Unstructured data is any document, file, graphic, image, text, report, form, video, or sound recording that has not been tagged or otherwise structured into rows and columns or records. Non-tabular data includes unstructured data as well as tagged data. This term has unfair connotations, as there is usually some structure in these formats, for instance, paragraphs and chapters.

According to many estimates, as much as 80% of all stored data is maintained outside of relational databases. Unstructured or semi-structured data presents as information stored in context. Some refer to data stored outside relational databases as "non-tabular" data. Of course, there is always some structure in which data provides information, and this structure may even be tabular in its presentation. No single term adequately describes the vast volume and diverse format of unstructured data.

Unstructured data is found in different kinds of electronic formats, including word processing documents, electronic mail, flat files, spreadsheets, XML files, transactional messages, reports, business graphics, digital images, microfiche, video recordings, and audio recordings. An enormous amount of unstructured data also exists in paper files.

10.2.2 Document / Record Management

Document / Record Management is the lifecycle management of the designated significant documents of the organization. Not all documents are significant as evidence of the organization's business activities and regulatory compliance.

While some hope technology will one day enable a paperless world, the world of today is certainly full of paper documents and records. Records management manages paper and microfiche / film records from their creation or receipt through processing, distribution, organization, and retrieval, to their ultimate disposition. Records can be physical, e.g. documents, memos, contracts, reports or microfiche; electronic, e.g. email content, attachments, and instant messaging; content on a website; documents on all types of media and hardware; and data captured in databases of all kinds. There are even hybrid records that combine formats such as aperture cards (paper record with a microfiche window imbedded with details or supporting material).

More than 90% of the records created today are electronic. Growth in email and instant messaging has made the management of electronic records critical to an organization. Compliance regulations and statutes, such as the U.S. Sarbanes-Oxley Act and E-Discovery Amendments to the Federal Rules of Civil Procedure, and Canada's Bill 198, are now concerns of corporate compliance officers who, in turn, have pushed for more standardization of records management practices within an organization.

Due to many privacy, data protection, and identity theft issues, records management processes must not retain, nor transport across international boundaries, certain data about individuals. Both market and regulatory pressures result in greater focus on records retention schedules, location, transport, and destruction.

The lifecycle of Document / Record Management includes the following activities:

- Identification of existing and newly created documents / records.

- Creation, Approval, and Enforcement of documents / records policies.

- Classification of documents / records.

- Documents / Records Retention Policy.

- Storage: Short and long term storage of physical and electronic documents / records.

- Retrieval and Circulation: Allowing access and circulation of documents / records in accordance with policies, security and control standards, and legal requirements.

- Preservation and Disposal: Archiving and destroying documents / records according to organizational needs, statutes, and regulations.

Data management professionals are stakeholders in decisions regarding classification and retention schemes, in order to support business level consistency between the base structured data that relates to specific unstructured data. For example: If finished output reports are deemed appropriate historic documentation, the structured data in an OLTP or warehousing environment may be relieved of storing the report's base data.

10.2.2.1 Plan for Managing Documents / Records

The practice of documents management involves planning at different levels of a document's lifecycle, from its creation or receipt, organization for retrieval, distribution, and archiving or disposition. Develop classification / indexing systems and taxonomies so that the retrieval of documents is easy. Create planning and policy around documents and records on the value of the data to the organization and as evidence of business transactions.

Establish, communicate, and enforce policies, procedures, and best practices for documents. Freedom of Information legislation in some jurisdictions establishes governmental agencies that handle citizens' requests for documents through a very formal process. These organizations also coordinate the evaluation of documents, and even parts of documents, for full or partial release and the timing of any release.

First, identify the responsible, accountable organizational unit for managing the documents / records. That unit develops a records storage plan for the short and long-term housing of records. The unit establishes and manages records retention policies according to company standards and government regulations. It coordinates the access and distribution of records internally and externally, and integrates best practices and process flows with other departments throughout the organization. The unit also creates a business continuity plan for vital documents / records.

Finally, the unit develops and executes a retention plan and policy to archive, such as selected records for long-term preservation. Records are destroyed at the end of their lifecycle according to operational needs, procedures, statutes, and regulations.

10.2.2.2 Implement Document / Record Management Systems for Acquisition, Storage, Access, and Security Controls

Documents can be created within a document management system or captured via scanners or OCR software. These electronic documents must be indexed via keywords or text during the capture process so that the document can be found. Meta-data, such as the dates the document was created, revised, stored, and the creator's name, is typically stored for each document. It could be extracted from the document automatically or added by the user. Bibliographic records of documents are descriptive structured data, typically in Machine-Readable Cataloging (MARC) format standard that are stored in library databases locally and made available through shared catalogues world-wide, as privacy and permissions allow.

Document storage includes the management of these documents. A document repository enables check-in and check-out features, versioning, collaboration, comparison, archiving, status state(s), migration from one storage media to another, and disposition. Documents can be categorized for retrieval using a unique document identifier or by specifying partial search terms involving the document identifier and / or parts of the expected meta-data.

Reports may be delivered through a number of tools, including printers, email, websites, portals, and messaging, as well as through a document management system interface. Depending on the tool, users can search by drill-downs, view, download / check-in and out, and print reports on demand. Report management can be facilitated by the ability to add / change / delete reports organized in folders. Report retention can be set for automatic purge or archival to another media, such as disk, CD-ROM, etc.

Since the functionality needed is similar, many document management systems include digital asset management. This is the management of digital assets such as audio, video, music, and digital photographs. Tasks involve cataloging, storage, and retrieval of digital assets.

Some document management systems have a module that may support different types of workflows, such as:

- Manual workflows that indicate where the user sends the document.

- Rules-based workflow, where rules are created that dictate the flow of the document within an organization.

- Dynamic rules that allow for different workflows based on content.

Document management systems may have a rights management module where the administrator grants access based on document type and user credentials. Organizations may determine that certain types of documents require additional security or control procedures. Security restrictions, including privacy and confidentiality restrictions, apply during the document's creation and management, as well as during delivery. An electronic signature ensures the identity of the document sender and the authenticity of the message, among other things. Some systems focus more on control and security of data and information, rather than on its access, use, or retrieval, particularly in the intelligence, military, and scientific research sectors. Highly competitive or highly regulated industries, such as the pharmaceutical and financial sectors, also implement extensive security and control measures.

There are schemes for levels of control based on the criticality of the data and the perceived harm that would occur if data were corrupted or otherwise unavailable. ANSI Standard 859 (2008) has three levels of control: formal (the most rigid), revision, or custody (the least rigid).

When trying to establish control on documents, the following criteria is recommended in ANSI 859. *Formal* control requires formal change initiation, thorough change evaluation for impact, decision by a change authority, and full status accounting of implementation and validation to stakeholders. *Revision* control is less formal, notifying stakeholders and incrementing versions when a change is required. *Custody* control is the least formal, merely requiring safe storage and a means of retrieval. Table 10.1 shows a sample list of data assets and possible control levels.

When determining which control level applies to data assets, ANSI 859 recommends use of the following criteria:

1. Cost of providing and updating the asset.

2. Project impact, when the change has significant cost or schedule consequences.

3. Other consequences of change to the enterprise or project.

4. Need to reuse the asset or earlier versions of the asset.

5. Maintenance of a history of change (when significant to the enterprise or the project).

10.2.2.3 Backup and Recover Documents / Records

The document / record management system needs to be included as part of the overall corporate backup and recovery activities for all data and information. It is critical that a document / records manager be involved in risk mitigation and management, and business continuity, especially regarding security for vital records. Risk can be classified as threats that partially or totally interrupt an organization from conducting normal operations. Use of near-online sites, hot sites, or cold sites can help resolve some of the issues. Disasters could include power outages, human error, network and hardware failure, software malfunction, malicious attack, as well as natural disasters. A Business Continuity Plan (sometimes called a Disaster Recovery Plan) contains written policies, procedures, and information designed to mitigate the impact of threats to all media of an organization's documents / records, and to recover them in the event of a disaster, to recover them in a minimum amount of time, and with a minimum amount of disruption.

Data asset	Formal	Revision	Custody
Action item lists		X	
Agendas			X
Audit findings		X	X
Budgets	X		
DD 250s			X
Final proposal			X
Financial data and reports	X	X	X
Human resources data		X	
Meeting minutes			X
Meeting notices, minutes, attendance lists		X	X
Project plans (including data management and configuration management plans)	X		
Proposal (in-process)		X	
Schedules	X		
Statements of work	X		
Trade studies		X	
Training material	X	X	
Working papers			X

Table 10.1 Sample Levels of Control for Documents per ANSI- 859

A vital records program provides the organization with access to the records necessary to conduct its business during a disaster, and to resume normal business afterward. Vital records must be identified, plans developed for protection and recovery, and the plans must be maintained. Business continuity exercises need to include vital record recovery. Employees and managers responsible for vital records require training. And internal audits need to be conducted to ensure compliance with the vital records program.

10.2.2.4 Retention and Disposition of Documents / Records

A document / records retention and disposition program defines the period of time during which documents / records for operational, legal, fiscal or historical value must be maintained. It defines when the documents / records are not active anymore and can be transferred to a secondary storage facility, such as off-site storage. The program specifies the processes for compliance, and the methods and schedules for the disposition of documents / records.

Documents / records retention presents software considerations. Electronic records may require the use of appropriate combinations of software versions and operating systems to enable access. Installation of new software versions or technological changes can create a risk of system breaches or complete loss of readability / usability.

Document / records managers must deal with privacy and data protection issues, and with identify theft of records. They ensure that there is no retention of personally identifiable data. This brings attention to how the records retention schedules are set up for destruction documents / records.

Legal and regulatory requirements must be considered when setting up document / record retention schedules. The digital data in electronic records make it well-suited for retrieval for civil and criminal legal cases. All types of electronic records listed above can be discovered for evidence, including e-mail, where people are often less careful than they should be.

Non-value-added information should be removed from the organization's holdings and disposed of to avoid wasting physical and electronic space, as well as the cost associated with its maintenance. Policy and procedures development and conformance are critical to good records management.

Many organizations do not give priority to removing non-value added information because:

- Policies are not adequate.
    - One person's non-valued-added information is another's valued information.
    - Inability to foresee future possible needs for current non-value-added physical and / or electronic records

- There is no buy- in for Records Management.
    - Inability to decide which records to delete.
    - Perceived cost of making a decision and removing physical and electronic records.
    - Electronic space is cheap. Buying more space when required is easier than archiving and removal processes.

10.2.2.5 Audit Document / Records Management

Document / records management requires auditing on a periodic basis to ensure that the right information is getting to the right people at the right time for decision making or performing operational activities. An example of sample audit measures is shown in Table 10.2.

Document / Records Management Component	Sample Audit Measure
Inventory	Each location in the inventory is uniquely identified.
Storage	Storage areas for physical documents / records have adequate space to accommodate growth.
Reliability and Accuracy	Spot checks are executed to confirm that the documents / records are an adequate reflection of what has been created or received.
Classification and Indexing Schemes	Meta-data and document file plans are well described.
Access and Retrieval	End users find and retrieve critical information easily.
Retention Processes	The retention schedule is structured in a logical way.
Disposition Methods	Documents / records are disposed of as recommended.
Security and Confidentiality	Breaches of document / record confidentiality and loss of documents / records are recorded as security incidents and managed appropriately.
Organizational understanding of documents / records management	Appropriate training is provided to stakeholders and staff as to the roles and responsibilities related to document / records management.

Table 10.2 Sample Audit Measures

An audit usually consists of:

- Defining organizational drivers and identifying the stakeholders that comprise the "why" of document / records management.

- Gathering data on the process (the "how"), once it is determined what to examine / measure and what tools to use (such as standards, benchmarks, interview surveys).

- Reporting the outcomes.

- Developing an action plan of next steps and timeframes.

10.2.3 Content Management

Content management is the organization, categorization, and structure of data / resources so that they can be stored, published, and reused in multiple ways.

Content includes data / information, that exists in many forms and in multiple stages of completion within its lifecycle. Content may be found on electronic, paper or other media. In the content's completed form, some content may become a matter of record for an organization and requires different protection in its lifecycle as a record.

The lifecycle of content can be active, with daily changes through controlled processes for creation, modification, and collaboration of content before dissemination. Depending on what type of content is involved, it may need to be treated formally (strictly stored, managed, audited, retained or disposed of), or informally.

Typically, content management systems manage the content of a website or intranet through the creation, editing, storing, organizing, and publishing of content. However, the term content has become broader in nature to include unstructured information and the technologies already discussed in this chapter. Many data management professionals may be involved with the various concepts of this section, such as aspects of XML.

10.2.3.1 Define and Maintain Enterprise Taxonomies (Information Content Architecture)

Many ideas exist about what information content architecture or information architecture is and what an Information Architect does. In general, it is the process of creating a structure for a body of information or content.

For a document or content management system, Content Architecture identifies the links and relationships between documents and content, specifies document requirements and attributes, and defines the structure of content in a document or content management system.

For website management, information content architecture is specific to the production of a website. It identifies the owner(s) of the publishable content, and the publication timeframe. A menu structure of the site is designed using a common navigational model.

When creating the information content architecture, taxonomy meta-data (along with other meta-data) is used. Meta-data management and data modeling techniques are leveraged in the development of a content model.

Taxonomy is the science or technique of classification. It contains controlled vocabulary that can help with navigation and search systems. Ideally, the vocabulary and the entities in an enterprise conceptual data model should coordinate. Taxonomies are developed from an ontological perspective of the world.

Taxonomies are grouped into four types:

- A flat taxonomy has no relationship among the controlled set of categories as the categories are equal. An example is a list of countries.

- A facet taxonomy looks like a star where each node is associated with the center node. Facets are attributes of the object in the center. An example is meta-data, where each attribute (creator, title, access rights, keywords, version, etc.) is a facet of a content object.

- A hierarchical taxonomy is a tree structure of at least two levels and is bi-directional. Moving up the hierarchy expands the category; moving down refines the category. An example is geography, from continent down to address.

- A network taxonomy organizes content into both hierarchical and facet categories. Any two nodes in a network taxonomy link based on their associations. An example is a recommender engine (…if you liked that, you might also like this…). Another example is a thesaurus.

An ontology is a type of model that represents a set of concepts and their relationships within a domain. Both declarative statements and diagrams using data modeling techniques can describe these concepts and relationships. Most ontologies describe individuals (instances), classes (concepts), attributes, and relations. It can be a collection of taxonomies, and thesauri of common vocabulary for knowledge representation and exchange of information. Ontologies often relate to a taxonomic hierarchy of classes and definitions with the subsumption relation, such as decomposing intelligent behavior into many simpler behavior modules and then layers.

Semantic modeling is a type of knowledge modeling. It consists of a network of concepts (ideas or topics of concern) and their relationships. An ontology, a semantic model that describes knowledge, contains the concepts and relationships together.

10.2.3.2 Document / Index Information Content Meta-data

The development of meta-data for unstructured data content can take many forms, mostly and pragmatically based on:

- Format(s) of the unstructured data. Often the format of the data dictates the method to access the data (such as Electronic index for electronic unstructured data).

- Whether search tools already exist for use with related unstructured data.

- Whether the meta-data is self-documenting (as in file systems). In this case development is minimal, as the existing tool is simply adopted.

- Whether existing methods and schemes can be adopted or adapted (as in library catalogs).

- Need for thoroughness and detail in retrieval (as in the pharmaceutical or nuclear industry). Therefore detailed meta-data at the content level might be necessary, and a tool capable of content tagging might be necessary.

Generally the maintenance of meta-data for unstructured data becomes the maintenance of a cross-reference of various local schemes to the official set of enterprise meta-data. Records managers and meta-data professionals recognize long term embedded methods exist throughout the organization for documents / records / content that must be retained for many years, but that these methods are too costly to re-organize. In some organizations, a centralized team maintains cross-reference schemes between records management indexes, taxonomies and even variant thesauri.

10.2.3.3 Provide Content Access and Retrieval

Once the content has been described by meta-data / key word tagging and classified within the appropriate Information Content Architecture, it is available for retrieval and use. Finding unstructured data in the company can be eased through portal technology that maintains meta-data profiles on users to match them with content areas.

A search engine is a class of software that searches for requested information and retrieves websites that have those terms within its content. One example is Google. It has several components: search engine software, spider software that roams the Web and stores the Uniform Resource Locators (URLs) of the content it finds, indexing of the encountered keywords and text, and rules for ranking. Search engines can be used to search within a content management system, returning content and documents that contain specified keywords. Dogpile.com is a search engine that presents results from many other search engines.

Another organizational approach is to use professionals to retrieve information through various organizational search tools. This unstructured data can be used for hearings, ad hoc retrievals, executive inquires, legislative or regulatory reporting needs, or a Securities Commission enquiry, to name a few. Sample meta-data tools include:

- Data models used as guides to the data in an organization, with subject areas assigned to organizational units.

- Document management systems.

- Taxonomies.

- Cross reference schemes between taxonomies.

- Indexes to collections (e.g. particular product, market or installation).

- Indexes to archives, locations, or offsite holdings.

- Search engines.

- BI tools that incorporate unstructured data.

- Enterprise and departmental thesauri.

- File system indexes.

- Project manager control records.

- Published reports libraries, contents and bibliographies, and catalogs.

- Ad hoc or regular management reports collections.

- Indexes of opinion polls.

- Recording management systems for hearings or other meetings.

- Product development archives.

Tim Berners-Lee, the inventor of the World Wide Web, published an article in Scientific American in May of 2001, suggesting the Web could be made more intelligent: a concept known as the Semantic Web. Context-understanding programs could find the pages that the user seeks. These programs rely on natural language, machine-readable information, 'fuzzy' search methods, Resource Description Format (RDF) meta-data, ontologies, and XML.

Extensible Markup Language (XML) facilitates the sharing of data across different information systems and the Internet. XML puts tags on data elements to identify the meaning of the data rather than its format (e.g. HTML). Simple nesting and references provide the relationships between data elements. XML namespaces provide a method to avoid a name conflict when two different documents use the same element names. Older methods of markup include SGML and GML, to name a few.

XML provides a language for representing both structured and unstructured data and information. XML uses meta-data to describe the content, structure, and business rules of any document or database.

The need for XML-capable content management has grown. Several approaches include the following:

- XML provides the capability of integrating structured data into relational databases with unstructured data. Unstructured data can be stored in a relational DBMS BLOB (binary large object) or in XML files.

- XML can integrate structured data with unstructured data in documents, reports, email, images, graphics, audio, and video files. Data modeling should take into account the generation of unstructured reports from structured data, and include them in creating data quality error-correction workflows, backup, recovery, and archiving.

- XML also can build enterprise or corporate portals, (Business-to-Business (B2B), Business-to-Customer (B2C)), which provide users with a single access point to a variety of content.

Computer applications cannot process unstructured data / content directly. XML provides identification and labeling of unstructured data / content so that computer applications can understand and process them. In this way, structured data appends to unstructured content. An Extensible Markup Interface (XMI) specification consists of rules for generating the XML document containing the actual meta-data and thus is a 'structure' for XML.

Unstructured and semi-structured data is becoming more important to data warehousing and business intelligence. Data warehouses and their data models may include structured indexes to help users find and analyze unstructured data. Some databases include the capacity to handle URLs to unstructured data that perform as hyperlinks when retrieved from the database table.

Keyed RDF structures are used by search engines to return a single result set from both databases and unstructured data management systems. However, using keyed RDF structures is not yet an industry standards-based method.

10.2.3.4 Govern for Quality Content

Managing unstructured data requires effective partnerships between data stewards, data professionals, and records managers, with similar dynamics to the governance of structured data. Business data stewards can help define web portals, enterprise taxonomies, search engine indexes, and content management issues.

The focus of data governance in an organization may include document and record retention policies, electronic signature policies, reporting formats, and report distribution policies. Data professionals implement and execute these and other policies to protect and leverage data assets found in unstructured formats. A key to meeting the business needs of the organization is to maximize the skill set of its records management professionals.

High quality, accurate, and up-to-date information will aid in critical business decisions. Timeliness of the decision-making process with high quality information may increase competitive advantage and business effectiveness.

Defining quality for any record or for any content is as elusive as it is for structured data.

- Who needs the information? Consider the availability to both those who originate the information and those who must use it.

- When is the information needed? Some information may be required with limited regularity, such as monthly, quarterly, or yearly. Other information may be needed every day or not at all.

- What is the format of the information? Reporting in a format that cannot be used effectively results in the information having no real value.

- What is the delivery mechanism? A decision must be made on whether to deliver the information or to make it accessible electronically through, for example, a message or a website.

10.3 Summary

The guiding principles for implementing document and content management into an organization, a summary table of the roles for each document and content management activity, and organization and cultural issues that may arise during document and content management are summarized below.

10.3.1 Guiding Principles

The implementation of the document and content management function into an organization follows three guiding principles:

- Everyone in an organization has a role to play in protecting its future. Everyone must create, use, retrieve, and dispose of records in accordance with the established policies and procedures.

- Experts in the handling of records and content should be fully engaged in policy and planning. Regulatory and best practices can vary significantly based on industry sector and legal jurisdiction.

- Even if records management professionals are not available to the organization, everyone can be trained and have an understanding of the issues. Once trained, business stewards and others can collaborate on an effective approach to records management.

10.3.2 Process Summary

The process summary for the document and content management function is shown in Table 10.3. The deliverables, responsible roles, approving roles, and contributing roles are shown for each activity in the document and content management function. The Table is also shown in Appendix A9.

Activities	Deliverables	Responsible Roles	Approving Roles	Contributing Roles
8.1 Document and Records Management				
8.1.1 Plan for Managing Documents / Records (P)	Document Management Strategy and Roadmap	Document System Managers, Records Managers	Data Governance Council	Data Architects, Data Analysts, Business Data Stewards

Activities	Deliverables	Responsible Roles	Approving Roles	Contributing Roles
8.1.2 Implement Document / Record Management Systems for Acquisition, Storage, Access, and Security Controls (O, C)	Document / Record Management Systems (including image and e-mail systems), Portals Paper and Electronic Documents (text, graphics, images, audio, video)	Document System Managers, Records Managers	Subject Matter Experts	
8.1.3 Backup and Recover Documents / Records (O)	Backup Files Business Continuity	Document Systems Managers, Records Managers		
8.1.4 Retain and Dispose Documents / Records (O)	Archive Files Managed Storage	Document Systems Managers, Records Managers		
8.1.5 Audit Document / Record Management (C)	Document / Record Management Audits	Audit Department, Management	Management	
8.2 Content Management				
8.2.1 Define and Maintain Enterprise Taxonomies (P)	Enterprise Taxonomies (Information Content Architecture)	Knowledge Managers	Data Governance Council	Data Architects, Data Analysts, Business Data Stewards
8.2.2 Document / Index Information Content Meta-data (D)	Indexed Keywords, Meta-data	Document Systems Managers, Records Managers		
8.2.3 Provide Content Access and Retrieval (O)	Portals, Content Analysis, Leveraged Information	Document Systems Managers, Records Managers	Subject Matter Experts	Data Architects, Data Analysts

Activities	Deliverables	Responsible Roles	Approving Roles	Contributing Roles
8.2.4 Govern for Quality Content (C)	Leveraged Information	Document Systems Managers, Records Managers	Business Data Stewards	Data Management Professionals

Table 10.3 Document and Content Management Process Summary

10.3.3 Organizational and Cultural Issues

Q1: Where in the organization should records management be placed?

A1: The records management function needs to be elevated organizationally and not seen as a low level or low priority function.

Q2: What are the most important issues that a document and content management professional needs to recognize?

A2: Privacy, data protection, confidentiality, intellectual property, encryption, ethical use, and identity are the important issues that document and content management professionals must deal with in cooperation with employees, management, and regulators.

10.4 Recommended Reading

The references listed below provide additional reading that support the material presented in Chapter 10. These recommended readings are also included in the Bibliography at the end of the Guide.

10.4.1 Document / Content Management

Aspey, Len and Michael Middleton. Integrative Document & Content Management: Strategies for Exploiting Enterprise Knowledge. 2003. IGI Global, ISBN-10: 1591400554, ISBN-13: 978-1591400554.

Boiko, Bob. Content Management Bible. Wiley, 2004. ISBN-10: 0764573713, ISBN-13: 978-07645737.

Jenkins, Tom, David Glazer, and Hartmut Schaper.. Enterprise Content Management Technology: What You Need to Know, 2004. Open Text Corporation, ISBN-10: 0973066253, ISBN-13: 978-0973066258.

Sutton, Michael J. D. Document Management for the Enterprise: Principles, Techniques, and Applications. Wiley, 1996, ISBN-10: 0471147192, ISBN-13: 978-0471147190.

10.4.2 Records Management

Alderman, Ellen and Caroline Kennedy . <u>The Right to Privacy</u>. 1997. Vintage, ISBN-10: 0679744347, ISBN-13: 978-0679744344.

Bearman, David. <u>Electronic Evidence: Strategies for Managing Records in Contemporary Organizations</u>. 1994. Archives and Museum Informatics. ISBN-10: 1885626088, ISBN-13: 978-1885626080.

Cox, Richard J. and David Wallace. <u>Archives and the Public Good: Accountability and Records in Modern Society</u>. 2002. Quorum Books, ISBN-10: 1567204694, ISBN-13: 978-1567204698.

Cox, Richard J. <u>Managing Records as Evidence and Information</u>. Quorum Books, 2000. ISBN 1-567-20241-4. 264 pages.

Dearstyne, Bruce. <u>Effective Approaches for Managing Electronic Records and Archives</u>. 2006. The Scarecrow Press, Inc. ISBN-10: 0810857421, ISBN-13: 978-0810857421.

Ellis, Judith, editor. <u>Keeping Archives</u>. Thorpe Bowker; 2 Sub edition. 2004. ISBN-10: 1875589155, ISBN-13: 978-1875589159.

Higgs, Edward. <u>History and Electronic Artifacts</u>. Oxford University Press, USA. 1998. ISBN-10: 0198236344, ISBN-13: 978-0198236344.

Robek. <u>Information and Records Management: Document-Based Information Systems</u>. Career Education; 4 edition. 1995. ISBN-10: 0028017935.

Wellheiser, Johanna and John Barton. <u>An Ounce of Prevention: Integrated Disaster Planning for Archives, Libraries and Records Centers</u>. Canadian Library Assn. 1987. ISBN-10: 0969204108, ISBN-13: 978-0969204107.

10.4.3 Enterprise Information Portals

Firestone, Joseph M. <u>Enterprise Information Portals and Knowledge Management</u>. Butterworth-Heineman, 2002. ISBN 0-750-67474-1. 456 pages.

Mena, Jesus, <u>Data Mining Your Website</u>, Digital Press, Woburn, MA, 1999, ISBN 1-5555-8222- 2.

10.4.4 Meta-data in Library Science

Baca, Murtha, editor. <u>Introduction to Metadata: Pathways to Digital Information</u>. Getty Information Institute, 2000. ISBN 0-892-36533-1. 48 pages.

Hillman, Diane I., and Elaine L. Westbrooks,. <u>Metadata in Practice</u>. American Library Association, 2004. ISBN 0-838-90882-9. 285 pages.

Karpuk, Deborah. <u>Metadata: From Resource Discovery to Knowledge Management</u>. Libraries Unlimited, 2007. ISBN 1-591-58070-6. 275 pages.

Liu, Jia. Metadata and Its Applications in the Digital Library. Libraries Unlimited, 2007. ISBN 1-291-58306-6. 250 pages.

10.4.5 Semantics in XML Documents

McComb, Dave. Semantics in Business Systems: The Savvy Manager's Guide. The Discipline Underlying Web Services, Business Rules and the Semantic Web. San Francisco, CA: Morgan Kaufmann Publishers, 2004. ISBN: 1-55860-917-2.

10.4.6 Unstructured Data and Business Intelligence

Inmon, William H. and Anthony Nesavich,. Tapping into Unstructured Data: Integrating Unstructured Data and Textual Analytics into Business Intelligence. Prentice-Hall PTR, 2007. ISBN-10: 0132360292, ISBN-13: 978-0132360296.

10.4.7 Standards

ANSI/EIA859 : Data Management.

ISO 15489-1:2001 Records Management -- Part 1: General.

ISO/TR 15489-2:2001 Records Management -- Part 2: Guidelines.

AS 4390-1996 Records Management.

ISO 2788:1986 Guidelines for the establishment and development of monolingual thesauri.

UK Public Record Office Approved Electronic Records Management Solution.

Victorian Electronic Records Strategy (VERS) Australia.

10.4.8 E-Discovery

http//:www.uscourts.gov/ruless/Ediscovery_w_Notes.pdf

http//:www.fjc.gov/public/home.nsf/pages/196

11 Meta-data Management

Meta-data Management is the ninth Data Management Function in the data management framework shown in Figures 1.3 and 1.4. It is the eighth data management function that interacts with and is influenced by the Data Governance function. Chapter 11 defines the meta-data management function and explains the concepts and activities involved in meta-data management.

11.1 Introduction

Meta-data is "data about data", but what exactly does this commonly used definition mean? Meta-data is to data what data is to real-life. Data reflects real life transactions, events, objects, relationships, etc. Meta-data reflects data transactions, events, objects, relationships, etc.

Meta-data Management is the set of processes that ensure proper creation, storage, integration, and control to support associated usage of meta-data.

To understand meta-data's vital role in data management, draw an analogy to a card catalog in a library. The card catalog identifies what books are stored in the library and where they are located within the building. Users can search for books by subject area, author, or title. Additionally, the card catalog shows the author, subject tags, publication date, and revision history of each book. The card catalog information helps to determine which books will meet the reader's needs. Without this catalog resource, finding books in the library would be difficult, time-consuming, and frustrating. A reader may search many incorrect books before finding the right book if a card catalog did not exist.

Meta-data management, like the other data management functions, is represented in a context diagram. The context diagram for meta-data management, shown in Figure 11.1, is a short-hand representation of the functions described in this chapter. Meta-data management activities are in the center, surrounded by the relevant environmental aspects. Key definitional concepts in meta-data management are at the top of the diagram.

Leveraging meta-data in an organization can provide benefits in the following ways:

1. Increase the value of strategic information (e.g. data warehousing, CRM, SCM, etc.) by providing context for the data, thus aiding analysts in making more effective decisions.

2. Reduce training costs and lower the impact of staff turnover through thorough documentation of data context, history, and origin.

3. Reduce data-oriented research time by assisting business analysts in finding the information they need, in a timely manner.

4. Improve communication by bridging the gap between business users and IT professionals, leveraging work done by other teams, and increasing confidence in IT system data.

5. Increase speed of system development's time-to-market by reducing system development life-cycle time.

6. Reduce risk of project failure through better impact analysis at various levels during change management.

7. Identify and reduce redundant data and processes, thereby reducing rework and use of redundant, out-of-date, or incorrect data.

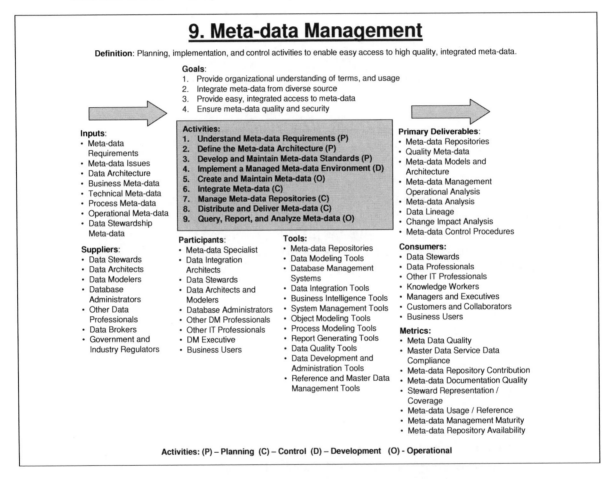

Figure 11.1 Meta-data Management Context Diagram

11.2 Concepts and Activities

Meta-data is the card catalog in a managed data environment. Abstractly, meta-data is the descriptive tags or context on the data (the content) in a managed data environment. Meta-data shows business and technical users where to find information in data repositories. Meta-data also provides details on where the data came from, how it got there, any transformations, and its level of quality; and it provides assistance with what the data really means and how to interpret it.

11.2.1 Meta-data Definition

Meta-data is information about the physical data, technical and business processes, data rules and constraints, and logical and physical structures of the data, as used by an organization. These descriptive tags describe data (e.g. databases, data elements, data models), concepts (e.g. business processes, application systems, software code, technology infrastructure), and the connections (relationships) between the data and concepts.

Meta-data is a broad term that includes many potential subject areas. These subject areas include:

1. Business analytics: Data definitions, reports, users, usage, performance.

2. Business architecture: Roles and organizations, goals and objectives.

3. Business definitions: The business terms and explanations for a particular concept, fact, or other item found in an organization.

4. Business rules: Standard calculations and derivation methods.

5. Data governance: Policies, standards, procedures, programs, roles, organizations, stewardship assignments.

6. Data integration: Sources, targets, transformations, lineage, ETL workflows, EAI, EII, migration / conversion.

7. Data quality: Defects, metrics, ratings.

8. Document content management: Unstructured data, documents, taxonomies, ontologies, name sets, legal discovery, search engine indexes.

9. Information technology infrastructure: Platforms, networks, configurations, licenses.

10. Logical data models: Entities, attributes, relationships and rules, business names and definitions.

11. Physical data models: Files, tables, columns, views, business definitions, indexes, usage, performance, change management.

12. Process models: Functions, activities, roles, inputs / outputs, workflow, business rules, timing, stores.

13. Systems portfolio and IT governance: Databases, applications, projects and programs, integration roadmap, change management.

14. Service-oriented architectuure (SOA) information: Components, services, messages, master data.

15. System design and development: Requirements, designs and test plans, impact.

16. Systems management: Data security, licenses, configuration, reliability, service levels.

11.2.1.1 Types of Meta-data

Meta-data is classified into four major types: business, technical and operational, process, and data stewardship.

Business meta-data includes the business names and definitions of subject and concept areas, entities, and attributes; attribute data types and other attribute properties; range descriptions; calculations; algorithms and business rules; and valid domain values and their definitions. Business meta-data relates the business perspective to the meta-data user.

Examples of business meta-data include:

- Business data definitions, including calculations.

- Business rules and algorithms, including hierarchies.

- Data lineage and impact analysis.

- Data model: enterprise level conceptual and logical.

- Data quality statements, such as confidence and completeness indicators.

- Data stewardship information and owning organization(s).

- Data update cycle.

- Historical data availability.

- Historical or alternate business definitions.

- Regulatory or contractual constraints.

- Reports lists and data contents.

- System of record for data elements.

- Valid value constraints (sample or list).

Technical and operational meta-data provides developers and technical users with information about their systems. Technical meta-data includes physical database table and column names, column properties, other database object properties, and data storage. The database administrator needs to know users patterns of access, frequency, and report / query execution time. Capture this meta-data using routines within a DBMS or other software.

Operational meta-data is targeted at IT operations users' needs, including information about data movement, source and target systems, batch programs, job frequency, schedule anomalies, recovery and backup information, archive rules, and usage.

Examples of technical and operational meta-data include:

- Audit controls and balancing information.

- Data archiving and retention rules.

- Encoding / reference table conversions.

- History of extracts and results.

- Identification of source system fields.

- Mappings, transformations, and statistics from the system of record to target data stores (OLTP, OLAP).

- Physical data model, including data table names, keys, and indexes.

- Program job dependencies and schedule.

- Program names and descriptions.

- Purge criteria.

- Recovery and backup rules.

- Relationships between the data models and the data warehouse / marts.

- Systems of record feeding target data stores (OLTP, OLAP, SOA).

- User report and query access patterns, frequency, and execution time.

- Version maintenance.

Process meta-data is data that defines and describes the characteristics of other system elements (processes, business rules, programs, jobs, tools, etc.).

Examples of process meta-data include:

- Data stores and data involved.

- Government / regulatory bodies.

- Organization owners and stakeholders.

- Process dependencies and decomposition.

- Process feedback loop documentation.

- Process name.

- Process order and timing.

- Process variations due to input or timing.

- Roles and responsibilities.

- Value chain activities.

Data stewardship meta-data is data about data stewards, stewardship processes, and responsibility assignments. Data stewards assure that data and meta-data are accurate, with high quality across the enterprise. They establish and monitor sharing of data.

Examples of data stewardship meta-data include:

- Business drivers / goals.

- Data CRUD rules.

- Data definitions - business and technical.

- Data owners.

- Data sharing rules and agreements / contracts.

- Data stewards, roles and responsibilities.

- Data stores and systems involved.

- Data subject areas.

- Data users.

- Government / regulatory bodies.

- Governance organization structure and responsibilities.

11.2.1.2 Meta-data for Unstructured Data

All data is somewhat structured, so the notion of unstructured meta-data is a misnomer. A better term is "meta-data for unstructured data." Unstructured data is highly structured, although using differing methods. Generally, consider unstructured data to be any data that is not in a database or data file, including documents or other media data. See Chapter 10 for more information on this topic.

Meta-data describes both structured and unstructured data. Meta-data for unstructured data exists in many formats, responding to a variety of different requirements. Examples of meta-data repositories describing unstructured data include content management applications, university websites, company intranet sites, data archives, electronic journals collections, and community resource lists. A common method for classifying meta-data in unstructured sources is to describe them as *descriptive meta-data, structural meta-data,* or *administrative meta-data.*

Examples of descriptive meta-data include:

- Catalog information.

- Thesauri keyword terms.

Examples of structural meta-data include:

- Dublin Core.

- Field structures.

- Format (Audio / visual, booklet).

- Thesauri keyword labels.

- XML schemas.

Examples of administrative meta-data include:

- Source(s).

- Integration / update schedule.

- Access rights.

- Page relationships (e.g. site navigational design).

Bibliographic meta-data, record-keeping meta-data, and preservation meta-data are all meta-data schemes applied to documents, but from different focuses. *Bibliographic meta-data* is the library card of the document. *Record-keeping meta-data* is concerned with validity and retention. *Preservation meta-data* is concerned with storage, archival condition, and conservation of material.

11.2.1.3 Sources of Meta-data

Meta-data is everywhere in every data management activity. The identification information on any data is meta-data that is of potential interest to some user group. Meta-data is integral to all IT systems and applications. Use these sources to meet technical meta-data requirements. Create business meta-data through user interaction, definition, and analysis of data. Add quality statements and other observations on the data to the meta-data repository or to source meta-data in IT systems through some support activity. Identify meta-data at an aggregate (such as subject area, system characteristic) or detailed (such as database column characteristic, code value) level. Proper management and navigation between related meta-data is an important usage requirement.

Primary sources of meta-data are numerous—virtually anything named in an organization. Secondary sources are other meta-data repositories, accessed using bridge software. Many data management tools create and use repositories for their own use. Their vendors also provide additional software to enable links to other tools and meta-data repositories, sometimes called bridge applications. However, this functionality mostly enables replication of meta-data between repositories, not true linkages.

11.2.2 Meta-data History 1990 - 2008

In the 1990s, some business managers finally began to recognize the value of meta-data repositories. Newer tools expanded the scope of the meta-data they addressed to include business meta-data. Some of the potential benefits of business meta-data identified in the industry during this period included:

- Providing the semantic layer between a company's systems, both operational and business intelligence, and their business users.

- Reducing training costs.

- Making strategic information, such as data warehousing, CRM, SCM, and so on, much more valuable as it aided analysts in making more profitable decisions.

- Creating actionable information.

- Limiting incorrect decisions.

The mid to late 1990's saw meta-data becoming more relevant to corporations who were struggling to understand their information resources. This was mostly due to the pending Y2K deadline, emerging data warehousing initiatives, and a growing focus around the World Wide Web. Efforts to try to standardize meta-data definition and exchange between applications in the enterprise were begun.

Examples of standardization include the CASE Definition Interchange Facility (CDIF) developed by the Electronics Industries Alliance (EIA) in 1995, and the Dublin Core Metadata Elements developed by the Dublin Core Metadata Initiative (DCMI) in 1995 in Dublin, Ohio. The first parts of ISO 11179 standard for Specification and Standardization of Data Elements were published in 1994 through 1999. The Object Management Group (OMG) developed the Common Warehouse Metadata Model (CWM) in 1998. Rival Microsoft supported the Metadata Coalitions' (MDC) Open Information Model in 1995. By 2000, the two standards merged into CWM. Many of the meta-data repositories began promising adoption of the CWM standard.

The early years of the 21st century saw the update of existing meta-data repositories for deployment on the web. Products also introduced some level of support for CWM. During this period, many data integration vendors began focusing on meta-data as an additional product offering. However, relatively few organizations actually purchased or developed meta-data repositories, let alone achieved the ideal of implementing an effective enterprise-wide Managed Meta-data Environment, as defined in *Universal Meta-data Models* for several reasons:

- The scarcity of people with real world skills.

- The difficulty of the effort.

- The less than stellar success of some of the initial efforts at some companies.

- Relative stagnation of the tool market after the initial burst of interest in the late 90's.

- The still less than universal understanding of the business benefits.

- The too heavy emphasis many in the industry placed on legacy applications and technical meta-data.

As the current decade proceeds, companies are beginning to focus more on the need for, and importance of, meta-data. Focus is also expanding on how to incorporate meta-data beyond the traditional structured sources and include unstructured sources. Some of the factors driving this renewed interest in meta-data management are:

- Recent entry into this market by larger vendors.

- The challenges that some companies are facing in trying to address regulatory requirements, such as Sarbanes-Oxley (U.S.), and privacy requirements with unsophisticated tools.

- The emergence of enterprise-wide initiatives like information governance, compliance, enterprise architecture, and automated software reuse.

- Improvements to the existing meta-data standards, such as the RFP release of the new OMG standard Information Management Metamodel (IMM) (aka CWM 2.0), which will replace CWM.

- A recognition at the highest levels, by some of the most sophisticated companies and organizations, that information is an asset (for some companies the most critical asset), that must be actively and effectively managed.

The history of meta-data management tools and products seems to be a metaphor for the lack of a methodological approach to enterprise information management that is so prevalent in organizations. The lack of standards and the proprietary nature of most managed meta-data solutions, cause many organizations to avoid focusing on meta-data, limiting their ability to develop a true enterprise information management environment. Increased attention given to information and its importance to an organization's operations and decision-making will drive meta-data management products and solutions to become more standardized. This driver gives more recognition to the need for a methodological approach to managing information and meta-data.

11.2.3 Meta-data Strategy

A meta-data strategy is a statement of direction in meta-data management by the enterprise. It is a statement of intent and acts as a reference framework for the development teams. Each user group has its own set of needs from a meta-data application. Working through a meta-data requirements development process provides a clear understanding of expectations and the reasons for the requirements.

Build a meta-data strategy from a set of defined components. The primary focus of the meta-data strategy is to gain an understanding of and consensus on the organization's key business drivers, issues, and information requirements for the enterprise meta-data program. The objective is to understand how well the current environment meets these requirements, both now and in the future.

The objectives of the strategy define the organization's future enterprise meta-data architecture. They also recommend the logical progression of phased implementation steps that will enable the organization to realize the future vision. Business objectives drive the meta-data strategy, which defines the technology and processes required to meet these objectives. The result of this process is a list of implementation phases driven by business objectives and prioritized by the business value they bring to the organization, combined with the level of effort required to deliver them. The phases include:

1. Meta-data Strategy Initiation and Planning: Prepares the meta-data strategy team and various participants for the upcoming effort to facilitate the process and improve results. It outlines the charter and organization of the meta-data strategy, including alignment with the data governance efforts, and establishes the communication of these objectives to all parties. Conduct the meta-data strategy development with the key stakeholders (business and IT) to determine / confirm the scope of the meta-data strategy and communicate the potential business value and objectives.

2. Conduct Key Stakeholder Interviews: The stakeholder interviews provide a foundation of knowledge for the meta-data strategy. Stakeholders would usually include both business and technical stakeholders.

3. Assess Existing Meta-data Sources and Information Architecture: Determines the relative degree of difficulty in solving the meta-data and systems issues identified in the interviews and documentation review. During this stage, conduct detailed interviews of key IT staff and review documentation of the system architectures, data models, etc.

4. Develop Future Meta-data Architecture: Refine and confirm the future vision, and develop the long-term target architecture for the managed meta-data environment in this stage. This phase includes all of the strategy components, such as organization structure, including data governance and stewardship alignment recommendations; managed meta-data architecture; meta-data delivery architecture; technical architecture; and security architecture.

5. Develop Phased MME Implementation Strategy and Plan: Review, validate, integrate, prioritize, and agree to the findings from the interviews and data analyses. Develop the meta-data strategy, incorporating a phased implementation approach that takes the organization from the current environment to the future managed meta-data environment.

11.2.4 Meta-data Management Activities

Effective meta-data management depends on data governance (see Chapter 3) to enable business data stewards to set meta-data management priorities, guide program investments, and oversee implementation efforts within the larger context of government and industry regulations.

11.2.4.1 Understand Meta-data Requirements

A meta-data management strategy must reflect an understanding of enterprise needs for meta-data. These requirements are gathered to confirm the need for a meta-data management environment, to set scope and priorities, educate and communicate, to guide tool evaluation and implementation, guide meta-data modeling, guide internal meta-data standards, guide provided services that rely on meta-data, and to estimate and justify staffing needs. Obtain these requirements from both business and technical users in the organization. Distill these requirements from an analysis of roles, responsibilities, challenges, and the information needs of selected individuals in the organization, not from asking for meta-data requirements.

11.2.4.1.1 Business User Requirements

Business users require improved understanding of the information from operational and analytical systems. Business users require a high level of confidence in the information obtained from corporate data warehouses, analytical applications, and operational systems. They need tailored access per their role to information delivery methods, such as reports, queries, push (scheduled), ad-hoc, OLAP, dashboards, with a high degree of quality documentation and context.

For example, the business term *royalty* is negotiated by the supplier and is factored into the amount paid by the retailer and, ultimately, by the consumer. These values represent data elements that are stored in both operational and analytical systems, and they appear in key financial reports, OLAP cubes, and data mining models. The definitions, usage, and algorithms need to be accessible when using royalty data. Any meta-data on royalty that is confidential or might be considered competitive information, requires controlled use by authorized user groups.

Business users must understand the intent and purpose of meta-data management. To provide meaningful business requirements, users must be educated about the differences between data and meta-data. It is a challenge to keep business users' focus limited to meta-data requirements versus other data requirements. Facilitated meetings (interviews and / or JAD sessions) with other business users with similar roles (e.g., the finance organization) are a very effective means of identifying requirements and maintaining focus on the meta-data and contextual needs of the user group.

Also critical to meta-data management success is the establishment of a data governance organization. The data governance organization is responsible for setting the direction and goals of the initiative and for making the best decisions regarding products, vendor support, technical architectures, and general strategy. Frequently, the Data Governance Council serves as the governing body for data and meta-data direction and requirements.

11.2.4.1.2 Technical User Requirements

High-level technical requirement topics include:

- Daily feed throughput: size and processing time.

- Existing meta-data.

- Sources – known and unknown.

- Targets.

- Transformations.

- Architecture flow – logical and physical.

- Non-standard meta-data requirements.

Technical users include Database Administrators (DBAs), Meta-data Specialists and Architects, IT support staff, and developers. Typically, these are the custodians of the corporate information assets. These users must understand the technical implementation of the data thoroughly, including both atomic-level details, data integration points, interfaces, and mappings. Additionally, they must understand the business context of the data at a sufficient level to provide the necessary support, including implementing the calculations or derived data rules and integration programs that the business users specify.

11.2.4.2 Define the Meta-data Architecture

Conceptually, all meta-data management solutions or environments consist of the following architectural layers: meta-data creation / sourcing, meta-data integration, one or more meta-data repositories, meta-data delivery, meta-data usage, and meta-data control / management.

A meta-data management system must be capable of extracting meta-data from many sources. Design the architecture to be capable of scanning the various meta-data sources and periodically updating the repository. The system must support the manual updates of meta-data, requests, searches, and lookups of meta-data by various user groups.

A managed meta-data environment should isolate the end user from the various and disparate meta-data sources. The architecture should provide a single access point for the meta-data repository. The access point must supply all related meta-data resources transparently to the user. Transparent means that the user can access the data without being aware of the differing environments of the data sources.

Design of the architecture of the above components depends on the specific requirements of the organization. Three technical architectural approaches to building a common meta-data repository mimic the approaches to designing data warehouses: centralized, distributed, and hybrid. These approaches all take into account implementation of the repository and how the update mechanisms operate. Each organization must choose the architecture that best suits their needs.

11.2.4.2.1 Centralized Meta-data Architecture

A centralized architecture consists of a single meta-data repository that contains copies of the live meta-data from the various sources. Organizations with limited IT resources, or those seeking to automate as much as possible, may choose to avoid this architecture option. Monitor processes and create a new set of roles in IT to support these new processes. Organizations with prioritization for a high degree of consistency and uniformity within the common meta-data repository can benefit from a centralized architecture.

Advantages of a centralized repository include:

- High availability, since it is independent of the source systems.

- Quick meta-data retrieval, since the repository and the query reside together.

- Resolved database structures that are not affected by the proprietary nature of third party or commercial systems.

- Extracted meta-data may be transformed or enhanced with additional meta-data that may not reside in the source system, improving quality.

Some limitations of the centralized approach include:

- Complex processes are necessary to ensure that changes in source meta-data quickly replicate into the repository.

- Maintenance of a centralized repository can be substantial.

- Extraction could require custom additional modules or middleware.

- Validation and maintenance of customized code can increase the demands on both internal IT staff and the software vendors.

11.2.4.2.2 Distributed Meta-data Architecture

A completely distributed architecture maintains a single access point. The meta-data retrieval engine responds to user requests by retrieving data from source systems in real time; there is no persistent repository. In this architecture, the meta-data management environment maintains the necessary source system catalogs and lookup information needed to process user queries and searches effectively. A common object request broker or similar middleware protocol accesses these source systems.

Advantages of distributed meta-data architecture include:

- Meta-data is always as current and valid as possible.

- Queries are distributed, possibly improving response / process time.

- Meta-data requests from proprietary systems are limited to query processing rather than requiring a detailed understanding of proprietary data structures, therefore minimizing the implementation and maintenance effort required.

- Development of automated meta-data query processing is likely simpler, requiring minimal manual intervention.

- Batch processing is reduced, with no meta-data replication or synchronization processes.

In addition, the following limitations exist for distributed architectures:

- No enhancement or standardization of meta-data is necessary between systems.

- Query capabilities are directly affected by the availability of the participating source systems.

- No ability to support user-defined or manually inserted meta-data entries since there is no repository in which to place these additions.

11.2.4.2.3 Hybrid Meta-data Architecture

A combined alternative is the hybrid architecture. Meta-data still moves directly from the source systems into a repository. However, the repository design only accounts for the user-added meta-data, the critical standardized items, and the additions from manual sources.

The architecture benefits from the near-real-time retrieval of meta-data from its source and enhanced meta-data to meet user needs most effectively, when needed. The hybrid approach lowers the effort for manual IT intervention and custom-coded access functionality to proprietary systems. The meta-data is as current and valid as possible at the time of use, based on user priorities and requirements. Hybrid architecture does not improve system availability.

The availability of the source systems is a limit, because the distributed nature of the back-end systems handles processing of queries. Additional overhead is required to link those initial results with meta-data augmentation in the central repository before presenting the result set to the end user.

Organizations that have rapidly changing meta-data, a need for meta-data consistency and uniformity, and a substantial growth in meta-data and meta-data sources, can benefit from a hybrid architecture. Organizations with more static meta-data and smaller meta-data growth profiles may not see the maximum potential from this architecture alternative.

Another advanced architectural approach is the *Bi-Directional Meta-data Architecture*, which allows meta-data to change in any part of the architecture (source, ETL, user interface) and then feed back from the repository into its original source. The repository is a broker for all updates. Commercial software packages are in development to include this internal feature, but the standards are still developing.

Various challenges are apparent in this approach. The design forces the meta-data repository to contain the latest version of the meta-data source and forces it to manage changes to the source, as well. Changes must be trapped systematically, then resolved.

Additional sets of program / process interfaces to tie the repository back to the meta-data source(s) must be built and maintained.

11.2.4.3 Meta-data Standards Types

Two major types of meta-data standards exist: industry or consensus standards, and international standards. Generally, the international standards are the framework from which the industry standards are developed and executed. A dynamic framework for meta-data standards, courtesy of Ashcomp.com is available on the DAMA International website, www.dama.org. The high-level framework in Figure 11.2 shows how standards are related and how they rely on each other for context and usage. The diagram also gives a glimpse into the complexity of meta-data standards and serves as a starting point for standards discovery and exploration.

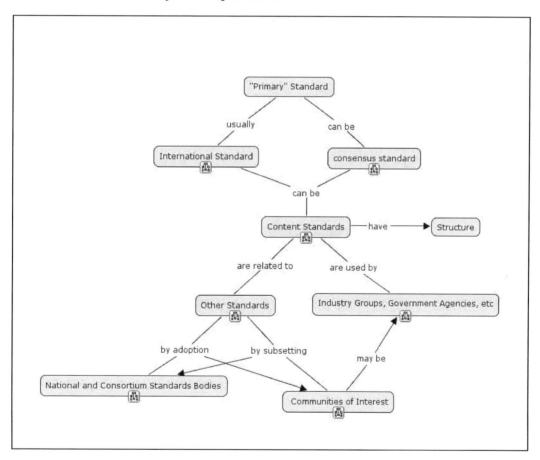

Figure 11.2 High Level Standards Framework

11.2.4.3.1 Industry / Consensus Meta-data Standards

Understanding the various standards for the implementation and management of meta-data in industry is essential to the appropriate selection and use of a meta-data solution for an enterprise. One area where meta-data standards are essential is in the exchange of data with operational trading partners. The establishment of the electronic data interchange (EDI) format represents an early meta-data format standard included in

EDI tools. Companies realize the value of information sharing with customers, suppliers, partners, and regulatory bodies. Therefore, the need for sharing common meta-data to support the optimal usage of shared information has spawned sector-based standards.

Vendors provide XML support for their data management products for data exchange. They use the same strategy to bind their tools together into suites of solutions. Technologies, including data integration, relational and multidimensional databases, requirements management, business intelligence reporting, data modeling, and business rules, offer import and export capabilities for data and meta-data using XML. While XML support is important, the lack of XML schema standards makes it a challenge to integrate the required meta-data across products. Vendors maintain their proprietary XML schemas and document type definitions (DTD). These are accessed though proprietary interfaces, so integration of these tools into a meta-data management environment still requires custom development.

Some noteworthy industry meta-data standards are:

1. OMG specifications: OMG is a nonprofit consortium of computer industry leaders dedicated to the definition, promotion, and maintenance of industry standards for interoperable enterprise applications. Companies, such as Oracle, IBM, Unisys, NCR, and others, support OMG. OMG is the creator of the CORBA middleware standard and has defined the other meta-data related standards:

   o Common Warehouse Meta-data (CWM): Specifies the interchange of meta-data among data warehousing, BI, KM, and portal technologies. CWM is based on UML and depends on it to represent object-oriented data constructs. The CWM has many components that are illustrated in Figure 11.3.

   o Information Management Metamodel (IMM): The next iteration of CWM, now under OMG direction and development, is expected to be published in 2009. It promises to bridge the gap between OO, data, and XML while incorporating CWM. It is aiming to provide traceability from requirement to class diagrams, including logical / physical models, and DDL and XML schemas.

   o MDC Open Information Model (OIM): A vendor-neutral and technology-independent specification of core meta-data types found in operational, data warehousing, and knowledge management environments.

   o The Extensible Markup Language (XML): The standard format for the interchange of meta-data using the MDC OIM.

   o Unified Modeling Language (UML) is the formal specification language for OIM

   o Structured Query Language (SQL): The query language for OIM.

- o Extensible Markup Interface (XMI): eases the interchange of meta-data between tools and repositories. XMI specification consists of rules for generating the XML document containing the actual meta-data and the XML DTD.

- o Ontology Definition Metamodel (ODM): A specification for formal representation, management, interoperability, and application of business semantics in support of OMG vision model driven architectures (MDA).

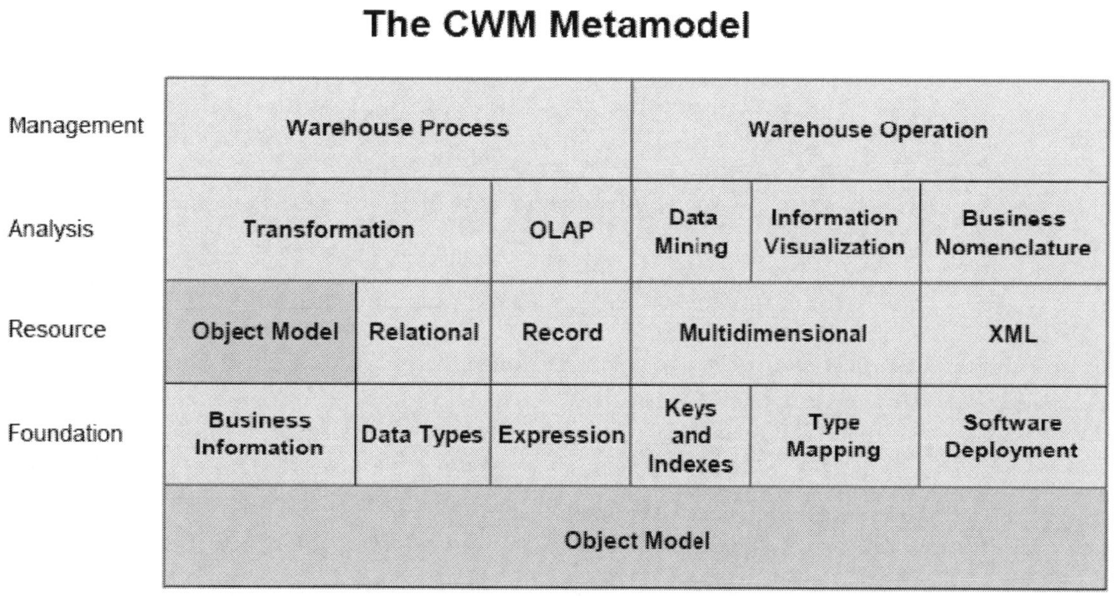

The CWM Metamodel

Management	Warehouse Process		Warehouse Operation		
Analysis	Transformation	OLAP	Data Mining	Information Visualization	Business Nomenclature
Resource	Object Model	Relational	Record	Multidimensional	XML
Foundation	Business Information	Data Types	Expression	Keys and Indexes	Type Mapping	Software Deployment
	Object Model				

Figure 11.3 CWM Metamodel [5]

2. World Wide Web Consortium (W3C) specifications: W3C has established the RDF (Relational Definition Framework) for describing and interchanging meta-data using XML. RDF focuses on capturing Web resources, plus other resources that are associated with a URL.

3. Dublin Core: Dublin Core Meta-data Initiative (DCMI) is a nonprofit forum for the consensus development of interoperable online meta-data standards for a variety of business and organizational purposes. It primarily focuses on the standardization of meta-data about online and Web resources, but is also useful for capturing meta-data from data warehouses and operational systems. The Dublin core builds on the Relational Description Framework (RDF).

4. Distributed Management Task Force (DTMF): Web-Based Enterprise Management (WBEM) is a set of management and Internet standard technologies developed to unify the management of distributed computing

---

[5] CWM Metamodel Reprinted with permission. Object Management Group, Inc. (C) OMG. 2009.

environments. It provides the ability for the industry to deliver a well-integrated set of standards-based management tools, facilitating the exchange of data across otherwise disparate technologies and platforms. One of the standards that comprise WBEM is the Common Information Model (CIM) standard–the data model for WBEM. CIM provides a common definition of management information for systems, networks, applications, and services, and allows for vendor extensions.

5. Meta-data standards for unstructured data are:

   o ISO 5964 - Guidelines for the establishment and development of multilingual thesauri.

   o ISO 2788 - Guidelines for the establishment and development of monolingual thesauri.

   o ANSI/NISO Z39.1 - American Standard Reference Data and Arrangement of Periodicals.

   o ISO 704 - Terminology work – Principles and methods.

6. Geospatial standards grew from a global framework called the Global Spatial Data Infrastructure, maintained by the U.S. Federal Geographic Data Committee (FGDC). The Content Standard for Digital Geospatial Metadata (CSDGM) is a U.S. initiative with oversight by the FGDC. The FGDC has a mandate that includes a data clearinghouse, spatial data standards, a National Digital Geospatial Data Framework, and partnerships for data acquisition.

7. The Australian New Zealand Land Information Council (ANZLIC) gave significant input to the ISO 9115:2003 Geographic Information: Metadata and ISO 19139:2003 Geographic Information: Metadata Implementation Specification.

8. In Europe, the geographic meta-data standards are centered on INSPIRE (Infrastructure for Spatial Information in Europe) committee and its work.

9. Industry sector meta-data standards are many and varied to meet particular problems or sector needs. Here are two sample sector standards:

   o Automotive industry: Modern-day Vehicle Identification Number systems are based on two related standards, ISO 3779 and ISO 3780 to define the 17 digit unique number. Each position of the 17 digits has a specific meaning and range of valid values. A variant European standard also exists.

   o Electric Utility industry: The Utility Common Information Model (CIM) is a standard data interchange structure for sharing power information including a message bus, and common data access specification between utilities in North America. The Electric Power Research Institute supports the Utility CIM.

Based on OMG's standards, Model Driven Architecture (MDA) separates business and application logic from platform technology. A platform-independent model of an application or system's business functionality and behavior can be realized on virtually any platform using UML and MOF (Meta-Object Facility) technology standards. In this architectural approach, there is a framework for application package vendors to adopt that permits flexibility in the package implementation, so that the product can meet varied market needs. The MDA has less direct impact on an organization's particular implementation of a package.

Organizations planning for meta-data solution deployment should adopt a set of established meta-data standards early in the planning cycle that are industry-based and sector-sensitive. Use the adopted standard in the evaluation and selection criteria for all new meta-data management technologies. Many leading vendors support multiple standards, and some can assist in customizing industry-based and / or sector-sensitive standards.

11.2.4.3.2 International Meta-data Standards

A key international meta-data standard is International Organization for Standardization ISO / IEC 11179 that describes the standardizing and registering of data elements to make data understandable and shareable.

The purpose of ISO / IEC 11179 is to give concrete guidance on the formulation and maintenance of discrete data element descriptions and semantic content (meta-data) that is useful in formulating data elements in a consistent, standard manner. It also provides guidance for establishing a data element registry.

The standard is important guidance for industry tool developers but is unlikely to be a concern for organizations who implement using commercial tools, since the tools should meet the standards. However, portions of each part of ISO / IEC 11179 may be useful to organizations that want to develop their own internal standards, since the standard contains significant details on each topic.

Relevant parts of the International Standard ISO / IEC 11179 are:

- Part 1: Framework for the Generation and Standardization of Data Elements.

- Part 3: Basic Attributes of Data Elements.

- Part 4: Rules and Guidelines for the Formulation of Data Definitions.

- Part 5: Naming and Identification Principles for Data Elements.

- Part 6: Registration of Data Elements.

11.2.4.4 Standard Meta-data Metrics

Controlling the effectiveness of the meta-data deployed environment requires measurements to assess user uptake, organizational commitment, and content coverage and quality. Metrics should be primarily quantitative rather than qualitative in nature.

Some suggested metrics on meta-data environments include:

- **Meta-data Repository Completeness:** Compare ideal coverage of the enterprise meta-data (all artifacts and all instances within scope) to actual coverage. Reference the Strategy for scope definitions.

- **Meta-data Documentation Quality:** Assess the quality of meta-data documentation through both automatic and manual methods. Automatic methods include performing collision logic on two sources, measuring how much they match, and the trend over time. Another metric would measure the percentage of attributes that have definitions, trending over time. Manual methods include random or complete survey, based on enterprise definitions of quality. Quality measures indicate the completeness, reliability, currency, etc., of the meta-data in the repository.

- **Master Data Service Data Compliance:** Shows the reuse of data in SOA solutions. Meta-data on the data services assists developers in deciding when new development could use an existing service.

- **Steward Representation / Coverage:** Organizational commitment to meta-data as assessed by the appointment of stewards, coverage across the enterprise for stewardship, and documentation of the roles in job descriptions.

- **Meta-data Usage / Reference:** User uptake on the meta-data repository usage can be measured by simple login measures. Reference to meta-data by users in business practice is a more difficult measure to track. Anecdotal measures on qualitative surveys may be required to capture this measure.

- **Meta-data Management Maturity:** Metrics developed to judge the meta-data maturity of the enterprise, based on the Capability Maturity Model (CMM) approach to maturity assessment.

- **Meta-data Repository Availability:** Uptime, processing time (batch and query).

11.2.4.5 Implement a Managed Meta-data Environment

Implement a managed meta-data environment in incremental steps in order to minimize risks to the organization and to facilitate acceptance.

Often, the first implementation is a pilot to prove concepts and learn about managing the meta-data environment. A pilot project has the added complexity of a requirements assessment, strategy development, technology evaluation selection, and initial implementation cycle that subsequent incremental projects will not have. Subsequent cycles will have roadmap planning, staff training and organization changes, and an incremental rollout plan with assessment and re-assessment steps, as necessary. Integration of meta-data projects into current IS / IT development methodology is necessary.

Topics for communication and planning for a meta-data management initiative include discussions and decisions on the strategies, plans, and deployment, including:

- Enterprise Information Management.

- Data Governance.

- Master data management.

- Data quality management.

- Data architecture.

- Content management.

- Business Intelligence / Data Warehousing.

- Enterprise Data Modeling.

- Access and distribution of the meta-data.

11.2.4.6 Create and Maintain Meta-data

Use of a software package means the data model of the repository does not need to be developed, but it is likely to need tailoring to meet the organization's needs. If a custom solution is developed, creating the data model for the repository is one of the first design steps after the meta-data strategy is complete and the business requirements are fully understood.

The meta-data creation and update facility provides for the periodic scanning and updating of the repository, in addition to the manual insertion and manipulation of meta-data by authorized users and programs. An audit process validates activities and reports exceptions.

If meta-data is a guide to the data in an organization, then its quality is critical. If data anomalies exist in the organization sources, and if these appear correctly in the meta-data, then the meta-data can guide the user through that complexity. Doubt about the quality of meta-data in the repository can lead to total rejection of the meta-data solution, and the end of any support for continued work on meta-data initiatives. Therefore, it is critical to deal with the quality of the meta-data, not only its movement and consolidation. Of course, quality is also subjective, so business involvement in establishing what constitutes quality in their view is essential.

Low-quality meta-data creates:

- Replicated dictionaries / repositories / meta-data storage.

- Inconsistent meta-data.

- Competing sources and versions of meta-data "truth".

- Doubt in the reliability of the meta-data solution systems.

High quality meta-data creates:

- Confident, cross-organizational development.

- Consistent understanding of the values of the data resources.

- Meta-data "knowledge" across the organization.

11.2.4.7 Integrate Meta-data

Integration processes gather and consolidate meta-data from across the enterprise, including meta-data from data acquired outside the enterprise. Integrate extracted meta-data from a source meta-data store with other relevant business and technical meta-data into the meta-data storage facility. Meta-data can be extracted using adaptors / scanners, bridge applications, or by directly accessing the meta-data in a source data store. Adaptors are available with many third party vendor software tools, as well as from the meta-data integration tool selected. In some cases, adaptors must be developed using the tool API's.

Challenges arise in integration that will require some form of appeal through the governance process for resolution. Integrating internal data sets, external data such as Dow Jones or government statistics organizations, and data sourced from non-electronic form-such as white papers, articles in magazines, or reports can raise numerous questions on quality and semantics.

Accomplish repository scanning in two distinct manners.

1. Proprietary interface: In a single-step scan and load process, a scanner collects the meta-data from a source system, then directly calls the format-specific loader component to load the meta-data into the repository. In this process, there is no format-specific file output and the collection and loading of meta-data occurs in a single step.

2. Semi-Proprietary interface: In a two-step process, a scanner collects the meta-data from a source system and outputs it into a format-specific data file. The scanner only produces a data file that the receiving repository needs to be able to read and load appropriately. The interface is a more open architecture, as the file is readable by many methods.

A scanning process produces and leverages several types of files during the process.

1. Control file: Containing the source structure of the data model.

2. Reuse file: Containing the rules for managing reuse of process loads.

3. Log files: Produced during each phase of the process, one for each scan / extract and one for each load cycle.

4. Temporary and backup files: Use during the process or for traceability.

Use a non-persistent meta-data staging area to store temporary and backup files. The staging area supports rollback and recovery processes, and provides an interim audit trail to assist repository managers when investigating meta-data source or quality issues. The staging area may take the form of a directory of files or a database. Truncate staging area database tables prior to a new meta-data feed that utilizes the staging table, or timestamp versions of the same storage format.

ETL tools used for data warehousing and Business Intelligence applications are often used effectively in meta-data integration processes.

11.2.4.8 Manage Meta-data Repositories

Implement a number of control activities in order to manage the meta-data environment. Control of repositories is control of meta-data movement and repository updates performed by the meta-data specialist. These activities are administrative in nature and involve monitoring and responding to reports, warnings, job logs, and resolving various issues in the implemented repository environment. Many of the control activities are standard for data operations, and interface maintenance.

Control activities include:

- Backup, recovery, archive, purging.

- Configuration modifications.

- Education and training of users and data stewards.

- Job scheduling / monitoring.

- Load statistic analysis.

- Management metrics generation and analysis.

- Performance tuning.

- Quality assurance, quality control.

- Query statistics analysis.

- Query / report generation.

- Repository administration.

- Security management.

- Source mapping / movement.

- Training on the control activities and query / reporting.

- User interface management.

- Versioning.

11.2.4.8.1 Meta-data Repositories

Meta-data repository refers to the physical tables in which the meta-data are stored. Implement meta-data repositories using an open relational database platform. This allows development and implementation of various controls and interfaces that may not be anticipated at the start of a repository development project.

The repository contents should be generic in design, not merely reflecting the source system database designs. Design contents in alignment with the enterprise subject area experts, and based on a comprehensive meta-data model. The meta-data should be as integrated as possible—this will be one of the most direct valued-added elements of the repository. It should house current, planned, and historical versions of the meta-data.

For example, the business meta-data definition for *Customer* could be "Anyone that has purchased a product from our company within one of our stores or through our catalog". A year later, the company adds a new distribution channel. The company constructs a Web site to allow customers to order products. At that point, the business meta-data definition for customer changes to "Anyone that has purchased a product from our company within one of our stores, through our mail order catalog or through the web."

11.2.4.8.2 Directories, Glossaries and Other Meta-data Stores

A *Directory* is a type of meta-data store that limits the meta-data to the location or source of data in the enterprise. Tag sources as system of record (it may be useful to use symbols such as "gold") or other level of quality. Indicate multiple sources in the directory. A directory of meta-data is particularly useful to developers and data super users, such as data stewardship teams and data analysts.

A *Glossary* typically provides guidance for use of terms, and a thesaurus can direct the user through structural choices involving three kinds of relationships: equivalence, hierarchy, and association. These relationships can be specified against both intra- and inter-glossary source terms. The terms can link to additional information stored in a meta-data repository, synergistically enhancing usefulness.

A multi-source glossary should be capable of the following:

- Storing terms and definitions from many sources.

- Representing relationships of sets of terms within any single source.

- Establishing a structure flexible enough to accommodate input from varying sources and relating new terms to existing ones.

- Linking to the full set of meta-data attributes recorded in the meta-data repository.

Other Meta-data stores include specialized lists such as source lists or interfaces, code sets, lexicons, spatial and temporal schema, spatial reference, and distribution of digital geographic data sets, repositories of repositories, and business rules.

11.2.4.9 Distribute and Deliver Meta-data

The meta-data delivery layer is responsible for the delivery of the meta-data from the repository to the end users and to any applications or tools that require meta-data feeds to them.

Some delivery mechanisms:

- Meta-data intranet websites for browse, search, query, reporting, and analysis.

- Reports, glossaries, other documents, and websites.

- Data warehouses, data marts, and BI tools.

- Modeling and software development tools.

- Messaging and transactions.

- Applications.

- External organization interface solutions (e.g. supply chain solutions).

The meta-data solution often links to a Business Intelligence solution, so that both the universe and currency of meta-data in the solution synchronizes with the BI contents. The link provides a means of integration into the delivery of the BI to the end user. Similarly, some CRM or other ERP solutions may require meta-data integration at the application delivery layer.

Occasionally, meta-data is exchanged with external organizations through flat files; however, it is more common for companies to use XML as transportation syntax through proprietary solutions.

11.2.4.10 Query, Report and Analyze Meta-data

Meta-data guides how we use data assets. We use meta-data in business intelligence (reporting and analysis), business decisions (operational, tactical, strategic), and in business semantics (what we say, what we mean - 'business lingo').

Meta-data guides how we manage data assets. Data governance processes use meta-data to control and govern. Information system implementation and delivery uses meta-data to add, change, delete, and access data. Data integration (operational systems, DW / BI systems) refers to data by its tags or meta-data to achieve that integration. Meta-data controls and audits data, process, and system integration. Database administration is an activity that controls and maintains data through its tags or meta-data layer, as does system and data security management. Some quality improvement activities are initiated through inspection of meta-data and its relationship to associated data.

A meta-data repository must have a front-end application that supports the search-and-retrieval functionality required for all this guidance and management of data assets. The interface provided to business users may have a different set of functional requirements than that for technical users and developers. Some reports facilitate future development such as change impact analysis, or trouble shoot varying definitions for data warehouse and business intelligence projects, such as data lineage reports.

11.3 Summary

The guiding principles for implementing meta-data management into an organization, a summary table of the roles for each meta-data management activity, and organization and cultural issues that may arise during meta-data management are summarized below.

11.3.1 Guiding Principles

The guiding principles for establishing a meta-data management function are listed below.

1. Establish and maintain a meta-data strategy and appropriate policies, especially clear goals and objectives for meta-data management and usage.

2. Secure sustained commitment, funding, and vocal support from senior management concerning meta-data management for the enterprise.

3. Take an enterprise perspective to ensure future extensibility, but implement through iterative and incremental delivery.

4. Develop a meta-data strategy before evaluating, purchasing, and installing meta-data management products.

5. Create or adopt meta-data standards to ensure interoperability of meta-data across the enterprise.

6. Ensure effective meta-data acquisition for both internal and external meta-data.

7. Maximize user access, since a solution that is not accessed or is under-accessed will not show business value.

8. Understand and communicate the *necessity* of meta-data and the purpose of each type of meta-data; socialization of the value of meta-data will encourage business usage.

9. Measure content and usage.

10. Leverage XML, messaging, and Web services.

11. Establish and maintain enterprise-wide business involvement in data stewardship, assigning accountability for meta-data.

12. Define and monitor procedures and processes to ensure correct policy implementation.

13. Include a focus on roles, staffing, standards, procedures, training, and metrics.

14. Provide dedicated meta-data experts to the project and beyond.

15. Certify meta-data quality.

11.3.2 Process Summary

The process summary for the meta-data management function is shown in Table 11.1. The deliverables, responsible roles, approving roles, and contributing roles are shown for each activity in the meta-data management function. The Table is also shown in Appendix A9.

Activities	Deliverables	Responsible Roles	Approving Roles	Contributing Roles
9.1 Understand Meta-data Requirements (P)	Meta-data requirements	Meta-data Specialists Data Stewards Data Architects and Modelers Database Administrators	Enterprise Data Architect, DM Leader, Data Stewardship Committee	Other IT Professionals Other DM Professionals
9.2 Define the Meta-data Architecture (P)	Meta-data architecture	Meta-data Architects, Data Integration Architects	Enterprise Data Architect, DM Leader, CIO Data Stewardship Committee Database Administrators	Meta-data Specialists, Other Data Mgmt. Professionals Other IT Professionals
9.3 Develop and Maintain Meta-data Standards (P)	Meta-data standards	Meta-data and Data Architects Data Stewards Database Administrators	Enterprise Data Architect, DM Leader, Data Stewardship Committee	Other IT Professionals Other DM Professionals

Activities	Deliverables	Responsible Roles	Approving Roles	Contributing Roles
9.4 Implement a Managed Meta-data Environment (D)	Meta-data metrics	Database Administrators	Enterprise Data Architect, DM Leader, Data Stewardship Committee	Other IT Professionals
9.5 Create and Maintain Meta-data (O)	Updated: • Data Modeling Tools • Database Management Systems • Data Integration Tools • Business Intelligence Tools • System Management Tools • Object Modeling Tools • Process Modeling Tools • Report Generating Tools • Data Quality Tools • Data Development and Administration Tools Reference and Master Data Management Tools	Meta-data Specialists Data Stewards Data Architects and Modelers Database Administrators	Enterprise Data Architect, DM Leader, Data Stewardship Committee	Other IT Professionals

Activities	Deliverables	Responsible Roles	Approving Roles	Contributing Roles
9.6 Integrate Meta-data (C)	Integrated Meta-data repositories	Integration Data Architects Meta-data Specialists Data Stewards Data Architects and Modelers Database Administrators	Enterprise Data Architect, DM Leader, Data Stewardship Committee	Other IT Professionals
9.7 Manage Meta-data Repositories (C)	Managed Meta-data repositories Administration Principles, Practices, Tactics	Meta-data Specialists Data Stewards Data Architects and Modelers Database Administrators	Enterprise Data Architect, DM Leader, Data Stewardship Committee	Other IT Professionals
9.8 Distribute and Deliver Meta-data (O)	Distribution of Meta-data Meta-data Models and Architecture	Database Administrators	Enterprise Data Architect, DM Leader, Data Stewardship Committee	Meta-data Architects
9.9 Query, Report and Analyze Meta-data (O)	Quality Meta-data Meta-data Management Operational Analysis Meta-data Analysis Data Lineage Change Impact Analysis	Data Analysts, Meta-data Analysts	Enterprise Data Architect, DM Leader, Data Stewardship Committee	Business Intelligence Specialists, Data Integration Specialists, Database Administrators, Other Data Mgmt. Professionals

Table 11.1 Meta-data Management Process Summary

11.3.3 Organizational and Cultural Issues

Many organizational and cultural issues exist for a meta-data management initiative. Organizational readiness is a major concern, as are methods for governance and control.

Q1: Meta-data Management is a low priority in many organizations. What are the core arguments or value-add statements for Meta-data management?

A1: An essential set of meta-data needs coordination in an organization. It can be structures of employee identification data, insurance policy numbers, vehicle identification numbers, or product specifications, which if changed, would require major overhauls of many enterprise systems. Look for that good example where control will reap immediate quality benefits for data in the company. Build the argument from concrete business-relevant examples.

Q2: How does Meta-data Management relate to Data Governance? Don't we govern through meta-data rules?

A2: Yes! Meta-data is governed much as data is governed, through principles, policies and effective and active stewardship. Read up on Data Governance in Chapter 3.

11.4 Recommended Reading

The references listed below provide additional reading that support the material presented in Chapter 11. These recommended readings are also included in the Bibliography at the end of the Guide.

11.4.1 General Reading

Brathwaite, Ken S. Analysis, Design, and Implementation of Data Dictionaries. McGraw-Hill Inc., 1988. ISBN 0-07-007248-5. 214 pages.

Collier, Ken. Executive Report, Business Intelligence Advisory Service, *Finding the Value in Metadata Management* (Vol. 4, No. 1), 2004. Available only to Cutter Consortium Clients, http://www.cutter.com/bia/fulltext/reports/2004/01/index.html.

Hay, David C. Data Model Patterns: A Metadata Map. Morgan Kaufmann, 2006. ISBN 0-120-88798-3. 432 pages.

Hillmann, Diane I. and Elaine L. Westbrooks, editors. Metadata in Practice. American Library Association, 2004. ISBN 0-838-90882-9. 285 pages.

Inmon, William H., Bonnie O'Neil and Lowell Fryman. Business Metadata: Capturing Enterprise Knowledge. 2008. Morgan Kaufmann ISBN 978-0-12-373726-7. 314 pages.

Marco, David, Building and Managing the Meta Data Repository: A Full Life-Cycle Guide. John Wiley & Sons, 2000. ISBN 0-471-35523-2. 416 pages.

Marco, David and Michael Jennings. Universal Meta Data Models. John Wiley & Sons, 2004. ISBN 0-471-08177-9. 478 pages.

Poole, John, Dan Change, Douglas Tolbert and David Mellor. Common Warehouse Metamodel: An Introduction to the Standard for Data Warehouse Integration. John Wiley & Sons, 2001. ISBN 0-471-20052-2. 208 pages.

Poole, John, Dan Change, Douglas Tolbert and David Mellor. Common Warehouse Metamodel Developer's Guide. John Wiley & Sons, 2003. ISBN 0-471-20243-6. 704 pages.

Ross, Ronald. Data Dictionaries And Data Administration: Concepts and Practices for Data Resource Management. New York: AMACOM Books, 1981. ISN 0-814-45596-4. 454 pages.

Tannenbaum, Adrienne. Implementing a Corporate Repository, John Wiley & Sons, 1994. ISBN 0-471-58537-8. 441 pages.

Tannenbaum, Adrienne. Metadata Solutions: Using Metamodels, Repositories, XML, And Enterprise Portals to Generate Information on Demand. Addison Wesley, 2001. ISBN 0-201-71976-2. 528 pages.

Wertz, Charles J. The Data Dictionary: Concepts and Uses, 2nd edition. John Wiley & Sons, 1993. ISBN 0-471-60308-2. 390 pages.

11.4.2 Meta-data in Library Science

Baca, Murtha, editor. Introduction to Metadata: Pathways to Digital Information. Getty Information Institute, 2000. ISBN 0-892-36533-1. 48 pages.

Hillmann, Diane I., and Elaine L. Westbrooks. Metadata in Practice. American Library Association, 2004. ISBN 0-838-90882-9. 285 pages.

Karpuk, Deborah. METADATA: From Resource Discovery to Knowledge Management. Libraries Unlimited, 2007. ISBN 1-591-58070-6. 275 pages.

Liu, Jia. Metadata and Its Applications in the Digital Library. Libraries Unlimited, 2007. ISBN 1-291-58306-6. 250 pages.

11.4.3 Geospatial Meta-data Standards

http://www.fgdc.gov/metadata/geospatial-metadata-standards.

11.4.4 ISO Meta-data Standards

ISO Standards Handbook 10, Data Processing—Vocabulary, 1982.

ISO 704:1987, Principles and methods of terminology.

ISO 1087, Terminology—Vocabulary.

ISO 2382-4:1987, Information processing systems—Vocabulary part 4.

ISO/IEC 10241:1992, International Terminology Standards—Preparation and layout.

FCD 11179-2, Information technology—Specification and standardization of data elements - Part 2: Classification for data elements.

ISO/IEC 11179-3:1994, Information technology—Specification and standardization of data elements - Part 3: Basic attributes of data elements.

ISO/IEC 11179-4:1995, Information technology—Specification and standardization of data elements - Part 4: Rules and guidelines for the formulation of data definitions.

ISO/IEC 11179-5:1995, Information technology—Specification and standardization of data elements - Part 5: Naming and identification principles for data elements.

ISO/IEC 11179-6:1997, Information technology—Specification and standardization of data elements - Part 6: Registration of data elements.

12 Data Quality Management

Data Quality Management (DQM) is the tenth Data Management Function in the data management framework shown in Figures 1.3 and 1.4. It is the ninth data management function that interacts with, and is influenced by, the Data Governance function. Chapter 12 defines the data quality management function and explains the concepts and activities involved in DQM.

12.1 Introduction

Data Quality Management (DQM) is a critical support process in organizational change management. Changing business focus, corporate business integration strategies, and mergers, acquisitions, and partnering can mandate that the IT function blend data sources, create gold data copies, retrospectively populate data, or integrate data. The goals of interoperability with legacy or B2B systems need the support of a DQM program.

Data quality is synonymous with information quality, since poor data quality results in inaccurate information and poor business performance. Data cleansing may result in short-term and costly improvements that do not address the root causes of data defects. A more rigorous data quality program is necessary to provide an economic solution to improved data quality and integrity.

In a program approach, these issues involve more than just correcting data. Instead, they involve managing the lifecycle for data creation, transformation, and transmission to ensure that the resulting information meets the needs of all the data consumers within the organization.

Institutionalizing processes for data quality oversight, management, and improvement hinges on identifying the business needs for quality data and determining the best ways to measure, monitor, control, and report on the quality of data. After identifying issues in the data processing streams, notify the appropriate data stewards to take corrective action that addresses the acute issue, while simultaneously enabling elimination of its root cause.

DQM is also a continuous process for defining the parameters for specifying acceptable levels of data quality to meet business needs, and for ensuring that data quality meets these levels. DQM involves analyzing the quality of data, identifying data anomalies, and defining business requirements and corresponding business rules for asserting the required data quality. DQM involves instituting inspection and control processes to monitor conformance with defined data quality rules, as well as instituting data parsing, standardization, cleansing, and consolidation, when necessary. Lastly, DQM incorporates issues tracking as a way of monitoring compliance with defined data quality Service Level Agreements.

The context for data quality management is shown in Figure 12.1.

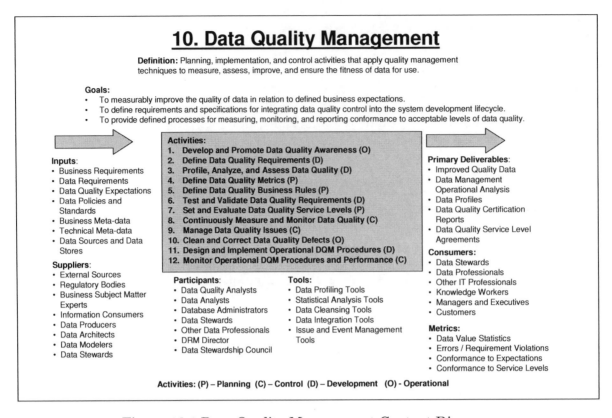

Figure 12.1 Data Quality Management Context Diagram

12.2 Concepts and Activities

Data quality expectations provide the inputs necessary to define the data quality framework. The framework includes defining the requirements, inspection policies, measures, and monitors that reflect changes in data quality and performance. These requirements reflect three aspects of business data expectations: a manner to record the expectation in business rules, a way to measure the quality of data within that dimension, and an acceptability threshold.

12.2.1 Data Quality Management Approach

The general approach to DQM, shown in Figure 12.2, is a version of the Deming cycle. Deming, one of the seminal writers in quality management, proposes a problem-solving model[6] known as 'plan-do-study-act' or 'plan-do-check-act' that is useful for data quality management. When applied to data quality within the constraints of defined data quality SLAs, it involves:

- Planning for the assessment of the current state and identification of key metrics for measuring data quality.

- Deploying processes for measuring and improving the quality of data.

---

[6] Deming, W. Edwards.

- Monitoring and measuring the levels in relation to the defined business expectations.

- Acting to resolve any identified issues to improve data quality and better meet business expectations.

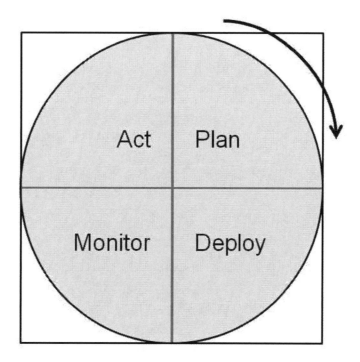

Figure 12.2 The Data Quality Management Cycle.

The DQM cycle begins by identifying the data issues that are critical to the achievement of business objectives, defining business requirements for data quality, identifying key data quality dimensions, and defining the business rules critical to ensuring high quality data.

In the plan stage, the data quality team assesses the scope of known issues, which involve determining the cost and impact of the issues and evaluating alternatives for addressing them.

In the deploy stage, profile the data and institute inspections and monitors to identify data issues when they occur. During this stage, the data quality team can arrange for fixing flawed processes that are the root cause of data errors, or as a last resort, correcting errors downstream. When it is not possible to correct errors at their source, correct errors at the earliest point in the data flow.

The monitor stage is for actively monitoring the quality of data as measured against the defined business rules. As long as data quality meets defined thresholds for acceptability, the processes are in control and the level of data quality meets the business requirements. However, if the data quality falls below acceptability thresholds, notify data stewards so they can take action during the next stage.

The act stage is for taking action to address and resolve emerging data quality issues.

New cycles begin as new data sets come under investigation, or as new data quality requirements are identified for existing data sets.

12.2.2 Develop and Promote Data Quality Awareness

Promoting data quality awareness means more than ensuring that the right people in the organization are aware of the existence of data quality issues. Promoting data quality awareness is essential to ensure buy-in of necessary stakeholders in the organization, thereby greatly increasing the chance of success of any DQM program.

Awareness includes relating material impacts to data issues, ensuring systematic approaches to regulators and oversight of the quality of organizational data, and socializing the concept that data quality problems cannot be solely addressed by technology solutions. As an initial step, some level of training on the core concepts of data quality may be necessary.

The next step includes establishing a data governance framework for data quality. Data governance is a collection of processes and procedures for assigning responsibility and accountability for all facets of data management, covered in detail in Chapter 3. DQM data governance tasks include:

- Engaging business partners who will work with the data quality team and champion the DQM program.

- Identifying data ownership roles and responsibilities, including data governance board members and data stewards.

- Assigning accountability and responsibility for critical data elements and DQM.

- Identifying key data quality areas to address and directives to the organization around these key areas.

- Synchronizing data elements used across the lines of business and providing clear, unambiguous definitions, use of value domains, and data quality rules.

- Continuously reporting on the measured levels of data quality.

- Introducing the concepts of data requirements analysis as part of the overall system development life cycle.

- Tying high quality data to individual performance objectives.

Ultimately, a Data Quality Oversight Board can be created that has a reporting hierarchy associated with the different data governance roles. Data stewards who align with business clients, lines of business, and even specific applications, will continue to promote awareness of data quality while monitoring their assigned data assets. The Data Quality Oversight Board is accountable for the policies and procedures for oversight of the data quality community. The guidance provided includes:

- Setting priorities for data quality.

- Developing and maintaining standards for data quality.

- Reporting relevant measurements of enterprise-wide data quality.

- Providing guidance that facilitates staff involvement.

- Establishing communications mechanisms for knowledge sharing.

- Developing and applying certification and compliance policies.

- Monitoring and reporting on performance.

- Identifying opportunities for improvements and building consensus for approval.

- Resolving variations and conflicts.

The constituent participants work together to define and popularize a data quality strategy and framework; develop, formalize, and approve information policies, data quality standards and protocols; and certify line-of-business conformance to the desired level of business user expectations.

12.2.3 Define Data Quality Requirements

Quality of the data must be understood within the context of 'fitness for use'. Most applications are dependent on the use of data that meets specific needs associated with the successful completion of a business process. Those business processes implement business policies imposed both through external means, such as regulatory compliance, observance of industry standards, or complying with data exchange formats, and through internal means, such as internal rules guiding marketing, sales, commissions, logistics, and so on. Data quality requirements are often hidden within defined business policies. Incremental detailed review and iterative refinement of the business policies helps to identify those information requirements which, in turn, become data quality rules.

Measuring conformance to 'fitness for use' requirements enables the reporting of meaningful metrics associated with well-defined data quality dimensions. The incremental detailed review steps include:

1. Identifying key data components associated with business policies.

2. Determining how identified data assertions affect the business.

3. Evaluating how data errors are categorized within a set of data quality dimensions.

4. Specifying the business rules that measure the occurrence of data errors.

5. Providing a means for implementing measurement processes that assess conformance to those business rules.

Segment the business rules according to the dimensions of data quality that characterize the measurement of high-level indicators. Include details on the level of granularity of the measurement, such as data value, data element, data record, and data table, that are required for proper implementation. Dimensions of data quality include:

- Accuracy: Data accuracy refers to the degree that data correctly represents the "real-life" entities they model. In many cases, measure accuracy by how the values agree with an identified reference source of correct information, such as comparing values against a database of record or a similar corroborative set of data values from another table, checking against dynamically computed values, or perhaps applying a manual process to check value accuracy.

- Completeness: One expectation of completeness indicates that certain attributes always have assigned values in a data set. Another expectation of completeness is that all appropriate rows in a dataset are present. Assign completeness rules to a data set in varying levels of constraint–mandatory attributes that require a value, data elements with conditionally optional values, and inapplicable attribute values. See completeness as also encompassing usability and appropriateness of data values.

- Consistency: Consistency refers to ensuring that data values in one data set are consistent with values in another data set. The concept of consistency is relatively broad; it can include an expectation that two data values drawn from separate data sets must not conflict with each other, or define consistency with a set of predefined constraints. Encapsulate more formal consistency constraints as a set of rules that specify consistency relationships between values of attributes, either across a record or message, or along all values of a single attribute. However, care must be taken not to confuse consistency with accuracy or correctness. Consistency may be defined between one set of attribute values and another attribute set within the same record (record-level consistency), between one set of attribute values and another attribute set in different records (cross-record consistency), or between one set of attribute values and the same attribute set within the same record at different points in time (temporal consistency).

- Currency: Data currency refers to the degree to which information is current with the world that it models. Data currency measures how "fresh" the data is, as well as correctness in the face of possible time-related changes. Measure data currency as a function of the expected frequency rate at which different data elements refresh, as well as verify that the data is up to date. Data currency rules define the "lifetime" of a data value before it expires or needs updating.

- Precision: Precision refers to the level of detail of the data element. Numeric data may need accuracy to several significant digits. For example, rounding and truncating may introduce errors where exact precision is necessary.

- Privacy: Privacy refers to the need for access control and usage monitoring. Some data elements require limits of usage or access.

- Reasonableness: Use reasonableness to consider consistency expectations relevant within specific operational contexts. For example, one might expect that the number of transactions each day does not exceed 105% of the running average number of transactions for the previous 30 days.

- Referential Integrity: Referential integrity is the condition that exists when all intended references from data in one column of a table to data in another column of the same or different table is valid. Referential integrity expectations include specifying that when a unique identifier appears as a foreign key, the record to which that key refers actually exists. Referential integrity rules also manifest as constraints against duplication, to ensure that each entity occurs once, and only once.

- Timeliness: Timeliness refers to the time expectation for accessibility and availability of information. As an example, measure one aspect of timeliness as the time between when information is expected and when it is readily available for use.

- Uniqueness: Essentially, uniqueness states that no entity exists more than once within the data set. Asserting uniqueness of the entities within a data set implies that no entity exists more than once within the data set and that a key value relates to each unique entity, and only that specific entity, within the data set. Many organizations prefer a level of controlled redundancy in their data as a more achievable target.

- Validity: Validity refers to whether data instances are stored, exchanged, or presented in a format that is consistent with the domain of values, as well as consistent with other similar attribute values. Validity ensures that data values conform to numerous attributes associated with the data element: its data type, precision, format patterns, use of a predefined enumeration of values, domain ranges, underlying storage formats, and so on. Validating to determine possible values is not the same as verifying to determine accurate values.

12.2.4 Profile, Analyze and Assess Data Quality

Prior to defining data quality metrics, it is crucial to perform an assessment of the data using two different approaches, bottom-up and top-down.

The bottom-up assessment of existing data quality issues involves inspection and evaluation of the data sets themselves. Direct data analysis will reveal potential data anomalies that should be brought to the attention of subject matter experts for validation and analysis. Bottom-up approaches highlight potential issues based on the results of automated processes, such as frequency analysis, duplicate analysis, cross-data set dependency, 'orphan child' data rows, and redundancy analysis.

However, potential anomalies, and even true data flaws may not be relevant within the business context unless vetted with the constituency of data consumers. The top-down approach to data quality assessment involves engaging business users to document their business processes and the corresponding critical data dependencies. The top-down approach involves understanding how their processes consume data, and which data elements are critical to the success of the business application. By reviewing the types of reported, documented, and diagnosed data flaws, the data quality analyst can assess the kinds of business impacts that are associated with data issues.

The steps of the analysis process are:

- Identify a data set for review.

- Catalog the business uses of that data set.

- Subject the data set to empirical analysis using data profiling tools and techniques.

- List all potential anomalies.

- For each anomaly:
  - o Review the anomaly with a subject matter expert to determine if it represents a true data flaw.
  - o Evaluate potential business impacts.

- Prioritize criticality of important anomalies in preparation for defining data quality metrics.

In essence, the process uses statistical analysis of many aspects of data sets to evaluate:

- The percentage of the records populated.

- The number of data values populating each data attribute.

- Frequently occurring values.

- Potential outliers.

- Relationships between columns within the same table.

- Relationships across tables.

Use these statistics to identify any obvious data issues that may have high impact and that are suitable for continuous monitoring as part of ongoing data quality inspection and control. Interestingly, important business intelligence may be uncovered just in this analysis step. For instance, an event in the data that occurs rarely (an outlier) may point to an important business fact, such as a rare equipment failure may be linked to a suspected underachieving supplier.

12.2.5 Define Data Quality Metrics

The metrics development step does not occur at the end of the lifecycle in order to maintain performance over time for that function, but for DQM, it occurs as part of the strategy / design / plan step in order to implement the function in an organization.

Poor data quality affects the achievement of business objectives. The data quality analyst must seek out and use indicators of data quality performance to report the relationship between flawed data and missed business objectives. Seeking these indicators introduces a challenge of devising an approach for identifying and managing "business-relevant" information quality metrics. View the approach to measuring data quality similarly to monitoring any type of business performance activity; and data quality metrics should exhibit the characteristics of reasonable metrics defined in the context of the types of data quality dimensions as discussed in a previous section. These characteristics include, but are not limited to:

- Measurability: A data quality metric must be measurable, and should be quantifiable within a discrete range. Note that while many things are measurable, not all translate into useful metrics, implying the need for business relevance.

- Business Relevance: The value of the metric is limited if it cannot be related to some aspect of business operations or performance. Therefore, every data quality metric should demonstrate how meeting its acceptability threshold correlates with business expectations.

- Acceptability: The data quality dimensions frame the business requirements for data quality, and quantifying quality measurements along the identified dimension provides hard evidence of data quality levels. Base the determination of whether the quality of data meets business expectations on specified acceptability thresholds. If the score is equal to or exceeds the acceptability threshold, the quality of the data meets business expectations. If the score is below the acceptability threshold, notify the appropriate data steward and take some action.

- Accountability / Stewardship: Associated with defined roles indicating notification of the appropriate individuals when the measurement for the metric indicates that the quality does not meet expectations. The business process owner is essentially the one who is accountable, while a data steward may be tasked with taking appropriate corrective action.

- Controllability: Any measurable characteristic of information that is suitable as a metric should reflect some controllable aspect of the business. In other words, the assessment of the data quality metric's value within an undesirable range should trigger some action to improve the data being measured.

- Trackability: Quantifiable metrics enable an organization to measure data quality improvement over time. Tracking helps data stewards monitor activities within the scope of data quality SLAs, and demonstrates the effectiveness of improvement activities. Once an information process is stable, tracking enables instituting statistical control processes to ensure predictability with respect to continuous data quality.

The process for defining data quality metrics is summarized as:

1. Select one of the identified critical business impacts.

2. Evaluate the dependent data elements, and data create and update processes associated with that business impact.

3. For each data element, list any associated data requirements.

4. For each data expectation, specify the associated dimension of data quality and one or more business rules to use to determine conformance of the data to expectations.

5. For each selected business rule, describe the process for measuring conformance (explained in the next section).

6. For each business rule, specify an acceptability threshold (explained in the next section).

The result is a set of measurement processes that provide raw data quality scores that can roll up to quantify conformance to data quality expectations. Measurements that do not meet the specified acceptability thresholds indicate nonconformance, showing that some data remediation is necessary.

12.2.6 Define Data Quality Business Rules

The process of instituting the measurement of conformance to specific business rules requires definition. Monitoring conformance to these business rules requires:

- Segregating data values, records, and collections of records that do not meet business needs from the valid ones.

- Generating a notification event alerting a data steward of a potential data quality issue.

- Establishing an automated or event driven process for aligning or possibly correcting flawed data within business expectations.

The first process uses assertions of expectations of the data. The data sets conform to those assertions or they do not. More complex rules can incorporate those assertions with actions or directives that support the second and third processes, generating a notification when data instances do not conform, or attempting to transform a data value identified as being in error. Use templates to specify these business rules, such as:

- Value domain membership: Specifying that a data element's assigned value is selected from among those enumerated in a defined data value domain, such as 2-Character United States Postal Codes for a STATE field.

- Definitional Conformance: Confirming that the same understanding of data definitions is understood and used properly in processes across the organization.

Confirmation includes algorithmic agreement on calculated fields, including any time, or local constraints, and rollup rules.

- Range conformance: A data element's assigned value must be within a defined numeric, lexicographic, or time range, such as greater than 0 and less than 100 for a numeric range.

- Format compliance: One or more patterns specify values assigned to a data element, such as the different ways to specify telephone numbers.

- Mapping conformance: Indicating that the value assigned to a data element must correspond to one selected from a value domain that maps to other equivalent corresponding value domain(s). The STATE data domain again provides a good example, since state values may be represented using different value domains (USPS Postal codes, FIPS 2-digit codes, full names), and these types of rules validate that "AL" and "01" both map to "Alabama."

- Value presence and record completeness: Rules defining the conditions under which missing values are unacceptable.

- Consistency rules: Conditional assertions that refer to maintaining a relationship between two (or more) attributes based on the actual values of those attributes.

- Accuracy verification: Compare a data value against a corresponding value in a system of record to verify that the values match.

- Uniqueness verification: Rules that specify which entities must have a unique representation and verify that one and only one record exists for each represented real world object.

- Timeliness validation: Rules that indicate the characteristics associated with expectations for accessibility and availability of data.

Other types of rules may involve aggregate functions applied to sets of data instances. Examples include validating reasonableness of the number of records in a file, the reasonableness of the average amount in a set of transactions, or the expected variance in the count of transactions over a specified timeframe.

Providing rule templates helps bridge the gap in communicating between the business team and the technical team. Rule templates convey the essence of the business expectation. It is possible to exploit the rule templates when a need exists to transform rules into formats suitable for execution, such as embedded within a rules engine, or the data analyzer component of a data-profiling tool, or code in a data integration tool.

12.2.7 Test and Validate Data Quality Requirements

Data profiling tools analyze data to find potential anomalies, as described in section 12.3.1. Use these same tools for rule validation as well. Rules discovered or defined during the data quality assessment phase are then referenced in measuring conformance as part of the operational processes.

Most data profiling tools allow data analysts to define data rules for validation, assessing frequency distributions and corresponding measurements, and then applying the defined rules against the data sets.

Reviewing the results, and verifying whether data flagged as non-conformant is truly incorrect, provides one level of testing. In addition, it is necessary to review the defined business rules with the business clients to make sure that they understand them, and that the business rules correspond to their business requirements.

Characterizing data quality levels based on data rule conformance provides an objective measure of data quality. By using defined data rules proactively to validate data, an organization can distinguish those records that conform to defined data quality expectations and those that do not. In turn, these data rules are used to baseline the current level of data quality as compared to ongoing audits.

12.2.8 Set and Evaluate Data Quality Service Levels

Data quality inspection and monitoring are used to measure and monitor compliance with defined data quality rules. Data quality SLAs (Service Level Agreements) specify the organization's expectations for response and remediation. Data quality inspection helps to reduce the number of errors. While enabling the isolation and root cause analysis of data flaws, there is an expectation that the operational procedures will provide a scheme for remediation of the root cause within an agreed-to timeframe.

Having data quality inspection and monitoring in place increases the likelihood of detection and remediation of a data quality issue before a significant business impact can occur.

Operational data quality control defined in a data quality SLA, includes:

- The data elements covered by the agreement.

- The business impacts associated with data flaws.

- The data quality dimensions associated with each data element.

- The expectations for quality for each data element for each of the identified dimensions in each application or system in the value chain.

- The methods for measuring against those expectations.

- The acceptability threshold for each measurement.

- The individual(s) to be notified in case the acceptability threshold is not met.The timelines and deadlines for expected resolution or remediation of the issue.

- The escalation strategy and possible rewards and penalties when the resolution times are met.

The data quality SLA also defines the roles and responsibilities associated with performance of operational data quality procedures. The operational data quality procedures provide reports on the conformance to the defined business rules, as well as monitoring staff performance in reacting to data quality incidents. Data stewards and the operational data quality staff, while upholding the level of data quality service, should take their data quality SLA constraints into consideration and connect data quality to individual performance plans.

When issues are not addressed within the specified resolution times, an escalation process must exist to communicate non-observance of the level of service up the management chain. The data quality SLA establishes the time limits for notification generation, the names of those in that management chain, and when escalation needs to occur. Given the set of data quality rules, methods for measuring conformance, the acceptability thresholds defined by the business clients, and the service level agreements, the data quality team can monitor compliance of the data to the business expectations, as well as how well the data quality team performs on the procedures associated with data errors.

12.2.9 Continuously Measure and Monitor Data Quality

The operational DQM procedures depend on available services for measuring and monitoring the quality of data. For conformance to data quality business rules, two contexts for control and measurement exist: in-stream and batch. In turn, apply measurements at three levels of granularity, namely data element value, data instance or record, and data set, making six possible measures. Collect in-stream measurements while creating the data, and perform batch activities on collections of data instances assembled in a data set, likely in persistent storage.

Provide continuous monitoring by incorporating control and measurement processes into the information processing flow. It is unlikely that data set measurements can be performed in-stream, since the measurement may need the entire set. The only in-stream points are when full data sets hand off between processing stages. Incorporate data quality rules using the techniques detailed in Table 12.1. Incorporating the results of the control and measurement processes into both the operational procedures and reporting frameworks enable continuous monitoring of the levels of data quality.

12.2.10 Manage Data Quality Issues

Supporting the enforcement of the data quality SLA requires a mechanism for reporting and tracking data quality incidents and activities for researching and resolving those incidents. A data quality incident reporting system can provide this capability. It can log the evaluation, initial diagnosis, and subsequent actions associated with data quality events. Tracking of data quality incidents can also provide performance reporting data, including mean-time-to-resolve issues, frequency of occurrence of issues, types of issues, sources of issues, and common approaches for correcting or eliminating problems. A good issues tracking system will eventually become a reference source of current and historic issues, their statuses, and any factors that may need the actions of others not directly involved in the resolution of the issue.

Granularity	In-stream	Batch
Data Element: Completeness, structural consistency, reasonableness	Edit checks in application Data element validation services Specially programmed applications	Direct queries Data profiling or analyzer tool
Data Record: Completeness, structural consistency, semantic consistency, reasonableness	Edit checks in application Data record validation services Specially programmed applications	Direct queries Data profiling or analyzer tool
Data Set: Aggregate measures, such as record counts, sums, mean, variance	Inspection inserted between processing stages	Direct queries Data profiling or analyzer tool

Table 12.1 Techniques for incorporating measurement and monitoring.

Many organizations already have incident reporting systems for tracking and managing software, hardware, and network issues. Incorporating data quality incident tracking focuses on organizing the categories of data issues into the incident hierarchies. Data quality incident tracking also requires a focus on training staff to recognize when data issues appear and how they are to be classified, logged, and tracked according to the data quality SLA. The steps involve some or all of these directives:

- Standardize data quality issues and activities: Since the terms used to describe data issues may vary across lines of business, it is valuable to standardize the concepts used, which can simplify classification and reporting. Standardization will also make it easier to measure the volume of issues and activities, identify patterns and interdependencies between systems and participants, and report on the overall impact of data quality activities. The classification of an issue may change as the investigation deepens and root causes are exposed.

- Provide an assignment process for data issues: The operational procedures direct the analysts to assign data quality incidents to individuals for diagnosis and to provide alternatives for resolution. The assignment process should be driven within the incident tracking system, by suggesting those individuals with specific areas of expertise.

- Manage issue escalation procedures: Data quality issue handling requires a well-defined system of escalation based on the impact, duration, or urgency of an issue. Specify the sequence of escalation within the data quality SLA. The incident tracking system will implement the escalation procedures, which helps expedite efficient handling and resolution of data issues.

- Manage data quality resolution workflow: The data quality SLA specifies objectives for monitoring, control, and resolution, all of which define a collection of operational workflows. The incident tracking system can support workflow management to track progress with issues diagnosis and resolution.

Implementing a data quality issues tracking system provides a number of benefits. First, information and knowledge sharing can improve performance and reduce duplication of effort. Second, an analysis of all the issues will help data quality team members determine any repetitive patterns, their frequency, and potentially the source of the issue. Employing an issues tracking system trains people to recognize data issues early in the information flows, as a general practice that supports their day-to-day operations. The issues tracking system raw data is input for reporting against the SLA conditions and measures. Depending on the governance established for data quality, SLA reporting can be monthly, quarterly or annually, particularly in cases focused on rewards and penalties.

12.2.11 Clean and Correct Data Quality Defects

The use of business rules for monitoring conformance to expectations leads to two operational activities. The first is to determine and eliminate the root cause of the introduction of errors. The second is to isolate the data items that are incorrect, and provide a means for bringing the data into conformance with expectations. In some situations, it may be as simple as throwing away the results and beginning the corrected information process from the point of error introduction. In other situations, throwing away the results is not possible, which means correcting errors.

Perform data correction in three general ways:

- Automated correction: Submit the data to data quality and data cleansing techniques using a collection of data transformations and rule-based standardizations, normalizations, and corrections. The modified values are committed without manual intervention. An example is automated address correction, which submits delivery addresses to an address standardizer that, using rules, parsing and standardization, and reference tables, normalizes and then corrects delivery addresses. Environments with well-defined standards, commonly accepted rules, and known error patterns, are best suited to automated cleansing and correction.

- Manual directed correction: Use automated tools to cleanse and correct data but require manual review before committing the corrections to persistent storage. Apply name and address cleansing, identity resolution, and pattern-based corrections automatically, and some scoring mechanism is used to propose a level of confidence in the correction. Corrections with scores above a particular level of confidence may be committed without review, but corrections with scores below the level of confidence are presented to the data steward for review and approval. Commit all approved corrections, and review those not approved to understand whether or not to adjust the applied underlying rules. Environments in which sensitive data sets require human oversight are good examples of where manual-directed correction may be suited.

- Manual correction: Data stewards inspect invalid records and determine the correct values, make the corrections, and commit the updated records.

12.2.12 Design and Implement Operational DQM Procedures

Using defined rules for validation of data quality provides a means of integrating data inspection into a set of operational procedures associated with active DQM. Integrate the data quality rules into application services or data services that supplement the data life cycle, either through the introduction of data quality tools and technology, the use of rules engines and reporting tools for monitoring and reporting, or custom-developed applications for data quality inspection.

The operational framework requires these services to be available to the applications and data services, and the results presented to the data quality team members. Data quality operations team members are responsible for four activities. The team must design and implement detailed procedures for operationalizing these activities.

1. Inspection and monitoring: Either through some automated process or via a manually invoked process, subject the data sets to measurement of conformance to the data quality rules, based on full-scan or sampling methods. Use data profiling tools, data analyzers, and data standardization and identity resolution tools to provide the inspection services. Accumulate the results and then make them available to the data quality operations analyst. The analyst must:
   o Review the measurements and associated metrics.
   o Determine if any acceptability thresholds exist that are not met.
   o Create a new data quality incident report.
   o Assign the incident to a data analyst for diagnosis and evaluation.

2. Diagnosis and evaluation of remediation alternatives: The objective is to review the symptoms exhibited by the data quality incident, trace through the lineage of the incorrect data, diagnose the type of the problem and where it originated, and pinpoint any potential root causes for the problem. The procedure should also describe how the data analyst would:
   o Review the data issues in the context of the appropriate information processing flows, and track the introduction of the error upstream to isolate the location in the processing where the flaw is introduced.
   o Evaluate whether or not there have been any changes to the environment that would have introduced errors into the system.
   o Evaluate whether or not there are any other process issues that contributed to the data quality incident.
   o Determine whether or not there are external data provider issues that have affected the quality of the data.
   o Evaluate alternatives for addressing the issue, which may include modification of the systems to eliminate root causes, introducing additional inspection and monitoring, direct correction of flawed data, or no action based on the cost of correction versus the value of the data correction.
   o Provide updates to the data quality incident tracking system.

3. Resolving the issue: Having provided a number of alternatives for resolving the issue, the data quality team must confer with the business data owners to select one of the alternatives to resolve the issue. These procedures should detail how the analysts:
   o Assess the relative costs and merits of the alternatives.
   o Recommend one of the alternatives.
   o Provide a plan for developing and implementing the resolution, which may include both modifying the processes and correcting flawed data.
   o Implement the resolution.
   o Provide updates to the data quality incident tracking system.

4. Reporting: To provide transparency for the DQM process, there should be periodic reports on the performance status of DQM. The data quality operations team will develop and populate these reports, which include:
   o Data quality scorecard, which provides a high-level view of the scores associated with various metrics, reported to different levels of the organization.
   o Data quality trends, which show over time how the quality of data is measured, and whether the quality indicator levels are trending up or down.
   o Data quality performance, which monitors how well the operational data quality staff is responding to data quality incidents for diagnosis and timely resolution.
   o These reports should align to the metrics and measures in the data quality SLA as much as possible, so that the areas important to the achievement of the data quality SLA are at some level, in internal team reports.

12.2.13 Monitor Operational DQM Procedures and Performance

Accountability is critical to the governance protocols overseeing data quality control. All issues must be assigned to some number of individuals, groups, departments, or organizations. The tracking process should specify and document the ultimate issue accountability to prevent issues from dropping through the cracks. Since the data quality SLA specifies the criteria for evaluating the performance of the data quality team, it is reasonable to expect that the incident tracking system will collect performance data relating to issue resolution, work assignments, volume of issues, frequency of occurrence, as well as the time to respond, diagnose, plan a solution, and resolve issues. These metrics can provide valuable insights into the effectiveness of the current workflow, as well as systems and resource utilization, and are important management data points that can drive continuous operational improvement for data quality control.

12.3 Data Quality Tools

DQM employs well-established tools and techniques. These utilities range in focus from empirically assessing the quality of data through data analysis, to the normalization of data values in accordance with defined business rules, to the ability to identify and resolve duplicate records into a single representation, and to schedule these inspections and changes on a regular basis. Data quality tools can be segregated into four categories of activities: Analysis, Cleansing, Enhancement, and Monitoring. The principal tools used are data profiling, parsing and standardization, data transformation, identity resolution and matching, enhancement, and reporting. Some vendors bundle these functions into more complete data quality solutions.

12.3.1 Data Profiling

Before making any improvements to data, one must first be able to distinguish between good and bad data. The attempt to qualify data quality is a process of analysis and discovery. The analysis involves an objective review of the data values populating data sets through quantitative measures and analyst review. A data analyst may not necessarily be able to pinpoint all instances of flawed data. However, the ability to document situations where data values look like they do not belong provides a means to communicate these instances with subject matter experts, whose business knowledge can confirm the existences of data problems.

Data profiling is a set of algorithms for two purposes:

- Statistical analysis and assessment of the quality of data values within a data set.

- Exploring relationships that exist between value collections within and across data sets.

For each column in a table, a data-profiling tool will provide a frequency distribution of the different values, providing insight into the type and use of each column. In addition, column profiling can summarize key characteristics of the values within each column, such as the minimum, maximum, and average values.

Cross-column analysis can expose embedded value dependencies, while inter-table analysis explores overlapping values sets that may represent foreign key relationships between entities. In this way, data profiling analyzes and assesses data anomalies. Most data profiling tools allow for drilling down into the analyzed data for further investigation.

Data profiling can also proactively test against a set of defined (or discovered) business rules. The results can be used to distinguish records that conform to defined data quality expectations from those that don't, which in turn can contribute to baseline measurements and ongoing auditing that supports the data quality reporting processes.

12.3.2 Parsing and Standardization

Data parsing tools enable the data analyst to define sets of patterns that feed into a rules engine used to distinguish between valid and invalid data values. Actions are triggered upon matching a specific pattern. Extract and rearrange the separate components (commonly referred to as "tokens") into a standard representation when parsing a valid pattern. When an invalid pattern is recognized, the application may attempt to transform the invalid value into one that meets expectations.

Many data quality issues are situations where a slight variance in data value representation introduces confusion or ambiguity. Parsing and standardizing data values is valuable. For example, consider the different ways telephone numbers expected to conform to a Numbering Plan are formatted. While some have digits, some have alphabetic characters, and all use different special characters for separation. People can recognize each one as being a telephone number. However, in order to determine if these numbers are accurate (perhaps by comparing them to a master customer directory) or to investigate whether duplicate numbers exist when there should be only one for each supplier, the values must be parsed into their component segments (area code, exchange, and line number) and then transformed into a standard format.

The human ability to recognize familiar patterns contributes to our ability to characterize variant data values belonging to the same abstract class of values; people recognize different types of telephone numbers because they conform to frequently used patterns. An analyst describes the format patterns that all represent a data object, such as Person Name, Product Description, and so on. A data quality tool parses data values that conform to any of those patterns, and even transforms them into a single, standardized form that will simplify the assessment, similarity analysis, and cleansing processes. Pattern-based parsing can automate the recognition and subsequent standardization of meaningful value components.

12.3.3 Data Transformation

Upon identification of data errors, trigger data rules to transform the flawed data into a format that is acceptable to the target architecture. Engineer these rules directly within a data integration tool or rely on alternate technologies embedded in or accessible from within the tool. Perform standardization by mapping data from some source pattern into a corresponding target representation. A good example is a "customer name," since names may be represented in thousands of different forms. A good standardization tool will be able to parse the different components of a customer name, such as given name, middle name, family name, initials, titles, generational designations, and then rearrange those components into a canonical representation that other data services will be able to manipulate.

Data transformation builds on these types of standardization techniques. Guide rule-based transformations by mapping data values in their original formats and patterns into a target representation. Parsed components of a pattern are subjected to rearrangement, corrections, or any changes as directed by the rules in the knowledge base. In fact, standardization is a special case of transformation, employing rules that capture context, linguistics, and idioms recognized as common over time, through repeated analysis by the rules analyst or tool vendor.

12.3.4 Identity Resolution and Matching

Employ record linkage and matching in identity recognition and resolution, and incorporate approaches used to evaluate "similarity" of records for use in duplicate analysis and elimination, merge / purge, house holding, data enhancement, cleansing and strategic initiatives such as customer data integration or master data management. A common data quality problem involves two sides of the same coin:

- Multiple data instances that actually refer to the same real-world entity.

- The perception, by an analyst or an application, that a record does not exist for a real-world entity, when in fact it really does.

In the first situation, something introduced similar, yet variant representations in data values into the system. In the second situation, a slight variation in representation prevents the identification of an exact match of the existing record in the data set.

Both of these situations are addressed through a process called similarity analysis, in which the degree of similarity between any two records is scored, most often based on weighted approximate matching between a set of attribute values in the two records. If the score is above a specified threshold, the two records are a match and are presented to the end client as most likely to represent the same entity. It is through similarity analysis that slight variations are recognized and data values are connected and subsequently consolidated.

Attempting to compare each record against all the others to provide a similarity score is not only ambitious, but also time-consuming and computationally intensive. Most data quality tool suites use advanced algorithms for blocking records that are most likely to contain matches into smaller sets, whereupon different approaches are taken to measure similarity. Identifying similar records within the same data set probably means that the records are duplicates, and may need cleansing and / or elimination. Identifying similar records in different sets may indicate a link across the data sets, which helps facilitate cleansing, knowledge discovery, and reverse engineering—all of which contribute to master data aggregation.

Two basic approaches to matching are deterministic and probabilistic. Deterministic matching, like parsing and standardization, relies on defined patterns and rules for assigning weights and scores for determining similarity. Alternatively, probabilistic matching relies on statistical techniques for assessing the probability that any pair of records represents the same entity. Deterministic algorithms are predictable in that the patterns matched and the rules applied will always yield the same matching determination. Tie performance to the variety, number, and order of the matching rules. Deterministic matching works out of the box with relatively good performance, but it is only as good as the situations anticipated by the rules developers.

Probabilistic matching relies on the ability to take data samples for training purposes by looking at the expected results for a subset of the records and tuning the matcher to self-adjust based on statistical analysis. These matchers are not reliant on rules, so the results may be nondeterministic. However, because the probabilities can be refined based on experience, probabilistic matchers are able to improve their matching precision as more data is analyzed.

12.3.5 Enhancement

Increase the value of an organization's data by enhancing the data. Data enhancement is a method for adding value to information by accumulating additional information about a base set of entities and then merging all the sets of information to provide a focused view of the data. Data enhancement is a process of intelligently adding data from alternate sources as a byproduct of knowledge inferred from applying other data quality techniques, such as parsing, identity resolution, and data cleansing.

Data parsing assigns characteristics to the data values appearing in a data instance, and those characteristics help in determining potential sources for added benefit. For example, if it can be determined that a business name is embedded in an attribute called name, then tag that data value as a business. Use the same approach for any situation in which data values organize into semantic hierarchies.

Appending information about cleansing and standardizations that have been applied provides additional suggestions for later data matching, record linkage, and identity resolution processes. By creating an associative representation of the data that imposes a meta-context on it, and adding detail about the data, more knowledge is collected about the actual content, not just the structure of that information. Associative representation makes more interesting inferences about the data, and consequently enables use of more information for data enhancement. Some examples of data enhancement include:

- Time / Date stamps: One way to improve data is to document the time and date that data items are created, modified, or retired, which can help to track historical data events.

- Auditing Information: Auditing can document data lineage, which also is important for historical tracking as well as validation.

- Contextual Information: Business contexts such as location, environment, and access methods are all examples of context that can augment data. Contextual enhancement also includes tagging data records for downstream review and analysis.

- Geographic Information: There are a number of geographic enhancements possible, such as address standardization and geocoding, which includes regional coding, municipality, neighborhood mapping, latitude / longitude pairs, or other kinds of location-based data.

- Demographic Information: For customer data, there are many ways to add demographic enhancements such as customer age, marital status, gender, income, ethnic coding; or for business entities, annual revenue, number of employees, size of occupied space, etc.

- Psychographic Information: Use these kinds of enhancements to segment the target population by specified behaviors, such as product and brand preferences, organization memberships, leisure activities, vacation preferences, commuting transportation style, shopping time preferences, etc.

12.3.6 Reporting

Inspection and monitoring of conformance to data quality expectations, monitoring performance of data stewards conforming to data quality SLAs, workflow processing for data quality incidents, and manual oversight of data cleansing and correction are all supported by good reporting. It is optimal to have a user interface to report results associated with data quality measurement, metrics, and activity. It is wise to incorporate visualization and reporting for standard reports, scorecards, dashboards, and for provision of ad hoc queries as part of the functional requirements for any acquired data quality tools.

12.4 Summary

The guiding principles for implementing DQM into an organization, a summary table of the roles for each DQM activity, and organization and cultural issues that may arise during database quality management are summarized below.

12.4.1 Setting Data Quality Guiding Principles

When assembling a DQM program, it is reasonable to assert a set of guiding principles that frame the type of processes and uses of technology described in this chapter. Align any activities undertaken to support the data quality practice with one or more of the guiding principles. Every organization is different, with varying motivating factors. Some sample statements that might be useful in a Data Quality Guiding Principles document include:

- Manage data as a core organizational asset. Many organizations go so far as to place data as an asset on their balance sheets.

- All data elements will have a standardized data definition, data type, and acceptable value domain.

- Leverage Data Governance for the control and performance of DQM.

- Use industry and international data standards whenever possible.

- Downstream data consumers specify data quality expectations.

- Define business rules to assert conformance to data quality expectations.

- Validate data instances and data sets against defined business rules.

- Business process owners will agree to and abide by data quality SLAs.

- Apply data corrections at the original source, if possible.

- If it is not possible to correct data at the source, forward data corrections to the owner of the original source whenever possible. Influence on data brokers to conform to local requirements may be limited.

- Report measured levels of data quality to appropriate data stewards, business process owners, and SLA managers.

- Identify a gold record for all data elements.

12.4.2 Process Summary

The process summary for the DQM function is shown in Table 12.2. The deliverables, responsible roles, approving roles, and contributing roles are shown for each activity in the data operations management function. The Table is also shown in Appendix A9.

Activities	Deliverables	Responsible Roles	Approving Roles	Contributing Roles
10.1 Develop and Promote Data Quality Awareness (O)	Data quality training Data Governance Processes Established Data Stewardship Council	Data Quality Manager	Business Managers DRM Director	Information Architects Subject Matter Experts
10.2 Define Data Quality Requirements ((D)	Data Quality Requirements Document	Data Quality Manager Data Quality Analysts	Business Managers DRM Director	Information Architects Subject Matter Experts
10.3 Profile, Analyze, and Assess Data Quality (D)	Data Quality Assessment Report	Data Quality Analysts	Business Managers DRM Director	Data Stewardship Council
10.4 Define Data Quality Metrics (P)	Data Quality Metrics Document	Data Quality Manager Data Quality Analysts	Business Managers DRM Director	Data Stewardship Council
10.5 Define Data Quality Business Rules (P)	Data Quality Business Rules	Data Quality Analysts	Business Managers DRM Director Data Quality Manager	Information Architects Subject Matter Experts Data Stewardship Council
10.6 Test and Validate Data Quality Requirements (D)	Data Quality Test Cases	Data Quality Analysts	Business Managers DRM Director	Information Architects Subject Matter Experts

Activities	Deliverables	Responsible Roles	Approving Roles	Contributing Roles
10.7 Set and Evaluate Data Quality Service Levels (P)	Data Quality Service Levels	Data Quality Manager	Business Managers DRM Director	Data Stewardship Council
10.8 Continuously Measure and Monitor Data Quality (C)	Data Quality Reports	Data Quality Manager	Business Managers DRM Director	Data Stewardship Council
10.9 Manage Data Quality Issues (C)	Data Quality Issues Log	Data Quality Manager Data Quality Analysts	Business Managers DRM Director	Data Stewardship Council
10.10 Clean and Correct Data Quality Defects (O)	Data Quality Defect Resolution Log	Data Quality Analysts	Business Managers DRM Director	Information Architects Subject Matter Experts
10.11 Design and Implement Operational DQM Procedures (D)	Operational DQM Procedures	Data Quality Manager Data Quality Analysts	Business Managers DRM Director	Information Architects Subject Matter Experts Data Stewardship Council
10.12 Monitor Operational DQM Procedures and Performance (C)	Operational DQM Metrics	Data Quality Manager Data Quality Analysts	Business Managers DRM Director	Data Stewardship Council

Table 12.2 Data Quality Management Process Summary

12.4.3 Organizational and Cultural Issues

Q1: Is it really necessary to have quality data if there are many processes to change the data into information and use the information for business intelligence purposes?

A1: The business intelligence value chain shows that the quality of the data resource directly impacts the business goals of the organization. The foundation of the value chain is the data resource. Information is produced from the data resource through information engineering, much the same as products are developed from raw materials. The information is used by the knowledge workers in an organization to provide the business intelligence necessary to manage the organization. The business intelligence is used to support the business strategies, which in turn support the business goals. Through the business intelligence value chain, the quality of the data directly impacts how successfully the business goals are met. Therefore, the emphasis for quality must be placed on the data resource, not on the process through information development and business intelligence processes.

Q2: Is data quality really free?

A2: Going back to the second law of thermodynamics, a data resource is an open system. Entropy will continue to increase without any limit, meaning the quality of the data resource will continue to decrease without any limit. Energy must be expended to create and maintain a quality data resource. That energy comes at a cost. Both the initial data resource quality and the maintenance of data resource quality come at a cost. Therefore, data quality is not free.

It is less costly to build quality into the data resource from the beginning, than it is to build it in later. It is also less costly to maintain data quality throughout the life of the data resource, than it is to improve the quality in major steps. When the quality of the data resource is allowed to deteriorate, it becomes far more costly to improve the data quality, and it creates a far greater impact on the business. Therefore, quality is not free; but, it is less costly to build in and maintain. What most people mean when they say that data quality is free is that the cost-benefit ratio of maintaining data quality from the beginning is less than the cost-benefit ratio of allowing the data quality to deteriorate.

Q3: Are data quality issues something new that have surfaced recently with evolving technology?

A3: No. Data quality problems have always been there, even back in the 80-column card days. The problem is getting worse with the increased quantity of data being maintained and the age of the data. The problem is also becoming more visible with processing techniques that are both more powerful and are including a wider range of data. Data that appeared to be high quality in yesterday's isolated systems now show their low quality when combined into today's organization-wide analysis processes.

Every organization must become aware of the quality of their data if they are to effectively and efficiently use that data to support the business. Any organization that considers data quality to be a recent issue that can be postponed for later consideration, is putting the survival of their business at risk. The current economic climate is not the time to put the company's survival on the line by ignoring the quality of their data.

Q4: Is there one thing to do more than any other for ensuring high data quality?

A4: The most important thing is to establish a single enterprise-wide data architecture, then build and maintain all data within that single architecture. A single enterprise-wide data architecture does not mean that all data are stored it one central repository. It does mean that all data are developed and managed within the context of a single enterprise-wide data architecture. The data can be deployed as necessary for operational efficiency.

As soon as any organization allows data to be developed within multiple data architectures, or worse yet, without any data architecture, there will be monumental problems with data quality. Even if an attempt is made to coordinate multiple data architectures, there will be considerable data quality problems. Therefore, the most important thing is to manage all data within a single enterprise-wide data architecture.

12.5 Recommended Reading

The references listed below provide additional reading that support the material presented in Chapter 12. These recommended readings are also included in the Bibliography at the end of the Guide.

Batini, Carlo, and Monica Scannapieco. <u>Data Quality: Concepts, Methodologies and Techniques</u>. Springer, 2006. ISBN 3-540-33172-7. 262 pages.

Brackett, Michael H. <u>Data Resource Quality: Turning Bad Habits into Good Practices</u>. Addison-Wesley, 2000. ISBN 0-201-71306-3. 384 pages.

Deming, W. Edwards. <u>Out of the Crisis</u>. The MIT Press, 2000. ISBN 0262541157. 507 pages.

English, Larry. <u>Improving Data Warehouse And Business Information Quality: Methods For Reducing Costs And Increasing Profits</u>. John Wiley & Sons, 1999. ISBN 0-471-25383-9. 518 pages.

Huang, Kuan-Tsae, Yang W. Lee and Richard Y. Wang. <u>Quality Information and Knowledge</u>. Prentice Hall, 1999. ISBN 0-130-10141-9. 250 pages.

Loshin, David. <u>Enterprise Knowledge Management: The Data Quality Approach</u>. Morgan Kaufmann, 2001. ISBN 0-124-55840-2. 494 pages.

Loshin, David. <u>Master Data Management</u>. Morgan Kaufmann, 2009. ISBN 0123742250. 288 pages.

Maydanchik, Arkady. <u>Data Quality Assessment</u>. Technics Publications, LLC, 2007 ISBN 0977140024. 336 pages.

McGilvray, Danette. Executing Data Quality Projects: Ten Steps to Quality Data and Trusted Information. Morgan Kaufmann, 2008. ISBN 0123743699. 352 pages.

Olson, Jack E. Data Quality: The Accuracy Dimension. Morgan Kaufmann, 2003. ISBN 1-558-60891-5. 294 pages.

Redman, Thomas. Data Quality: The Field Guide. Digital Press, 2001. ISBN 1-555-59251-6. 256 pages.

13 Professional Development

Professional development, though not one of the ten data management functions, is crucial for development of a data management profession. Chapter 13 discusses the characteristics of a data management professional and the various components of professionalism: professional organization membership, education and training for continuing education, certification program, ethics, and the notable members in the data management profession.

13.1 Characteristics of a Profession

Data management is an emerging legitimate profession in the information technology field. A profession is defined as an occupational calling (vocation) requiring specialized knowledge and skills, or the body of persons engaged in that vocation. Today's data management professionals feel some sense of calling and commitment about the importance of data as a resource. This calling and commitment makes data management a vocation, not "just a job." Aspiring data management professionals are needed and most welcome in the field.

Several recent studies show that recognized professions, including medicine, law, the clergy, the military, engineering, architecture, nursing, and accounting, share common features. Some of these common features include:

1. A professional *society* or guild for the communal support of professionals.

2. The publication of a recognized consensus *body of knowledge*.

3. A professional *degree* or emphasis available from an accredited higher education institution using a *curriculum* validated by the professional society.

4. Registration of fitness to practice via voluntary *certification* or mandatory licensing.

5. Availability of *continuing education* and an expectation of continuing skills development for professionals.

6. The existence of a specific *code of ethics*, often with a formal oath of commitment to this code, and including an obligation to society beyond occupational expectations.

7. *Notable members* of the profession well known to the public, recognized for their professionalism.

Aspiring data management professionals are encouraged to:

1. Join DAMA International and participate in their local DAMA chapter.

2. Be familiar with the DAMA-DMBOK Guide and the DAMA Dictionary of Data Management.

3. Attend the annual DAMA International Symposium (Now the Enterprise Data World) and / or other professional conferences, workshops, seminars and technical courses each year.,

4. Earn the Certified Data Management Professional (CDMP) designation.

5. Obtain an undergraduate or graduate degree in computer science or management information systems with an emphasis in data management, and / or support the development of such programs in local colleges and universities.

6. Strive to maintain the highest ethical standards of professional behavior.

13.2 DAMA Membership

DAMA International, the Data Management Association, is the world's premiere organization for data management professionals worldwide. DAMA International is an international not-for-profit membership organization, with over 7500 members in 40 chapters around the globe. To find a chapter near you, go to the DAMA International website, www.dama.org.

DAMA International seeks to mature the data management profession in several ways, including:

- In partnership with Wilshire Conferences, the DAMA International Symposium (Now the Enterprise Data World) is the largest annual professional data management conference in the world.

- In partnership with IRMUK, the DAMA International Symposium Europe is the largest European professional data management conference.

- In partnership with ICCP, DAMA International offers a professional certification program, recognizing Certified Data Management Professionals (CDMPs). DAMA publishes study guides for these exams.

- The CDMP certification exams, developed by DAMA International members, are also used by The Data Warehouse Institute (TDWI) in their Certified Business Intelligence Professional (CBIP) program.

- The DAMA International Education Committee's award winning Data Management Curriculum Framework offers guidance on how North American colleges and universities can teach data management as part of their IT and MIS curricula.

- In partnership with the IS 2002 Model Curriculum authors, and based on DAMA International's Model Curriculum Framework, expand the IS 2002 Model Curriculum to include the topics of Data Quality, Data Warehousing, and Meta-data.

- In partnership with the DAMA Chicago chapter, DAMA International publishes the Guidelines to Implementing Data Resource Management.

- DAMA International publishes The <u>DAMA Dictionary of Data Management</u>, a sister publication of the DAMA-DMBOK Guide. The Dictionary is the Glossary for the DAMA-DMBOK Guide. The Dictionary is available separately in CD-ROM format.

- Publication of this DAMA-DMBOK Guide document in CD-ROM format.

13.3 Continuing Education and Training

Professionals in any field participate in continuing education to stay current with best practices and to further develop specialized skills. Some data management training is focused on developing skills with specific technology products. DAMA International and other professional organizations provide education in product-neutral concepts, methods, and techniques.

DAMA International holds annual Symposium conferences in the United States, United Kingdom, and Australia. There are plans for additional international conferences in the future. In addition, DAMA International Chapters in over 20 countries sponsor speakers who present educational topics at local meetings.

Data management professionals should subscribe to professional magazines and online newsletters, and should be well read on data management and related topics.

13.4 Certification

Professional certification is an indication of knowledge, skills, and experience in a field. DAMA International and the Institute for Certification of Computing Professionals (ICCP) have jointly constructed the Certified Data Management Professional (CDMP) designation. The certification program gives data management professionals the opportunity to show professional growth that can enhance their personal and career goals. DAMA International's certification effort is coordinated with the model education curriculum and with work being done to define job ladders for the data management field.

DAMA International is a constituent member of the ICCP, a consortium of professional IT associations creating international standards and certification credentials since 1973. The ICCP offers internationally recognized product and vendor neutral certification programs that test stringent industry fundamentals for the computing profession. The ICCP office administers the testing and recertification programs for the CDMP.

13.4.1 How Do You Obtain a CDMP?

The CDMP certification process is as follows:

1. Obtain information and the application (<u>www.dama.org</u> or <u>www.iccp.org</u>).

2. Fill out the application.

3. Arrange to take the exam(s) through DAMA or ICCP. Internet testing is available through the ICCP office.

4. Pass the IS Core exam (required).

5. Pass two specialty exams.

6. At least one of the data specialty exams taken must be from the following list:
    a. Data Management
    b. Data Warehousing
    c. Database Administration
    d. Data and Information Quality

7. Meet the experience and education qualifications.

8. Sign the ICCP code of ethics.

13.4.2 CDMP Examination Criteria

Three ICCP exams must be passed with the scores shown in Table 13.1

Score	Credential Earned
Pass all exams at 50% or higher	CDMP Practitioner Certificate
Pass all exams at 70% or higher	CDMP Mastery Certificate

Table 13.1 ICCP Exam Score Requirements

The *CDMP Practitioner* certification is awarded to professionals who scored above 50% on all three exams. These individuals can contribute as a team member on assigned tasks, for they have a working knowledge of concepts, skills, and techniques in a particular data specialization.

The *CDMP Mastery* certification is awarded to professionals who scored 70% or higher on all three exams. These individuals have the ability to lead and mentor a team of professionals, as they have mastered the concepts, skills, and practices of their data specialization.

Exams may be retaken to improve your score and go from the Practitioner to the Mastery certificate level. You may be able to substitute selected vendor certifications for up to one specialty exam.

13.4.3 Additional CDMP Certification Criteria

The criteria shown in Table 13.2 must also be met in order to qualify for the CDMP:

CDMP Criteria	CDMP Practitioner Certificate	CDMP Mastery Certificate
# Years Data management professional Work Experience	2	4+

CDMP Criteria	CDMP Practitioner Certificate	CDMP Mastery Certificate
Substitute Up to 2 Years – Bachelor or Master Degree in an appropriate discipline for Work Experience	2	2
Recertification Required	Yes	Yes
Continuing Professional Education / Activity Required	120 hours every 3-year cycle	120 hours every 3-year cycle
ICCP Code of Ethics	Yes	Yes

Table 13.2 CDMP Certification Criteria

13.4.4 CDMP Qualifying Examinations

CDMP certification candidates must take three qualifying examinations. The IS Core exam must be one of these three exams. The other two exams are chosen by candidates based on their work experience. Table 13.3 shows which Data Management Functions are covered as topics in each specialty exam in the CDMP program.

13.4.5 Accepted Vendor Training Certifications

Any of the following certifications may be substituted for one of the "candidate's choice" specialty exams required for the CDMP. Other certification programs may be accepted, but need to be evaluated. Check with the ICCP office or the DAMA contacts.

IBM:

- IBM Certified Database Administrator–DB2 Universal Database.

- IBM Certified Advanced Database Administrator–DB2 Universal Database.

- IBM Certified Solutions Expert–DB2 Universal Database.

- IBM Certified Solutions Expert–DB2 Content Manager.

Information Engineering Services Pty Ltd:

- Certified Business Data Modeler.

Insurance Data Management Association (IDMA):

- Certified Insurance Data Manager.

Microsoft:

- Microsoft Certified Database Administrator.

NCR (Teradata):

- Teradata Certified Professional.

CDMP Program Specialty Exams	DAMA – DMBOK Data Management Functions									
	Data Governance	Data Architecture Management	Data Development	Data operations management	Data Security Management	Reference and Data Management	Data Warehousing and Business Intelligence Management	Document Content Management	Meta-data Management	Data Quality Management
Data Management	X	X	X			X	X		X	X
Database Administration				X	X					
Systems Development			X							
Data Warehousing							X			
Business Intelligence and Analytics							X			
Data and Information Quality	X									X
Systems Security					X					
Zachman Enterprise Architecture Framework[2]		X								
Business Process Management							X			

Table 13.3 CDMP Examination Topics

Oracle:

- Oracle (xx) Certified Professional.

- Oracle(xx) Database Administrator Certified Professional (for Practitioner Level CDMP).

- Oracle(xx) Database Administrator Certified Master (for Mastery Level CDMP).

Project Management Institute:

- Project Management Professional (PMP).

- Certified Associate in Project Management (CAPM).

13.4.6 Preparation for Taking Exams

Preparing to take the ICCP exams can be done in various ways:

- Sponsor ICCP Exam Review courses for your DAMA chapter membership.

- Refer to the exam subject outlines (at level 1 and 2) posted on http://www.iccp.org/iccpnew/outlines.html to become familiar with the subject coverage of each exam.

- Contact the ICCP (office@iccp.org) for the CDMP Study Guide, which covers all the exams in the CDMP program and has sample exams / questions for self-study. Also, ICCP sells the DAMA International Data Management Exam Study Guide and the Data Warehousing Exam Study Guide.

13.4.7 Taking CDMP Exams

ICCP testing can be done anywhere in the world with an approved ICCP Proctor to verify physical identity and supervise / monitor the examination.

The ICCP exams are offered at the DAMA International Symposiums (Now the Enterprise Data World).

A DAMA chapter can set up exam sessions during their chapter meetings. A volunteer proctor is needed from the chapter. A proctor is an individual authorized by ICCP to oversee the writing of an exam by an ICCP exam taker. This person must meet specific guidelines (http://www.iccp.org/iccpnew/testing.html) and be willing to supervise the person taking the exam. The ICCP reserves the right to reject proposed proctors. Contact office@iccp.org or phone 847.299.4227 or 800.843.8227 for assistance in determining an appropriate proctor.

Exams may also be taken via the Internet; contact the ICCP as noted above for more information.

The exams run off the USB drive of an individual's laptop. There are 110 multiple choice questions to answer in 90 minutes. One hundred questions are scored and 10 are beta questions included for future test development. You will not know which type of question you are answering. Questions and possible distracting answers are randomly listed in a different order for each exam taker. Therefore, although this guide contains sample questions that allow for "all or none of the above" type answers meant for study purposes, this type of answer will not be available to choose from on the actual exam.

Computer based testing allows for immediate scoring after the exam is taken. An ICCP Performance Profile is then available for downloading, and one will be sent later to the individual by the ICCP. This Profile shows your exam strengths and weaknesses.

13.4.8 Professional Development / Recertification

To keep your CDMP current, you must earn 120 approved contact hours of continuing education over a 3-year period. Many educational activities count, including DAMA

Symposiums and chapter meetings. For further information, contact the ICCP (office@iccp.org) for an ICCP Recertification Guidelines Booklet or go to www.iccp.org/iccpnew/Recertification%20Guidelines2005.pdf.

Table 13.4 identifies some example of how to earn these credits.

Activity	ICCP Recertification Credits
Formal educational institutions	1 Quarter Hour = 8 credits 1 Semester Hour = 12 credits 1 Continuing Education Unit (CEU) = 10
Independent organized programs Professional society meetings, seminars, conferences	Count time of education program content
Teaching, lecturing, presenting Self-study programs Published article, book	For each activity category, credit limited to 60 recertification credits / 3 year period
Sit for other ICCP examinations	Depends on exam score: 70% or higher = 60 credits 60 - 69% = 30 credits 50 - 59% = 20 credits Less than 50 % = 0 credits

Activity	ICCP Recertification Credits
As a volunteer, (non-compensated) serve as an Elected Official, Committee / Council Member of a Professional Organization.	You could serve as an elected official, committee or council member for a professional organization, e.g. DAMA, ICCP or another professional organization. For documentation / auditing purposes, a letter or certificate from the professional organization is required. 20 Credits Allowed Per 3 year Cycle: 1. Serve as an elected officer for a professional organization. • Minimum three months of participation: 2 recertification credits per calendar year. (No credits are awarded for service less than three months) • Minimum six months of participation: 5 recertification credits per calendar year. • Twelve months of participation: 10 recertification credits per calendar year. 2. Serve as a volunteer / appointed committee / council member for a professional organization. • Minimum three months of participation: 1 recertification credit per calendar year. (No credits are awarded for service less than three months) • Minimum six months of participation: 3 recertification credits per calendar year. • Twelve months of participation: 5 recertification credits per calendar year.

Table 13.4 Ways to Earn CDMP Professional Development / Recertification Credits

Recertification credits can be entered online through the Professional Development Transmittal Form, http://www.iccp.org/cgi-bin/pdform.php. Your DAMA International chapter can also keep track of meeting attendance for the purpose of recertification and submit on a timely basis. An annual maintenance fee to ICCP is required for keeping track of your recertification credits. You will receive an annual transcript from the ICCP.

13.5 Professional Ethics

As data management professionals, we inherently accept a personal obligation to the profession and its members, and to all who use data and information. Information consumers expect data to possess certain qualities (completeness, accuracy, validity, etc.). Likewise, our information consumers, data stewards, managers, and colleagues expect professional qualities of honesty, integrity, trustworthiness, respect, maturity, courtesy, and cooperation. Through our combined behaviors, we present the professional "face" of data management to others. Data management professionals should strive to maintain the highest ethical and professional conduct.

Data management professionals have traditionally dismissed any responsibility for the ways data is used by business people. Generally, professional responsibility for data has been limited to making data and information 'fit for use' for a particular business purpose. But what are those purposes, and are they ethical? Is it possible for business to be continually aware of the potential technical or process breaches of ethics in their planned data use? Business data consumers are not solely responsible for ethical breaches; data management professionals play an advisory role in the ethical use of data. Ethical handling of data includes a legal framework, activities involving dataset handling, and the framing of the questions of analysis without bias. [7]

When discussing the ethical handling of data, the handling of personal data (e.g. name, address, religious affiliation, sexual orientation) and privacy (access or restriction to this information) are key topics. Much has been written of the U.S. Sarbanes-Oxley, HIPPA, Canada Bill 198, and other laws emerging in the 1990's for our protection; it is available for review for further information.

There are two types of ethics: compelled ethics and imposed ethics. Compelled ethics are those that are part of an internal personal code of responsibility. Imposed ethics are those forced on us by law or regulation. These two ethics frameworks are a way to understanding the approaches to privacy law in Canada and the United States, and are profiled below to show how two countries have developed similar but differing approaches. Refer to local law when developing corporate policy for handling personal data and privacy.

Under United States self regulatory regimes, organizations design and implement their own privacy programs based on the criteria set down by the Federal Trade Commission (FTC):

- Notice: Data collectors must disclose their information practices before collecting personal information from consumers.

- Choice: Consumers must be given options with respect to whether and how personal information collected from them may be used for purposes beyond those for which the information was provided.

---

[7] From FIT FOR USE TO A FAULT Deborah Henderson, Tandum Lett, Anne Marie Smith and Cora Zeeman. MITIQ 2008. The MIT 2008 Information Quality Industry Symposium, Boston, Mass. July 2008

- Access: Consumers should be able to view and contest the accuracy and completeness of data collected about them.

- Security: Data collectors must take reasonable steps to assure that information collected from consumers is accurate and secure from unauthorized use.

- Enforcement: The use of a reliable mechanism to impose sanctions for noncompliance with these fair information practices.

Canadian privacy law is a hybrid of a comprehensive regime of privacy protection along with industry self regulation. PIPEDA (Personal Information Protection and Electronic Documents Act) covers all businesses who collect, use, and disseminate personal information in the course of commercial activities. It stipulates rules, with exceptions, that organizations must follow in the collection, use, and dissemination of personal information.

The 10 guidelines below are statutory obligations that all organizations that collect, use and disseminate personal information must follow:

- Accountability: An organization is responsible for personal information under its control and must designate an individual to be accountable for the organization's compliance with the principle.

- Identifying Purposes: An organization must identify the purposes for which personal information is collected at or before the time the information is collected.

- Consent: An organization must obtain the knowledge and consent of the individual for the collection, use, or disclosure of personal information, except where inappropriate.

- Limiting Collection, Use, Disclosure, and Retention: The collection of personal information must be limited to that which is necessary for the purposes identified by the organization. Information shall be collected by fair and lawful means. Personal information shall not be used or disclosed for purposes other than those for which it was collected, except with the consent of the individual or as required by law. Personal information shall be retained only as long as necessary for the fulfillment of those purposes.

- Accuracy: Personal information must be as accurate, complete, and up-to-date as is necessary for the purposes for which it is to be used.

- Safeguards: Personal information must be protected by security safeguards appropriate to the sensitivity of the information.

- Openness: An organization must make specific information about its policies and practices relating to the management of their personal information readily available to individuals.

- Individual Access: Upon request, an individual shall be informed of the existence, use, and disclosure of his or her personal information, and shall be given access to that information. An individual shall be able to challenge the accuracy and completeness of the information and have it amended as appropriate.

- Challenging Compliance: An individual shall be able to address a challenge concerning compliance with the above principles to the designated individual or individuals accountable for the organization's compliance.

In Canada, the federal privacy commissioner has the sole responsibility for handling privacy complaints against organizations. However, they fill an ombudsman role wherein decisions are recommendations and not legally binding and decisions have no precedential value, even within their own office.

As data professionals involved in business intelligence (BI), we are actively involved in the following types of analyses:

- *Who* people are, including terrorist and criminal identification.

- *What* people do, including profiling.

- *When* people do it, including timing of data analysis, bias, accuracy.

- *Where* people do it, including profiling and corralling choices.

- *How* people are treated, including outcomes of analysis, such as scoring and preference tracking, that will tag them as ultimately privileged or not for future business.

It is right to ask whether these activities are ethical or not, and to explore the implications to the community before proceeding with the work. Often, though the decision to proceed is confirmed, the manner in which to proceed may be changed. The data may be made anonymous, the private information removed from the file, the security on the files tightened or confirmed, and a review of the local and other applicable privacy law reviewed. Figure 13.1 summarizes the evaluation of ethical risks.

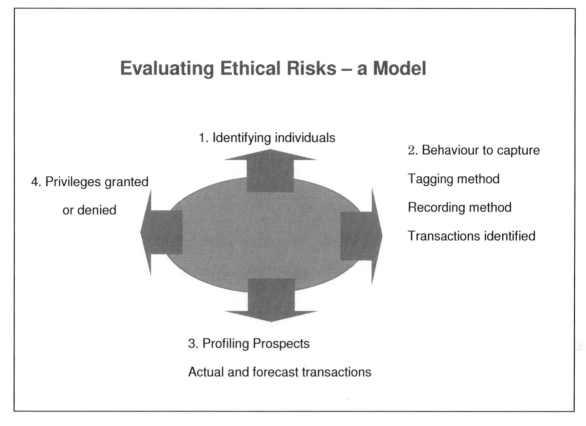

Figure 13.1 Ethical Risk Model for Projects

Be aware of the following traps to ethical handling of information.

- Hunch and Search: The analyst has a hunch and wants to satisfy that hunch, but only uses data that satisfies their hunch.

- Data Collection for Pre-defined result: The analyst is pressured to collect data and produce results based on pre-defined desires.

- Biased use of data collected: Data is used to satisfy a chosen approach; data is manipulated for a chosen approach.

In summary, business users may not be aware of "where the data comes from" and ethical issues may not be obvious to them. Automated monitoring is not sufficient protection from unethical activities; the analysts, themselves, need to reflect on possible bias. Cultural norms and ethics in the workplace influence corporate behavior – learn and use the ethical risk model. DAMA International encourages data professionals to take a professional stand, and present the risk situation to business leaders; they just might not have thought about these implications in their work.

13.6 Notable Data Management Professionals

Since its inception in 1988, DAMA International has recognized data management professionals who have made significant, demonstrable contributions to the data management field by honoring them with a DAMA Individual Achievement Award.

13.6.1 Lifetime Achievement Award

The Lifetime Achievement Award recognizes an individual for significant contributions to the data management profession over the course of his / her lifetime. The highest honor bestowed by DAMA International.

2002	John Zachman
2006	Michael Brackett

13.6.2 Professional Achievement Award

The Professional Achievement Award was formerly known as the Individual Achievement Award. It recognizes a DAMA International member who has made significant, demonstrable contributions to the data management profession.

1988	John Zachman
1988	Walter Vitale
1991	Jo Meador
1992	Gary Schudt
1993	Belkis Leong-Hong
1995	Ronald Ross
1996	Barbara von Halle
1997	Clive Finkelstein
1998	Larry English
1999	Claudia Imhoff
2000	Peter Chen
2001	Peter Aiken
2001	E.F. "Ted" Codd
2002	Davida Berger
2002	William (Bill) H. Inmon
2003	Graeme Simsion
2004	Len Silverston
2005	Claudia Imhoff
2006	Patricia Cupoli
2007	Robert Seiner
2008	David Marco
2009	Jaylene McCandlish

13.6.3 Government Achievement Award

The Government Achievement Award recognizes a DAMA International member working in the public sector for data management leadership and practice.

2004	Dr. John D. Graham
2005	Judith Newton
2008	Suzanne Acar
2009	Glenn Thomas

13.6.4 Academic Achievement Award

The Academic Achievement Award recognizes a DAMA International member from academia for outstanding research or theoretical contributions in the field of data management.

2003	Dr. Terry Halpin
2004	Dr. Richard Nolan
2005	Dr. Richard Wang
2006	Dr. Gordon Everest
2007	Dr. Herbert Longnecker
2008	Dr. John Talburt
2009	Eva Smith

13.6.5 DAMA Community Award

The DAMA Community Award recognizes a DAMA International member who has gone beyond the call of volunteer service to the DAMA organization and its membership.

2003	Brett Champlin
2004	Larry Dziedzic
2005	Dr. Peter Aiken
2006	Len Silverston
2007	Jack Olson
2008	Michael Scofield
2009	Mark Mosley

Afterword

To echo John Zachman's opening comment in the Foreword: Wow, what a truly monumental piece of work!

The DAMA-DMBOK Guide is the first of its kind in the data management profession, even though other Bodies of Knowledge exist in other professions. The development of a formal data management profession from a collection of different disciplines requires, actually mandates, that a Body of Knowledge be developed. That is exactly what was done here.

Is the first DAMA-DMBOK Guide perfect? No. But, it is a major step in the right direction. DAMA, including both DAMA International and the DAMA Foundation, has 'driven the stake' and made a stand on what should comprise a formal, certified, recognized, and respected data management profession. The contents of the first DAMA-DMBOK Guide will be evaluated, revised, and released in updated versions.

It was not easy pulling the first DAMA-DMBOK Guide together. Several hundred people were involved in developing and reviewing the contents, and preparing the final manuscript for publication. These people came from different disciplines, different professional backgrounds, and different operating environments. All had different ideas and thoughts about what should be included in a formal data management profession. However, in staying with the theme of *professionals creating the profession*, the input of a wide variety of professionals needed to be considered.

You probably noticed some inconsistencies as you read through the DAMA-DMBOK Guide. These inconsistencies are the result of including the thoughts and ideas of many data management professionals. Although attempts were made at consistency, at least with respect to the over-style, the objective was to avoid forcing the thoughts of a few on the many. It is better to surface the inconsistencies among professionals, evaluate them, decide on the best approach, and include the refinements in revisions to the DAMA-DMBOK Guide.

The evolution of the data management profession and the DAMA-DMBOK Guide is quite interesting. In the middle and late 1990's concern was growing about the development of a formal data management profession. A number of data management professionals felt that if we, the professionals, did not develop our own formal data management profession, that someone else would develop it for us. Those were very disconcerting times.

In the early 2000's a few of us in DAMA had a vision of a formal, certified, recognized, and respected data management profession. We developed an education curriculum, began formal certifications, established a Foundation, and prepared mission statements. We decided to develop a Body of Knowledge (BOK), which quickly evolved to a Complete Body of Knowledge (CBOK).

Subsequently, a discussion evolved about branding products that DAMA developed. Accordingly, the Data Management Body of Knowledge (DMBOK) was established. Further branding led to the DAMA-DMBOK. When we initially looked at the contents of a complete body of knowledge, it was clear that it could not be put into a single document. Hence, the DAMA-DMBOK Guide was conceived as a guide to the complete body of knowledge for data management.

The DAMA-DMBOK Guide was such a daunting task that development actually began with the DAMA Dictionary of Data Management published in 2008. The Dictionary, like the DAMA-DMBOK Guide is not perfect and will be revised. However, it was a start and formed the foundation for the DAMA-DMBOK Guide published in 2009. Plans are already under way to enhance the Dictionary and the Guide.

The evolution of a formal data management profession can only continue if the professionals are actively involved. I encourage each of you to become involved in the evolution of a formal data management profession, and encourage your fellow professionals to become involved. It is only through the active involvement of data management professionals that a truly viable data management profession will evolve and survive.

Michael Brackett
Lilliwaup, Washington
January, 2009

A1 Data Management Suppliers

Function	Suppliers
1. Data Governance	• Business Executives • IT Executives • Data Stewards • Regulatory Bodies
2. Data Architecture Management	• Executives • Data Stewards • Data Producers • Information Consumers
3. Data Development	• Data Stewards • Subject Matter Experts • IT Steering Committee • Data Governance Council • Data Architects and Analysts • Software Developers • Data Producers • Information Consumers
4. Data operations Management	• Executives • IT Steering Committee • Data Governance Council • Data Stewards • Data Architects and Modelers • Software Developers
5. Data Security Management	• Data Stewards • IT Steering Committee • Data Stewardship Council • Government • Customers
6. Reference and Master Data Management	• Steering Committees • Business Data Stewards • Subject Matter Experts • Data Consumers • Standards Organizations • Data Providers
7. Data Warehouse and Business Intelligence Management	• Executives and Managers • Subject Matter Experts • Data Governance Council • Information Consumers (Internal and External) • Data Producers • Data Architects and Analysts
8. Document and Content Management	• Employees • External parties

Function	Suppliers
9. Meta-data Management	• Data Stewards • Data Architects • Data Modelers • Database Administrators • Other Data Professionals • Data Brokers • Government and Industry Regulators
10. Data Quality Management	• External Sources • Regulatory Bodies • Business Subject Matter Experts • Information Consumers • Data Producers • Data Architects • Data Modelers • Data Stewards

A2 Data Management Inputs

Function	Inputs
1. Data Governance	<ul><li>Business Goals</li><li>Business Strategies</li><li>IT Objectives</li><li>IT Strategies</li><li>Data Needs</li><li>Data Issues</li><li>Regulatory Requirements</li></ul>
2. Data Architecture Management	<ul><li>Business Goals</li><li>Business Strategies</li><li>Business Architecture</li><li>Process Architecture</li><li>IT Objectives</li><li>IT Strategies</li><li>Data Strategies</li><li>Data Issues</li><li>Data Needs</li><li>Technical Architecture</li></ul>
3. Data Development	<ul><li>Business Goals and Strategies</li><li>Data Needs and Strategies</li><li>Data Architecture</li><li>Process Architecture</li><li>Application Architecture</li><li>Technical Architecture</li></ul>
4. Data operations Management	<ul><li>Data Requirements</li><li>Data Architecture</li><li>Data Models</li><li>Legacy Data</li></ul>
5. Data Security Management	<ul><li>Business Goals</li><li>Business Strategy</li><li>Business Rules</li><li>Business Process</li><li>Data Strategy</li><li>Data Privacy Issues</li><li>Related IT Policies and Standards</li></ul>
6. Reference and Master Data Management	<ul><li>Business Drivers</li><li>Data Requirements</li><li>Policy and Regulations</li><li>Standards</li><li>Code Sets</li><li>Master Data</li><li>Transactional Data</li></ul>

Function	Inputs
7. Data Warehouse and Business Intelligence Management	• Business Drivers • BI Data and Access Requirements • Data Quality Requirements • Data Security Requirements • Data Architecture • Technical Architecture • Data Modeling Standards and Guidelines • Transactional Data • Master and Reference Data • Industry and External Data
8. Document and Content Management	• Text Documents • Reports • Spreadsheets • Email • Instant Messages • Faxes • Voicemail • Images • Video recordings • Audio recordings • Printed paper files • Microfiche
9. Meta-data Management	• Meta-data Requirements • Meta-data Issues • Data Architecture • Business Meta-data • Technical Meta-data • Process Meta-data • Operational Meta-data • Data Stewardship Meta-data
10. Data Quality Management	• Business Requirements • Data Requirements • Data Quality Expectations • Data Policies and Standards • Business Meta-data • Technical Meta-data

A3 Data Management Participants

Function	Participants
1. Data Governance	• Executive Data Stewards • Coordinating Data Stewards • Business Data Stewards • Data Professionals • DM Executive • CIO
2. Data Architecture Management	• Data Stewards • Subject Matter Experts (SMEs) • Data Architects • Data Analysts and Modelers • Other Enterprise Architects • DM Executive and Managers • CIO and Other Executives • Database Administrators • Data Model Administrator
3. Data Development	• Data Stewards and SMEs • Data Architects and Analysts • Database Administrators • Data Model Administrators • Software Developers • Project Managers • DM Executives and Other IT Management
4. Data operations Management	• Database Administrators • Software Developers • Project Managers • Data Stewards • Data Architects and Analysts • DM Executives and Other IT Management • IT Operators
5. Data Security Management	• Data Stewards • Data Security Administrators • Database Administrators • BI Analysts • Data Architects • DM Leader • CIO / CTO • Help Desk Analysts
6. Reference and Master Data Management	• Data Stewards • Subject Matter Experts • Data Architects • Data Analysts • Application Architects • Data Governance Council • Data Providers • Other IT Professionals

Function	Participants
7. Data Warehouse and Business Intelligence Management	<ul><li>Business Executives and Managers</li><li>DM Execs and Other IT Mgmt</li><li>BI Program Manager</li><li>SMEs and Other Info Consumers</li><li>Data Stewards</li><li>Project Managers</li><li>Data Architects and Analysts</li><li>Data Integration (ETL) Specialists</li><li>BI Specialists</li><li>Database Administrators</li><li>Data Security Administrators</li><li>Data Quality Analysts</li></ul>
8. Document and Content Management	<ul><li>All Employees</li><li>Data Stewards</li><li>DM Professionals</li><li>Records Management Staff</li><li>Other IT Professionals</li><li>Data Management Executive</li><li>Other IT Managers</li><li>Chief information Officer</li><li>Chief Knowledge Officer</li></ul>
9. Meta-data Management	<ul><li>Meta-data Specialist</li><li>Data Integration Architects</li><li>Data Stewards</li><li>Data Architects and Modelers</li><li>Database Administrators</li><li>Other DM Professionals</li><li>Other IT Professionals</li><li>DM Executive</li></ul>
10. Data Quality Management	<ul><li>Data Quality Analysts</li><li>Data Stewards</li><li>Other Data Professionals</li><li>DRM Director</li><li>Data Stewardship Council</li></ul>

A4 Data Management Tools

Function	Tools
1. Data Governance	<ul><li>Intranet Website</li><li>E-Mail</li><li>Meta-data Tools</li><li>Issue Management Tools</li></ul>
2. Data Architecture Management	<ul><li>Data Modeling Tools</li><li>Model Management Tool</li><li>Meta-data Repository</li><li>Office Productivity Tools</li></ul>
3. Data Development	<ul><li>Data Modeling Tools</li><li>Database Management Systems</li><li>Software Development Tools</li><li>Testing Tools</li><li>Model Management Tools</li><li>Configuration Management Tools</li><li>Office Productivity Tools</li></ul>
4. Data operations Management	<ul><li>Database Management Systems</li><li>Data Development Tools</li><li>Database Administration Tools</li><li>Office Productivity Tools</li></ul>
5. Data Security Management	<ul><li>Database Management System</li><li>Business Intelligence Tools</li><li>Application Frameworks</li><li>Identity Management Technologies</li><li>Change Control Systems</li></ul>
6. Reference and Master Data Management	<ul><li>Reference Data Management Applications</li><li>Master Data Management Applications</li><li>Data Modeling Tools</li><li>Process Modeling Tools</li><li>Meta-data Repositories</li><li>Data Profiling Tools</li><li>Data Cleansing Tools</li><li>Data Integration Tools</li><li>Business Process and Rule Engines</li><li>Change Management Tools</li></ul>

Function	Tools
7. Data Warehouse and Business Intelligence Management	<ul><li>Business Executives and Managers</li><li>DM Execs and Other IT Mgmt</li><li>BI Program Manager</li><li>SMEs and Other Info Consumers</li><li>Data Stewards</li><li>Project Managers</li><li>Data Architects and Analysts</li><li>Data Integration (ETL) Specialists</li><li>BI Specialists</li><li>Database Administrators</li><li>Data Security Administrators</li><li>Data Quality Analysts</li></ul>
8. Document and Content Management	<ul><li>All Employees</li><li>Data Stewards</li><li>DM Professionals</li><li>Records Management Staff</li><li>Other IT Professionals</li><li>Data Management Executive</li><li>Other IT Managers</li><li>Chief information Officer</li><li>Chief Knowledge Officer</li></ul>
9. Meta-data Management	<ul><li>Meta-data Repositories</li><li>Data Modeling Tools</li><li>Database Management Systems</li><li>Data Integration Tools</li><li>Business Intelligence Tools</li><li>System Management Tools</li><li>Object Modeling Tools</li><li>Process Modeling Tools</li><li>Report Generating Tools</li><li>Data Quality Tools</li><li>Data Development and Administration Tools</li><li>Reference and Master Data Management Tools</li></ul>
10. Data Quality Management	<ul><li>Data Profiling Tools</li><li>Statistical Analysis Tools</li><li>Data Cleansing Tools</li><li>Data Integration Tools</li><li>Issue and Event Management Tools</li></ul>

A5 Data Management Primary Deliverables

Function	Primary Deliverables
1. Data Governance	<ul><li>Data Policies</li><li>Data Standards</li><li>Resolved Issues</li><li>Data Mgmt Projects and Services</li><li>Quality Data and Information</li><li>Recognized Data Value</li></ul>
2. Data Architecture Management	<ul><li>Enterprise Data Model</li><li>Information Value Chain Analysis</li><li>Database Architecture</li><li>Data Integration / MDM Architecture</li><li>DW / BI Architecture</li><li>Meta-data Architecture</li><li>Enterprise Taxonomies and Namespaces</li><li>Document Management Architecture</li><li>Meta-data</li></ul>
3. Data Development	<ul><li>Data Requirements and Business Rules</li><li>Logical Data Models and Specifications</li><li>Physical Data Models and Specifications</li><li>Meta-data (Business and Technical)</li><li>Data Modeling and DB Design Standards</li><li>Data Model and DB Design Reviews</li><li>Version Controlled Data Models</li><li>Test Data</li><li>Development and Test Databases</li><li>Information Products</li><li>Data Access Services</li><li>Data Integration Services</li><li>Migrated and Converted Data</li></ul>
4. Data operations Management	<ul><li>DBMS Technical Environments</li><li>Dev / Test, QA, and Production Databases</li><li>Externally Sourced Data</li><li>Database Performance</li><li>Data Recovery Plans</li><li>Business Continuity</li><li>Data Retention Plan</li><li>Archived and Purged Data</li></ul>
5. Data Security Management	<ul><li>Data Security Policies</li><li>Data Privacy and Confidentiality Standards</li><li>User Profiles, Passwords and Memberships</li><li>Data Security Permissions</li><li>Data Security Controls</li><li>Data Access Views</li><li>Document Classifications</li><li>Authentication and Access History</li><li>Data Security Audits</li></ul>

Function	Primary Deliverables
6. Reference and Master Data Management	• Master and Reference Data Requirements • Data Models and Documentation • Reliable Reference and Master Data • "Golden Record" Data Lineage • Data Quality Metrics and Reports • Data Cleansing Services
7. Data Warehouse and Business Intelligence Management	• DW / BI Architecture • Data Warehouses • Data Marts and OLAP Cubes • Dashboards and Scorecards • Analytic Applications • File Extracts (for Data Mining / Stat. Tools) • BI Tools and User Environments • Data Quality Feedback Mechanism / Loop
8. Document and Content Management	• Managed records in many media formats • E-discovery records • Outgoing letters and emails • All contracts and financial documents • Policies and procedures • Audit trails and logs • Meeting minutes • Formal reports • Significant memoranda
9. Meta-data Management	• Meta-data Repositories • Quality Meta-data • Meta-data Models and Architecture • Meta-data Management Operational Analysis • Meta-data Analysis • Data Lineage • Change Impact Analysis • Meta-data Control Procedures
10. Data Quality Management	• Higher Quality Data • Data Management Operational Analysis • Data Profiles • Data Quality Certification Reports

A6 Data Management Consumers

Function	Consumers
1. Data Governance	• Data Producers • Knowledge Workers • Managers and Executives • Data Professionals • Customers
2. Data Architecture Management	• Data Stewards • Data Architects • Data Analysts • Database Administrators • Software Developers • Project Managers • Data Producers • Knowledge Workers • Managers and Executives
3. Data Development	• Data Producers • Knowledge Workers • Managers and Executives • Customers • Data Professionals • Other IT Professionals
4. Data operations Management	• Data Creators • Information Consumers • Enterprise Customers • Data Professionals • Other IT Professionals
5. Data Security Management	• Data Producers • Knowledge Workers • Managers • Executives • Customers • Data Professionals
6. Reference and Master Data Management	• Application Users • BI and Reporting Users • Application Developers and Architects • Data Integration Developers and Architects • BI Developers and Architects • Vendors, Customers, and Partners
7. Data Warehouse and Business Intelligence Management	• Knowledge Workers • Managers and Executives • External Customers • Internal Systems • Data Professionals • Other IT Professionals

Function	Consumers
8. Document and Content Management	• Business and IT users • Government regulatory agencies • Senior management • External customers
9. Meta-data Management	• Data Stewards • Data Professionals • Other IT Professionals • Knowledge Workers • Managers and Executives • Customers and Collaborators
10. Data Quality Management	• Data Stewards • Data Professionals • Other IT Professionals • Knowledge Workers • Managers and Executives • Customers

A7 Data Management Metrics

Function	Metrics
1. Data Governance	• Data Value • Data Management Cost • Achievement of Objectives • # of Meetings Held • # of Decisions Made • Steward Representation / Coverage • Data Professional Headcount • Data Management Process Maturity
2. Data Architecture Management	•
3. Data Development	•
4. Data operations Management	• Availability • Performance
5. Data Security Management	•
6. Reference and Master Data Management	• Reference and Master Data Quality • Change Activity • Issues, Costs, Volume • Use and Re-Use • Availability • Data Steward Coverage
7. Data Warehouse and Business Intelligence Management	• Usage Metrics • Customer / User Satisfaction • Subject Area Coverage %s • Response / Performance Metrics
8. Document and Content Management	• Return on investment • Key Performance Indicators • Balanced Scorecards
9. Meta-data Management	• Meta Data Quality • Master Data Service Data Compliance • Meta-data Repository Contribution • Meta-data Documentation Quality • Steward Representation / Coverage • Meta-data Usage / Reference • Meta-data Management Maturity • Meta-data Repository Availability
10. Data Quality Management	• Data Value Statistics • Errors / Requirement Violations • Conformance to Expectations • Conformance to Service Levels

A8 Software Product Classes

Classes of Technology	Description
Database Management Systems (DBMS)	• Relational Database Management Systems (RDBMS). • Multi-Dimensional Database Management Systems (MDBMS). • Object-Oriented Database Management Systems (OODBMS). • Hierarchical Database Management Systems. • Network Database Management Systems.
Modeling and Meta-data Tools	• Data Modeling Tools. • Model Management Tools. • Process Modeling Tools. • Object Modeling Tools. • Meta-data Repositories. • Glossaries. • Directories. • Taxonomies.
Data Development and Administration tools	• Database Development Tools. • Database Administration Tools. • Testing Tools. • Software Configuration Management Tools (source code library and version control). • Issue and Defect Management Tools. • Project Management Tools.
Data Integration Tools	• Data Movement Tools (ETL). • Enterprise Application Integration (EAI) Tools. • Data Transparency Tools.
Data Quality Tools	• Data Profiling Tools. • Data Cleansing Tools.
Business Intelligence Tools	• Ad Hoc Query and Reporting Tools. • Enterprise Reporting Tools. • Online Analytical Processing (OLAP) Tools. • Desktop OLAP Tools. • Multi-Dimensional OLAP (MOLAP) Tools. • Relational OLAP (ROLAP) Tools. • Statistical Analysis Tools. • Data Mining / Predictive Analysis Tools. • Scenario Modeling Tools. • Specialized Analytical Applications (Analytics). • Executive Information Systems. • Business Performance Management Tools.
Reference and Master Data Management Tools	• Master Data Management System Environments. • Customer Data Integration Solutions. • Product Data Integration Solutions. • Dimensional Hierarchy Management Tools.

A9 Summary Process Tables

The process summary tables from each chapter have been included in an Appendix to provide a ready reference to all the processes. The codes in parentheses is P for Planning, D for Develop and Deploy, O for Operate, and C for Control.

A9.1 Data Governance

Activities	Deliverables	Responsible Roles	Approving Roles	Contributing Roles
1.1.1 Understand Strategic Enterprise Data Needs (P)	Strategic Enterprise Data Needs	DM Executive	Data Governance Council, CIO	Data Stewards, Data management professionals
1.1.2 Develop and Maintain the Data Strategy (P)	Data Strategy – Vision, Mission, Bus. Case, Goals, Objectives, Principles, Components, Metrics, Implementation Roadmap	DM Executive	Data Governance Council, CIO	Data Stewards, Data management professionals
1.1.3 Establish Data Management Professional Roles and Organizations (P)	Data Management Services organizations and staff	CIO	Data Governance Council	DM Executive
1.1.4 Establish Data Governance and Stewardship Organizations (P)	Data Governance Council, Data Stewardship Committee, Data Stewardship Teams	DM Executive, CIO, Data Governance Council	Senior Mgmt	Data Stewards, Data management professionals
1.1.5 Identify and Appoint Data Stewards (P)	Business Data Stewards, Coordinating Data Stewards, Executive Data Stewards	DM Executive, Executive Data Stewards	Data Governance Council	Coordinating Data Stewards, Data management professionals

Activities	Deliverables	Responsible Roles	Approving Roles	Contributing Roles
1.1.6 Develop, Review and Approve Data Policies, Standards, and Procedures (P)	Data Policies, Data Standards, Data Management Procedures	DM Executive	Data Governance Council, CIO	Data Stewardship Committee, Data Stewardship Teams, Data management professionals
1.1.7 Review and Approve Data Architecture (P)	Adopted Enterprise Data Model, Related Data Architecture	Data Governance Council	Data Governance Council, CIO	Enterprise Data Architect, Data Stewardship Committee, Data Stewards, Data Architects, DM Executive
1.1.8 Plan and Sponsor Data Management Projects and Services (P)	Data Management Projects, Data Management Services	Data Governance Council	Data Governance Council, CIO, IT Steering Committee	DM Executive, Data management professionals, Data Stewards
1.1.9 Estimate Data Asset Value and Associated Costs (P)	Data Asset Value Estimates, Data Mgmt. Cost Estimates	Data Stewards	Data Governance Council	DM Executive, Data management professionals
1.2.1 Supervise Data Professional Organizations and Staff (C)	Data Management Services organization(s) and staff	DM Executive(s)	CIO	Data management professionals
1.2.2 Coordinate Data Governance Activities (C)	Data Governance Organization Schedules, Meetings, Agendas, Documents, Minutes	DM Executive, Enterprise Data Architect, Data Architects	Data Governance Council, Data Stewardship Committee, Data Stewardship Teams, CIO	Data management professionals

Activities	Deliverables	Responsible Roles	Approving Roles	Contributing Roles
1.2.3 Manage and Resolve Data Related Issues (C)	Issue Log, Issue Resolutions	Data Stewardship Teams, Data Stewardship Committee, Data Governance Council	Data Stewardship Teams, Data Stewardship Committee, Data Governance Council	DM Executive, Data management professionals
1.2.4 Monitor and Ensure Regulatory Compliance (C)	Compliance Reporting, Non-compliance Issues	Data management professionals	Data Governance Council	DM Executive, CIO
1.2.5 Communicate, Monitor and Enforce Conformance with Data Policies, Standards, Procedures, and Architecture (C)	Policy / Standards / Arch / Procedure Communication, Non-conformance Issues	Data management professionals, Data Stewards	Data Governance Council, Data Stewardship Committee	DM Executive
1.2.6 Oversee Data Management Projects and Services (C)		DM Executive	Data Governance Council	Data management professionals
1.2.7 Communicate and Promote the Value of Data and Data Management (C)	Data Management Website, Data Management Newsletter, Understanding and Recognition	DM Executive, Data management professionals, Data Stewards, CIO	Data Governance Council	Data Stewards

A9.2 Data Architecture Management

Activities	Deliverables	Responsible Roles	Approving Roles	Contributing Roles
2.1 Understand Enterprise Information Needs (P)	Lists of essential information requirements	Enterprise Data Architect, Business SME's	Data Governance Council, Data Architecture Steering Committee, DM Executive, CIO	
2.2 Develop and Maintain the Enterprise Data Model (P)	Enterprise Data Model: • Subject Area Model • Conceptual Model • Logical Model • Glossary	Enterprise Data Architect	Data Governance Council, Data Architecture Steering Committee, DM Executive, CIO	Data Architects, Data Stewards / Teams
2.3 Analyze and Align With Other Business Models (P)	Information Value Chain Analysis Matrices • Entity / Function • Entity / Org and Role • Entity / Application	Enterprise Data Architect	Data Governance Council, Data Architecture Steering Committee, DM Executive, CIO	Data Architects, Data Stewards / Teams, Enterprise Architects
2.4 Define and Maintain the Data Technology Architecture (P)	Data Technology Architecture (Technology, Distribution, Usage)	Enterprise Data Architect	DM Executive, CIO,Data Architecture Steering Committee, Data Governance Council	Database Administrators, Other Data Management. Professionals

Activities	Deliverables	Responsible Roles	Approving Roles	Contributing Roles
2.5 Define and Maintain the Data Integration Architecture (P)	Data Integration Architecture • Data Lineage / Flows • Entity Lifecycles	Enterprise Data Architect	DM Executive, CIO, Data Architecture Steering Committee, Data Governance Council	Database Administrators, Data Integration Specialists, Other Data Management Professionals
2.6 Define and Maintain the Data Warehouse / BI Architecture (P)	Data Warehouse / Business Intelligence Architecture	Data Warehouse Architect	Enterprise Data Architect, DM Executive, CIO, Data Architecture Steering Committee, Data Governance Council	Business Intelligence Specialists, Data Integration Specialists, Database Administrators, Other Data Management. Professionals
2.7 Define and Maintain Enterprise Taxonomies and Namespaces	Enterprise Taxonomies, XML Namespaces, Content Management Standards	Enterprise Data Architect	DM Executive, CIO, Data Architecture Steering Committee, Data Governance Council	Other Data Architects, Other Data Management Professionals
2.8 Define and Maintain the Meta-data Architecture (P)	Meta-data Architecture	Meta-data Architect	Enterprise Data Architect, DM Executive, CIO, Data Architecture Steering Committee, Data Governance Council	Meta-data Specialists, Other Data Management. Professionals

A9.3 Data Development

Activities	Deliverables	Responsible Roles	Approving Roles	Contributing Roles
3.1.1 Analyze Information Requirements (D)	Information Requirement Specification Statements	Data Architects, Data Analysts	Data Stewards	Data Stewards, Other SMEs
3.1.2 Develop and Maintain Conceptual Data Models (D)	Conceptual Data Model Diagrams and Reports	Data Architects, Data Analysts	Data Stewards, Data Architects	Data Stewards, Other SMEs
3.1.3 Develop and Maintain Logical Data Models (D)	Logical Data Model Diagrams and Reports	Data Architects, Data Analysts, Data Modelers	Data Stewards, Data Architects	Data Stewards, Other SMEs
3.1.4 Develop and Maintain Physical Data Models (D)	Physical Data Model Diagrams and Reports	Data Architects, Data Modelers, DBAs	DBAs, Data Architects	Software Developers
3.2.1 Design Physical Databases (D)	DDL Specifications, OLAP Cube Specs, XML schemas	DBAs, Application Architects, Software Developers	Data Architects, DBAs, Application Architects	Data Analysts, Data Modelers, Software Developers
3.2.2 Design Information Products (D)	Application Screens, Reports	Software Developers	Application Architects	Data Analysts, DBAs
3.2.3 Design Data Access Services (D)	Data Access Service Design Specifications	Software Developers, DBAs	Application Architects, Data Architects	Data Analysts, DBAs
3.2.4 Design Data Integration Services (D)	Source-to-Target Maps, ETL Design Specs, Conversion Designs	Data Integration Specialists, DBAs, Data Analysts	DBAs, Data Architects, Application Architects	Data Analysts, Data Stewards, DBAs
3.3.1 Develop Data Modeling and Database Design Standards (P)	Data Modeling Standards Documents, Database Design Standards Documents	Data Architects, Data Analysts, Data Modelers, DBAs	DM Executive, Data Governance Council	Data Stewards, Application Architects, Software Developers

Activities	Deliverables	Responsible Roles	Approving Roles	Contributing Roles
3.3.2 Review Data Model and Database Design Quality (C)	Design Review Findings	Data Architects, Data Analysts, Data Modelers, DBAs	DM Executive, Project Manager	Application Architects, Software Developers
3.3.3 Manage Data Model Versioning and Integration (C)	Model Management Libraries and Contents	Data Model Administrators, Data Modelers	Data Architects, DM Executive	Data Analysts, DBAs
3.4.1 Implement Development and Test Database Changes (D)	Dev and Test DB Environments, Database Tables, Other DB Objects	DBAs	DM Executive	Data Architects, Data Analysts, Software Developers
3.4.2 Create and Maintain Test Data (D)	Test Databases, Test Data	DBAs, Data Analysts, Software Developers, Test Analysts	Data Architects, Application Architects, Data Stewards	Data Stewards, Software Developers, Data Analysts
3.4.3 Migrate and Convert Data (D)	Migrated and Converted Data	DBAs, Software Developers	Data Stewards, Data Architects	Data Analysts
3.4.4 Build and Test Information Products (D)	Information Products: Screens, Reports	Software Developers	Data Stewards, Application Architects, Data Architects	DBAs, Data Analysts
3.4.5 Build and Test Data Access Services (D)	Data Access Services (interfaces)	Software Developers	Data Architects, Application Architects	DBAs
3.4.6 Build and Test Data Integration Services (D)	Data Integration Services (ETL, etc.)	Data Integration Specialists	Data Stewards, Data Architects	DBAs, Data Analysts
3.4.7 Validate Information Requirements (D)	Validated Requirements, User Acceptance Signoff	Data Stewards, Testing Specialists	Data Stewards	Data Analysts, Data Architects, DBAs

Activities	Deliverables	Responsible Roles	Approving Roles	Contributing Roles
3.4.8 Prepare for Data Deployment (D)	User Training, User Documentation	Data Stewards, Business SMEs, Training Specialists, Data Analysts	Data Stewards, Data Architects	Data Stewards, Data Architects, DBAs

A9.4 Data Operations Management

Activities	Deliverables	Responsible Roles	Approving Roles	Contributing Roles
4.1.1 Implement and Control Database Environments	Production database environment maintenance, managed changes to production databases, releases	DBAs	DM Executive	System programmers, data stewards, data analysts, software developers, project managers
4.1.2 Acquire Externally Sourced Data (O)	Externally sourced data	DBAs, data analysts, data stewards	Data Governance Council	Data stewards, data analysts
4.1.3 Plan for Data Recovery (P)	Data availability SLAs, data recovery plans	DBAs	DM Executive, Data Governance Council	
4.1.4 Backup and Recover Data (O)	Database backups and logs,restored databases,business continuity	DBAs	DM Executive	
4.1.5 Set Database Performance Service Levels (P)	Database performance SLAs	DBAs	DM Executive, Data Governance Council	
4.1.6 Monitor and Tune Database Performance (O)	Database performance reporting, Database performance	DBAs		

Activities	Deliverables	Responsible Roles	Approving Roles	Contributing Roles
4.1.7 Plan for Data Retention (P)	Data retention plan, storage management procedures	DBAs	DM Executive	Storage management specialists
4.1.8 Archive, Retrieve and Purge Data (O)	Archived data, retrieved data, purged data	DBAs	DM Executive	
4.1.9 Manage Specialized Databases (O)	Geospatial databases, CAD / CAM databases, XML databases, object databases	DBAs	DM Executive	Data stewards, Subject matter experts
4.2.1 Understand Data Technology Requirements (P)	Data technology requirements	Data architect, DBAs	DM Executive	Data stewards, other IT professionals
4.2.2 Define the Database Architecture (P) (same as 2.3)	Data technology architecture	Data architect	DM Executive, Data Governance Council	DBAs, data analysts, data stewards
4.2.3 Evaluate Data Technology (P)	Tool evaluation findings, tool selection decisions	Data analysts, DBAs	DM Executive, Data Governance Council	Data stewards, other IT professionals
4.2.4 Install and Administer Data Technology (O)	Installed technology	DBAs	DM Executive	Data analysts, other data professionals
4.2.5 Inventory and Track Data Technology Licenses (C)	License inventory	DBAs	DM Executive	Other data professionals
4.2.6 Support Data Technology Usage and Issues (O)	Identified and resolved technology issues	DBAs	DM Executive	Other data professionals

A9.5 Data Security Management

Activities	Deliverables	Responsible Roles	Approving Roles	Contributing Roles
5.1 Understand Data Security Needs and Regulatory Requirements (P)	Data Security Requirements and Regulations	Data Stewards, DM Executive, Security Administrators	Data Governance Council	Data Stewards, Legal Department, IT Security
5.2 Define Data Security Policy (P)	Data Security Policy	Data Stewards, DM Executive, Security Administrators	Data Governance Council	Data Stewards, Legal Department, IT Security
5.3 Define Data Security Standards (P)	Data Security Standards	Data Stewards, DM Executive, Security Administrators	Data Governance Council	Data Stewards, Legal Department, IT Security
5.4 Define Data Security Controls and Procedures (D)	Data Security Controls and Procedures	Security Administrators	DM Executive	Data Stewards, IT Security
5.5 Manage Users, Passwords and Group Membership (C)	User Accounts, Passwords, Role Groups	Security Administrators, DBAs	Management	Data Producers, Data Consumers, Help Desk
5.6 Manage Data Access Views and Permissions (C)	Data Access Views Data Resource Permissions	Security Administrators, DBAs	Management	Data Producers, Data Consumers, Software Developers, Management, Help Desk
5.7 Monitor User Authentication and Access Behavior (C)	Data Access Logs, Security Notification Alerts, Data Security Reports	Security Administrators, DBAs	DM Executive	Data Stewards, Help Desk
5.8 Classify Information Confidentiality (C)	Classified Documents, Classified Databases	Document Authors, Report Designers, Data Stewards	Management	Data Stewards
5.9 Audit Data Security (C)	Data Security Audit Reports	Data Security Auditors	Data Governance Council, DM Executive	Security Administrators, DBAs, Data Stewards

A9.6 Reference and Master Data Management

Activities	Deliverables	Responsible Roles	Approving Roles	Contributing Roles
6.1 Understand Reference Data Integration Needs (P)	Reference and Master Data Requirements	Business Analysts	Stakeholders, Data Governance Council	Business Data Stewards, Subject Matter Experts
6.2 Identify Reference Data Sources and Contributors (P)	Description and Assessment of Sources and Contributors	Data Architects, Data Stewards	Data Governance Council	Data Analysts, Subject Matter Experts
6.3 Define and Maintain the Data Integration Architecture (P)	Reference and Master Data Integration Architecture and Roadmap	Data Architects	Data Governance Council	Application Architects, Data Stewards
	Data Integration Services Design Specifications	Data Architects, Application Architects	IT Management	Other IT Professionals, Stakeholders
6.4 Implement Reference and Master Data Management Solutions (D)	Reference Data Management Applications and Databases, Master Data Management Application and Databases	Application Architects, Data Architects	Data Governance Council	Other IT Professionals
	Data Quality Services	Application Architects, Data Architects	Data Governance Council	Data Analysts, Other IT Professionals
	Data Replication and Access Services for Applications	Data Architects, Application Architects, Integration	Data Governance Council	Data Analysts, Other IT Professionals

Activities	Deliverables	Responsible Roles	Approving Roles	Contributing Roles
	Data Replication Services for Data Warehousing	Developers		
6.5 Define and Maintain Match Rules (P)	Record Matching Rules (Functional Specifications)	Business Analysts, Data Architects, Business Data Stewards	Data Governance Council	Application Architects, Subject Matter Experts
6.6 Establish Golden Records (C)	Reliable Reference and Master Data	Data Stewards	Stakeholders	Data Analysts, Data Architects, Subject Matter Experts, Other IT Professionals
	Cross-Reference Data	Data Stewards	Stakeholders	Data Analysts, Subject Matter Experts
	Data Lineage Reports	Data Architects	Data Stewards	Data Analysts
	Data Quality Reports	Data Analysts	Data Stewards, Stakeholders	Data Architects
6.7 Define and Maintain Hierarchies and Affiliations (C)	Defined Hierarchies and Affiliations	Data Stewards	Stakeholders	Data Analysts, Data Providers
6.8 Plan and Implement Integration of New Sources (D)	Data Source Quality and Integration Assessments	Data Analysts, Data Architects, Application Architects	Data Stewards, IT Management	Data Providers, Subject Matter Experts

Activities	Deliverables	Responsible Roles	Approving Roles	Contributing Roles
	Integrated new data source	Data Architects, Application Architects	Data Stewards, Stakeholders	Data Analysts, Other IT Professionals
6.9 Replicate and Distribute Reference and Master Data (O)	Replicated Data	Data Architects, Application Architects	Data Stewards, Stakeholders,	Data Analysts, Other IT Professionals
6.10 Manage Changes to Reference and Master Data (C)	Change Request Procedures	Data Architects	Data Governance Council, Data Stewards	Other IT Professionals, Stakeholders
	Change Requests and Responses	Data Stewards	Data Governance Council	Stakeholders, Data Analysts, Data Architects, Application Architects
	Change Request Metrics	Data Architects	Data Stewards, Data Governance Council	Data Analysts, Other IT Professionals

A9.7 Data Warehouse and Business Intelligence Management

Activities	Deliverables	Responsible Roles	Approving Roles	Contributing Roles
7.1 Understand Business Intelligence Information Needs (P)	DW-BIM Project Requirements	Data / BI Analyst, BI Program Manager, SME	Data Steward, Business Executives and Managers	Meta-Data Specialist, Business Process Lead

Activities	Deliverables	Responsible Roles	Approving Roles	Contributing Roles
7.2 Define the Data Warehouse / BI Architecture (P) (same as 2.1.5)	Data Warehouse / Business Intelligence Architecture	Data Warehouse Architect, Business Intelligence Architect	Enterprise Data Architect, DM Executive, CIO, Data Architecture Steering Committee, Data Governance Council	Business Intelligence Specialists, Data Integration Specialists, DBAs, Other Data Mgmt. Professionals, IT architects
7.3 Implement Data Warehouses and Data Marts (D)	Data Warehouses, Data Marts, OLAP Cubes	Business Intelligence Specialists	Data Warehouse Architect, Data Stewardship Teams	Data Integration Specialists, DBAs, Other Data Mgmt. Professionals, Other IT Professionals
7.4 Implement Business Intelligence Tools and User Interfaces (D)	BI Tools and User Environments, Query and Reporting, Dashboards, Scorecards, Analytic Applications, etc.	Business Intelligence Specialists	Data Warehouse Architect, Data Stewardship Committee, Data Governance Council, Business Executives and Managers	Data Warehouse Architect, Other Data Mgmt. Professionals,, Other IT Professionals
7.5 Process Data for Business Intelligence (O)	Accessible Integrated Data, Data Quality Feedback Details	Data Integration Specialists	Data Stewards	Other Data Mgmt. Professionals, Other IT Professionals
7.6 Monitor and Tune Data Warehousing Processes (C)	DW Performance Reports	DBAs, Data Integration Specialists		IT Operators

Activities	Deliverables	Responsible Roles	Approving Roles	Contributing Roles
7.7 Monitor and Tune BI Activity and Performance (C)	BI Performance Reports, New Indexes, New Aggregations	Business Intelligence Specialists, DBAs, Business Intelligence Analysts		Other Data Mgmt. Professionals, IT Operators, IT Auditors

A9.8 Document and Content Management

Activities	Deliverables	Responsible Roles	Approving Roles	Contributing Roles
8.1 Document and Records Management				
8.1.1 Plan for Managing Documents / Records (P)	Document Management Strategy and Roadmap	Document System Managers, Records Managers	Data Governance Council	Data Architects, Data Analysts, Business Data Stewards
8.1.2 Implement Document / Record Management Systems for Acquisition, Storage, Access, and Security Controls (O, C)	Document / Record Management Systems (including image and e-mail systems), Portals, Paper and Electronic Documents (text, graphics, images, audio, video)	Document System Managers, Records Managers	Subject Matter Experts	
8.1.3 Backup and Recover Documents / Records (O)	Backup Files, Business Continuity	Document Systems Managers, Records Managers		
8.1.4 Retain and Dispose Documents / Records (O)	Archive Files, Managed Storage	Document Systems Managers, Records Managers		

Activities	Deliverables	Responsible Roles	Approving Roles	Contributing Roles
8.1.5 Audit Document / Record Management (C)	Document / Record Management Audits	Audit Department, Management	Management	
8.2 Content Management				
8.2.1 Define and Maintain Enterprise Taxonomies (P)	Enterprise Taxonomies (Information Content Architecture)	Knowledge Managers	Data Governance Council	Data Architects, Data Analysts, Business Data Stewards
8.2.2 Document / Index Information Content Meta-data (D)	Indexed Keywords, Meta-data	Document Systems Managers, Records Managers		
8.2.3 Provide Content Access and Retrieval (O)	Portals, Content Analysis, Leveraged Information	Document Systems Managers, Records Managers	Subject Matter Experts	Data Architects, Data Analysts
8.2.4 Govern for Quality Content (C)	Leveraged Information	Document Systems Managers, Records Managers	Business Data Stewards	Data Management Professionals

A9.9 Meta-data Management

Activities	Deliverables	Responsible Roles	Approving Roles	Contributing Roles
9.1 Understand Meta-data Requirements (P)	Meta-data requirements	Meta-data Specialists Data Stewards Data Architects and Modelers Database Administrators	Enterprise Data Architect, DM Leader, Data Stewardship Committee	Other IT Professionals Other DM Professionals

Activities	Deliverables	Responsible Roles	Approving Roles	Contributing Roles
9.2 Define the Meta-data Architecture (P)	Meta-data architecture	Meta-data Architects, Data Integration Architects	Enterprise Data Architect, DM Leader, CIO Data Stewardship Committee Database Administrators	Meta-data Specialists, Other Data Mgmt. Professionals Other IT Professionals
9.3 Develop and Maintain Meta-data Standards (P)	Meta-data standards	Meta-data and Data Architects Data Stewards Database Administrators	Enterprise Data Architect, DM Leader, Data Stewardship Committee	Other IT Professionals Other DM Professionals
9.4 Implement a Managed Meta-data Environment (D)	Meta-data metrics	Database Administrators	Enterprise Data Architect, DM Leader, Data Stewardship Committee	Other IT Professionals

Activities	Deliverables	Responsible Roles	Approving Roles	Contributing Roles
9.5 Create and Maintain Meta-data (O)	Updated: • Data Modeling Tools • Database Management Systems • Data Integration Tools • Business Intelligence Tools • System Management Tools • Object Modeling Tools • Process Modeling Tools • Report Generating Tools • Data Quality Tools • Data Development and Administration Tools Reference and Master Data Management Tools	Meta-data Specialists Data Stewards Data Architects and Modelers Database Administrators	Enterprise Data Architect, DM Leader, Data Stewardship Committee	Other IT Professionals
9.6 Integrate Meta-data (C)	Integrated Meta-data repositories	Integration Data Architects Meta-data Specialists Data Stewards Data Architects and Modelers Database Administrators	Enterprise Data Architect, DM Leader, Data Stewardship Committee	Other IT Professionals

Activities	Deliverables	Responsible Roles	Approving Roles	Contributing Roles
9.7 Manage Meta-data Repositories (C)	Managed Meta-data repositories Administration Principles, Practices, Tactics	Meta-data Specialists Data Stewards Data Architects and Modelers Database Administrators	Enterprise Data Architect, DM Leader, Data Stewardship Committee	Other IT Professionals
9.8 Distribute and Deliver Meta-data (O)	Distribution of Meta-data Meta-data Models and Architecture	Database Administrators	Enterprise Data Architect, DM Leader, Data Stewardship Committee	Meta-data Architects
9.9 Query, Report and Analyze Meta-data (O)	Quality Meta-data Meta-data Management Operational Analysis Meta-data Analysis Data Lineage Change Impact Analysis	Data Analysts, Meta-data Analysts	Enterprise Data Architect, DM Leader, Data Stewardship Committee	Business Intelligence Specialists, Data Integration Specialists, Database Administrators, Other Data Mgmt. Professionals

A9.10 Data Quality Management

Activities	Deliverables	Responsible Roles	Approving Roles	Contributing Roles
10.1 Develop and Promote Data Quality Awareness (O)	Data quality training Data Governance Processes Established Data Stewardship Council	Data Quality Manager	Business Managers DRM Director	Information Architects Subject Matter Experts

Activities	Deliverables	Responsible Roles	Approving Roles	Contributing Roles
10.2 Define Data Quality Requirements ((D)	Data Quality Requirements Document	Data Quality Manager Data Quality Analysts	Business Managers DRM Director	Information Architects Subject Matter Experts
10.3 Profile, Analyze, and Assess Data Quality (D)	Data Quality Assessment Report	Data Quality Analysts	Business Managers DRM Director	Data Stewardship Council
10.4 Define Data Quality Metrics (P)	Data Quality Metrics Document	Data Quality Manager Data Quality Analysts	Business Managers DRM Director	Data Stewardship Council
10.5 Define Data Quality Business Rules (P)	Data Quality Business Rules	Data Quality Analysts	Business Managers DRM Director Data Quality Manager	Information Architects Subject Matter Experts Data Stewardship Council
10.6 Test and Validate Data Quality Requirements (D)	Data Quality Test Cases	Data Quality Analysts	Business Managers DRM Director	Information Architects Subject Matter Experts
10.7 Set and Evaluate Data Quality Service Levels (P)	Data Quality Service Levels	Data Quality Manager	Business Managers DRM Director	Data Stewardship Council
10.8 Continuously Measure and Monitor Data Quality (C)	Data Quality Reports	Data Quality Manager	Business Managers DRM Director	Data Stewardship Council
10.9 Manage Data Quality Issues (C)	Data Quality Issues Log	Data Quality Manager Data Quality Analysts	Business Managers DRM Director	Data Stewardship Council
10.10 Clean and Correct Data Quality Defects (O)	Data Quality Defect Resolution Log	Data Quality Analysts	Business Managers DRM Director	Information Architects Subject Matter Experts

Activities	Deliverables	Responsible Roles	Approving Roles	Contributing Roles
10.11 Design and Implement Operational DQM Procedures (D)	Operational DQM Procedures	Data Quality Manager Data Quality Analysts	Business Managers DRM Director	Information Architects Subject Matter Experts Data Stewardship Council
10.12 Monitor Operational DQM Procedures and Performance (C)	Operational DQM Metrics	Data Quality Manager Data Quality Analysts	Business Managers DRM Director	Data Stewardship Council

A10 Standards

The standards listed in the selected reading from each chapter have been combined into a single appendix and sorted in alphabetical order by the standard name for ready reference.

A10.1 Non-United States Privacy Laws:

Argentina: Personal Data Protection Act of 2000 (aka Habeas Data).

Austria: Data Protection Act 2000, Austrian Federal Law Gazette Part I No. 165/1999 (DSG 2000).

Australia: Privacy Act of 1988.

Brazil: Privacy currently governed by Article 5 of the 1988 Constitution.

Canada: The Privacy Act - July 1983, Personal Information Protection and Electronic Data Act (PIPEDA) of 2000 (Bill C-6).

Chile: Act on the Protection of Personal Data, August 1998.

Columbia: No specific privacy law, but the Columbian constitution provides any person the right to update and access their personal information.

Czech Republic: Act on Protection of Personal Data (April 2000) No. 101.

Denmark: Act on Processing of Personal Data, Act No. 429, May 2000.

Estonia: Personal Data Protection Act, June 1996, Consolidated July 2002.

European Union: Data Protection Directive of 1998.

European Union: Internet Privacy Law of 2002 (DIRECTIVE 2002/58/EC).

Finland: Act on the Amendment of the Personal Data Act (986) 2000.

France: Data Protection Act of 1978 (revised in 2004).

Germany: Federal Data Protection Act of 2001.

Greece: Law No.2472 on the Protection of Individuals with Regard to the Processing of Personal Data, April 1997.

Hong Kong: Personal Data Ordinance (The "Ordinance").

Hungary: Act LXIII of 1992 on the Protection of Personal Data and the Publicity of Data of Public Interests.

Iceland: Act of Protection of Individual; Processing Personal Data (Jan 2000).

Ireland: Data Protection (Amendment) Act, Number 6 of 2003.

India: Information Technology Act of 2000.

Italy: Data Protection Code of 2003 Italy: Processing of Personal Data Act, Jan. 1997.

Japan: Personal Information Protection Law (Act).

Japan: Law for the Protection of Computer Processed Data Held by Administrative Organizations, December 1988.

Korea: Act on Personal Information Protection of Public Agencies Act on Information and Communication Network Usage.

Latvia: Personal Data Protection Law, March 23, 2000.

Lithuania: Law on Legal Protection of Personal Data (June 1996).

Luxembourg: Law of 2 August 2002 on the Protection of Persons with Regard to the Processing of Personal Data.

Malaysia: Common Law principle of confidentiality Draft Personal data Protection Bill Banking and Financial Institutions Act of 1989 privacy provisions.

Malta: Data Protection Act (Act XXVI of 2001), Amended March 22, 2002, November 15, 2002 and July 15, 2003.

New Zealand: Privacy Act, May 1993; Privacy Amendment Act, 1993; Privacy Amendment Act, 1994.

Norway: Personal Data Act (April 2000) - Act of 14 April 2000 No. 31 Relating to the Processing of Personal Data (Personal Data Act).

Philippines: No general data protection law, but there is a recognized right of privacy in civil law.

Poland: Act of the Protection of Personal Data (August 1997).

Singapore: The E-commerce Code for the Protection of Personal Information and Communications of Consumers of Internet Commerce.

Slovak Republic: Act No. 428 of 3 July 2002 on Personal Data Protection.

Slovenia: Personal Data Protection Act , RS No. 55/99.

South Korea: The Act on Promotion of Information and Communications Network Utilization and Data Protection of 2000.

Spain: ORGANIC LAW 15/1999 of 13 December on the Protection of Personal Data.

Switzerland: The Federal Law on Data Protection of 1992.

Sweden: Personal Data Protection Act (1998:204), October 24, 1998.

Taiwan: Computer Processed Personal data Protection Law - applies only to public institutions.

Thailand: Official Information Act (1997) for state agencies (Personal data Protection bill under consideration).

Vietnam: The Law on Electronic Transactions (Draft: Finalized in 2006).

A10.2 United States Privacy Laws:

Americans with Disabilities Act (ADA).

Cable Communications Policy Act of 1984 (Cable Act).

California Senate Bill 1386 (SB 1386).

Children's Internet Protection Act of 2001 (CIPA).

Children's Online Privacy Protection Act of 1998 (COPPA).

Communications Assistance for Law Enforcement Act of 1994 (CALEA).

Computer Fraud and Abuse Act of 1986 (CFAA).

Computer Security Act of 1987 - (Superseded by the Federal Information Security Management Act (FISMA).

Consumer Credit Reporting Reform Act of 1996 (CCRRA) - Modifies the Fair Credit Reporting Act (FCRA).

Controlling the Assault of Non-Solicited Pornography and Marketing (CAN-SPAM) Act of 2003.

Electronic Funds Transfer Act (EFTA).

Fair and Accurate Credit Transactions Act (FACTA) of 2003.

Fair Credit Reporting Act.

Federal Information Security Management Act (FISMA).

Federal Trade Commission Act (FTCA).

Driver's Privacy Protection Act of 1994.

Electronic Communications Privacy Act of 1986 (ECPA).

Electronic Freedom of Information Act of 1996 (E-FOIA).

Fair Credit Reporting Act of 1999 (FCRA).

Family Education Rights and Privacy Act of 1974 (FERPA; also known as the Buckley Amendment).

Gramm-Leach-Bliley Financial Services Modernization Act of 1999 (GLBA).

Privacy Act of 1974.

Privacy Protection Act of 1980 (PPA).

Right to Financial Privacy Act of 1978 (RFPA).

Telecommunications Act of 1996.

Telephone Consumer Protection Act of 1991 (TCPA).

Uniting and Strengthening America by Providing Appropriate Tools Required to Intercept and Obstruct Terrorism Act of 2001 (USA PATRIOT Act).

Video Privacy Protection Act of 1988.

A10.3 Industry-Specific Security and Privacy Regulations:

Financial Services: Gramm-Leach-Bliley Act (GLBA), PCI Data Security Standard.

Healthcare and Pharmaceuticals: HIPAA (Health Insurance Portability and Accountability Act of 1996) and FDA 21 CFR Part 11.

Infrastructure and Energy: FERC and NERC Cybersecurity Standards, the Chemical Sector Cyber Security Program and Customs-Trade Partnership against Terrorism (C-TPAT).

Federal Government: FISMA and related NSA Guidelines and NIST Standard.

A10.4 Standards

ANSI/EIA859 : Data Management.

AS 4390-1996 Records Management.

CAN-SPAM - Federal law regarding unsolicited electronic mail.

FCD 11179-2, Information technology—Specification and standardization of data elements - Part 2: Classification for data elements.

ISO 1087, Terminology—Vocabulary.

ISO 15489-1:2001 Records Management—Part 1: General.

ISO 2382-4:1987, Information processing systems—Vocabulary part 4.

ISO 2788:1986 Guidelines for the establishment and development of monolingual thesauri.

ISO 704:1987, Principles and methods of terminology.

ISO Standards Handbook 10, Data Processing—Vocabulary, 1982.

ISO/IEC 10241:1992, International Terminology Standards—Preparation and layout.

ISO/IEC 11179-3:1994, Information technology—Specification and standardization of data elements - Part 3: Basic attributes of data elements.

ISO/IEC 11179-4:1995, Information technology—Specification and standardization of data elements - Part 4: Rules and guidelines for the formulation of data definitions.

ISO/IEC 11179-5:1995, Information technology—Specification and standardization of data elements - Part 5: Naming and identification principles for data elements.

ISO/IEC 11179-6:1997, Information technology—Specification and standardization of data elements - Part 6: Registration of data elements.

ISO/TR 15489-2:2001 Records Management -- Part 2: Guidelines.

UK Public Record Office Approved Electronic Records Management Solution.

Victorian Electronic Records Strategy (VERS) Australia.

Bibliography

The selected reading from each chapter has been combined into a single bibliography and sorted in alphabetical order by author to provide a ready reference.

Adamson, Christopher and Michael Venerable. Data Warehouse Design Solutions. John Wiley & Sons, 1998. ISBN 0-471-25195-X. 544 pages.

Adamson, Christopher. Mastering Data Warehouse Aggregates: Solutions for Star Schema Performance. John Wiley & Sons, 2006. ISBN 0-471-77709-9. 345 pages.

Adelman, Sid and Larissa T. Moss. Data Warehouse Project Management. Addison-Wesley Professional, 2000. ISBN 0-201-61635-1. 448 pages.

Adelman, Sid and others. Impossible Data Warehouse Situations: Solutions from the Experts. Addison-Wesley, 2002. ISBN 0-201-76033-9. 432 pages.

Adelman, Sid, Larissa Moss, and Majid Abai. Data Strategy. Addison-Wesley, 2005. ISBN 0-321-24099-5. 384 pages.

Afyouni, Hassan A. Database Security and Auditing: Protecting Data Integrity and Accessibility. Course Technology, 2005. ISBN 0-619-21559-3.

Aiken, Peter and M. David Allen. XML in Data Management: Understanding and Applying Them Together. Morgan Kaufmann, 2004. ISBN 0-12-45599-4.

Alderman, Ellen and Caroline Kennedy . The Right to Privacy. 1997. Vintage, ISBN-10: 0679744347, ISBN-13: 978-0679744344.

Ambler, Scott W. and Pramodkumar J. Sadalage. Refactoring Databases: Evolutionary Database Design. Addison-Wesley, 2006. ISBN 0-321-29353-3.

Ambler, Scott. Agile Database Techniques: Effective Strategies for the Agile Software Developer. Wiley & Sons, 2003. ISBN 0-471-20283-5.

Anderson, Ross J. Security Engineering: A Guide to Building Dependable Distributed Systems. Wiley, 2008. ISBN 0-470-06852-6.

Aspey, Len and Michael Middleton. Integrative Document & Content Management: Strategies for Exploiting Enterprise Knowledge. 2003. IGI Global, ISBN-10: 1591400554, ISBN-13: 978-1591400554.

Avison, David and Christine Cuthbertson. A Management Approach to Database Applications. McGraw Hill, 2002. ISBN 0-077-09782-3.

Axelrod, C. Warren. Outsourcing Information Security. Artech House, 2004. ISBN 0-58053-531-3.

Baca, Murtha, editor. Introduction to Metadata: Pathways to Digital Information. Getty Information Institute, 2000. ISBN 0-892-36533-1. 48 pages.

Barry, Douglas K. <u>Web Services and Service-Oriented Architectures: The Savvy Manager's Guide</u>. Morgan Kaufmann, 2003. ISBN 1-55860-906-7.

Batini, Carlo, and Monica Scannapieco. <u>Data Quality: Concepts, Methodologies and Techniques</u>. Springer, 2006. ISBN 3-540-33172-7. 262 pages.

Bean, James. <u>XML for Data Architects: Designing for Reuse and Integration</u>. Morgan Kaufmann, 2003. ISBN 1-558-60907-5. 250 pages.

Bearman, David. <u>Electronic Evidence: Strategies for Managing Records in Contemporary Organizations</u>. 1994. Archives and Museum Informatics. ISBN-10: 1885626088, ISBN-13: 978-1885626080.

Benson, Robert J., Tom Bugnitz, and Bill Walton. <u>From Business Strategy to IT Action: Right Decisions for a Better Bottom Line</u>. John Wiley & Sons, 2004. ISBN 0-471-49191-8. 309 pages.

Bernard, Scott A. <u>An Introduction to Enterprise Architecture, 2nd Edition</u>. Authorhouse, 2005. ISBN 1-420-88050-0. 351 pages.

Berson, Alex and Larry Dubov. <u>Master Data Management and Customer Data Integration for a Global Enterprise</u>. McGraw-Hill, 2007. ISBN 0-072-26349-0. 400 pages.

Biere, Mike. <u>Business Intelligence for the Enterprise</u>. IBM Press, 2003. ISBN 0-131-41303-1. 240 pages.

Bischoff, Joyce and Ted Alexander. <u>Data Warehouse: Practical Advice from the Experts</u>. Prentice-Hall, 1997. ISBN 0-135-77370-9. 428 pages.

Bloem, Jaap, Menno van Doorn, and Piyush Mittal. <u>Making IT Governance Work in a Sarbanes-Oxley World</u>. John Wiley & Sons, 2005. ISBN 0-471-74359-3. 304 pages.

Boddie, John. <u>The Information Asset: Rational DP Funding and Other Radical Notions</u>. Prentice-Hall (Yourdon Press Computing Series), 1993. ISBN 0-134-57326-9. 174 pages.

Boiko, Bob. <u>Content Management Bible</u>. Wiley, 2004. ISBN-10: 0764573713, ISBN-13: 978-07645737.

Brackett, Michael H. <u>Data Resource Quality: Turning Bad Habits into Good Practices</u>. Addison-Wesley, 2000. ISBN 0-201-71306-3. 384 pages.

Brackett, Michael H. <u>Practical Data Design</u>. Prentice Hall, 1990. ISBN 0-136-90827-6.

Brackett, Michael. <u>Data Sharing Using A Common Data Architecture</u>. New York: John Wiley & Sons, 1994. ISBN 0-471-30993-1. 478 pages.

Brackett, Michael. <u>The Data Warehouse Challenge: Taming Data Chaos</u>. New York: John Wiley & Sons, 1996. ISBN 0-471-12744-2. 579 pages.

Brathwaite, Ken S. <u>Analysis, Design, and Implementation of Data Dictionaries</u>. McGraw-Hill Inc., 1988. ISBN 0-07-007248-5. 214 pages.

Bruce, Thomas A. Designing Quality Databases with IDEF1X Information Models. Dorset House, 1991. ISBN 10:0932633188. 584 pages.

Bryce, Milt and Tim Bryce. The IRM Revolution: Blueprint for the 21st Century. M. Bryce Associates Inc., 1988. ISBN 0-962-11890-7. 255 pages.

Cabena, Peter, Hadjnian, Stadler, Verhees and Zanasi. Discovering Data Mining: From Concept to Implementation. Prentice Hall, 1997. ISBN-10: 0137439806

Calder, Alan and Steve Watkins. IT Governance: A Manager's Guide to Data Security and BS 7799/ISO 17799, 3rd Edition. Kogan Page, 2005. ISBN 0-749-44414-2.

Carbone, Jane. IT Architecture Toolkit. Prentice Hall, 2004. ISBN 0-131-47379-4. 256 pages.

Carlis, John and Joseph Maguire. Mastering Data Modeling - A User-Driven Approach. Addison Wesley, 2000. ISBN 0-201-70045-X.

Caserta, Joe and Ralph Kimball. The Data Warehouse ETL Toolkit: Practical Techniques for Extracting, Cleaning, Conforming and Delivering Data. John Wiley & Sons, 2004. ISBN 0-764-56757-8. 525 pages.

Castano, Silvana, Maria Grazia Fugini, Giancarlo Martella, and Pierangela Samarati. Database Security. Addison-Wesley, 1995. ISBN 0-201-59375-0.

Celko, Joe. Joe Celko's SQL for Smarties: Advanced SQL Programming, 3rd Edition. ISBN 10: 0123693799. 840 pages.

Celko, Joe. Joe Celko's Trees and Hierarchies in SQL for Smarties. Morgan Kaufmann, 2004. ISBN 1-558-60920-2.

Chisholm, Malcolm. How to Build a Business Rules Engine: Extending Application Functionality Through Metadata Engineering. Morgan Kaufmann, 2003. ISBN 1-558-60918-0.

Chisholm, Malcolm. Managing Reference Data in Enterprise Databases: Binding Corporate Data to the Wider World. Morgan Kaufmann, 2000. ISBN 1-558-60697-1. 389 pages.

Coad, Peter. Object Models: Strategies, Patterns And Applications, 2nd Edition. Prentice Hall PTR, 1996. ISBN 0-13-840117-9.

Collier, Ken. Executive Report, Business Intelligence Advisory Service, Finding the Value in Metadata Management (Vol. 4, No. 1), 2004. Available only to Cutter Consortium Clients, http://www.cutter.com/bia/fulltext/reports/2004/01/index.html.

Cook, Melissa. Building Enterprise Information Architectures: Re-Engineering Information Systems. Prentice Hall, 1996. ISBN 0-134-40256-1. 224 pages.

Correy, Michael J. and Michael Abby. Oracle Data Warehousing: A Practical Guide to Successful Data Warehouse Analysis, Build and Roll-Out. TATA McGraw-Hill, 1997. ISBN 0-074-63069-5.

Covey, Stephen R. The 7 Habits of Highly Effective People. Free Press, 2004. ISBN 0743269519. 384 Pages.

Cox, Richard J. and David Wallace. Archives and the Public Good: Accountability and Records in Modern Society. 2002. Quorum Books, ISBN-10: 1567204694, ISBN-13: 978-1567204698.

Cox, Richard J. Managing Records as Evidence and Information. Quorum Books, 2000. ISBN 1-567-20241-4. 264 pages.

DAMA Chicago Chapter Standards Committee, editors. Guidelines to Implementing Data Resource Management, 4th Edition. Bellevue, WA: The Data Management Association (DAMA International), 2002. ISBN 0-9676674-1-0. 359 pages.

Date, C. J. An Introduction to Database Systems, 8th Edition. Addison-Wesley, 2003. ISBN 0-321-19784-4.

Date, C. J. and Hugh Darwen. Databases, Types and the Relational Model: The Third Manifesto, 3rd Edition. Addison Wesley, 2006. ISBN 0-321-39942-0.

Date, C. J., What Not How: The Business Rules Approach To Application Development. Addison-Wesley, 2000. ISBN 0-201-70850-7.

Date, C. J., with Hugh Darwen. A Guide to the SQL Standard, 4th Edition. Addison-Wesley, 1997. ISBN 0-201-96426-0.

DeAngelis, Carla. Data Modeling with Erwin. Indiana: Sams Publishing, 2000. ISBN 0-672-31868-7.

Dearstyne, Bruce. Effective Approaches for Managing Electronic Records and Archives. 2006. The Scarecrow Press, Inc. ISBN-10: 0810857421, ISBN-13: 978-0810857421.

Delmater, Rhonda and Monte Hancock Jr. Data Mining Explained, A Manager's Guide to Customer-Centric Business Intelligence. Digital Press, Woburn, MA, 2001. ISBN 1-5555-8231-1.

Deming, W. Edwards. Out of the Crisis. The MIT Press, 2000. ISBN 0262541157. 507 pages.

Dennis, Jill Callahan. Privacy and Confidentiality of Health Information. Jossey-Bass, 2000. ISBN 0-787-95278-8.

DM Review Magazine–www.dmreview.com. Note: www.dmreview.com is now www.information-management.com.

Dorsey, Paul. Enterprise Data Modeling Using UML. McGraw-Hill Osborne Media, 2007. ISBN 0-072-26374-1.

Dreibelbis, Allen, Eberhard Hechler, Ivan Milman, Martin Oberhofer, Paul van Run, and Dan Wolfson. Enterprise Master Data Management: An SOA Approach to Managing Core Information. IBM Press, 2008. ISBN 978-0-13-236625-0. 617 pages.

Dunham, Jeff. Database Performance Tuning Handbook. McGraw-Hill, 1998. ISBN 0-07-018244-2.

Durell, William R. Data Administration: A Practical Guide to Successful Data Management. New York: McGraw-Hill, 1985. ISBN 0-070-18391-0. 202 pages.

Dyche, Jill and Evan Levy. Customer Data Integration: Reaching a Single Version of the Truth. John Wiley & Sons, 2006. ISBN 0-471-91697-8. 320 pages.

Dyche, Jill. E-Data: Turning Data Into Information With Data Warehousing. Addison-Wesley, 2000. ISBN 0-201-65780-5. 384 pages.

Eckerson, Wayne W. Performance Dashboards: MEassuring, Monitoring, and Managing Your Business. Wiley, 2005. ISBN-10: 0471724173. 320 pages.

EIM Insight, published by The Enterprise Information Management Institute– http://eiminstitute.org

Ellis, Judith, editor. Keeping Archives. Thorpe Bowker; 2 Sub edition. 2004. ISBN-10: 1875589155, ISBN-13: 978-1875589159.

English, Larry. Improving Data Warehouse And Business Information Quality: Methods For Reducing Costs And Increasing Profits. John Wiley & Sons, 1999. ISBN 0-471-25383-9. 518 pages.

Entsminger, Gary. The Tao Of Objects. M & T Books, 1990. ISBN 1-55851-155-5.

Erl, Thomas. Service-Oriented Architecture: A Field Guide to Integrating XML and Web Services. Prentice Hall, 2004. ISBN 0-131-42898-5.

Erl, Thomas. Service-Oriented Architecture: Concepts, Technology and Design. Prentice Hall, 2004. ISBN 0-131-85858-0.

Finkelstein, Clive and Peter Aiken. Building Corporate Portals with XML. McGraw-Hill, 1999. ISBN 10: 0079137059. 512 pages.

Finkelstein, Clive. An Introduction to Information Engineering: From Strategic Planning to Information Systems. Addison-Wesley, 1990. ISBN 0-201-41654-9.

Finkelstein, Clive. Enterprise Architecture for Integration: Rapid Delivery Methods and Techniques. Artech House Mobile Communications Library, 2006. ISBN 1-580-53713-8. 546 pages.

Finkelstein, Clive. Information Engineering: Strategic Systems Development. Addison-Wesley, 1993. ASIN B000XUA41C.

Firestone, Joseph M. Enterprise Information Portals and Knowledge Management. Butterworth-Heineman, 2002. ISBN 0-750-67474-1. 456 pages.

Fleming, Candace C. and Barbara Von Halle. The Handbook of Relational Database Design. Addison Wesley, 1989. ISBN 0-201-11434-8.

Gertz, Michael and Sushil Jajodia. Handbook of Database Security: Applications and Trends. Springer, 2007. ISBN 0-387-48532-5.

Gill, Harjinder S. and Prekash C. Rao. The Official Guide To Data Warehousing. Que, 1996. ISBN 0-789-70714-4. 382 pages.

Goldberg, Adele and Kenneth S, Rubin. Succeeding With Objects. Addison-Wesley, 1995. ISBN 0-201-62878-3.

Graham, Ian, Migrating To Object Technology. Addison-Wesley, 1995. ISBN 0-201-59389-0.

Hackathorn, Richard D. Enterprise Database Connectivity. Wiley Professional Computing, 1993. ISBN 0-4761-57802-9. 352 pages.

Hackney, Douglas. Understanding and Implementing Successful Data Marts. Addison Wesley, 1997. ISBN 0-201-18380-3. 464 pages.

Hagan, Paula J., ed. EABOK: Guide to the (Evolving) Enterprise Architecture Body of Knowledge. MITRE Corporation, 2004. 141 pages. A U.S. federally-funded guide to enterprise architecture in the context of legislative and strategic requirements. Available for free download at
http://www.mitre.org/work/tech_papers/tech_papers_04/04_0104/04_0104.pdf

Halpin, Terry, Ken Evans, Pat Hallock, and Bill McLean. Database Modeling with Microsoft Visio for Enterprise Architects. Morgan Kaufmann, 2003. ISBN 1-558-60919-9.

Halpin, Terry. Information Modeling and Relational Databases: From Conceptual Analysis to Logical Design. Morgan Kaufmann, 2001. ISBN 1-558-60672-6.

Harrington, Jan L. Relational Database Design Clearly Explained, 2nd Edition. Morgan Kaufmann, 2002. ISBN 1-558-60820-6.

Hay, David C. Data Model Patterns: A Metadata Map. Morgan Kaufmann, 2006. ISBN 0-120-88798-3. 432 pages.

Hay, David C. Data Model Patterns: Conventions of Thought. Dorset House Publishing, 1996. ISBN 0-932633-29-3.

Hay, David C. Requirements Analysis From Business Views to Architecture. Prentice Hall, 2003. ISBN 0-120-28228-6.

Henderson, Deborah, Tandum Lett, Anne Marie Smity, and Cora Zeeman. Fit For Use to a Fault. The MIT 2008 Information Quality Industry Symposium (MIT 2008), Boston, Mass. July 2008.

Hernandez, Michael J. Database Design for Mere Mortals: A Hands-On Guide to Relational Database Design, 2nd Edition. Addison-Wesley, 2003. ISBN 0-201-75284-0.

Higgs, Edward. History and Electronic Artifacts. Oxford University Press, USA. 1998. ISBN-10: 0198236344, ISBN-13: 978-0198236344.

Hillmann, Diane I. and Elaine L. Westbrooks, editors. Metadata in Practice. American Library Association, 2004. ISBN 0-838-90882-9. 285 pages.

Hoberman, Steve. Data Modeling Made Simple: A Practical Guide for Business & Information Technology Professionals. Technics Publications, LLC, 2005. ISBN 0-977-14000-8.

Hoberman, Steve. The Data Modeler's Workbench. Tools and Techniques for Analysis and Design. John Wiley & Sons, 2001. ISBN 0-471-11175-9.

Hoffer, Jeffrey A., Joey F.. George, and Joseph S. Valacich. Modern Systems Analysis and Design, 4th Edition. Prentice Hall, 2004. ISBN 0-131-45461-7.

Hoffer, Jeffrey, Mary Prescott, and Fred McFadden. Modern Database Management, 7th Edition. Prentice Hall, 2004. ISBN 0-131-45320-3. 736 pages.

Horrocks, Brian and Judy Moss. Practical Data Administration. Prentice-Hall International, 1993. ISBN 0-13-689696-0.

Howson, Cindi. "The Business Intelligence Market". http://www.biscorecard.com/. Requires annual subscription to this website.

http//:www.fjc.gov/public/home.nsf/pages/196

http//:www.uscourts.gov/ruless/Ediscovery_w_Notes.pdf

http://www.fgdc.gov/metadata/geospatial-metadata-standards.

http://www.olapcouncil.org/research/resrchly.htm

Huang, Kuan-Tsae, Yang W. Lee and Richard Y. Wang. Quality Information and Knowledge. Prentice Hall, 1999. ISBN 0-130-10141-9. 250 pages.

Humphrey, Watts S. Managing The Software Process. Addison Wesley, 1989. ISBN 0-201-18095-2.

Imhoff, Claudia, Lisa Loftis and Jonathan G. Geiger. Building the Customer-Centric Enterprise: Data Warehousing Techniques for Supporting Customer Relationship Management. John Wiley & Sons, 2001. ISBN 0-471-31981-3. 512 pages.

Imhoff, Claudia, Nicholas Galemmo and Jonathan G. Geiger. Mastering Data Warehouse Design: Relational and Dimensional Techniques. John Wiley & Sons, 2003. ISBN 0-471-32421-3. 456 pages.

Inmon, W. H. Advanced Topics in Information Engineering. John Wiley & Sons - QED, 1989. ISBN 0-894-35269-5.

Inmon, W. H. and Richard D. Hackathorn. Using the Data Warehouse. Wiley-QED, 1994. ISBN 0-471-05966-8. 305 pages.

Inmon, W. H. Building the Data Warehouse, 4th Edition. John Wiley & Sons, 2005. ISBN 0-764-59944-5. 543 pages.

Inmon, W. H. Building the Operational Data Store, 2nd edition. John Wiley & Sons, 1999. ISBN 0-471-32888-X. 336 pages.

Inmon, W. H. Information Engineering For The Practitioner. Prentice-Hall (Yourdon Press), 1988. ISBN 0-13-464579-0.

Inmon, W. H., Claudia Imhoff and Ryan Sousa. The Corporate Information Factory, 2nd edition. John Wiley & Sons, 2000. ISBN 0-471-39961-2. 400 pages.

Inmon, William H. and Anthony Nesavich,. Tapping into Unstructured Data: Integrating Unstructured Data and Textual Analytics into Business Intelligence. Prentice-Hall PTR, 2007. ISBN-10: 0132360292, ISBN-13: 978-0132360296.

Inmon, William H., Bonnie O'Neil and Lowell Fryman. Business Metadata: Capturing Enterprise Knowledge. 2008. Morgan Kaufmann ISBN 978-0-12-373726-7. 314 pages.

Inmon, William H., John A. Zachman and Jonathan G. Geiger. Data Stores, Data Warehousing and the Zachman Framework. McGraw-Hill, 1997. ISBN 0-070-31429-2. 358 pages.

IT Governance Institute. Control Objectives for Information and related Technology (CobiT©). www.isaca.org/cobit

Jacobson, Ivar, Maria Ericsson, and Agneta Jacobson. The Object Advantage. Addison-Wesley, 1995. ISBN 0-201-42289-1.

Jaquith, Andrew. Security Metrics: Replacing Fear, Uncertainty and Doubt. Addison-Wesley, 2007. ISBN 0-321-349998-9.

Jenkins, Tom, David Glazer, and Hartmut Schaper.. Enterprise Content Management Technology: What You Need to Know, 2004. Open Text Corporation, ISBN-10: 0973066253, ISBN-13: 978-0973066258.

Karpuk, Deborah. Metadata: From Resource Discovery to Knowledge Management. Libraries Unlimited, 2007. ISBN 1-591-58070-6. 275 pages.

Kent, William. Data and Reality: Basic Assumptions in Data Processing Reconsidered. Authorhouse, 2000. ISBN 1-585-00970-9. 276 pages.

Kepner, Charles H. and Benjamin B. Tregoe. The New Rational Manager. Princeton Research Press, 1981. 224 pages.

Kerr, James M. The IRM Imperative. John Wiley & Sons, 1991. ISBN 0-471-52434-4.

Kimball, Ralph and Margy Ross. The Data Warehouse Toolkit: The Complete Guide to Dimensional Modeling, 2nd edition. New York: John Wiley & Sons, 2002. ISBN 0-471-20024-7. 464 pages.

Kimball, Ralph and Richard Merz. The Data Webhouse Toolkit: Building the Web-Enabled Data Warehouse. John Wiley & Sons, 2000. ISBN 0-471-37680-9. 416 pages.

Kimball, Ralph, Laura Reeves, Margy Ross and Warren Thornwaite. The Data Warehouse Lifecycle Toolkit: Expert Methods for Designing, Developing and Deploying Data Warehouses. John Wiley & Sons, 1998. ISBN 0-471-25547-5. 800 pages.

Kline, Kevin, with Daniel Kline. SQL in a Nutshell. O'Reilly, 2001. ISBN 0-471-16518-2.

Kroenke, D. M. Database Processing: Fundamentals, Design, and Implementation, 10th Edition. Pearson Prentice Hall, 2005. ISBN 0-131-67626-3. 696 pages.

Krogstie, John, Terry Halpin, and Keng Siau, editors. Information Modeling Methods and Methodologies: Advanced Topics in Database Research. Idea Group Publishing, 2005. ISBN 1-591-40375-8.

Landoll, Douglas J. The Security Risk Assessment Handbook: A Complete Guide for Performing Security Risk Assessments. CRC, 2005. ISBN 0-849-32998-1.

Lankhorst, Marc. Enterprise Architecture at Work: Modeling, Communication and Analysis. Springer, 2005. ISBN 3-540-24371-2. 334 pages.

Litchfield, David, Chris Anley, John Heasman, and Bill Frindlay. The Database Hacker's Handbook: Defending Database Servers. Wiley, 2005. ISBN 0-764-57801-4.

Liu, Jia. Metadata and Its Applications in the Digital Library. Libraries Unlimited, 2007. ISBN 1-291-58306-6. 250 pages.

Loshin, David. Enterprise Knowledge Management: The Data Quality Approach. Morgan Kaufmann, 2001. ISBN 0-124-55840-2. 494 pages.

Loshin, David. Master Data Management. Morgan Kaufmann, 2008. ISBN 98-0-12-374225-4. 274 pages.

Loshin, David. Master Data Management. Morgan Kaufmann, 2009. ISBN 0123742250. 288 pages.

Lutchen, Mark. Managing IT as a Business: A Survival Guide for CEOs. John Wiley & Sons, 2003. ISBN 0-471-47104-6. 256 pages.

Maizlish, Bryan and Robert Handler. IT Portfolio Management Step-By-Step: Unlocking the Business Value of Technology. John Wiley & Sons, 2005. ISBN 0-471-64984-8. 400 pages.

Malik, Shadan. Enterprise Dashboards: Design and Best Practices for IT. Wiley, 2005. ISBN 0471738069. 240 pages.

Marco, David and Michael Jennings. Universal Meta Data Models. John Wiley & Sons, 2004. ISBN 0-471-08177-9. 478 pages.

Marco, David, Building and Managing the Meta Data Repository: A Full Life-Cycle Guide. John Wiley & Sons, 2000. ISBN 0-471-35523-2. 416 pages.

Martin, James and Joe Leben. Strategic Data Planning Methodologies, 2nd Edition. Prentice Hall, 1989. ISBN 0-13-850538-1. 328 pages.

Martin, James. Information Engineering Book 1: Introduction. Prentice-Hall, 1989. ISBN 0-13-464462-X. Also see Book 2: Analysis and Design and Book 3: Design and Construction.

Martin, James. Information Engineering Book II: Planning and Analysis. Prentice-Hall, Inc., 1990. Englewoood Cliffs, New Jersey.

Mattison, Rob, Web Warehousing & Knowledge Management. McGraw Hill, 1999. ISBN 0-070-41103-4. 576 pages.

Mattison, Rob. Understanding Database Management Systems, 2nd Edition. McGraw-Hill, 1998. ISBN 0-07-049999-3. 665 pages.

Maydanchik, Arkady. Data Quality Assessment. Technics Publications, LLC, 2007 ISBN 0977140024. 336 pages.

McComb, Dave. Semantics in Business Systems: The Savvy Manager's Guide. The Discipline Underlying Web Services, Business Rules and the Semantic Web. San Francisco, CA: Morgan Kaufmann Publishers, 2004. ISBN: 1-55860-917-2.

McGilvray, Danette. Executing Data Quality Projects: Ten Steps to Quality Data and Trusted Information. Morgan Kaufmann, 2008. ISBN 0123743699. 352 pages.

Melton, Jim and Stephen Buxton. Querying XML: XQuery, XPath and SQL/XML in Context. Morgan Kaufmann, 2006. ISBN 1-558-60711-0.

Mena, Jesus, Data Mining Your Website, Digital Press, Woburn, MA, 1999, ISBN 1-5555-8222- 2.

Morgan, Tony. Business Rules and Information Systems: Aligning IT with Business Goals. Addison-Wesley, 2002. ISBN 0-201-74391-4.

Morris, Henry. Analytic Applications and Business Performance Management. DM Review Magazine, March, 1999. www.dmreview.com. Note: www.dmreview.com is now www.information-management.com.

Moss, Larissa T. and Shaku Atre. Business Intelligence Roadmap: The Complete Project Lifecycle for Decision-Support Applications. Addison-Wesley, 2003. ISBN 0-201-78420-3. 576 pages.

Muller, Robert. J. Database Design for Smarties: Using UML for Data Modeling. San Francisco, CA, USA, Morgan Kaufmann, 1999. ISBN 1-558-60515-0.

Mullins, Craig S. Database Administration: The Complete Guide to Practices and Procedures. Addison-Wesley, 2002. ISBN 0-201-74129-6. 736 pages.

National Information Standards Association (NISO), ANSI/NISO Z39.19-2005: Guidelines for the Construction, Format, and Management of Monolingual Controlled Vocabularies. 2005. 172 pages. www.niso.org

Newton, Judith J. and Daniel Wahl, editors. Manual For Data Administration. Washington, DC: GPO, NIST Special Publications 500-208, Diane Publishing Co., 1993. ISBN 1-568-06362-8.

Olson, Jack E. Data Quality: The Accuracy Dimension. Morgan Kaufmann, 2003. ISBN 1-558-60891-5. 294 pages.

Parsaye, Kamran and Mark Chignell. Intelligent Database Tools and Applications: Hyperinformation Access, Data Quality, Visualization, Automatic Discovery. John Wiley & Sons, 1993. ISBN 0-471-57066-4. 560 pages.

Pascal, Fabian, Practical Issues In Database Management: A Reference For The Thinking Practitioner. Addison-Wesley, 2000. ISBN 0-201-48555-9. 288 pages.

Peltier, Thomas R. Information Security Policies and Procedures: A Practitioner's Reference, 2nd Edition. Auerbach, 2004. ISBN 0-849-31958-7.

Perks, Col and Tony Beveridge. Guide to Enterprise IT Architecture. Springer, 2002. ISBN 0-387-95132-6. 480 pages.

Piedad, Floyd, and Michael Hawkins. High Availability: Design, Techniques and Processes. Prentice Hall, 2001. ISBN 0-13-096288-0.

Poe, Vidette, Patricia Klauer and Stephen Brobst. Building A Data Warehouse for Decision Support, 2nd edition. Prentice-Hall, 1997. ISBN 0-137-69639-6. 285 pages.

Ponniah, Paulraj. Data Warehousing Fundamentals: A Comprehensive Guide for IT Professionals. John Wiley & Sons – Interscience, 2001. ISBN 0-471-41254-6. 528 pages.

Poole, John, Dan Change, Douglas Tolbert and David Mellor. Common Warehouse Metamodel: An Introduction to the Standard for Data Warehouse Integration. John Wiley & Sons, 2001. ISBN 0-471-20052-2. 208 pages.

Poole, John, Dan Change, Douglas Tolbert and David Mellor. Common Warehouse Metamodel Developer's Guide. John Wiley & Sons, 2003. ISBN 0-471-20243-6. 704 pages.

Purba, Sanjiv, editor. Data Management Handbook, 3rd Edition. Auerbach, 1999. ISBN 0-849-39832-0. 1048 pages.

Redman, Thomas. Data Quality: The Field Guide. Digital Press, 2001. ISBN 1-555-59251-6. 256 pages.

Reingruber, Michael. C. and William W. Gregory. The Data Modeling Handbook: A Best-Practice Approach to Building Quality Data Models. John Wiley & Sons, 1994. ISBN 0-471-05290-6.

Riordan, Rebecca M. Designing Effective Database Systems. Addison-Wesley, 2005. ISBN 0-321-20903-3.

Rob, Peter, and Carlos Coronel. Database Systems: Design, Implementation, and Management, 7th Edition. Course Technology, 2006. ISBN 1-418-83593-5. 688 pages.

Robek. Information and Records Management: Document-Based Information Systems. Career Education; 4 edition. 1995. ISBN-10: 0028017935.

Ross, Jeanne W., Peter Weill, and David Robertson. Enterprise Architecture As Strategy: Creating a Foundation For Business Execution. Harvard Business School Press, 2006. ISBN 1-591-39839-8. 288 pages.

Ross, Ronald G. Business Rules Concepts, 2nd Edition. Business Rule Solutions, 2005. ISBN 0-941-04906-X.

Ross, Ronald G. Principles of the Business Rule Approach. Addison-Wesley, 2003. ISBN 0-201-78893-4.

Ross, Ronald. Data Dictionaries And Data Administration: Concepts and Practices for Data Resource Management. New York: AMACOM Books, 1981. ISN 0-814-45596-4. 454 pages.

Rud, Olivia Parr. Data Mining Cookbook: Modeling Data for Marketing, Risk and Customer Relationship Management. John Wiley & Sons, 2000. ISBN 0-471-38564-6. 367 pages.

Schekkerman, Jaap. How to Survive in the Jungle of Enterprise Architecture Frameworks: Creating or Choosing an Enterprise Architecture Framework. Trafford, 2006. 224 pages. ISBN 1-412-01607-X.

Schmidt, Bob. Data Modeling for Information Professionals. Prentice Hall, 1999. ISBN 0-13-080450-9.

SearchDataManagement.com white paper library–
http://go.techtarget.com/r/3762877/5626178

Shostack, Adam and Andrew Stewart. The New School of Information Security. Addison-Wesley, 2008. ISBN 0-321-50278-7.

Silverston, Len. The Data Model Resource Book, Volume 1: A Library of Universal Data Models for All Enterprises, 2nd Edition, John Wiley & Sons, 2001. ISBN 0-471-38023-7.

Silverston, Len. The Data Model Resource Book, Volume 2: A Library of Data Models for Specific Industries, 2nd Edition. John Wiley & Sons, 2001. ISBN 0-471-35348-5.

Simsion, Graeme C. and Graham C. Witt. Data Modeling Essentials, 3rd Edition. Morgan Kaufmann, 2005. ISBN 0-126-44551-6.

Spewak, Steven and Steven C. Hill, Enterprise Architecture Planning. John Wiley & Sons -QED, 1993. ISBN 0-471-59985-9. 367 pages.

Sutton, Michael J. D. Document Management for the Enterprise: Principles, Techniques, and Applications. Wiley, 1996, ISBN-10: 0471147192, ISBN-13: 978-0471147190.

Tannenbaum, Adrienne. Implementing a Corporate Repository, John Wiley & Sons, 1994. ISBN 0-471-58537-8. 441 pages.

Tannenbaum, Adrienne. Metadata Solutions: Using Metamodels, Repositories, XML, And Enterprise Portals to Generate Information on Demand. Addison Wesley, 2001. ISBN 0-201-71976-2. 528 pages.

Taylor, David. Business Engineering With Object Technology. New York: John Wiley, 1995. ISBN 0-471-04521-7

Taylor, David. Object Oriented Technology: A Manager's Guide. Reading, MA: Addison-Wesley, 1990. ISBN 0-201-56358-4

Teorey, Toby , Sam Lightstone, and Tom Nadeau. Database Modeling and Design, 4th Edition. Morgan Kaufmann, 2006. ISBN 1-558-60500-2.

Thalheim, Bernhard. Entity-Relationship Modeling: Foundations of Database Technology. Springer, 2000. ISBN 3-540-65470-4.

The Data Administration Newsletter (TDAN)–*http://www.TDAN.com*

The Open Group, TOGAF: The Open Group Architecture Framework, Version 8.1 Enterprise Edition. The Open Group. (www.opengroup.org). ISBN 1-93-16245-6. 491 pages.

Thomas, Gwen. Alpha Males and Data Disasters: The Case for Data Governance. Brass Cannon Press, 2006. ISBN-10: 0-978-6579-0-X. 221 pages.

Thomsen, Erik. OLAP Solutions: Building Multidimensional Information Systems, 2nd edition. Wiley, 2002. ISBN-10: 0471400300. 688 pages.

Thuraisingham, Bhavani. Database and Applications Security: Integrating Information Security and Data Management. Auerbac Publications, 2005. ISN 0-849-32224-3.

Van der Lans, Rick F. Introduction to SQL: Mastering the Relational Database Language, 4th Edition. Addison-Wesley, 2006. ISBN 0-321-30596-5.

Van Grembergen, Wim and Steven Dehaes. Enterprise Governance of Information Technology: Achieving Strategic Alignment and Value. Springer, 2009. ISBN 0-387-84881-5, 360 pages.

Van Grembergen, Wim and Steven Dehaes. Implementing Information Technology Governance: Models, Practices and Cases. IGI Publishing, 2007. ISBN 1-599-04924-3, 255 pages.

Van Grembergen, Wim and Steven Dehaes. Strategies for Information Technology Governance. IGI Publishing, 2003. ISBN 1-591-40284-0. 406 pages.

Vitt, Elizabeth, Michael Luckevich and Stacia Misner. **Business Intelligence**. Microsoft Press, 2008. ISBN 073562660X. 220 pages.

Von Halle, Barbara. Business Rules Applied: Building Better Systems Using the Business Rules Approach. John Wiley & Sons, 2001. ISBN 0-471-41293-7.

Watson, Richard T. Data Management: Databases And Organization, 5th Edition. John Wiley & Sons, 2005. ISBN 0-471-71536-0.

Weill, Peter and Jeanne Ross. IT Governance: How Top Performers Manage IT Decision Rights for Superior Results. Harvard Business School Press, 2004. ISBN 1-291-39253-5. 288 pages.

Wellheiser, Johanna and John Barton. An Ounce of Prevention: Integrated Disaster Planning for Archives, Libraries and Records Centers. Canadian Library Assn. 1987. ISBN-10: 0969204108, ISBN-13: 978-0969204107.

Wertz, Charles J. The Data Dictionary: Concepts and Uses, 2nd edition. John Wiley & Sons, 1993. ISBN 0-471-60308-2. 390 pages.

Westerman, Paul. Data Warehousing: Using the Wal-Mart Model. Morgan Kaufman, 2000. ISBN 155860684X. 297 pages.

Whitman, Michael R. and Herbert H. Mattord. Principles of Information Security, Third Edition. Course Technology, 2007. ISBN 1-423-90177-0.

Wirfs-Brock, Rebecca, Brian Wilkerson, and Lauren Wiener. Designing Object-Oriented Software. NJ: Prentice Hall, 1990. ISBN 0-13-629825-7.

Wremble, Robert and Christian Koncilia. Data Warehouses and Olap: Concepts, Architectures and Solutions. IGI Global, 2006. ISBN: 1599043645. 332 pages.

Zachman, John A. "A Framework for Information Systems Architecture", IBM_Systems Journal, Vol. 26 No. 3 1987, pages 276 to 292. IBM Publication G321-5298. Also available in a special issue of the IBM Systems Journal, "Turning Points in Computing: 1962-1999", IBM Publication G321-0135, pages 454 to 470 http://researchweb.watson.ibm.com/journal/sj/382/zachman.pdf.

Zachman, John A. and John F. Sowa,. "Extending and Formalizing the Framework for Information Systems Architecture", IBM Systems Journal. Vol. 31 No. 3 1992, pages 590 – 616. IBM Publication G321-5488.

Zachman, John A. The Zachman Framework: A Primer for Enterprise Engineering and Manufacturing. Metadata Systems Software Inc., Toronto, Canada. eBook available only in electronic form from www.ZachmanInternational.com.

Zachman, John. "A Concise Definition of the Enterprise Framework." Zachman International, 2008. Article in electronic form available for free download at http://www.zachmaninternational.com/index.php/home-article/13#thezf.

Index

49593062R00238

Made in the USA
Lexington, KY
11 February 2016